Public Power-
Private Life

A memoir and history
of public power
in the twentieth century

By Alex Radin

To my parents,
Joseph and Mollie Radin,
for the values they held,
and for their fortitude
in immigrating
to a land of freedom
and opportunity.

Contents

Introduction

I met Alex Radin 26 years ago. The Chairman of the House Rules Committee had been defeated and I, as the committee's majority counsel, was looking for a job. A friend and fellow House staffer encouraged me to contact the American Public Power Association and apply for the position of legislative counsel. I knew little about energy, and even less about public power, but I followed his advice. And so began my career with APPA and my friendship with Alex Radin. What I envisioned as a short stop on my path to a law firm became my profession. I hold Alex responsible for this. And for this I am indebted to him.

As one of approximately 25 members of the APPA staff at that time, there was little formality within the office, and even less bureaucracy. Alex was accessible. For me and others on the staff, he was a teacher, mentor and friend. In a rather classic "seeing the trees not the forest" phenomenon, during my first few years at APPA, I didn't fully appreciate his role in the public power movement. Nor did I appreciate the incredible role he played in the positive, pro-consumer role of public power in America in the second half of the 20th century.

I lived through and participated in several of the political struggles so vividly portrayed by Alex in this book. I learned of others through conversations with him and his deputy, successor and my predecessor as the leader of APPA, Larry Hobart. Yet, reading the manuscript and reflecting on public power's role in America as recounted in this book, my appreciation for what he personally and public power have contributed to our country, continues to grow.

Not long ago, in a ceremony sponsored by the University of Tennessee, Chattanooga, hosted by and held at APPA's offices in Washington, I welcomed the guests to the "House that Alex built." As readers of this book will see, Alex truly did build APPA. When he retired in 1986, APPA's then-general counsel Northcut Ely noted that the institution, APPA, is but the shadow of the man. How true.

But for Alex Radin, public power as an institution and APPA as its voice would not be what it is today. The book you are about to read tells this story. Alex promised to write this book when he retired almost 20 years ago. I'm glad he finally got around to it. Public power's (and Alex's) contributions to politics and policy in America in the last 50 years would not be complete if this history were left unwritten.

Alan H. Richardson
President & CEO
American Public Power Association

Author's Note

This book is a memoir of my experiences in an era that witnessed some of the most significant events in the history of America—events well known to most Americans. In the main, however, this is an account of landmark events that occurred during my association for half a century with an important institution that is not well known and understood outside of the electric industry—public power.

For some, the term public power may conjure the vision of political power. Others may associate public power with electricity. Because utilities that generate and deliver electricity are generally regarded as "public utilities," many people mistakenly regard as "public power" the "public utilities" that are privately or investor-owned. These privately owned companies are the largest sector of the utility industry. They serve about 73 percent of all electric consumers. They are not part of the public power sector.

Public power refers to the segment of the electric industry that is owned by government institutions. They can be federal agencies such as the Tennessee Valley Authority or Bonneville Power Administration; state entities such as the Lower Colorado River Authority in Texas or the New York Power Authority; public utility districts, which primarily serve counties, especially in the state of Washington; or cities such as Los Angeles, Memphis, Seattle or Orlando, which distribute electricity to their respective citizens.

When I joined the staff of the American Public Power Association in 1948, public power was best known for the federal program, which developed hydroelectric power as part of water resource development that also included flood control, navigation, irrigation and recreation.

The program was started at the turn of the 20th century, but it expanded and attracted national attention in the 1930s, when it was a highly controversial part of the New Deal. Although it was savagely attacked, the federal government's role as a producer of public power also was regarded as a "movement" that attracted supporters who defended it with religious-like zeal.

The oldest version of public power developed in 1882, at the initiation of central station electric service. When communities were not furnished electricity by private companies, or were charged exorbitant rates, citizens exercised their right to provide electricity for themselves by establishing municipally owned utilities. Today, these municipal electric systems, together with public utility districts and state-owned utilities, exist throughout the United States, and number more than 2,000. Many buy a substantial portion of their wholesale power from the federal power systems; others generate their own power or buy it at wholesale from other utilities or independent power producers and distribute it to their respective communities.

Although they serve only about 15 percent of the nation's electric consumers, public power utilities have had an enormous influence on the electric industry and the nation's economy. Because they provide institutional competition for private power companies, publicly owned utilities serve as a "yardstick" of performance and rates.

The American Public Power Association, established in 1940, is the national organization that represents the interests of the public power utilities. I was associated with APPA for more than 38 years, 35 as executive director.

Another important segment of the electric industry consists of about 900 rural electric cooperatives. They provide service to approximately 12 percent of the populace. Although they are sometimes regarded as part of public power, they are actually private, nonprofit organizations.

In its totality, the electric industry is one of the largest and most vital in the United States. In 2000 it had a net plant investment of about $482 billion and annual revenues in excess of $236 billion.

It is not surprising that much of this book deals with issues affecting Congress and executive and regulatory agencies. The electric industry— whether it is privately, publicly or cooperatively owned—is essential to the functioning of our society, it is affected with the public interest, and it is therefore subject to government control and oversight. The degree of such control will continue to be the subject of intense public policy debates.

Because electricity is essential to the nation's well being, a strong public power presence is vital. It offers a proven alternative means of providing electric power. It prods other sectors of the industry and serves as a testing ground for new concepts. It is a bulwark against monopoly control of an essential service.

The period during which I served in the public power sector was one of the most exciting and eventful eras in the history of the electric industry. There are now new challenges. The lessons learned from history should be useful in setting a path for the future of public power and the entire electric industry.

Acknowledgments

I am indebted to many people, foremost my wife Carol, for their support and assistance in completing this book. From the outset, Carol encouraged me and patiently endured my periods of emotional detachment while I transported myself to a different era. She also did the initial editing, giving me valuable advice on style, grammar and syntax. More significantly, she offered the perspective of a layperson so the book might be of interest to a wider audience than the aficionados of public power.

My sons, Jay and Bill, were a constant source of encouragement and Bill suggested the book's title. My brother, Jacob, provided details about our family and documented facts about my mother and father. My cousin, Freda Charp, was the source of information about my father's family. My sister-in-law, Anna Jacobson, filled in details about the family of my first wife, Sara.

The book could not have been completed without the invaluable assistance of the excellent staff of the American Public Power Association. Alan Richardson, president and CEO, read and gave me comments on draft chapters, and encouraged me to complete the book. David Penn, executive vice president, likewise was supportive. Alan made available a number of members of the staff to assist me. All were helpful, but the indispensable person was Jeanne LaBella, vice president, publishing, who served as my editor. Among her many attributes was her ability to make sensible, much-needed cuts, in the absence of which the book would have been about 25 percent longer and far less readable. She devoted many hours to this project while continuing her other responsibilities and was always good-natured and judicious. It was a joy working with her.

Mary Rufe, library director, and Mary Fumento, assistant librarian, also were invaluable. They cheerfully provided much source material from the APPA library and researched many difficult questions about obscure information. The following members of the APPA staff read the entire manuscript, caught factual errors, corrected typos, and suggested clarifications: Chris Eckl, Michele Ghosh, Ron Lunt, Diane Moody, Shelley Padilla, Eileen Peerless, Theresa Pugh, Bob Thomas and Bob Varela. Bob Thomas, art director, designed the cover and photo layouts, and Richard Geltman, general counsel, provided valuable legal advice.

A number of friends and former colleagues read portions of the manuscript and provided useful insights; others furnished important information and perspectives through interviews. This group included Don Allen of Duncan and Allen, and Frances Francis of Spiegel & McDiarmid, Washington attorneys for a number of public power utilities; David Angevine, who as an employee of the Kansas City, Kansas, Board of Public Utilities, was involved in the creation of

APPA; Dr. James Banner, author and former professor of history at Princeton University; Charles Bartlett, syndicated columnist and former Washington correspondent of *The Chattanooga Times*; Ellen Berman, president of the Consumer Energy Council of America; Herbert Blinder, former director of technical services at APPA; J.D. Brown, former deputy executive director of APPA; S. David Freeman, chairman of the California Power Authority and formerly chief executive officer of several large public power utilities, including the Tennessee Valley Authority and the Los Angeles Department of Water and Power; Skila Harris, director, TVA; Dr. Dale Haworth, retired member of the faculty of Carleton College; Larry Hobart, a long-time associate who succeeded me as executive director of APPA; Steve Johnson, executive director, Washington Public Utility Districts Association; Llewellyn King, publisher of *The Energy Daily*; Dr. Dale Klein, who served with me as a member of the Monitored Retrievable Storage Review Commission and is currently assistant to the secretary of the Department of Defense; Robert McKinney, a former president of APPA and retired general manager of the Cowlitz County Public Utility District, Longview, Wash.; Leroy Michael, former associate general manager of the Salt River Project, Phoenix, Ariz.; Gary K. Miller, author and senior information specialist of Energy Northwest; Vic Parrish, chief executive officer, Energy Northwest; Charles Ross, former member of the Federal Power Commission; Deborah Sliz, former APPA director of government relations and currently partner, Morgan Meguire; Lee C. White, assistant special counsel to President Kennedy, special counsel to President Johnson, and former chair of the Federal Power Commission; and Steve Wright, administrator of the Bonneville Power Administration.

This book in large part is a narrative about issues in which APPA was involved during the 38 years that I was associated with that organization. As executive director, I was the principal spokesperson, and am quoted in the book. However, whatever I was able to accomplish would not have been possible without the efforts of a loyal and able staff and dedicated officers and members of APPA who contributed so much to the success of the organization. I am especially indebeted to Jim Grahl, J.D. Brown and Larry Hobart, who served successively as my deputy, and whose support, counsel and friendship were invaluable.

Despite the advice and reviews by esteemed friends and colleagues, I presume that the book contains errors and omissions, for which I take responsibility.

Alex Radin
February 2003

Chapter 1

Immigrant Parents

My father was born in Starobin, near Minsk, Belarus (formerly part of the Soviet Union); my mother's birthplace was Amdur (or Indura), Poland. I first saw light in Chattanooga, Tennessee. The contrast between the cultures of a Jewish ghetto in an Eastern European *shtetl* (village) during the latter part of the 19th century and a black ghetto in a small southern city in the 1920s defines the gulf that separates the early experiences of my parents and me.

I can only imagine the environment in which my parents grew up. They were not talkative about their youth. My father died when I was 10 years old. Although my mother lived until she was in her mid-80s, only once—late in life—did she tell me about the odyssey from her *shtetl* to the United States, and I did not have the foresight to make notes of her story.

The nearest I have come to a vicarious experience of my parents' youth was in 1959, during a trip to the Soviet Union with a United States Senate delegation. Our group spent a few days traveling on the Volga and Don rivers, and we stopped long enough at one village to disembark and stroll through the town. Seeing the wooden houses, muddy streets, animals wandering through the town, and older women wearing babushkas, I felt that I had been transported to my father's *shtetl*. I could not avoid the thought that I might have grown up there, were it not for my father's initiative in leaving Russia.

•

My father, Joseph (Joe) Radin, whom I called Papa, came from a reasonably prosperous family. He had two brothers and four sisters. All of his siblings were gentle, thoughtful people of integrity. My father was probably the most studious of the lot, having been a *Yeshivah bocher* (student of the Torah) before he left Russia.

My paternal great-grandfather established the family in Starobin, about 20 miles from Minsk. He acquired land and built two houses with gardens. The houses, which adjoined each other, were built for his two sons, one of whom was Hessel, my grandfather. Hessel was married to Esther Rachel Rubnitz, my grandmother.

In Russia, Hessel was known as a "handler." He bought goods (farm produce, fish, etc.) in Starobin and drove them in a covered wagon to Minsk, where he sold his merchandise. Then he bought other goods in Minsk for sale in Starobin. Each round trip to Minsk took about two weeks.

Starobin was then a village of about 100 families, many of whom were named Rubnitz. My Aunt Lena, Papa's sister, said that the Gentiles and the Jews got along well, and she remembered playing with Gentile children.

Hessel apparently did well as a "handler" and made several trips to the United States to visit his children, who had moved here. The last trip was in 1907, when he accompanied Lena. He remained in the United States for several months, working in New York City as a tailor and presser, and sleeping at night in the shop. After a while, he realized that the younger generation would outshine him in the United States. In Starobin, he was important; in New York, he was not. He returned to Starobin.

My father's family name was Rutgun (sometimes spelled Rodgon or Rodgen). One of my uncles had this explanation of the name: Russian Jews did not have surnames. Census takers arbitrarily assigned names to the family, frequently using words to describe objects they observed when they visited a family. Because "rutgun" means "red hen" in Russian, my uncle surmised that when a census taker came to the home of my forefathers, he saw a red hen on the grounds and gave that name to the family. I believed this story for many years, but in the course of writing this memoir, I was told by a student of Russian that "rutgun" does not mean "red hen." But it makes a good story. When Papa came to the United States he changed his name to Radin. He selected that name because he saw it on a sign over a shop in New York and concluded that Radin was more Americanized than Rutgun.

•

Like all young Jewish men in Russia, Papa was subject to the czar's dreaded draft. Life was hard in the Russian army, especially for Jews, who frequently were victims of pogroms carried out by Cossacks. Jews were terrorized by the Cossacks and many used drastic means to evade military service. To avoid conscription, my father escaped from Russia when he was in his late teens. His flight was a harrowing experience. Dogs brayed at his heels as he fled across the border.

Papa landed at Ellis Island on January 9, 1907, at the age of 19, and settled in New York City, where he worked in a cigar factory. He moved to Chattanooga, Tennessee, after a short time.

Like many immigrants, he followed a relative who had settled in Chattanooga. Many Jewish immigrants who came to the United States dispersed to the hinterlands to seek their fortunes. Following a practice of their forebears in Eastern Europe, the immigrants became peddlers, going from one small town to another to sell their wares. Frequently, they transported their goods in horse-drawn carts. When they came to a city or town they liked, they settled there and established small businesses. Sometimes, as was the case with two of my mother's cousins, they were the only Jews in a small town. In order to buy kosher food or to meet other Jews, they made weekly pilgrimages to larger nearby towns.

When an immigrant felt he had roots in a community, he invited relatives and friends to join him. That is how my father came to Chattanooga—through his cousin, Joe Kress. Like his cousin, my father opened a grocery store in a black neighborhood—one of the few means of livelihood available to foreigners. Kress undoubtedly helped him get established in business.

Once he had his own store, Papa encouraged other members of his family to move to Chattanooga, and he set them up in the grocery business. His sister, Fannie, and her family came to Chattanooga from Detroit, where Fannie's husband had been doing manual labor in a furniture warehouse. Papa apparently was not concerned about competition, because he helped his sister's family open a grocery store only one block from his own business. Papa also brought two younger brothers to Chattanooga and helped them buy grocery stores in black neighborhoods within a few blocks of his store.

•

My mother, Mollie Pernat, came from a poor family in Amdur. She had two sisters—one older and one younger—and an older brother. Her family was never well off. Their situation was made desperate by the death of her father when she was a child. Her mother subsisted by cleaning houses and doing other menial chores. Mom came to North America with an older sister, Neshke. They had a rough voyage in steerage and were sick during much of the trip. Mom and her sister settled in Montreal, where Neshke's husband had moved earlier. At the time, my mother was only 10 or 12 years old. She promptly went to work in a garment sweatshop. Because she was a minor, she was told to hide in a rest room when child labor inspectors came to the factory. The trauma of hiding probably had a lasting effect, because throughout her life she was fearful of authorities.

My awareness of Mom's apprehension of authority was etched in my memory when I took her on a tour of the Capitol shortly after I moved to Washington. I thought that she would be impressed by the experience. To my dismay, I found that she was uncomfortable and wanted to hurry through the tour. She was visibly relieved when we left the building.

Like my father, my mother was a person of integrity. She also was kind and generous—as she demonstrated on many occasions during the Great Depression when she gave food and other assistance to poor blacks in the neighborhood where our grocery store was located. She had a limited education, but learned to write and read Yiddish. She spoke English fairly well, but was not fluent in writing English. The hardships experienced in her childhood did not embitter her, but toughened her to endure the adversities she was to face later.

When Mom was in her late teens, she came to Chattanooga to visit a relative. By that time, she had moved with her sister, Neshke, to Kingston, New York. During her visit to Chattanooga, she met my father. They probably had a rather short courtship, and relatives or friends undoubtedly tried to arrange a marriage. However, Papa was somewhat shy and was diffident about proposing. In fact, the story (perhaps apocryphal) is that my mother had already boarded the train that was to take her back to Kingston when my father, at the last minute, came to the railroad station, proposed to her on the train and induced her to disembark so they could get married. The only vestige of the wedding ceremony that I ever saw was a pressed flower that was preserved in one of my father's books.

Mom and Papa were quiet people. From time to time they had disagreements, but I rarely, if ever, heard them quarrel or raise their voices. Their differences stemmed primarily from the fact that my father was more gregarious than my mother. Occasionally, he wanted to visit friends or relatives, while my mother preferred to stay home, usually with the excuse that she didn't want to leave her mother, who lived with us from time to time.

In addition to having a love of music, my father read quite a bit, both books and a Jewish newspaper, the *Forward*, which was considered by some to be a socialist publication. My mother also read the Jewish newspaper, but her favorite articles were the "Bintle Briefs," an early Jewish version of the Ann Landers column. Many letters in the column—

at least those that my mother discussed—were about immigrant families whose Americanized sons and daughters abandoned their parents or were ashamed to associate with them after the children had made it in American society. This scenario was of obvious concern to my parents and their friends. They were worried that they, too, might ultimately be abandoned by their children who were growing up in a different culture.

It was not until many years into my adulthood that I fully appreciated the impact my parents' unquestioning love had on me. Their complete acceptance of me was their greatest gift. It gave me a sense of confidence that compensated to a large degree for my feelings of insecurity, born of other circumstances.

·

From this union of two immigrants, I was born on June 14, 1921, in a modest house that my parents rented near their grocery store. The only memorabilia I have from my infancy is a small silver cup and spoon that were given to my parents by relatives, in honor of my birth.

My brother Jacob, who was called Jake or Jakie, had preceded me by five years. He was born February 18, 1916. One of his earliest memories was a celebration after the armistice was declared at the end of World War I. My mother and father were witnessing a parade in Chattanooga when fireworks went off. My mother was so frightened that she rushed into a store with Jake to protect him.

When I was an infant, my parents moved to an apartment located over our grocery on Tenth Street in Chattanooga. I have no recollection of the house where I was born, but I have vivid memories of Tenth Street, which was my home for the first 10 years of my life.

Chapter 2

Early Days on Tenth Street

Tenth Street was the center of my universe and a symbol of the formative period of my life. It shaped my social outlook, indirectly influenced my choice of a career and left scars that have never completely healed.

Tenth Street was in the heart of a black ghetto. It was definitely on "the wrong side of the tracks." Our living quarters above the store consisted of a kitchen, a bathroom, two bedrooms and a combination living-dining room. With the exception of the kitchen, which had a coal-burning stove, all of the rooms were heated by fireplaces. My parents, my brother Jake, and I all shared one bedroom. Most of the time my grandmother occupied the second bedroom. In those years privacy didn't have the sanctity that it does today.

The living-dining room was used on rare occasions for company, although sometimes I could hear my mother and father conversing there in the evenings after Jake and I went to bed. It was furnished with a ponderous dining room table and chairs, a cabinet, and a sofa covered in black leather. My immigrant parents referred to the sofa as a "lunge" (lounge). It was not until I was in junior high school that I learned the correct pronunciation of "lounge." I was called upon to read aloud and pronounced the word as I had heard it at home—much to my embarrassment, but to the amusement of my classmates.

Before I was born, these limited quarters were used several times to house families of relatives who were brought to the United States by my father. The relatives would stay for three or four weeks, until permanent lodging was found for them. In one case, a cousin was born in this apartment. I don't know how my parents managed to accommodate so many people in such a small space, but they never complained.

Despite these Spartan living quarters, I have some happy memories of those times. Even today, I can recall the warm feeling of being bathed, as an infant, in a large washtub in the kitchen, where water was heated on top of a coal-burning range. I also savored the times when I had a cold or other illness and had to be confined to bed. To comfort me, Mom treated me to high-quality crayons, which I was allowed to use in bed during my recuperation.

The apartment was secondary to the store, where we spent most of our time. The store had many features of a home. The rear one-quarter was separated from the front by a large refrigerated display case for meats and dairy products. This area became a living space where we had a small kitchen. There, I ate almost all of my meals, read books, and later worked on model airplanes. This part of the store was inviting in the winter because it was heated by a pot-bellied stove, later replaced by what we regarded as a luxurious circulating heater fired by coal.

Drawing was another diversion I enjoyed. In the late 1920s, Admiral Richard Byrd received a great deal of publicity about his exploration of the Antarctic region. My father avidly followed his adventures. He read newspaper articles to me about the expedition and showed me pictures of the frozen Antarctic wasteland. It was rather easy to draw this barren landscape, and I often used it as the subject of my art. I also copied favorite cartoons from the newspaper, and compiled a notebook of these drawings.

Mom and Papa were not particularly fond of pets—especially dogs, considering my father's encounter with them in escaping from Russia. However, to control mice, my parents had pet cats. They bred a number of litters. One of the delights of my childhood was to play with and watch the kittens, to which I became quite devoted—so much so that I once wrote a poem about a favorite kitten.

At the time I was growing up, I thought the store was spacious, but when I returned there as an adult I was surprised by its smallness. It could not have been more than about 15 to 20 feet wide, and perhaps 25 to 30 feet long. It had two large front windows, one of which was used to display fruits and vegetables, the other to display "dry goods"—items of clothing and other "notions." The window that was used to display fruit was emblazoned with the words "J. Radin" in a semicircle, and underneath, "Groceries, Fresh Meats, Dry Goods."

Adjacent to the front of the store and on the rear were two duplex houses that my parents owned to provide a source of rental income. Wedged between the rear of the store and one of the duplexes was a small shed used by my family to store coal and other items. At one point, I had visions of a more grandiose use of the shed. At a picnic, I was treated to a ride on a pony, and was given a ticket to a raffle for the pony. I had dreams of winning the pony and converting the shed to a stable.

The duplexes were rented to black families. I occasionally went into these houses and others in the neighborhood. The visits gave me insights I have not forgotten about urban poverty. Our own housing was hardly grand, but it was sumptuous compared with that of our tenants. We had running water, electricity and inside toilets. Our neighbors had none of these amenities. For lighting, they used kerosene lamps and pumped water from wells in the rear of the houses. Occupants of two of the houses had to share the use of an outside privy that was adjacent to the basement of our adjoining store. This much-used facility frequently overflowed, and the stench was nauseating until the privy was repaired. (I pitied the local Jewish immigrant plumber who did this nasty repair work, but he was later rewarded when he developed a thriving plumbing business.)

•

The customers of our store were very poor, barely eking out a living. Men were engaged mainly in manual labor, the women in housework for "white folks"—jobs requiring long hours at meager pay. They had money only for the barest necessities—certainly none for telephones or radios (television, of course, had not been invented). Their diversions consisted primarily of going to church. If they occasionally had enough money to go to a movie theater, they were relegated either to a "colored" movie house or to the balcony of a "white" theater. Living under such conditions, it is not surprising that some sought refuge in drinking cheap bootleg liquor. Fights broke out frequently, often spilling out into the streets. Switchblade knives were the weapons of choice.

Election Day provided a slight additional income for many of the blacks. Local political bosses paid their poll tax, plus an additional dollar, and blacks were rounded up and taken to the polls.

Blacks also sought to obtain extra income by playing the numbers—gambling that was illegal, but commonplace. Runners to collect money for numbers plied the neighborhood and when a lucky person "hit," it was the source of rejoicing.

My parents more or less accepted the role of the blacks—this being before the era of civil rights. Occasionally, they would make derogatory comments about their black neighbors and customers, but generally they treated them with respect, if not pity, and accorded them extensions of credit, which were repaid with few exceptions.

Mom and Papa never attempted to exploit their customers, who reciprocated by referring deferentially to my father as "Mr. Joe" and to my mother as "Miss Mollie." One incident especially impressed me as indicative of the feelings our customers had for my parents. Shortly after Papa's death, Mom received an anonymous letter from a person who enclosed $10—a large sum in those days. The writer said that this money was in payment for a debt long owed to my parents, and was being remitted because of the compassion this person felt for my mother in her bereavement.

We sold mostly staples, such as basic canned food, meats, white bread (5 cents a loaf), milk (5 cents a pint, 10 cents a quart), and a few fruits and vegetables. Because they were considered a luxury, fruits were sold mostly during the Christmas season. At that time, we also offered specialties, such as English walnuts and Brazil nuts. Even our African-American customers referred to Brazil nuts as "nigger toes."

Meats consisted largely of spare ribs, neck bones, pigs' feet, bologna, pork chops and ham; steaks were unheard of. One of the more popular meats, because it was so cheap, was fatback—largely pork fat from which one could slice bacon containing meager quantities of lean meat. Other staples in considerable demand were lard, which we ladled from a large metal container, and a yellow cheese, which was cut from a large, round "hog's head." We also handled a product that I found repulsive—chitterlings (or chitlins), which were the small intestines of pigs.

During the Depression, one of the more popular items was peanut butter, which we served from a large metal container. Customers could buy a small quantity that we ladled into a paper container. For a penny they could purchase a peanut butter "sandwich"—peanut butter between two crackers.

Chickens were sold live, by weight, from a coop, and were killed by customers who wrung their necks (not a pretty sight). I disliked handling chickens, because of the sometimes-difficult task of attempting to hold them still while they were being weighed. There was always the danger, too, that the chickens would decide to defecate while I was holding them. Fortunately, the chicken coop was moved outside the store during the summer—a relief for our olfactory senses.

We sold kerosene, or coal oil, which our customers used for lamps. We pumped the coal oil into metal containers from a large orange tank at the rear of the store.

Cigarettes were a luxury. Few of our customers could afford to buy an entire pack, so we sold individual cigarettes for one cent each. Our most popular tobacco products were snuff (used mainly by women), and chewing tobacco, which we sometimes cut in small triangles so that it was more affordable.

We sold women's dresses, stockings, bloomers and panties; men's denim overalls and shirts; candy, chewing gum, school supplies, soft drinks and a few toys, such as marbles. During one Christmas season we stocked a few cuckoo clocks (probably because they fascinated my father). I enjoyed winding them up and seeing the cuckoo spring out at the appointed hour, to the accompaniment of a loud, "cuckoo, cuckoo."

•

Jake and I worked in the store and virtually lived there. It was the center of my limited social life, which consisted largely of playing with cousins who lived nearby or with black children in the neighborhood. My favorite game was marbles. To my parents' chagrin, I freely gave away store merchandise—marbles, candy and chewing gum—to my playmates. I generally enjoyed playing with the black kids, but occasionally I would get into a fistfight with one of them, usually over a game of marbles.

The store had interesting nooks and crannies that allowed me to exercise my imagination. A large closed storage compartment under a window display space for fruits and vegetables became a cave where I could hide. An indentation in this same area served as a place where I could pretend to lead a band, or play drums.

The long hours of operation left little time for family socializing. The store was open from 6 a.m. to 9 p.m. daily, and until about 11:30 p.m. on Saturday. On weekdays, after the store was closed, we went to the local curb market to buy produce for the following day. On Sunday, the store was open only until 3 p.m.

The highlight of the year was the celebration of the two major Jewish holidays—Rosh Hashanah and Yom Kippur. The seven-day-a-week routine of operating a grocery store was broken during these holidays, when the Jewish-owned stores closed. Although my father was a *Yeshivah bocher* in Russia, he was not especially observant of orthodox Jewish customs, except during these holidays. On Rosh Hashanah and Yom Kippur we went to the synagogue. Mainly, though, these holidays were an opportunity for us to be together in a relaxed setting as a family, and have a sit-down meal in our home rather than in back of the store.

Rosh Hashanah offered another diversion. It is not as holy a day as Yom Kippur, and Orthodox Jews observed the occasion for two days. After spending a day and a half in *shul* (synagogue), many Jewish families established the tradition of going to the premier local movie theater, the Tivoli, on the afternoon of the second day of Rosh Hashanah. Such an activity was not strictly kosher; consequently, we sneaked off to the movie house. We frequently saw other Jewish families taking part in this forbidden activity, too, but to respect their (and our) privacy, we rarely acknowledged their presence, nor did they greet us. We were aware that we were indulging in sacrilegious behavior, but this rare opportunity to spend time with our parents in entertainment outside of the grocery store made us relish the experience.

My father's interest in music brightened our lives. He taught himself to play a mandolin (which I still have), and he was one of the first of his contemporaries to buy a wind-up record player. His favorite recordings were of violinists and opera singers. We listened to opera stars such as Luisa Tetrazzini, Amelita Galli-Curci and Enrico Caruso. My father's favorite violinists were Mischa Elman, Jascha Heifitz and the child prodigy, Yehudi Menuhin. Menuhin was the envy of all Jewish parents, especially those who had sons.

Jewish mores dictated that all Jewish boys study the violin and girls the piano. Jake began violin lessons at an early age. When I was eight years old, my father took me to Lester Cohn, one of the favorite violin teachers at the Cadek Conservatory, which was founded by a talented Czech family of musicians. Cohn carefully examined my hands and proclaimed that my fingers were excellent for the violin. He particularly admired the pads at the ends of my fingers, which he said were especially suitable for obtaining a good tone quality from the violin. (I am sure he found similar attributes in all of his prospective pupils.) I took up the violin and won a gold medal, which I still have, at my first annual recital.

Thereafter I began to lose enthusiasm. My music studies ended at the end of the second year, when I played with an ensemble. I barely touched the bow to the strings during the recital, because I was under the mistaken impression that if I could hear myself, my playing must be standing out above that of the other musicians. Since I was not overly proud of my performance, the last thing I wanted the audience to hear was my scraping away on the strings. At the completion of the program, when recognition was given to the students, I did not receive another medal or other award. Lacking this incentive, I lost interest in the violin and after my father's death gave up the instrument.

Although I did not fulfill Jewish parents' fondest hope—that their boys would become prodigies such as Menuhin—I enjoyed hearing music, and it became one of my principal interests. Jake continued to progress. Playing violin (and later, viola) has been a continuing source of pleasure to him and to those who have heard him.

Sunday afternoons or evenings also provided other diversions, such as strolling and window shopping in Chattanooga's main business area—Market Street. A highlight of this activity was a stop at George K. Brown's ice cream parlor, whose antiseptic décor featured a white marble floor, white walls and bent iron ice cream chairs and tables. The main attraction was the large counter where ice cream and sodas were dispensed. At George K. Brown's, I became a life-long devotee of ice cream and chocolate sodas.

Some Sunday afternoons we visited the Chickamauga Civil War battlefields near Chattanooga. For these occasions we dressed in our Sunday best clothes.

•

A grammar school was on College Hill, about two blocks from the grocery store. It was segregated, of course, and the white teachers would frequently stop at the store before or after work. My parents befriended them and they permitted me to enroll in the school about half a year before I otherwise would have been eligible. Because of my age or my feelings about living above the grocery store on Tenth Street, I had difficulty adjusting socially to school, initially. I also was at a disadvantage because neither my parents nor I were familiar with some of the conventions of the white Gentile kids who constituted the overwhelming majority of students. My first major embarrassment was at Easter in the first grade. Each kid was asked to bring an egg to school and I dutifully relayed this information to my mother. Not realizing that we were supposed to bring hard-boiled eggs that presumably would have been dyed or decorated, my mother sent me off with a raw egg, which I carefully carried to school. However, after I arrived I put the egg in my pocket and sat down at my desk—with disastrous consequences.

When I was in the second grade, I learned a lesson that made a lasting impression on me. I was seated in the back of the classroom, and observed that during an arithmetic test some of my fellow students were looking up answers to a quiz on a crib sheet attached to the test. This seemed to be an easy way to get the correct answers, provided one knew how to relate the answers to the questions. Unfortunately, I had not been briefed on this technique, and got completely bollixed up. When I turned in my paper, the teacher, Miss Acuff, immediately discerned that I had used the crib sheet.

Miss Acuff was an attractive person whom I admired (in fact, I had a crush on her), and when she asked me to remain after class I knew something was wrong. Without being too severe in rebuking me, she made it clear that cheating was strictly verboten, and that I could better answer the questions on my own rather than via the crib sheet. Duly embarrassed, and afraid that I would get caught if I ever tried it again, I foreswore cheating forever. (The honest approach seemed to work better anyhow; I never figured out how to use the crib sheet.)

Chapter 3

Papa's Death

Life changed abruptly on Friday, July 13, 1931, about a month after my 10th birthday. Early in the afternoon, Papa's sister, Aunt Fannie, rushed into our store, frantic and distraught. A great *umglick* (tragedy) had occurred, she wailed. Papa had died. She received the news in a telephone call from the sanatorium in Nashville, where my father had been staying for several weeks. The sanatorium had tried first to reach my mother, but was unable to do so, and therefore had called my aunt.

This is how Jake recalls hearing the news:

> That summer I was taking a course in Harmony at the Cadek Conservatory of Music in Chattanooga. Having played the violin since I was eight or nine, I was told by my teacher, Lester Cohn, that I should learn something about music theory.
>
> Around noon on July 13 I stood behind the counter in the store, harmony book and exercise tablet in front of me, ready to try my hand at the six-four chord.
>
> There was a sudden shriek and wailing. I moved to the door to see what was going on. There was Fannie running toward our store, her open apron flying, screaming, "Er is gestorben. Yossele is gestorben" (He is dead. Joe is dead.). Fannie had received the fateful telephone call from Nashville. Mom broke down.
>
> I don't know what I did. For me this was the end of Harmony, which became a hated word.

•

Pandemonium broke out as my mother and aunt vented their grief. Although I was caught up in the tragedy, I was also bewildered. I was not prepared for the news. I knew that my father had been ill and that he had to be located in a quiet place, away from Tenth Street. But death was unknown to me and I had repressed the idea that he was in a terminal condition, even though I had warnings.

A couple of months earlier, my parents had returned to the store after seeing Papa's heart doctor. They were distraught, because the doctor had told them that he had a short time to live, perhaps only six weeks. My mother was angry because the doctor had been so blunt and unfeeling about my father's condition. She thought that Papa's knowledge of the grievous state of his health aggravated his condition and brought on depression.

Until I heard this shocking information, I didn't know that my father was in such peril. So far as I could tell, he was an active, vibrant person who lived a normal life. Later, my mother said that Papa had injured his heart while dogs chased him as he escaped from Russia. I doubt that this experience explained his problem. Jake subsequently told me that my father suffered a heart ailment because he had contracted a serious case of flu during an epidemic that swept the United States in 1918, near the close of World War I. Mom also confided to Jake that Papa had typhoid fever before they were married and she thought this illness contributed to his heart condition. She learned about his typhoid fever after they were wed and resented the fact that she had not been informed prior to their marriage.

After Papa and Mom disclosed the doctor's news to Jake and me, Mom persuaded Papa to go upstairs to our living quarters to rest. As Mom and Jake escorted Papa to the rear of the store to the stairway leading to our apartment, they passed a large scale used to weigh heavy bags of sugar, beans and other staples. Papa lunged for one of the black iron balancing weights, seized it and attempted to strike himself on the head. Mom quickly thwarted his movements and she and Jake escorted Papa upstairs. As they climbed the stairs, Papa cried and attempted to bump his head against the wall of the stairwell. My terrified mother concluded that Papa was in danger of committing suicide, and was apprehensive whenever he was out of her sight.

•

After the initial trauma, there were no further incidents of this nature. However, major changes began to take place. The doctor said Papa should be in a more serene setting, removed from the stresses and strains of the grocery business. Because his sister, Aunt Fannie, and her family lived in a new house in a quiet, wooded neighborhood not too distant from Tenth Street, Papa moved to Aunt Fannie's house. Despite the more pleasant surroundings, this must have been a depressing environment for Papa. Mom, Jake and my uncle and aunt were tied up all day at their grocery stores. My father therefore was alone most of the time, giving him ample opportunity to ruminate about his fate.

After a few weeks, Papa moved to the City View Sanatorium in Nashville, about 140 miles from Chattanooga. This was supposedly a tranquil place where he would have constant care. Blocking out the doctor's prediction about my father's imminent death, I presumed that Papa would recuperate within a short time and return home.

Uncle Harry, Papa's brother, drove Mom and Papa to Nashville to admit him to the sanatorium, and they asked me to come with them. Until then, I had not been outside of the immediate vicinity of Chattanooga, so I thought the trip to Nashville would be an adventure, despite the seriousness of the situation. After seeing that my father was admitted to the sanatorium, my mother, Uncle Harry and I spent the night in a downtown Nashville hotel near the state capitol. Sleeping in a hotel for the first time, looking out the window at a busy street and the state capitol, walking around a strange city with my mother and uncle and eating at a restaurant were all exhilarating new experiences.

Before returning to Chattanooga the following day, we visited my father and said our good-byes. Located on spacious grounds in a park-like setting outside the city, the sanatorium appeared to be an attractive place, but I overheard disturbing references to the fact that some of the patients suffered from mental illnesses.

After Papa was admitted to the sanatorium, Mom made regular trips to Nashville to visit him. Because she could not drive, the automobile trip presented a problem. My uncle could not get away from his store often; consequently, Mom sometimes hired a young neighborhood black man to drive us. Jake tended the store when my mother went to Nashville. After my first travel adventure, I found the subsequent long drives boring. I was not privy to all the discussions between Mom and Papa during our visits, but I did hear Papa's occasional complaints. He was especially concerned about the emotionally disturbed people who were there. After a while, Papa also began to have delusions. He complained that he heard voices of members of the family—especially his brothers and sisters—who came to the sanatorium at night but did not visit him.

•

I do not recall how long my father was at the sanatorium before he died, but it was probably not more than a few weeks or a month. During this period, my mother assumed complete responsibility for operating the grocery store. Jake took a more prominent role, too, and I pitched in to a limited extent. It was a lonely period—a foretaste of what was to come.

Because Papa died on a Friday and Jews could not be buried on the Sabbath, the funeral was held on Sunday. On the day of the funeral, a large black limousine drove up to the grocery store and picked up Mom, Jake, me and Aunt Lena, Papa's sister. We drove first to Wann's Funeral Home, where we pulled up behind a black hearse carrying Papa's casket. The hearse and our limousine led the procession to the cemetery. (I was so traumatized by the sight of the black hearse and limousine that, many years later, when my first wife, Sara, died, I insisted that we use a white hearse and limousine. I did not want my sons to have a memory of those foreboding black vehicles.)

When we arrived at the gravesite, there were Hebrew prayers and much wailing and crying. Immigrant Jews from Eastern Europe made no effort to restrain their expressions of grief. My most searing memory of the funeral was the sight of my father's corpse, wrapped in a white shroud, being placed in a simple wooden coffin (as prescribed by Jewish custom) in the newly dug grave. When that happened, Mom and others began to shriek. My mother appeared at one point to want to step into the grave to join my father and had to be restrained. At another point in the funeral, someone who was officiating made a cut in the lapels of the suit coats Jake and I were wearing. This symbolic tear in our familial relationships was another part of Jewish tradition.

After several friends and relatives made soulful, tearful remarks, the service was concluded when Jake and I read the *Kaddish*, or mourner's prayer. I had only limited exposure to Hebrew school, and could not read the *Kaddish* in Hebrew, but Jake and I stumbled through a transliterated version. Leaving the cemetery, we all washed our hands, as was customary.

That evening, and for several evenings thereafter, Mom, Jake, I and relatives and friends "sat *shiva*" (or mourning) at Aunt Fannie's house. *Shiva* consisted of reciting prayers every evening at the home of the bereaved by a *minyan* (10 adult males) and the performance of other rituals, such as covering mirrors in the home. After several days of *shiva,* Jake and I continued to say Kaddish at the morning and evening services at the local orthodox synagogue. This experience did not greatly endear me to the practice of Judaism. Because of my father's illness, and because a *bar mitzvah* was not a big deal in those days, neither Jake nor I was *bar mitzvahed*, and we had limited exposure to *cheder* (Hebrew school). Consequently, we were unable to take an active part in the daily services at the synagogue. Failing to understand a word of Hebrew, I regarded the entire service as meaningless. Members of the congregation performed by rote, mouthing Hebrew words that, for the most part, they did not understand.

Jake and I were supposed to say *Kaddish* for a year after Papa's death. However, after school started, my mother paid a fee to the *shammes* (caretaker) at the synagogue, who read the *Kaddish* for us, and we were absolved from having to attend services twice a day.

•

After the funeral, Mom, Jake and I were asked by Aunt Fannie and her husband, Uncle Barnet (pronounced "Bonnet"), to live in their house for a short time until we could find an apartment of our own (it was considered unsafe for us to continue to live above the store). Moving out of the apartment over the grocery store was a welcome relief. I relished the opportunity to live in a real house, surrounded by grass and trees, and be in the company of an aunt, uncle and cousins. I was relieved to have a respite from Tenth Street.

The pain of my father's death was eased considerably, for a short interval, by the presence of my Aunt Lena, Papa's sister, who lived in New York City. She came to Chattanooga for the funeral, and remained for an extended visit to help Mom, Jake and me during this trying period. Lena was in Chattanooga for about a month, and I became attached to her. She possessed virtually all of the characteristics that I felt my mother lacked. Although Lena was an immigrant like my mother, she spoke English well, dressed stylishly, was attractive and had a lively personality. She also took a keen interest in politics and other affairs of the day. Not having been married, and not having children, she yearned for attachment with kids, and she and I immediately took to each other. She accompanied me to movies and other activities. If we were walking near my school and encountered classmates, I was proud to introduce her.

Lena worked in the garment industry. She apparently was an excellent seamstress and made expensive fashionable clothing for women. She was active in the International Ladies Garment Workers Union and in left-wing politics and could probably be described as a socialist. Lena's political views, and later the philosophy of President Franklin D. Roosevelt's New Deal, were important influences in shaping my political orientation.

Lena made a considerable sacrifice by taking a leave of absence from her job in New York to be with our family. However, after about a month, she informed us that she would have to return home. Our prospective separation was a devastating experience for both Lena and me. On the final afternoon of her stay in Chattanooga, she took me to a movie.

Mindful of her departure the next day, I could not enjoy the occasion. I was deeply saddened by the thought that she would soon be leaving. We walked home from the theater in mournful silence. Even so, I did not then realize how much I would miss her and how the mood and tempo of my life would change after her departure.

•

For a month or more after Papa died, we continued to live with Aunt Fannie and her family—an experience that temporarily masked the extent of the tragedy that had befallen Mom, Jake and me. But it soon became apparent that sharing the house with Fannie's family was an imposition on them. So Mom found an apartment on Seventh Street, several blocks from our store, in a predominantly white neighborhood. The apartment was on the second floor of a relatively new, red brick building with modern amenities. It had a porch in the front and a small grassy plot in the back where Jake and I and others occasionally played touch football.

Mom's way of dealing with Papa's death was to shut it out as best she could. She rarely mentioned him and she tried to conceal from Jake and me anything having to do with his death. Several months after Papa died, a man visited the store a few times and engaged in muted conversation with Mom. She did not tell us the subject of their talks, but I later deduced that they had been talking about a tombstone for my father's grave. I am sure she went to the cemetery for the unveiling, but neither Jake nor I was asked to go. We never talked about Papa or overtly grieved. It was not until three decades later, when I saw a therapist, that I broke down and wept uncontrollably about my father's death.

Although we continued to be lonely and isolated, life returned somewhat to normal when school started that fall. Our teacher asked us to tell what had happened to us during the summer vacation, and I told about my father's death, but without emotion. I recounted with some pride my adventure in going to Nashville and visiting my father in the sanatorium. Later in the year, I was elected class president. I learned how to call the meeting to order, and to follow other procedures that were a necessary part of running a meeting. I even learned some of *Robert's Rules of Order*. This sixth grade experience stood me in good stead many years later, when my professional responsibilities required me to lead meetings.

Because of his heart condition, Papa was not able to buy life insurance. Mom inherited the grocery store and the property immediately surrounding it. Thanks to Mom's willingness to work long hours and deprive herself, we never lacked for food, clothing or other necessities.

Housing was the only area in which I felt somewhat deprived. Our apartment was clean and comfortable, but in a poor neighborhood and I did not feel comfortable inviting friends to visit me in our home, and certainly not in the store.

By 1932, a year after Papa's death, the economic depression had worsened considerably. Even in the normally poverty-stricken Tenth Street we began to feel the increasingly severe impact of the Depression, and later, the exhilaration of the election of Franklin D. Roosevelt and the advent of the New Deal.

Chapter 4

The Great Depression and the New Deal

The Great Depression was under way in 1932, but for a brief period, the seriousness of the times was masked by an exciting adventure. Partially, if not entirely, out of *rachmones* (pity) over loss of my father, Uncle Harry invited me to accompany him in the summer of 1932 on a trip to Paterson, New Jersey, to visit Aunt Celia Freedman and her family. From Paterson, I was to have a reunion with Aunt Lena in New York City. Except for trips to Nashville, I had not been outside Chattanooga's immediate environs.

The journey took 18 hours on a train powered by a coal-fired steam locomotive that belched black smoke into the air and into the open windows of our non-air-conditioned coach. After a few hours, our clothes were grimy with black soot. Nevertheless, I was riveted to the window, excited to see unfamiliar towns and terrain. I had my first glimpse of Washington on this trip. We changed trains at Union Station and had time to go outside to see the Capitol building. This brief view of Washington was enough to convince me that I wanted to return to see more of the city, although I never dreamed then that I would spend most of my life in the nation's capital.

Our train arrived in Newark, New Jersey, and we took a bus to Paterson. To a more sophisticated person, Paterson would have been no big deal, but it opened new worlds for me.

Aunt Celia's husband, Louis Freedman, was the prosperous owner of an electrical appliance store in downtown Paterson. His store offered a sharp contrast to neighborhood grocery stores in the Chattanooga ghettos. Unlike my Chattanooga relatives, Uncle Louis dressed well. He was "Americanized" and spoke English without an accent. The Freedman's house was more impressive than any I had ever seen. It was large and well furnished and located in a neighborhood that teemed with life. Although

Paterson was not a large city, it was close to New York and had some of the attributes of that city, such as bustling communities and a delicatessen displaying a greater variety of delicacies than those available in Chattanooga.

My reunion with Lena was the most gratifying aspect of the trip. She lived in the Brighton Beach section of New York and after I had spent a few days in Paterson, she came to escort me to New York, to stay in her apartment and to tour the city. As we crossed the Hudson River by ferry from Hoboken, I was excited by the skyscrapers and riverboats and the hustle and bustle of New York. In anticipation of the trip, Uncle Harry bought me a small camera, thereby introducing me to what became a life-long interest in photography. Some of my first photos were taken on this trip.

Lena took me on a tour of the sights of the city: the Statue of Liberty, the Hayden Planetarium, Radio City Music Hall, Wall Street, the Metropolitan Museum, and a trip through Manhattan on the upper deck of a Fifth Avenue bus. My most lasting impressions of Radio City Music Hall were the opulence of the magnificent hall, the dancing Rockettes and the novelty of electric hand dryers in the men's room.

Eating at restaurants and delicatessens was a new experience. The dish that impressed me the most was a cream cheese sandwich. Another unique experience was eating at the Horn and Hardart automat, where food was displayed in glass-fronted compartments and diners could drop a nickel, dime or quarter into the slot to retrieve a meal or snack.

•

After this brief interlude in New York, I returned to a dreary, lonely life in Chattanooga centered about the grocery store. Almost imperceptibly at first, the signs of the deepening Depression began to appear. Our customers had less and less money to spend, even for bare necessities.

Another sign of the Depression was the increasing number of robberies and hold-ups. Uncle Joe Prebul, who was married to Mom's sister, Edith, was more gutsy than most grocery store owners, and thwarted attempted hold-ups by engaging in gun battles with robbers. Fortunately, he was a good shot and emerged unscathed. Closer to home, a customer in Aunt Fannie's store, just a block from ours, was killed by a police officer as he resisted arrest.

There was violence in the streets too. Once, after we had closed the store and were driving home, a fight erupted in the street. As we passed the scene of the fight, Jake blew the horn and one of the angry participants threw a rock through the window on the driver's side of the car. The shattering glass cut Jake's face and we rushed to the emergency room of a nearby hospital. Fortunately, Jake was not hurt badly.

Because of the robberies and violence, Mom engaged a black man in the neighborhood—Mr. Bostick—to guard the store in the evenings. Bostick was a strong but gentle person. His presence gave us a feeling of security. He also relieved the tedium of tending to the store. A native of the Bahamas, he had worked as a stevedore before coming to Chattanooga. The life of a stevedore was entirely foreign to me and I was entranced by his stories about far-away places. Although a number of neighborhood grocery stores were held up, ours never was, perhaps because of Bostick's presence. I also believed (perhaps naively) that there was some honor among thieves, and that they would not prey upon a widow. This was in an era when one rarely, if ever, heard of attacks on women or elderly persons. If a suspicious person entered the store, Mom would tell Jake and me to go outside.

For whatever reasons—perhaps a confluence of fundamentalist religion and a desire to protect the interests of larger stores—the Chattanooga police enforced the "blue laws," which prohibited merchants from doing business on Sunday. This was a serious blow to smaller merchants, because the long hours we operated were one of the major reasons we were competitive. Mom and other small merchants flaunted the law by allowing customers to enter the store through a back door on Sunday mornings. This led to tense moments. When we observed a patrol car cruising nearby, we asked the customers to huddle in the rear of the store so the police could not see them. Fortunately, we escaped any citations.

The most direct impact of the Depression was the bank holiday proclaimed early in the Roosevelt administration. Aside from the store and rental property, Mom's assets consisted of about $2,000 in savings. For a period of several years, Mom was denied access to this money. Eventually, most of the savings were returned but, at the time, we did not know whether the money would ever be available.

The bank closing was my first tangible evidence of the coming of the New Deal. Although it was a disheartening experience, other actions gave us hope. Stamps similar to today's food stamps were issued to the needy, but confronted us with an ethical dilemma. They were to be used only for food. We were pressured by customers to accept the stamps for prohibited products, such as tobacco or clothing. Although we normally abided by the rules, I suspect that at times Mom permitted some customers to use the stamps for items other than food.

Other manifestations of the New Deal also became evident. The most impressive was the creation of the Tennessee Valley Authority. Chickamauga Dam on the Tennessee River, about seven miles upstream from Chattanooga, was one of the earliest TVA construction projects. As work on the dam progressed, Jake and I found another venue for our Sunday afternoon outings. We drove to an observation point near the dam and spent hours watching the construction.

Gleaming white refrigerators and washing machines, manifestations of the New Deal's rural electrification program, began to appear on the front porches of Tennessee farmhouses. They were a mark of pride to the homeowners, who were delighted to have electricity.

Construction of dams created the need for high-voltage transmission towers to move electricity to people throughout the region. Today, these towers are regarded by some as a blight on the landscape, but in that era they were a welcome sign of progress.

During that period I got my first taste of opposition by the power companies to public power. There was to be a referendum in Chattanooga on the issue of establishing a municipal electric distribution system that would buy power from TVA and distribute it at retail within the city. Establishment of such a utility would be in competition with the privately owned Tennessee Electric Power Company (TEPCO), and ultimately could (and did) result in the takeover of that company's system in Chattanooga. At the height of the campaign, the refrigeration system for the meat display case in our store needed repairs and TEPCO sent a serviceman to do the work. After he finished, he lectured us about the dangers of setting up a publicly owned electric utility, which he said would be inefficient and would not provide the reliable service we were accustomed to receiving from TEPCO. Many years later I recalled this incident when I worked for the American Public Power Association and was repeatedly confronted with similar arguments against public power.

Perhaps the most important impact of the New Deal was intangible, but very real: an infusion of hope in the lives of the people. President Roosevelt's actions and personality gave us faith. We believed him when he said "the only thing we have to fear is fear itself." We relied on radio to convey the mood and character of a person, as well as the substance of the message. Roosevelt's voice was reassuring and his fireside chats conveyed such warmth and intimacy that he seemed to be present in our homes. These feelings were reinforced when we saw his smiling face and jaunty demeanor in newspaper photos or newsreels.

•

The Depression affected my schooling and my professional career. Early in the Depression, I entered junior high school. I felt overwhelmed by the much larger school, changing classes each period, rushing to lockers and gym classes where we were handed a basketball and told to play a game with rules and objectives unknown to me. The only bright spot in the seventh grade was a class in mechanical drawing. I enjoyed the course tremendously and had visions of becoming an architect or engineer. However, because of the Depression, an advanced course in mechanical drawing was dropped in the eighth grade, ending my serious interest in this subject. In lieu of mechanical drawing, I began to work on the school newspaper, which ultimately led me to become a newspaper reporter.

Gradually the tedium of the Depression was relieved by other diversions. I took up building model airplanes and spent almost every weekend at the kitchen table in the back of the store building a model. Another diversion was going to rehearsals of the Chattanooga Symphony Orchestra. Jake was one of the orchestra's founders and served as concertmaster or assistant concertmaster. I often accompanied him to rehearsals, which deepened my appreciation for music. Rehearsals heightened our suspense about the concert, as we wondered how some of the more difficult passages would turn out at the performance. The French horn solo in the second movement of Tchaikovsky's Fifth Symphony was especially challenging. It is a haunting, soulful melody, but the French horn is not an easy instrument to play, and the solo can be ruined by a flubbed rendition. Robert Shinbaum played this part flawlessly during the final rehearsal, but then flubbed several notes at the concert. Shinbaum's speaking voice was superior to his French horn playing. He later became a radio announcer and his mellifluous voice was heard on NBC under the name Robert Sherry.

At rehearsals, I learned a few phrases and terms used by musicians in critiquing their performance. These were useful to me later when I was a newspaper reporter. The city editor tapped me occasionally to review a symphony concert as a substitute for the paper's regular music reviewer. I managed to include in my reviews every one of the few terms I knew.

The highlight of the Chattanooga Symphony Orchestra's performances was a concert at which Jake was the soloist, playing Lalo's Symphony Espagnole. He practiced this work diligently (customers at our store became very familiar with this work), but Mom and I were nervous before the Sunday afternoon concert at Chattanooga High School auditorium. However, Jake played flawlessly and received an enthusiastic ovation. His performance was favorably reviewed (not by me) the following morning on the front page of *The Chattanooga Times*. Mom did her share of sobbing during the performance, as she gleaned *naches* (pride) from her son's performance.

•

At the height of the Depression a cousin from New York arrived unexpectedly in the store one day. Jack Arnold (his real name was Arnovitz) had a strong influence on my life. He was the son of Mom's older sister, Neshke, and lived in Coney Island. He was about the same age as Jake and was an aspiring journalist. He had found it impossible to get a job in New York. Without informing us in advance, he hitchhiked to Chattanooga to see if he could find employment.

He arrived one summer day after a heavy downpour. Because of the rain, the chicken coop had been moved into the store and the odor was strong. Suddenly, the sun shone brightly and into the store appeared this handsome but bedraggled person. We were shocked when he introduced himself, but he was a self-possessed, voluble person, and we felt comfortable with him almost immediately. In fact, he was a welcome addition to our family, which was starved for companionship.

Jack was an anomaly. He spoke with an accent quite different from the one I was accustomed to. He had hitchhiked from New York to Chattanooga and had spent some nights sleeping in barns. Jack was a strong-willed, self-proclaimed, highly verbal Communist who was not reticent about expounding his views. His vigor and enthusiasm were stimulating and I was fascinated with him as a personality. He brought excitement into our humdrum lives. He had not been able to land a job at New York newspapers, so he was pleasantly surprised when prospective employers at Chattanooga's two daily papers interviewed him. However, jobs were scarce and because of Jack's limited experience, he did not get a job as a reporter in Chattanooga.

After several weeks, he gave up the quest for a position on a local newspaper. In desperation, he went to work helping the Jewish owner of a grocery store in a black neighborhood. Jake and I never liked working in the grocery store and we never intended to make a career of it, but we thought that it was an honorable calling. Not so, Jack. Every evening after he returned to our store from work, he would regale us with stories about how the black people were oppressed or exploited by the owner of the store where he worked. To him, the situation was a typical case of class warfare and substantiated Communist dogma.

It was no surprise several weeks later when Jack decided to return to New York. I was saddened at his departure. I thought some of his views were extreme, but many of his pronouncements seemed reasonable, given the circumstances of the Depression. I learned a lot from Jack. His enthusiasm, idealism and dedication to a cause were an inspiration. Jack proselytized to the end of his visit. His parting gift to Jake was a copy of Lenin's "Imperialism—The State and Revolution."

Shortly after he returned to New York, Jack joined the Abraham Lincoln Brigade and went to Spain to fight with the Loyalists. The Spanish Civil War was a *cause celebre* at that time and in many ways foreshadowed the line-up of forces in World War II. The Spanish fascist, Francisco Franco, attempted to overthrow the monarchy in Spain and received direct assistance from Hitler. The Soviet Union sided with the Spanish Loyalists and they and their supporters from other countries sent troops and other assistance to the Loyalists. The Abraham Lincoln Brigade was organized in the United States as part of the aid to the Loyalists.

I corresponded some with Jack after he left Chattanooga. Sadly, within a short time after he arrived in Spain, his family reported that he was missing in action. His brother asked us and other friends to write the State Department to see if they could find out anything about him, but our efforts were to no avail.

Despite the fact that the Spanish Loyalists and the Abraham Lincoln Brigade were fighting the fascist Franco and Hitler's minions, the State Department seemed little interested in helping relatives of members of the Abraham Lincoln Brigade. Jack was never heard from, and was presumed to have been killed, which was not surprising. Members of the Abraham Lincoln Brigade had a great deal of fervor for their cause, but they lacked training or weapons.

Chapter 5

Life In A Small Southern Town

After the initial shock of Papa's death and the trauma of the Depression years, I began to enjoy various activities in Chattanooga.

In terms of physical setting, Chattanooga (population about 120,000) was a pleasant place to live. It is surrounded by picturesque mountains and hills, and the Tennessee River meanders through the city. From the top of nearby Lookout Mountain, one is supposed to be able to see seven states.

Chattanooga also is rich in history. It was the site of important battles fought during the Civil War (referred to in the South as the War Between the States). Civil War cannons and battlefields were within easy walking or driving distance of our home. Across the street from the elementary school that I attended was a southern mansion that had been used by Gen. Grant as his headquarters during the nearby battles. It had been converted into a funeral home at the time I was in school.

As I grew older, many opportunities for recreation and entertainment were opened to me. I frequently hiked in the mountains with friends. Late in the Depression, a family of actors—the Peruccis—moved to Chattanooga, took over the Bijou theater and began presenting comedies in repertory, thereby providing some comic relief from the agony of those times. The price of admission was low; for a pittance, Chattanoogans could enjoy a couple hours of laughs.

The prime movie theater was the Tivoli. Along with first-run films, it featured live entertainment. Jake and I never bothered to go to the movies at the beginning of the feature picture; instead, we entered the theater whenever it was convenient, and we stayed until we had seen a complete show. If a film was especially good, we might see it twice —or more. Once, we were so entranced with the Marx brothers that we stayed through more than two performances—much to Mom's dismay. After three or four hours, she was understandably concerned about our whereabouts.

The Community Concert series introduced me to a number of famous performers. It brought to Chattanooga such notables as singers Lawrence Tibbett and Lily Pons, the Ted Shawn dance ensemble (Martha Graham may have performed with this group, too), and ballet companies. My most memorable experience was the performance by Marian Anderson. I will never forget her regal demeanor and her magnificent voice.

I was not active in sports, but there was a period when I was an avid fan of Chattanooga's minor league baseball team, the Lookouts. The game was enlivened by many special events promoted by the team's imaginative owner, Joe Engle. To make up for the team's deficiencies, Engle arranged a number of stunts. On one occasion, he hired a woman who pitched to Babe Ruth in an exhibition game – and struck him out. He also hung birdcages with live birds in the stadium. His biggest promotion was raffling a new, completely furnished house.

Aside from these attractions, Engle managed to hire a few colorful players. Most notable was a swashbuckling first baseman, "Mule" Shirley. He played with a verve that made him a crowd pleaser. Unfortunately, he could not stay away from hard liquor, and fell victim to what the local newspapers politely referred to as "Joe Barleycorn." It was a sad day for the fans when he was fired.

In addition to following the Lookouts, I enjoyed going to football games of the University of Chattanooga's Moccasins. Because of Jake, I had a special reason to be interested in the "Mocs." To enroll at the university, Jake needed a scholarship, and the only opportunity that was open to him for financial aid was to capitalize on his musical ability. However, musical scholarships were offered only to members of the marching band. As a violinist, Jake obviously couldn't qualify, but he was told that he would be granted a scholarship if he learned to play the flugelhorn, a bugle with valves similar to the cornet.

Jake worked diligently on the flugelhorn – enough to be accepted by the band, but his practice sessions in the back of the store were excruciating to hear. Considering his rudimentary knowledge of the instrument, it is surprising that he was able to play and march at the same time – but play and march he did, both in parades through downtown Chattanooga and on the football field. Despite Jake's lack of proficiency with the flugelhorn, I was proud to see him in his handsome uniform, complete with a purple cape lined in gold, and a cap with a shiny black bill and gold braid.

After Papa died, we moved quite a bit, mainly for economic reasons.

For several years we lived in an apartment house about two blocks from the store, on Cedar Street. Our house was one of four units in the building. It had a living room, a kitchen, a bathroom and two bedrooms—one for me and Jake, and a second for Mom. Since we ate most of our meals at the store, we rarely used the kitchen. The principal activity in the apartment, other than sleeping, was listening to the radio on Sunday evenings.

From here we moved to a nicer apartment on Poplar Street, in a better part of town. The building had a front and side yard that I appreciated. It was a considerable step up from our previous abode. It had more modern appurtenances, such as central heating, and was located on a tree-lined street. It was only about half a block from a walled, block-long estate that was the home of Mr. and Mrs. Adolph S. Ochs, publisher of *The Chattanooga Times* and *The New York Times*. At the time we lived nearby, the Ochs family had moved to New York, but they retained this home for their occasional visits to Chattanooga. The only drawback to the apartment was that it had only one bedroom, which was used by Jake and me. Mom slept in a large closet that contained a pullout bed, but she was content to make this sacrifice.

Unfortunately, I enjoyed this home for only a short time. Mom's sister, Edith, wanted us and her family to rent separate units of a duplex a couple of blocks away. It was also on Cedar Street. Mom, Jake and I were less than enthusiastic about this move, but Edith continued to agitate, and Mom finally relented.

Our new home had no central heat. It had fireplaces and a coal-burning stove in the kitchen. In the winter, Mom arose early (before Jake and I were awake) and fired up the kitchen stove and the fireplace in our bedroom before she walked to the store. By the time Jake and I were ready to get dressed for school, the house was warm.

We had two bedrooms—one for me and Jake, the other for Mom, who shared the room with her mother, who lived with us from time to time. We were in close quarters, so I could hear what transpired in Mom's bedroom. I did not like my *bubbeh* (grandmother) because I thought she was too demanding of my mother, and I was ashamed of her dress, which was a throwback to the *shtetl* from which she came. I especially resented the fact that several times each night she awakened my mother and asked her to turn her on one side or the other. I can still recall Bubbeh's wailing, "Mollie, Mollie, Mollie." Several times I openly expressed my anger at *bubbeh's* selfishness in disturbing the little sleep that Mom enjoyed, but Mom was stoic and never complained. She felt she was doing her duty.

We lived on Cedar Street until my second or third year of college, when Aunt Edith and Uncle Joe Prebul decided to buy a house on Cameron Hill that had a commanding view of downtown Chattanooga. It was considered one of the more desirable places to live in Chattanooga.

The Prebuls offered to fix up an apartment in the lower level of their house for our family. I overcame any objections I had to sharing a home with the Prebuls because of the attractiveness of the house and the neighborhood. But there was an overriding—if not openly stated—lure of this location: It was next door to the home of Sara Gordon and her family. By this time I had become rather deeply involved with Sara, and it appealed to me (and to her) for us to be neighbors.

●

I was never deeply involved in Judaism as a religion, but I could not escape the fact that I was Jewish and part of the Jewish community in Chattanooga. Mom and Papa frequently spoke Yiddish to each other, but usually addressed us in English. They spoke to us in Yiddish only when they wanted to give us information that was not intended for the ears of our customers.

Our family did not celebrate many Jewish holidays, but all of our social and business contacts were with Jews. In public school I began to have a few Gentile friends, but for the most part the Jewish community in Chattanooga—especially the immigrants—felt isolated socially from the Gentiles. I was not conscious that I was overtly a victim of anti-Semitism, but nevertheless I had the feeling that there was an invisible barrier between the Jewish and Gentile communities.

In addition to occasional attendance at holiday services at the synagogue, my earliest involvement with a Jewish institution was my participation in *cheder* (Hebrew school). The principal purpose of going to *cheder* was to learn to read Hebrew with sufficient proficiency to take part in services at the synagogue, and ultimately to prepare for *bar mitzvah*. No real effort was made to teach Hebrew as a language. Occasionally, there were also minimal lectures about the Bible.

Classes at the *cheder* were held after school at the Young Men's Hebrew Association (the Jewish version of the YMCA). They were chaotic. The active pubescent or pre-pubescent students had no interest in learning to read Hebrew. After being pent up in school all day, they were a rowdy, boisterous lot. They spent most of their time running up and down stairs, in and out of doors, and jumping out of windows—all to the accompaniment of a cacophony of screaming and shouting. I felt sorry for the teachers.

Most of our family's contacts, other than those with relatives and customers, were with Jewish merchants and others who provided necessary services. Mom kept a kosher house and we were given the feeling that we might be poisoned, or at least banned from Heaven if we ate *traif* (non-kosher food). Mom went to a Jewish butcher for meat, and her chickens were killed by a *schochet* (one who was licensed to kill animals in a humane manner, as prescribed by Jewish law). For baked goods we had a choice of two Jewish bakeries—Miller's New York Bakery, and a competitor who chose the name of Manhattan Bakery. The latter offered a more eclectic variety of baked goods that appealed to some *goyim* (Gentiles).

Another Jewish merchant was the father of someone whom I later became closely associated with, personally and professionally. He was Morris Freeman, father of S. David Freeman, who has had an illustrious career in public power as chairman of the Tennessee Valley Authority and head of several large local public power utilities. Dave's father owned a shop, and sold and repaired umbrellas.

Freeman's real passion was politics and social commentary. He had strong ideas about politics (as does Dave) and spent a great deal of time expressing his views by writing letters to the editor of *The Chattanooga Times*. He composed the letters in Yiddish and Dave or his younger brother, Harold, translated them into English.

Mom told me that Mr. Freeman and Papa, both *Yeshiva bochers*, frequently got together to discuss the Torah. There could have been an even closer link between Mr. Freeman and my family. Mom said that mutual friends in Chattanooga had tried to arrange a *shidech* (marriage) between Mr. Freeman and my Aunt Lena, but Lena rejected the proposal.

•

Jews were represented in almost all types of businesses and service trades. By far the largest aggregation of Jews was in the grocery business, almost exclusively in black ghettos. That was an easy entry-level business for immigrants, because it required relatively little capital and was a service that few others were willing to provide, given the hours and working conditions. Later, when liquor was legalized, some of the grocery store owners (including my wife Sara's father) went into the liquor business, which became quite lucrative, especially during World War II.

Jews who were born in America succeeded in owning much larger and more prestigious enterprises, or were involved in white-collar professions. Jews owned two large downtown department stores, Miller's and Effron's (the latter owned by Sara's uncle), and the Boy's Shop, the preeminent place for the purchase of clothing for young men. The Solomon and Borisky families owned a chain of theaters, and a leading doctor was Phil Livingston (whose name had been changed from Levinson, to make him more acceptable outside of the Jewish community).

Members of the Siskin family were among the more important local business leaders. The patriarch of this family was an immigrant who began as a scrap or junk peddler, handling mainly steel or other metal products. During World War II, when there was an urgent demand for steel, the Siskin enterprise—which by that time had been taken over by the two sons of the original owner—was converted to a steel mill and became highly profitable.

The most prominent Jewish-owned enterprise was *The Chattanooga Times*, which belonged to Adolph S. Ochs, who later bought *The New York Times* when it was about to go bankrupt and built it into a renowned institution.

•

The stratification of Jews in business and social circles was reflected in the congregations of the three synagogues. Jews of German heritage, who had become the most Americanized and most prosperous members of the Jewish community, were members of the reform congregation. They were the top drawer of Jewish society. Generally, they looked down upon Eastern European immigrants, who spoke English poorly and for the most part operated grocery stores in the black neighborhoods. German and Eastern European Jews rarely, if ever, moved in the same social circles.

The reform temple was a bequest of the Ochs family, and appropriately was named in honor of Adolph and his wife, Bertha. When there was an occasion for a rabbi to be called upon to participate in a civic function, Rabbi Feinstein of the Ochs temple was almost always selected.

Being of Eastern European parentage, I never went to the Ochs Temple, but Jake performed there once a year. He was engaged to play Kol Nidre at the year's highest holiday, Yom Kippur. The orthodox congregation to which my family belonged, the B'nai Zion Synagogue, would not have countenanced playing a musical instrument in *shul* during the High Holy Days.

Most Jews from Eastern Europe and their families went to the orthodox B'nai Zion Synagogue. When I went to the *shul* while Papa was still living, the service was conducted in Hebrew and I did not understand a word that was spoken. But Jake and I dutifully sat through the entire proceeding, while Mom was in the balcony with other women, as was the custom at that time.

As an increasing number of American-born children went to *shul*, their parents pressured leaders of the congregation to introduce more English into the services and to have a rabbi who could deliver a sermon in English. Consequently, several years after Papa died, the congregation hired Rabbi Israel Gerstein, who was well educated and spoke English fluently. He and his young, attractive wife were popular with the congregation, and his initial sermons were well received.

After a few years, however, the novelty of having a "modern" rabbi wore off, and attendance, other than during the High Holy Days, began to dwindle. Even during Rosh Hashanah and Yom Kippur, some of the younger members of the congregation stood outside to socialize during portions of the service. Since the High Holy Days came at the beginning of the fall season, they were also a convenient occasion for members of the congregation, especially the younger ones, to display their new outfits.

During the early part of Rabbi Gerstein's tenure, he organized a Junior Congregation and I became involved, primarily, I suppose, because the group afforded social interactions. In addition to attending Sunday school (of itself quite an innovation for an orthodox synagogue), I participated in special meetings of the Junior Congregation, and was elected its president. My principal responsibility was to attend the Friday evening services and make announcements about activities of our group. It was not a demanding task, but I took it seriously and carefully prepared my brief remarks. The elders, impressed with my stage presence, were complimentary. The experience gave me confidence later in addressing audiences.

Although they were not affiliated with the B'nai Zion Synagogue, two other important Jewish groups consisted primarily of members of this orthodox congregation. They were the Zionists and the Pioneer Women, a women's auxiliary of the Zionists. Sara's parents were ardent Zionists. One of their proudest moments came when Golda Meir, some years before the state of Israel was established, visited Chattanooga to promote the Zionist cause, and spent the night with Sara's parents, the Gordons. Lacking sufficient beds, Golda slept with Sara. Little did the Gordons dream that Golda would one day be a key figure in the establishment of the state of Israel and would become its prime minister.

In general, members of the reform temple seemed to eschew the Zionist cause. German Jews were concerned that their advocacy of the establishment of the state of Israel could open them to the accusation that they were giving less than 100 percent allegiance to the United States. At least, that was the rationale given by the Eastern European Jews.

In addition to the Ochs Temple and the B'nai Zion Synagogue, a third venue of religious activity centered about the "Little *Schul*," which was in a small house several blocks from our grocery store. This congregation consisted primarily of persons who leaned to the left, politically. The "Little *Shul*" also served as the locale for meetings of the *Arbeiter Ring*, the Workman's Circle, which was sympathetic to socialist concepts. In fact, some people regarded members of the Workmen's Circle as "Reds," but I doubt whether any were card-carrying Communists. Members of other congregations looked down upon those associated with the "Little *Shul*."

Although there were many advantages in growing up in Chattanooga, I felt increasingly confined by the clannishness of the society and the separation between the Jewish and Gentile communities. I believed that, regardless of my ability, I would always be considered in Chattanooga as coming from "the wrong side of the tracks"—a Jewish boy from Tenth Street. I also felt opportunities were limited in what I had chosen as my profession—journalism—and that I had to seek my fortune in a larger, more cosmopolitan environment. The advent of World War II hastened my departure from Chattanooga.

Chapter 6

Newspaper Days

My New York cousin, Jack Arnold, sparked my interest in becoming a newspaper reporter. From his descriptions, I concluded that it would be a glamorous career that would introduce me to many facets of life.

In my first year at Chattanooga High School, I joined the staff of the school newspaper, where I learned the rudiments of writing a news story. By the end of my junior year I had been sufficiently active at the school paper to run for the elective position of editor. My principal opponent was a friend, David Shavin. To my regret, David won the election. However, we remained friends and he asked me to work with him. I consented, but only if he appointed me associate editor. He readily agreed.

While I was in high school, I began submitting articles on a freelance basis to the local afternoon newspaper, *The Chattanooga News*. My most notable success was a story about Earl Browder, who was a candidate for president of the United States on the Communist Party ticket. Browder spoke at the local radio station, WDOD (Wonderful Dynamo of Dixie), and I interviewed him at the studio after his radio address. The lead to my story was that Browder was like Hitler in appearance (both had small mustaches and similar hairstyles and facial characteristics), but that was where the similarity ended. In political views they were diametrically opposed, and while Hitler was surrounded by legions of supporters, Browder traveled alone.

The *News* published the story under a two-column headline and my by-line. I promptly sent the story to my cousin Jack, who had not yet left New York to join the Abraham Lincoln Brigade. Jack responded promptly. He criticized me for comparing Browder to Hitler, but said that of course I had to do so because the *News* was a capitalist publication. However, he complimented me on the remainder of the story. (Sadly, in the hysteria of the McCarthy era many years later, I destroyed Jack's letter while I was working for the Department of State in Washington.)

Emboldened by my success in placing several articles with the *News*, I mustered enough courage to apply for a non-paying job as a reporter in the summer between my junior and senior years of high school. In those days, aspiring reporters commonly worked without pay to gain experience and pave the way to a salaried job. The city editor, Cecil Holland, a dour person who later became city editor of *The Washington Star*, accepted my offer. So each morning I went to the city room and waited for an assignment. However, I was given few opportunities. After a few weeks of boredom and feeling ignored, I decided to quit my job.

•

My experience at the *News* did not dampen my enthusiasm for a journalism career. My opportunity came after I graduated from high school and was enrolled at the University of Chattanooga, where I had received a scholarship. Financial considerations and the need to be available to help Mom in the store ruled out even the thought of my going to college elsewhere.

Enrollment at UC offered the prospect of a position at *The Chattanooga Times*, which employed a university student to act as campus correspondent. Fortunately, the person who filled this position immediately prior to my matriculation was Bob Cassell, a friend of Jake's. Cassell graduated in the spring of the year that I enrolled, so the position was open when I prepared to enter the university. Cassell gave me pointers on how to apply.

Editor Julian LaRose Harris, who had had a distinguished career as a journalist, hired the campus correspondent. I wrote him a letter asking for an appointment, and within a few days his secretary advised me of a time when I could see him. Harris had a reputation for being a tough, irascible person and I approached our meeting with a great deal of trepidation. Cassell told me that Harris respected a person who stood up to him. He encouraged me not to be overawed by Harris and to maintain my composure regardless of any critical comments. In preparation for the meeting, I carefully rehearsed the presentation I would make. True to Cassell's warning, Harris was brusque, but he was not unkind. I said my piece as I had rehearsed it and did my best to remain calm in the presence of this formidable man. Shortly thereafter, I was hired.

I was fortunate to be asked to report to Ed Sussdorf, the city editor. At that time, books and movies portrayed city editors as rough, foul-mouthed autocrats who frantically screamed orders to reporters. Sussdorf was not in this mold. He was a gentle, soft-spoken, white haired, fiftyish man who rarely displayed anger.

The city room where local reporters and copy editors worked was large, perhaps 30 by 50 feet or more. At one end was a horseshoe-shaped copy desk where six or seven editors worked on stories sent to them by the city editor or managing editor. Those on the copy desk wrote headlines and subheads, and made up the paper, as well as edited copy.

After the copy desk completed its work, the articles were sent to a composing room on another floor, where linotypists converted the stories into hot metal type, which was placed on a large table and made up into pages. Needless to say, the process was far different from today's computer-driven printing.

By far the larger part of the room was where the reporters and city editor worked. Each reporter had a battered green desk furnished sparsely with a telephone and a manual typewriter. Desks were arranged in clusters, one butting up against another. The only art in the room was a large wall calendar advertising a local funeral home. The calendar was adorned with a color painting of Jesus staring at the ceiling with a beatific expression. By late afternoon or early evening, when reporters had returned from their beats in anticipation of the 11 p.m. deadline, the decibel level in the city room was high as reporters banged away on their typewriters or talked to news sources. At first, I found it difficult to concentrate in the midst of this noise and conversation, but after a while I was able to tune out these sounds.

I was hired as a "stringer," a term derived from the fact that at the end of each month I pasted together in a single "string" all of my stories that had been published. The "string" was measured and I was paid 10 cents per column inch.

Initially, my principal activities as campus correspondent consisted of writing articles about speeches given before the weekly assembly of students, who numbered about 600. I also covered other events, such as the hiring of new faculty members, grants awarded the university, recognition received by faculty and students and plans for the university's expansion.

As campus correspondent I had unusual entrée to the president of the university, Dr. Archie M. Palmer, who had been installed in this office the same year that I matriculated. Palmer was anxious to make a good impression on the community, so he welcomed me to his office and gave me leads to news stories. He was a gregarious person and, in a relatively short time, I came to know him and his family well. He later played a key role in my life.

My first big break as campus correspondent came at the end of my freshman year, when I covered the commencement address. The principal speaker was Tennessee Gov. Prentiss Cooper. He was a colorless orator, but because of his position his speech made news. My story appeared the next day on the front page. Many years later, I worked closely with his son, Jim Cooper, who served several terms as a Congressman from Tennessee.

Scoring a major scoop was the highlight of my sophomore year. The story involved the naming of the winners of the annual contest to determine the Bachelor of Ugliness and Miss UC. Contrary to the impression given by its name, the Bachelor of Ugliness was the highest honor bestowed by the university on a male student. The selection of the Bachelor of Ugliness and Miss UC was decided by a vote of the student body. Results of the balloting were kept secret until their publication a couple of days later in the college newspaper.

The story was especially interesting that year because the leading candidate for Bachelor of Ugliness was a popular student who had attained high academic standing, despite the fact that he had worked his way through college busing dishes and doing other chores in the student commons.

I was determined to scoop the university's newspaper. After the voting closed, I spent several hours on the telephone, calling student officers who knew the results of the election. They were diffident about revealing the outcome, but judging by the manner in which they responded to my questions, I was convinced, by early evening, that I knew the identity of the winners. So I went to the university commons with a photographer who took a picture of the new Bachelor of Ugliness as he swept the floor.

After writing the story I was so excited that I could not sleep that night. When I heard the newspaper plop on our front porch early the next morning, I rushed outside, picked it up, and was overjoyed to see that my by-lined story and the accompanying photo were on the front page.

I was elated, but paid a price. The editors of the university newspaper and some of the Big Men on Campus were furious at me for scooping the school paper on a story that they considered theirs.

•

As time went on, I found more and more subjects for articles at the university, and consequently spent an increasing amount of time at the paper. One afternoon, the city editor asked if I would like an assignment outside of the university beat. I jumped at the chance, even though it merely involved accompanying a photographer to get the names and identifications of people who were the subjects of a photo. I was to write cutlines for the picture.

After this experience, Sussdorf began giving me other assignments. At first, they were routine, such as covering speakers at local service clubs or churches. Gradually, I was assigned more important stories. One was an interview with a high ranking federal government official from Washington who had come to Chattanooga to attend a meeting. I asked him what I thought were intelligent and relevant questions, and at the end of the interview he turned to me and asked, "How old are you?"

I said that I was 19—or perhaps I fudged and said I was 20, in order to appear more mature.

"God, I'm in the hands of a kid," he responded.

Because of my interest in the subject, Sussdorf assigned me to cover several stories about music and musicians. One of the most memorable was an interview with the composer, Percy Grainger. I was to meet him at the railroad station, but when his train arrived he was nowhere to be found. I waited for quite a while and finally saw him walking toward the terminal along the railroad tracks. When I caught up with him, he explained that because he liked to walk, he had disembarked when the train stopped for a short time outside of Chattanooga, so that he could walk the remainder of the way.

When the St. Louis Symphony Orchestra came to town, I was assigned to interview its conductor, Vladimir Golschmann, who was well known. On one occasion, I jumped into the big time of music reviewing. The Philadelphia Symphony Orchestra, under the baton of its legendary conductor, Leopold Stokowski, was to perform in Knoxville at the University of Tennessee. Jake and I decided to go to the concert, and I volunteered to review it for the *Times*.

The principal work on the program was Tchaikovsky's Sixth Symphony, the *Pathetique*. It was a dazzling performance. Stokowski had an imperious demeanor that immediately commanded the respect and attention of his audience (not to mention the musicians). He did not use a baton, and his hands were the most expressive of any conductor I had seen. He was in complete mastery of the orchestra, which responded to every nuance of his direction.

Another off-campus story that I developed involved a local artist, Maurice Grosser, who later attained national recognition not only for his achievements as an artist, but also as the writer of the scenario of an opera by Virgil Thompson. Grosser loved to ride a motorcycle and he began driving into Chattanooga's black ghettos to paint some of the hovels and stores there. I heard about his activities through one of my uncles whose store was the subject of a Grosser painting. Grosser achieved celebrity status in the black ghettos. When he roared into a location to paint, the blacks would set up a chant: "Here come the motorcycle paintin' man." Grosser's work made the subject of a good feature story, accompanied by a photo of him at work in the ghetto.

When some of my distant relatives visited Chattanooga from South Africa, they were the subjects of an interview about life in that far distant country.

Politics also interested me. I took advantage of a trip to New York with Jake to stop off in Washington, where I interviewed Estes Kefauver, the congressman who represented Chattanooga. Later, as a U.S. senator, Kefauver became nationally known for his televised hearings on crime and his campaign for the presidency.

This was my second visit to Washington and again I was impressed with the city's monumental buildings and broad avenues and the sophisticated people on the streets of the capital. It was a special thrill to visit the Senate gallery, witness a debate and gawk at some of the better-known senators.

After my interview with Kefauver, Jake and I drove to New York and stayed at a YMCA. I carried a portable typewriter and after we had checked into a small room, I noisily typed late into the night, writing a story about my interview with Kefauver. I hurriedly mailed my story the next morning. The *Times* did not have a Washington correspondent, so my article from Washington made news.

•

By the time I had completed my junior year at UC, my pay as a stringer was averaging about $20 a week, as much as that of a beginning reporter. Sussdorf therefore offered me a full-time job at that salary. I had already been working almost as many hours as a regular reporter, so I accepted the position.

I continued my studies at UC, but cut back my academic schedule, even though this would delay my graduation for perhaps a half-year. I had classes at the university in the morning and worked at the T*imes* from 3-11 p.m. At first, I substituted for reporters who had a day off. This routine gave me an opportunity to learn a number of beats, such as downtown (the Chamber of Commerce and other business activities), city hall, the county courthouse, and police.

I was assigned to the police beat two evenings a week. I checked in with Sussdorf at 3 p.m., then went to a local car rental garage to pick up the car the *Times* had assigned to its police reporter. Emblazoned on the side with *The Chattanooga Times* logo, the car was equipped with a police radio, siren and flashing lights. As a 20-year-old, I felt a sense of empowerment having this vehicle at my disposal. However, I was warned to use the siren and flashing lights only if I were rushing to an emergency.

As a green kid reporter, I quickly found that seasoned cops looked upon me with disdain. After going to police headquarters, I first examined the police blotter to see who had been arrested. If I questioned the desk sergeant about the details of an arrest, he would either ignore me or respond in monosyllables. After a time, I realized I could gain the confidence of the police if I brought them information.

I found myself responding to calls from the police radio about accidents or fires. The police and firemen on the scene were as unresponsive as those in the headquarters.

The police reporter doubled as a photographer and I enjoyed this aspect of working the beat. The paper's staff photographer coached me on the use of a 3x5 Speed Graphic camera with a large flash attachment. Armed with this bulky equipment and a copious supply of throwaway flash bulbs, each of which could be used only once, I successfully took pictures of accidents.

The *Times* reported only crime news involving white people, as was the custom of southern newspapers. Street fights and murders were fairly common among the black population, but we reported them only in very unusual circumstances; when we did, the blacks were identified by race.

Because many of the police regarded Jews as only a notch above blacks in social standing, my work as a police reporter triggered my anxiety about coming from a Jewish family that operated a grocery store in a black ghetto. When I stopped at our store for dinner, I was uneasy about parking the *Times'* police car in front. I was concerned that if a police patrol car drove by, the officers would see the *Times'* car and identify me as coming from "the wrong side of the tracks." So I ate hastily and moved on as quickly as I could.

I did not enjoy being a police reporter, nor did my work with the police enhance my regard for them. The only gratification I received from this assignment was in riding around town late at night and experiencing a sense of excitement in being active when most people were asleep. I also liked to be at the paper at 11 p.m., hear the roar of the presses, and know that I was among the first people in the city to see tomorrow's newspaper.

By 1940, war had broken out in Europe, and increasing attention was given to military preparations. Although President Roosevelt continued to reassure the American people that he would not send troops to Europe to fight in its wars, the draft had been instituted, and new military training camps were being built. (Jake was among the first to be called.)

Newspapers always look for the local angle of a national story. The *Times* found such an angle in the military preparations taking place about seven miles from Chattanooga, at Fort Oglethorpe, Georgia. This was a relatively small cavalry training center. Before the mechanization of the military through the use of tanks, jeeps and other motorized vehicles, the cavalry was an important component of the Army. But with the advent of the German panzer divisions, which were overrunning one European country after another, the cavalry was less useful. In fact, many cavalry outfits were being converted to motorized units.

Nonetheless, the cavalry base at Fort Oglethorpe was part of the nation's military machine. As war preparations accelerated, I was assigned to cover Fort Oglethorpe regularly and was there almost every day. The fort was also an induction center for draftees and a considerable amount of news was generated at the base.

I found coverage of the military activities interesting and relevant to impending events. My principal news source was the colonel who commanded the base. He was a swashbuckling tyrant who relished his role. He told me that war would be good for the military, because it would offer many opportunities for advancement. This prediction was borne out in his case. He was later shifted to a motorized unit and became a brigadier general.

The colonel loved publicity and was a good source of news. I had only one unpleasant incident with him. A *Times* staff photographer took a photo of him that made him look like a fierce bulldog. His eyes were popped out and he appeared to be growling. When the photo was published, he told me in no uncertain terms that it was never to be used again. A few weeks later, I wrote a story about him, and Sussdorf, without my knowledge, pulled the same picture out of the file and used it to accompany my article.

When I met with the colonel the next day, he acted like the bulldog portrayed in his picture. As I entered his office, he jumped up from his desk, grabbed me by the collar, pulled me close to his face, and shouted, "I thought I told you never to use that picture of me. If you print it again, I'll kill you."

I apologized profusely, but couldn't explain to him that the use of the photo was not my decision. However, his desire for publicity was stronger than his anger about the publication of the picture and we quickly reestablished a good working relationship.

•

I also covered other nearby military installations, such as a large new Army training center being built near Tullahoma, Tennessee. War preparations were stimulating the economy. It was not until the war that the United States finally emerged from the Depression, despite advances made in the New Deal. I covered war games in middle Tennessee. These lasted several weeks and brought together military units and thousands of soldiers from many sections of the country. Major General George S. Patton commanded the maneuvers. Patton had already achieved fame because he was such a colorful figure. He was articulate and a good phrasemaker and would have been excellent in producing sound bites for television.

I joined Patton's forces as they came near Chattanooga. I will never forget the excitement of my first night of riding with the convoy as it proceeded to the site of the maneuvers. I rode near the end of a long convoy of vehicles, and it was awesome to see this line of vehicles snaking through the hills of Tennessee. Red taillights were visible for miles. I could understand how a military leader might be intoxicated with the power at his command.

Patton held regular press conferences and he did not disappoint the media. The first press conference I attended was in a wooded area and Patton expounded on his views of leadership qualities. He compared an army to spaghetti and said that the role of the leader was to be out front, to pull the spaghetti forward. The leader should never be in the rear and attempt to push the spaghetti.

Patton drove the press as hard as he worked his troops. We stayed in tents and awoke before dawn each day to join a convoy to the scene of a mock battle. Windshields were removed from all vehicles because Patton believed they would reflect sunlight and reveal the location of troops to the enemy. Consequently, when we were awakened before sunrise to join a troop movement, we sat in dew-covered seats and shivered in the jeeps as they sped along the highways.

Major publications such as *Time* and *Life* magazines, *The New York Times*, and wire services such as Associated Press, United Press and the International News Service sent their star reporters to cover this event. Some reporters had already become famous for their coverage of the war in Europe. I was undoubtedly the youngest and least seasoned of the lot and I felt inadequate. Because of my age and inexperience, I was not accepted by the other reporters. I was excluded from their camaraderie, much of which consisted of story telling at night, accompanied by heavy drinking. As we traveled together, they included me when they passed around a flask, but after one or two swigs, I had had enough.

Despite my handicaps, I managed to keep up with the group and file stories every night. On one occasion, however, I committed a terrible blunder. A few days after I joined the maneuvers, I heard rumors of a serious accident in which two soldiers reportedly were killed. It was difficult to get the facts, but I overheard the veteran reporters talking about the accident and was afraid that I would be scooped. As we paused in the town of Bell Buckle, Tennessee, I hurried to a public phone in a general store and called in the story about these deaths.

By this time, the *Times* was in fierce competition with its rival, *The*

Chattanooga News-Free Press, an afternoon newspaper, and had begun publication of *The Evening Times* as well as the morning paper. Because of the time that the accident story broke, my article appeared in *The Evening Times,* which played up news in a more sensational manner than the staid morning paper. *The Evening Times* featured my story under an eight-column banner across the top of the front page.

My gratification in attaining such prominent treatment of my story quickly turned sour. Shortly thereafter, I learned that there had been no fatalities. The managing editor of *The Evening Times* understandably was embarrassed by my story. Probably the roughest reprimand that I had ever received during my newspaper days greeted me when I returned to the city room after about a week at the maneuvers.

Another negative legacy from my experience covering the Patton maneuvers was the onset of a back problem that has persisted for the remainder of my life. My doctor thought that the early morning rides in the jeep, while I was sitting on a damp seat, precipitated the problem, which was diagnosed as a degenerated disc. I am convinced that the tension of covering the maneuvers contributed to this ailment.

My last sighting of General Patton was at the conclusion of the maneuvers. Ever colorful and in the limelight, Patton stood in the middle of a main street intersection directing traffic as the armored vehicles under his command lumbered through a small town.

•

The biggest bonus of working for the *Times* was the opportunity it afforded me to associate with editors, reporters and photographers during an impressionable period of my life.

One of the most important influences was the editor, Julian LaRose Harris. He was the son of Joel Chandler Harris, author of the Uncle Remus stories, which had attained national acclaim, especially in the South. They were tales, such as the B'rer Rabbit story, told by African Americans in the Southern Negro dialect. (They would probably be considered politically incorrect today.)

Before coming to the *Times*, Harris held a number of important positions. He was reputed to be the youngest managing editor in the history of the *Atlanta Constitution*. He left that paper to become publisher of a newspaper in Columbus, Georgia, where he led a fight against the Ku Klux Klan. He was rewarded for his courage with a Pulitzer Prize, but fighting the Klan was not popular in the South. As a result, he ultimately lost the paper. However, he went on to become a reporter for the *New York Herald Tribune*, covering the Versailles Peace Conference at the conclusion of World War I.

Harris' exacting standards of writing and editing were an exceptionally strong incentive to reporters to perform at their best. He read the paper carefully and each day the in-box for reporters contained a few pink notes from him. When he was critical of one of my stories, I was downcast, but when I received a congratulatory note or he complimented me verbally, I felt exhilarated for days. Yet, he was such an imposing figure that I had to steel myself to retain my composure whenever I was in his presence.

In addition to his excellence as an editor, Harris continued to demonstrate his commitment to principle—as he had done in fighting the Ku Klux Klan. In 1940, he rose to the occasion when *The New York Times* endorsed Wendell Willkie in his race against Roosevelt, who was running for his third term. *The New York Times* supported Willkie, and told Harris that *The Chattanooga Times* should do likewise.

Harris refused. In protest, he and the chief editorial writer took a leave of absence during the campaign and *The Chattanooga Times* published editorials written in New York. Despite the fact that he was officially on leave, Harris continued to come to the newspaper daily and direct its operations. The leave therefore was somewhat of a sham, but it took courage for him to express his difference openly with the owner of the paper.

•

Another person who influenced me greatly was George F. Hull, the paper's chief photographer. A tall, lanky person endowed with tremendous energy, George was an excellent photographer who could easily have become a member of the staff of a large metropolitan daily or a magazine such as *Life*, to which he contributed occasionally. However, George enjoyed the lifestyle of a small town and spurned offers from more prestigious publications. He had one of the keenest minds of anyone I had ever met and a sharp, subtle wit. He was a voracious reader and could carry on an intelligent discourse about many subjects.

George also was an avid gardener. In addition to being the paper's chief photographer, he wrote a weekly gardening column and two books about bonsai. He practiced gardening by buying a few acres of land in an area several miles beyond one of Chattanooga's suburbs. Lacking money to build a home at that time, George and his wife, Florence, planned where they would site their house and designed a landscape plan and planted trees and shrubbery that conformed to the plan. Knowing that the landscaping would require many years to mature, he decided to install plantings immediately so they would be well developed by the time the house was built.

While awaiting the time when he could afford to construct the house, George erected a small tool shed that was large enough to accommodate bunk beds for him, his wife, and later their daughter, Leslie. They spent weekends in their gardens, and frequently Sara and I worked alongside them.

George finally accumulated enough money to begin construction of the house, but at first he could afford only to build a double garage, which they would need ultimately. The family used the garage as living quarters for several years before George was able to build the house. He did most of the work himself—carpentry, plumbing and electrical wiring, which he learned to do by reading handbooks.

Among other things, George gave me a significant lesson in management. He said that before Harris became editor, the *Times'* editorial staff was in disarray and was demoralized. When Harris became editor, he fired only one person, but by the power of his own management ability and the excellence of his editing, he completely turned the paper around.

Fred Hixson was the paper's chief political writer. A short, roly-poly, round-faced person who had a small black mustache, Fred always looked somewhat disheveled, but had an innocent, cherubic expression on his face. He lived, ate and breathed politics, whether it was local, regional or national. He had a unique way of generating a story. He came to the office briefly about noon, then left to make a few personal calls at the county courthouse or city hall. His real work began on the telephone when he returned to the office about 3 p.m. He would call a political leader and ask whether he had heard what another political leader had said about some subject. After getting a comment from the second person, he would relay it to a third, fourth or fifth person, but with each call the story was embellished. After a few hours, Fred had precipitated a full-blown controversy that had originated with a rather innocuous remark.

He pursued a story with the determination of a raging bull. One of the legendary stories about him stemmed from the time when he was a cub reporter writing about an accident. Before members of the family had been notified about a fatality, Fred called the wife of the victim, opening the conversation with the question, "Are you the widow?"

Travis Hedrick was another reporter who made a strong impression on me. Chattanooga had well-organized labor unions in the 1930s and 1940s, and Travis covered the labor beat. His most interesting stories were about labor conflicts in coal mining areas, especially in Harlan County, Kentucky. Coal companies there fiercely resisted the work of labor organizers and met attempts at unionization with violence. Travis covered these stories as objectively as he could, but it was obvious that he was sympathetic to the miners. He came back from Harlan or other coal mining regions with harrowing details about working conditions. He also described how the miners were forced to buy food and other necessities from a company-owned store. Many of the miners were so deeply in debt that they had no alternative except to continue to work in the mines in order to repay their obligations at the company store.

Many years later, when I was executive director of the American Public Power Association, I visited coal fields in Tennessee and Kentucky and saw first hand some of the conditions endured by miners in an earlier era. My interest at that time was in strip mining, which inflicted greater damage to the environment than to the workers. But I also saw the abandoned "dog holes" where miners once burrowed their way into holes so small that they could not stand erect. From these holes they painstakingly dug out coal, lump by lump. It was hard to believe that human beings had been subjected to such intolerable conditions and I could understand Travis' rage.

It was not surprising that Travis later came to Washington to join the staff of the *Federated Press*, which was regarded as a left-wing news service and, during the McCarthy era, was charged with being Communist-dominated. I saw Travis from time to time after he and I had moved to Washington, but I regret that during the hysteria of the McCarthy era, when I worked for the State Department, I dropped my association with him.

Another reporter, Rufus Terral, covered the Tennessee Valley Authority and became a life-long friend. He wrote with grace, wit and perception. Occasionally, he wrote editorials. Although they were not signed, his editorials could be identified by their wry, subtle humor, and their elegant style. He left the *Times* to work briefly for the Tennessee Valley Authority and was then hired by the *St. Louis Post-Dispatch*, which at that time vigorously advocated creation of a Missouri Valley Authority, patterned after TVA. Rufus spent most of his time in St. Louis trying to drum up support for the establishment of an MVA. He also wrote a book on the subject. The effort, however, was unsuccessful.

There was a great deal of camaraderie among members of the paper's staff and frequent parties. Although I was the youngest reporter, I gradually was included.   Coupled with my academic work at the university, and my developing relationship with Sara, my days at the *Times* were exciting.

Chapter 7

Sara

My love affair with Sara Gordon had its origins in the Polish *shtetl* of Amdur, birthplace of Mom and Sara's mother, Bessie (usually called by her Yiddish name, Bashke). Mom was only a few years older than Bashke. They knew each other in Amdur, but were not close friends. Mom was poor and her family lived in a different part of town than Bashke, who came from a family of relatively prosperous merchants.

Even if circumstances had brought them together, their friendship did not have time to develop, because Mom left Amdur at a much earlier age than Bashke. Mom was only 10 or 12 when she emigrated. Bashke was 22, married to Wolf Gordon and the mother of one child, Anna, age 2, when she arrived in the United States in 1922, a year after I was born.

By a quirk of fate, Mom and Bashke both settled in Chattanooga. Mom arrived there about eight years before Bashke, after having lived in Montreal and Kingston, New York. Like most Jews, the Gordons moved to Chattanooga because of family connections. Two of Bashke's brothers—Louis and David Effron—had settled there earlier. By the time the Gordons arrived, the Effrons were well established as owners of a small department store on Market Street, in the heart of Chattanooga's downtown business section.

Wolf initially worked for the Effrons as a stock clerk. However, he had been a successful trader in pelts in Poland and did not consider the position at Effrons befitting his background and experience. The Effrons helped the Gordons establish a dry goods store, which unfortunately went bankrupt after a few years.

Although they had not seen each other for about 15 years and were not close friends, the Amdur connection brought Mom and Bashke together after the Gordons arrived in Chattanooga. For a short time, the Gordons stayed with our family in the apartment above the store. Our families also were together occasionally through activities in the close-knit Jewish community. After their unsuccessful stint in the dry goods business, the Gordons rented a grocery store owned by my father and his brother in the "flats" section of town, near the Tennessee River. They later bought a store in a more desirable neighborhood only about three blocks from the house where I lived as a teenager.

When I was six or seven years old, Bashke brought Sara with her when she visited Mom. Sara was about a year and a half younger than me, but apparently I made a favorable impression on her, even at that tender age. Much later, Bashke told me that after that encounter, Sara periodically asked her mother to take her to see the *shaineh yingel* (pretty boy). I do not recall those meetings, but in my early teens I saw Sara occasionally at small parties, at Sunday school, or at events sponsored by the Junior Congregation of our *schul*.

Initially, I was not taken with Sara. As a young teenager, she was pudgy, had a round face and was rather undistinguished looking. She made overtures toward me, but I did not respond. Her feelings toward me became most obvious at a party held on her 13th or 14th birthday. About a half dozen boys and an equal number of girls were invited to a party at the Gordons' house. Each girl was handed a box of cookies and other goodies that she was to share with one of the boys. A small ceramic female doll about three-and-a-half inches tall was attached to each box with a ribbon. Underneath the doll was the name of the boy with whom the girl was to dine. Sara arranged the pairing and my name was under the doll attached to her box. So Sara and I went off to a corner of the room to partake of the confections. The event apparently had much greater significance for Sara than it did for me, because she kept the doll for the remainder of her life. I still have it.

•

After the party, I saw Sara from time to time, but we did not date and I seldom thought of her. However, my feelings changed dramatically when I was a sophomore in college and Sara was a high school senior. One spring day, while I was walking home from the campus of the University of Chattanooga, I saw Sara about a half-block ahead of me. I still have a clear mental picture of the exact location. She was on Sixth Street, near the Bijou Theater. Her personal appearance had been transformed dramatically since I had last seen her. The once chubby teenager had become a slender, statuesque, stylishly dressed, attractive young woman.

A week or two later a college classmate, Leo Mennen, invited me to spend the weekend at the mountain cabin of his sister, Fannie, who was an artist. Leo was infatuated with Sara and she was to be his date. He invited his cousin to be my date. I readily accepted. (I suspect that Sara had planted the idea of inviting me.)

The weekend was idyllic. Although Sara was Leo's date, she was not overly taken with him and I was not entranced with Leo's cousin. The four of us were together most of the time, but I related mostly to Sara, joking with her at card games and talking with her as much as I could without antagonizing Leo. Our experience was enhanced by the ambience of the location. Fannie's cabin was in a remote area in the mountains of north Georgia. Her place was called Plumb Nelly. In the language of the mountain folks, the cabin was "plumb" out of Tennessee and "nelly" out of Georgia. The cabin was located at the edge of a bluff and commanded a beautiful view of the mountains and valleys. It had no electricity or running water. If the cabin had been in Chattanooga, I would have considered it primitive and looked upon it with disdain. But in this enchanted setting, the use of kerosene lamps and the need to pump water from a well enhanced the experience.

I also was attracted to the mountaineers who lived in this area. They were descendants of Englishmen. Because of their isolation, they used language that had many throwbacks to the Elizabethan era. When they wanted to indicate that the forthcoming winter would be extraordinarily cold, they said, "The fish are going to be looking through glass this winter."

The locals had what I regarded as a unique way of fox hunting. At night, they mounted their horses and rode to a high elevation, accompanied by their dogs. When they reached a suitable spot, they let the dogs loose to hunt fox. The hunters did not chase the dogs and the fox. Instead, they remained on their horses and listened as the dogs pursued the animal. They could tell how the hunt was proceeding by the barking of the dogs. The sounds also indicated when the dogs had treed a fox, signaling the end of the hunt. No shots were fired; the hunters did not carry guns.

The four of us hiked, met the locals and had a grand time. The area was becoming an artists' colony, and one of the neighbors whom we visited was Frank Baisden, head of the art department at UC.

I would have been attracted to Sara in any event, but this bucolic setting played an important part in stimulating my infatuation. After we returned to Chattanooga, I began to see Sara often. When I was a junior at the University of Chattanooga, she enrolled there as a freshman and I saw her on campus. We went to dinner, movies and parties. Occasionally, she would accompany me on an assignment for the *Times*, which violated the newspaper rules.

Sara loved the outdoors and we hiked often in the mountains near Chattanooga. She usually brought sandwiches, but in colder weather we grilled hot dogs or hamburgers and roasted marshmallows—a unique experience for me, since these delicacies were unknown in my home. One of our most memorable experiences was a car trip we took with another couple to Atlanta to see New York's Metropolitan Opera perform Wagner's *Tristan and Isolde*.

The Met's performance of this magnificent opera was impressive, but my most specific memory has to do with the physique of the stars—Laurence Melchior and Kirsten Flagstad. Unlike most opera singers today, both were exceptionally portly and had difficulty getting their arms around each other when they embraced. Because of his girth, Melchior also experienced difficulty in stooping to retrieve his sword when he dropped it while Flagstad was singing an aria.

After the opera, we went to a popular hangout in Atlanta, the Pig and Whistle, for a late snack before returning to Chattanooga. In those days before interstate highways, the drive from Atlanta to Chattanooga took more than three hours and by the time we arrived at Sara's house it was practically dawn. Nevertheless, after such an exhilarating experience, we spent time petting in the car parked in front of her house. Unbeknownst to us, her parents, who were concerned about her late return, were anxiously looking out the window to await her arrival. As she entered her house, Sara learned that they had watched from their house as we smooched in the car.

●

Sara was not beautiful by Hollywood standards, but she was attractive. She was about five-feet, seven-inches tall, and was proud that her bust-waist-hips measurements were the same as those of leading movie actresses. I was drawn to her by her appearance, but even more by her personality. She was lively and outgoing and made friends easily. In a group, she quickly became the center of attention. She was strong-willed, outspoken and opinionated, and could easily captivate an audience. People confided in her almost immediately after they met her. She also had a mercurial personality, but I did not learn this until later.

By contrast, I was shy. While I desperately wanted to break out of my Tenth Street environment, I found it difficult to do so in a social setting. Sara helped me emerge from my shell and enter more easily into friendships. In a sense, she was my crutch.

My relationship with Sara also opened me to a different emotional milieu revolving about her family. I had been brought up in a family that was quiet and reserved—just the opposite from Sara's home environment. Where my mother was shy and retiring, Bashke was outgoing and aggressive. She was highly emotional and had no compunction about expressing her feelings. Within a 10-minute period she could be both crying and laughing.

An ardent leader in the Pioneer Women's Club, a pro-Zionist group, Bashke viewed most people and events through the prism of being a Jew. Her social life was tied exclusively to the Jewish community and she tended to think of names in a Jewish context. Thus, during the height of popularity of the singers Jeanette MacDonald and Nelson Eddy, she always referred to the latter as Neddy Elson. Like many other Eastern European Jews, she frequently pronounced a "w" as a "v." Thus, when she was informed that her granddaughter, Naomi, had been accepted at Wellesley, she promptly responded, "Vellesley? Vots Vellesley?"

Sara's father, Wolf, also was an outgoing, strong-willed person and an ardent Zionist. Wolf's sometimes-gruff exterior did not obscure his compassionate soul. Like Bashke, he expressed his warmth openly in his relationships with his family and his loyalty to friends.

I rarely heard my mother and father argue. But considering the fact that both Bashke and Wolf were highly charged emotionally—especially Bashke—it is not surprising that occasionally when I walked past the Gordons' grocery store on the way to my house, I could hear them screaming at each other during a fierce argument. However, there was never any question about their love for each other.

Mom rarely entertained, but the Gordons seemed to have company almost every night. They had a large kitchen, and several nights a week a group of Wolf's close friends came over to play pinochle in the kitchen. They had a joyous camaraderie, bantering continuously while they dealt the cards. They also had serious discussions, usually about the prospects for establishment of the state of Israel. All were Zionists, but Wolf also had a personal connection. Several of his relatives had emigrated to what was then Palestine and had become well established there. After the state of Israel was established, one of Wolf's brothers was appointed to a sub-cabinet position in the department of transportation. Another became the president of a bank.

While Wolf and his friends told stories, gossiped, joked and had serious conversations, Bashke was busy cooking. In a few minutes she could make a horrible mess of the kitchen. Never mind; the resulting pastries were delectable.

Bashke was the last of 16 children, but only four had survived by the time Bashke came to the United States. Because Bashke's mother bore children over such a long period of years, one nephew, Masha Lazer Gilluli, was about the same age as Bashke. He also settled in Chattanooga and he and Bashke were close. Masha Lazer (pronounced as if it were one word, Mayshalazer), was a tall, handsome man, with an engaging personality. When he came to the United States, he changed his name and frequently introduced himself in a slow, deliberate, mock pompous manner, as "Morris L. Gill." Nevertheless, all of his friends called him Masha Lazer. Before he came to the United States, he was a crack chess player in Poland. He was so good that he became a professional and people placed bets on him. I played chess with him only once. He beat me in three moves.

In addition to his prowess at chess, Masha Lazer liked to sing. Almost every time I saw him, he proclaimed that he had just learned a new *lied* (song) and would promptly perform with a twinkle in his eyes and a smile on his face. He took obvious delight in both the lyrics and the melody.

•

As our relationship developed, Sara began to broach the subject of marriage. At that time, a young woman who had attained the age of 21 and was not married was considered an old maid. So it was not surprising that Sara raised the issue. However, I was still in college and did not feel secure enough emotionally or financially to make a commitment. At the approach of her 19th birthday, Sara was insistent that we become engaged. Recognizing my reluctance (I was 20 years old), she argued that we would not get married immediately; in fact, we could delay the wedding for a year or two. She merely wanted the commitment and a sense of certainty.

Although I had some reluctance, I finally acceded. In the manner of those times, I met with her father and expressed my intentions. By then he knew me quite well, so he didn't ask many questions, except about my prospects for the future. I told him how much money I was making and that I wanted to be a newspaper reporter. Because Sara was insistent on our getting married, he gave his blessing. However, I had the feeling that he and Bashke probably would have preferred Sara to be matched with an older man who was well established in business. No slouch as a matchmaker, Bashke from time to time had introduced Sara to prospective mates, one being a diamond merchant in New York with whom Bashke had family connections. But her efforts were to no avail.

Sara's mind was made up.

Prior to my talk with Wolf, I told Mom about my intentions. She was hesitant because of my age. Although she did not express her feelings openly, it was clear that she also had the understandable reluctance of a widowed mother to lose her son. However, she had known Sara for many years, liked her, and gave her blessing. With these formalities taken care of, I went shopping for an engagement ring at a local jewelry store. With my meager earnings, almost all of which I had saved, I had accumulated enough money to buy a modest diamond ring, which I presented to Sara on January 17, 1942, her 19th birthday. The presentation, of course, was no surprise, but it added certainty to our commitment.

In May 1942, while I was a senior at the University of Chattanooga, I was offered a job in Washington by Dr. Palmer, president of the University of Chattanooga, who had been called to Washington shortly after the United States entered World War II. He had been named associate director of the Food Rationing Division of the Office of Price Administration and wanted me to work in his division. I expected that sooner or later I would be called into the army, but felt that this would be an exceptional opportunity to get Washington experience, even for a short period. I quit my job at the *Times*, terminated my academic work and moved to Washington. I assumed that I would complete my college education later, which I did after World War II.

Our separation changed any notion Sara and I might have had about waiting a year or two to get married. After I left Chattanooga, we agreed that I would return to get married on July 13, 1942, which happened to be the first birthday of Naomi, Sara's first niece, of whom she was especially fond. However, as that date approached, I was not emotionally ready to undertake this commitment. Furthermore, July 13 was the anniversary of my father's death, and I did not feel right about getting married on that date. I was in turmoil and thought long and hard about the matter. After much soul-searching, I wrote Sara a long letter explaining that I wanted to delay our wedding.

As might have been expected, my letter was a bombshell. Sara was very upset about the delay and broke out with a case of hives. Bashke and Wolf also were distraught. However, after further correspondence, Sara and I decided that in the interim, she would come to Washington to work as a secretary for a war agency. Jobs were plentiful in Washington and Sara already had experience working as a secretary in Chattanooga. She rented a room in a house in southeast Washington about a block from my apartment. (Living together was not an option in those days. It was not socially acceptable behavior, and our parents would have frowned upon it. To carry out the prevailing standards of morality, Sara's landlady would not let me go beyond the living room of her home.)

Washington was a bustling, exciting city in the war years. The downtown area, especially Pennsylvania Avenue and F and G streets, was mobbed with people during the evening. There were several palatial movie theaters, at least three of which had stage shows along with the movies. Sara and I frequently ate together in downtown Washington after work and occasionally we would go to the National Theater to see a play. Sometimes Sara would come to the apartment I shared with Mac Maguire, a colleague at the Food Rationing Division, and would cook dinner or a Sunday brunch. However, we had little opportunity to spend time alone. My reservations about getting married gradually diminished and by late summer we decided to get married that fall.

On Labor Day weekend, we returned to Chattanooga and were wed in a simple ceremony at Rabbi Gerstein's home on September 6, 1942. Only family members were present. Because we had to return to work immediately, our honeymoon consisted of one night at a rustic lodge in Gatlinburg, Tennessee, in the Smoky Mountains. Gatlinburg at that time was a small, quaint village—not the tawdry tourist mecca it subsequently became. With the gas rationing that was in effect at that time, Wolf made a real sacrifice by loaning us his car—and especially his gas coupons—to make the trip to Gatlinburg.

Chapter 8

War Years

Dr. Palmer's call in May 1942 offering me a job in the Food Rationing Division of the Office of Price Administration had an air of urgency. The United States had been at war for only six months and was still gearing up for vastly increased production of materiel required for the armed services. To assure that critically needed food and supplies were available for the military and that there was equitable distribution to civilians, the government instituted rationing of certain commodities. Controls were inaugurated to prevent price gouging of goods in short supply. These programs were administered by the Office of Price Administration.

Millions of people were desperately needed to carry out the domestic as well as military objectives. Because I had a relatively high draft number, I was among the pool of men who had not yet been called to military service. My job with the Food Rationing Division was hardly crucial to winning the war, but every person's efforts were needed. Palmer therefore asked me to report for work as soon as possible.

Within a week, I boarded a train and headed for Washington. Palmer had already purchased a home in Chevy Chase, Maryland, a Washington suburb, but his family and furniture had not arrived, so he invited me to stay with him in his house (which was empty except for cots, folding chairs and a card table) until I could find other living quarters.

Despite my arrangement with Palmer, I knew that I would soon have to move to a more permanent residence. As the train approached Washington, I bought a local newspaper and examined the want ads for apartments. I was dismayed to find that many ads included the words, "Gentiles only." I had not seen such a reference in publications in the Deep South. Washington was considered a southern city that practiced racial segregation, but I was not prepared for religious discrimination in housing, especially in the home of the New Deal. The words "Gentiles only" reinforced my insecurity.

When I arrived at Union Station, I immediately took a streetcar to Palmer's office. The Food Rationing Division was located in a temporary building—called Tempo T—at the corner of Seventh Street and Independence Avenue, where the Air and Space Museum now stands. A number of temporary buildings were erected in downtown Washington to house the many new war agencies. Most were adjacent to the Mall or in small urban parks.

The Food Rationing Division issued coupons to citizens so they could obtain meat, sugar and other foods. Rationing was administered on the local level by appointed boards that were guided by regulations promulgated by the Office of Price Administration in Washington. Where there was room for interpretation of the regulations, the local rationing boards decided the number and type of coupons that were to be issued to individuals, businesses and other establishments. I was assigned to a procedures unit charged with describing, in lay terms, regulations written by lawyers. We also devised procedures for carrying out the regulations. Palmer assumed that I would be qualified for this assignment because of my writing experience, but the work was different from that of a reporter.

My position with the Food Rationing Division necessitated in-depth knowledge of arcane regulations—rather boring stuff. I was irritated by the necessity to work closely with lawyers, who reviewed my drafts to be certain that I had correctly interpreted the regulations. The attorneys scrutinized my work word-for-word, far more carefully than my editors at the *Times*, and I regarded them as nit-pickers. In time, however, I began to appreciate them. They were very bright; many were graduates of Yale Law School. They taught me a discipline in thinking and writing that proved invaluable later. I was also impressed with the thorough consideration that they and their colleagues gave to the impact of government programs on the citizens.

After several months, I was asked to write a short weekly newsletter that was distributed to the entire Food Rationing Division in Washington and to OPA regional offices. This did not require legal review, was more akin to my work as a newspaper reporter, and was more satisfying. The newsletter had an informal style and contained information about prospective regulations, personnel changes and other developments. Field office staff especially appreciated having advance information about changes being considered in Washington.

•

During the war, the work week was extended to six days, so there was little time for leisure activities. The office routine was markedly different from that of a newspaper reporter and I found the adjustment difficult. As a reporter, I spent much of the day outside of the office on my beat, meeting with many different people. As a bureaucrat, I was mostly confined to a desk. The physical environment was not pleasant, either. The "tempos," as they were called, were unattractive two-story buildings that provided only the basic necessities. Lacking air conditioning, the second floor became unbearably hot during some mid-summer days. Despite wartime pressures, employees occasionally were dismissed to prevent heat exhaustion.

Although the war caused relatively few shortages and inconveniences, we were constantly reminded of it by seeing the large number of uniformed men and women on the streets. As I looked out my office window, I saw a steady procession of troop trains headed to or from Union Station. I wondered what those men were thinking and speculated that in the not-too-distant future I might be on a troop train.

My only extra-curricular activity in the office was acting as a shop steward for a union of government employees. Joining the union came naturally, because I had been a member of the Newspaper Guild when I worked for the *Times*. George Hull, the *Times'* photographer, had convinced me of the desirability of joining the guild after he had described the deplorable conditions that pressmen and linotype operators had endured before they had organized a union.

•

My colleagues at the Office of Price Administration were not what I had anticipated. I was a dedicated supporter of the New Deal and assumed that everyone who worked in the government was sympathetic to the Roosevelt administration. Not so, at least in my division. Most of the staff had worked in some aspect of the food industry and many came to Washington only because wartime conditions had eliminated their jobs. Their interests were not nearly as broad as those of my former colleagues at the newspaper. Their views on economic and social issues were conservative and they continually railed about government service and the workings of the bureaucracy.

Mac Maguire, one of my co-workers, grew up in Maine, but before he came to Washington he had worked in New York for the Atlantic and Pacific Tea Company in advertising and marketing. Maguire was a slight, somewhat retiring person who was at least 15 years older than me. He was my housemate for a while. After I had slept on a cot in Palmer's house for about a week, I welcomed Maguire's invitation to share his apartment in southeast Washington until he could move his family here.

Maguire and I did not have much in common. Occasionally, he invited a young couple who lived next door to come over in the evening for drinks. I was bored with their conversation, which consisted mainly of chitchat about household matters. I had thought that everybody in Washington talked about politics and government affairs.

Another colleague, Doug Boyle, had been involved in restaurant management. From him I learned the difference between "back of the house" (the kitchen) and "front of the house" (the seating area of a restaurant). This distinction was important in rationing sugar because of the different demands of the "back of the house" and "front of the house."

Another co-worker was a scion of the Wolfenson family, which operated fancy grocery stores in Kansas City, Missouri. Wolfenson had an aloof, aristocratic bearing and was especially contemptuous of Roosevelt and the New Deal. Before coming to Washington, he worked in OPA's Seattle regional office and had fallen in love with that part of the country. The only positive aspect of our relationship was my delight in hearing him recount stories about that region's lush vegetation, beautiful flowers, and spectacular scenery. Years later I had many occasions to travel to the Northwest and likewise fell in love with that part of the United States.

Maguire, Boyle, Wolfenson and I were in a carpool and our differing political views quickly came to the forefront as we drove to and from work. I read the liberal tabloid *PM*. One of *PM*'s columnists was I.F. ("Izzy") Stone, an especially articulate and persuasive defender of the New Deal. I was influenced by Stone and writers for other publications who espoused similar positions. My opinions were diametrically opposed to those of my fellow carpoolers and I frequently engaged in heated arguments with them. One of the most acrimonious was triggered when I commented that someone who had made millions of dollars by successfully marketing hamburgers was overly compensated by comparison with doctors, scientists, educators and others who made what I thought were much more significant contributions to society. As staunch believers in unbridled capitalism, Maguire, Boyle and Wolfenson were deeply offended by my comments. They probably thought I was a Communist—an opinion undoubtedly reinforced by the fact that I had joined a union of government employees.

•

Fortunately, several months after I joined the staff of the Food Rationing Division, Robert C. Davenport was named head of the unit in which I worked. His arrival was like a breath of fresh air. A career government employee, Bob was an ardent New Dealer, although he had arrived at his political views from an unlikely background. Prior to his government service, he had been an organizer for a college fraternity. His personality was well suited to that job. He was lively and had a keen sense of humor. I enjoyed working for Bob, but he was somewhat quixotic. Occasionally, just as I was about to complete an assignment, he decided that it should be done differently. He asked me to discard my work and start afresh in a new direction. Although I was sometimes disheartened, I was not offended by the abrupt change because of Bob's enthusiasm and imaginative approach.

One day at lunch Bob introduced me to a Washington institution, the Cooperative Bookstore, which offered discounts to members. Located in northwest Washington in an old house on 17th Street, the store had a congenial atmosphere and occasionally sponsored lectures. I became a member. Later, in the days of McCarthyism, the Cooperative Bookstore was branded as a communist front and federal employees who were members were considered suspect in their efforts to obtain security clearances.

Bob and I quickly became friends and after Sara and I were married, we occasionally visited him and his young family on the weekends. They lived in Tauxemont, a new cooperative community in a wooded area about seven miles south of Alexandria, Virginia, near Mount Vernon.

Sara and I worked with the Davenports in their garden. We helped plant shrubs and flowers, moved dirt and performed other such chores. As a reward for our efforts, we were invited to stay for dinner. A special treat was their homemade ice cream. Little did Sara and I dream that our friendship with Bob and our experiences at Tauxemont would lead to an important milestone in our lives. After the war, Bob became a developer, completed Tauxemont, and began to build Hollin Hills, where Sara and I bought our first home from Bob.

•

Although I was not enamored of my work with the Food Rationing Division, I enjoyed the excitement of living in wartime Washington. I could feel the energy as I disembarked from the train. The war necessitated the creation of a number of new government agencies, and the city was teeming with civilians and military personnel. At night, the sidewalks in the downtown area—Pennsylvania Avenue. and F and G streets between 7th and 15th streets Northwest—were packed. Opportunities for entertainment far surpassed those available in Chattanooga. In the summer, the Watergate concerts, performed on a barge anchored on the Potomac River beside Memorial Bridge, were a popular form of entertainment. Rock Creek Parkway, which separated the barge from the steps leading up to Lincoln Memorial, was closed to traffic during the concerts, and reserved chairs were placed on the street. However, most of the audience sat in the unreserved section on the stone steps rising from the parkway. Some people rented canoes from a boathouse in Georgetown and paddled to the area near the barge where they anchored to hear the concert. The sight at nightfall was picturesque, especially at the end of the performance when lights in each canoe traced a trail on the water back to Georgetown.

Another form of entertainment was the chamber music concerts in Meridian Hill Park on 16th Street. This beautiful formal garden, offering a spectacular view of the city, was an idyllic setting for the performances.

Downtown Washington was enlivened by an active shopping district consisting of five major department stores, many specialty shops and a variety of restaurants, night clubs and theaters. When Sara and I wanted to splurge, our favorite restaurant was one that went by the name 823, which was the restaurant's address on 15th Street. Palmer introduced me to 823 on my first night in Washington and I liked its ambience and the fact that it featured live music by an attractive woman violinist and a pianist. The restaurant originally was called the Bavarian Inn, but with the advent of the war with Germany, the owners changed the name to one that had a more neutral connotation. Nevertheless, the restaurant retained its murals depicting life in Bavaria.

Although President Roosevelt—and especially his wife, Eleanor—made significant gestures toward racial equality, Washington nevertheless remained a segregated city. Blacks were not served in "white" restaurants, and were seated in the balconies of theaters or in movie houses serving black patrons exclusively. They also had to ride in the back of the trolleys and buses, drink from water fountains marked "colored," and use separate toilet facilities. With few exceptions, blacks held only menial jobs in government agencies, and were assigned to segregated units in the armed services. Although there may have been some socializing between the races in homes, there could not have been any fraternization in the segregated restaurants or other public places.

When I moved to Washington, I realized that it was a southern city and retained the practices of the Deep South, but I was nevertheless disappointed that discrimination against blacks was not noticeably different than that practiced in Chattanooga.

•

Sara and I did not have to look for an apartment after we were married.

My housemate, Maguire, found more desirable accommodations in an adjacent building and his family joined him. Sara and I took over the unit Maguire and I had shared. It was in a relatively new red brick, three-story building. Our apartment was in the basement, and had a living room, bedroom, kitchen and bathroom. Because most of the living room was below ground, it had small, high windows. The bedroom, which had larger windows, overlooked a parking lot. The Spartan furniture, which Maguire or a previous owner had bought from Sears, was acceptable and I assumed the modest payments on the remaining amount of the debt.

After we were married, Sara continued her job as a secretary in a war agency that dealt with economic matters. We had no car, so we commuted either by bus or car pool. The area where we lived is now a predominantly black neighborhood.

Each day when I came home from work I immediately examined the mail to see whether I had received a notice from my draft board in Chattanooga. In late March 1943 the suspense was over. Because my legal residence was in Chattanooga, I was ordered to report to the induction station at Fort Oglethorpe, Georgia. Sara and I promptly returned to Chattanooga.

·

After we arrived in Chattanooga and before my induction, I called some of the officers I had known when I covered Fort Oglethorpe as a newspaper reporter and told them I would be coming through the induction center there. They asked what I had been doing in Washington and when I told them of my work in the Food Rationing Division, one officer said they could use me in post headquarters. Food for troops was not rationed, but the post had to deal with some aspects of rationing for the commissary and other purposes. They had been perplexed about some of the details of rationing and thought I could be helpful in administering the program.

I was almost certain that I would be classified for limited service and would not be sent into combat. In high school and college I had serious allergy problems that caused me to sneeze a great deal and required that I take desensitization shots. Additionally, the back problem that began when I was a reporter traveling with General Patton's troops had been diagnosed as a degenerated disc and this condition, too, limited my physical activities. When I was processed through the induction center, I was not surprised that I was classified for limited service. Officers at Fort Oglethorpe thereupon requested my assignment to the post rationing office. Thus began my inauspicious military career.

I was not sent to another camp for basic training, but instead was given limited training at Fort Oglethorpe, consisting primarily of close order drill, hiking and practicing at a rifle range. I learned how to make a bunk bed the Army way and performed such ennobling chores as latrine and guard duty. I also learned the rudiments of fire fighting.

I worked at first in the quartermaster's office handling rationing details. I was a private, but did the work that had been performed by an officer—not an uncommon experience in the Army. After several weeks, unless I had guard duty or other special assignments, I was permitted to leave the post after work and spend the night at the apartment in Chattanooga where Sara lived. I had to return to the post in time for reveille at 6 a.m., necessitating an early morning bus ride.

John Clay Lovett, who was an attorney for the Tennessee Valley Authority before he joined the Army, also was stationed at Fort Oglethorpe. He and his wife, Lunelle, had an apartment about a block from the Gordons' house, where Sara had her apartment. Lovett and I became friends and we frequently walked briskly or ran down Cameron Hill in the early morning hours to catch our bus to the post. Lovett came from a prominent family of lawyers who had practiced for many years in Benton, Kentucky, in the law firm of Lovett, Lovett and Lovett, located in the Lovett Building. Although he had graduated from Harvard Law School, he retained some of the unsophisticated ways of a small town lawyer. He was a great raconteur and at the slightest provocation would regale friends with hilarious stories about judges and lawyers in the rural South.

•

Another friend at Fort Oglethorpe was Fats Everett, whose nickname reflected his weight of more than 300 pounds. A native of the small town of Union City in West Tennessee, Fats held a minor local political position before his Army induction. He aspired to be a congressman or governor and believed that military service would advance his career. However, he had been rejected several times because the Army had no uniform large enough for him. He finally persuaded the Army to accept him and a uniform was made to order. Fats was a jolly, gregarious person with a booming voice. He not only knew most of his constituents by name, he also memorized their license plate numbers. Armed with this information, he would shout a personal greeting to the driver of an oncoming car as the two vehicles passed.

I was also friendly with the flamboyant Sgt. Early Maxwell, who worked in the public affairs office of the post headquarters. Maxwell was a former reporter for the *Memphis Commercial Appeal,* but before his military service he had worked as a sports and entertainment promoter. He claimed to know many prominent entertainers of that era, including Bob Hope. When Maxwell learned of my newspaper background, he asked that I be transferred to his office. By that time I was bored with the routine of the rationing program, so I gladly accepted his offer. In my new assignment, I did photography as well as public relations.

Shortly after going to the public affairs office, I was assigned to a War Department program to combat the growing problem of absenteeism of civilians working in war industries, of which there were many in the South. The War Department, through its industrial services branch, asked the Army's Fourth Service Command headquarters in Atlanta to assign personnel at posts in the command (which included Fort Oglethorpe) to work on this program. By that time, I had been promoted to the rank of sergeant and was ordered to report to Capt. Tom Sawyer of the Fourth Service Command headquarters to do advance work for a series of military shows that were to be held in the Southeast near important war production industries. I spent most of the remainder of my military service in this assignment, traveling thousands of miles—by car, bus and train—throughout the Southeast.

Captain Sawyer, who had been a corporate executive in Atlanta before joining the armed forces, was a genial person who did not follow military conventions, one of which prohibited fraternization between officers and enlisted men. When duty required us to be in Atlanta, I spent the night in his luxurious home. However, I was still assigned to Fort Oglethorpe and returned there between my travels.

We arranged logistics and advance publicity for the shows. The presentations generally were held in baseball fields and the highlight was a mock battle that showcased various types of Army equipment used in ground warfare. Troops advanced under cover of a smoke screen and fired blank ammunition. The noise and action aroused the audiences, which cheered the soldiers after each performance. After the demonstrations, a soldier who had just returned from combat in Europe described some of his experiences. Finally, an officer pitched the importance of maintaining the production of war materiel.

I had my doubts about the value of these productions, but Army surveys before and after the events showed that they reduced absenteeism for a significant period.

This assignment led me to new experiences. Besides writing press releases, I was interviewed on radio stations in towns where the shows were to be held and was master of ceremonies of some events. I also occasionally wrote scripts. I found especially interesting my visits to many newspaper offices to talk with reporters about forthcoming shows. There were no surprises in dealing with the metropolitan newspapers, but it was an eye opener to see how small weekly papers were published. One day I walked into the office of a weekly and saw that the editor was frantically taking notes while he sat close to a small radio, listening intently to a news broadcast. After he finished this chore, he turned to me and explained that he was obtaining information for a story he was writing on the latest developments in the war in Europe. Having worked for a newspaper that received a continuing stream of teletype reports on national and international developments from the Associated Press and United Press, I thought it was amusing that this weekly paper had to rely on a commercial radio report as the source of its news.

While working in the industrial services branch, I developed an enduring friendship with Jonas Silverstone, one of the sergeants in the Fourth Service Command headquarters in Atlanta. Jonas enjoyed writing scripts, even though he was circumscribed in what he could do. Before his induction into the Army, Jonas had been a successful New York lawyer who represented many prominent actors, such as Peter Lorre and Julie Harris, as well as producers and others in the entertainment world. He developed a close relationship with his clients, many of whom had troubled personal lives. They frequently called Jonas at all hours of the day or night to ask his advice about personal problems. Jonas aspired to be a playwright, and was grateful that the Army shows offered him limited opportunities to be creative. Jonas and I spent many hours talking about ideas he had for plays and what he would write after the war.

While doing the advance work for one show, I learned a painful lesson about the sensitivity of race relations. The Army was segregated and only white service men participated in most of the shows for which I did advance work. However, on one occasion we did advance work for a black unit, which was to appear in a black theater. In preparation for this event, I met with a black battle-hardened veteran from New York. Because I did not approve of segregation, I perhaps unwittingly overcompensated in my dealings with this soldier. In our discussion, I used the word "Nigra," which is how the more enlightened people of the South referred to Negroes. The sergeant was incensed by my use of this term and I thought he would hit me. I apologized profusely and he soon calmed down. I never again used the word.

•

During this period, Sara got a job as a reporter for *The Chattanooga*

Times. She had no previous newspaper experience, but was a good writer, especially of feature stories, and did well. She was imaginative, and her engaging personality was an asset. While with the *Times*, she covered campaign events and became friendly with Estes Kefauver, then a Congressman who represented the district that included Chattanooga. He later became a well-known U.S. senator and a candidate for vice president on the Democratic ticket with former Illinois Gov. Adlai Stevenson.

When the war ended in August 1945, I began to think seriously about the resumption of my civilian career. I had kept in touch with Palmer, who left the Office of Price Administration during the latter part of the war to become associate director of the Foreign Service Planning Division of the Department of State. After the armistice with Japan was signed, I called him and he offered me a position in his division. Although I did not entirely understand the specifics of the job, I was attracted by the notion of working at the State Department and relished the opportunity to live in Washington again.

The armed services were being demobilized and Palmer asked for my immediate release so I could go to work as soon as possible for the State Department. The War Department granted his request and in September 1945 I was mustered out of service.

As I looked back on my military service, I had regrets and ambivalent feelings. I felt fortunate to have survived the war unscathed. But I was not proud of my military service, even though I received several letters of commendation for my work with the industrial services branch. Because of physical problems, I probably never would have seen front-line service, yet I was embarrassed to have spent the war in a safe, relatively cushy environment while others risked their lives. In the security of retrospect, I felt I should have made an effort to serve in a more active capacity.

Sara and I spent our last night in Chattanooga at the Gordons' home, before taking a train to Washington. Before I went to sleep that night I looked out for a long time at the quiet city, heard the mournful horn of a train and realized that Chattanooga, with the many memories it held, would probably never be my home again.

Chapter 9

A Washington Bureaucrat

Fats Everett had been discharged from the Army and was working in Washington as chief of staff for Sen. Tom Stewart of Tennessee when I was released from the service. Fats lived at the Colonial Hotel, a small establishment at the corner of 15th and M streets. At his recommendation, Sara and I decided to move there until we could find an apartment.

After the restrictions of Army life, we enjoyed the freedom of wandering in the city and getting acclimated to post-war Washington, which had a less frantic air than we had experienced previously. Sidewalks were less crowded, traffic moved at a more leisurely pace and fewer uniformed men and women were on the streets.

We quickly got a first-hand introduction to the current international political scene. India was in the throes of becoming independent from the British Empire and, fortunately for us, three or four Indians were staying at the Colonial Hotel. Sara and I frequently saw them at breakfast. In her customary ingratiating manner, Sara became friendly with them and we had stimulating conversations. Although the Indians had dark skin, they were not discriminated against. Because of our upbringing in the South, it was a new experience for us to sit at the same table in a public place with people of a different color.

I reported for work immediately at the State Department and within a week I also enrolled at George Washington University to complete requirements for my bachelor of arts degree. Meanwhile, Sara spent the days shopping for an apartment in Virginia, where we had decided to live.

Because of wartime restrictions on construction, housing was scarce. We needed an apartment on a bus route. Even if we could have afforded a car, they were in short supply because manufacture of civilian automobiles had been suspended during the war. Fortunately, Sara made a good impression on the manager of Lee Gardens, which was on a convenient bus route in nearby Arlington. It was a desirable place to live. By comparison with our wartime apartment in southeast Washington, Lee Gardens was a significant step up. Our unit on the third floor had a large living room, a bedroom, a bath, and a small kitchen and dining area. It was light and airy, with parquet floors and the grounds of the building were nicely landscaped. Our rent was $65 a month—not considered inexpensive at that time.

When we moved to Chattanooga during my time in the Army, the Gordons had purchased a modicum of second-hand furniture for us. They shipped this furniture to us in Arlington and with the addition of a few other items and clever decorating, Sara made the new apartment attractive.

•

My job with the State Department began with a stimulating week-long orientation. A number of the top brass of the department made presentations. I was especially impressed with Charles E. Bohlen, who later became ambassador to the Soviet Union. Later, another person who made a lasting impression on me was Alger Hiss. At that time, Hiss was still basking in the glory of his accomplishments; it was not until later that he was accused of being a Communist agent and was the center of a congressional investigation and a trial that captured the attention of the world. I met Hiss only briefly while we were waiting for an elevator. Unlike most pompous high-level officials in the State Department, Hiss cordially greeted me and another young colleague. I was taken with his friendly, outgoing nature, even in this brief encounter.

The orientation sessions were held in the ornate Indian Treaty Room of the main State Department building, which is now the Eisenhower Executive Office Building, adjacent to the White House. The décor of the room was enhanced by elaborately carved gilded embellishments on the door frames. The room was two stories high, and a narrow balcony with a decorative wrought iron balustrade was cantilevered from the second floor. During the Eisenhower administration, the Indian Treaty Room was the site of Ike's press conferences and was frequently seen on television.

I was assigned to the Foreign Service Planning Division, in which Palmer served as associate director. The division, part of the Office of Foreign Service, handled administrative planning. It did not have the prestige of offices dealing with diplomatic work, so we were relegated to the Walker Johnson Building on New York Avenue, about a half-block from the State Department building. However, I frequently had lunch or went to meetings at "main State," and was impressed with this historic structure, which was built in the late 19th century and originally housed the War, Navy and State departments. With its graceful stairways, marble floors, wide corridors and large offices, main State had the staid, quiet air of what I imagined to be the foreign offices in a European country. The building had one incongruous note, however. In this pre-air conditioning era, saloon-type louvered swinging doors were installed in the doorways leading from the corridors to individual offices.

The government was confronted with the problem of determining the future of wartime agencies that had been established to deal with some aspects of foreign affairs. Congress and the Truman administration debated whether agencies such as the Office of War Information and those concerned with economic policy and foreign aid should be retained and, if so, whether they should be absorbed into the State Department or reincarnated as separate entities.

I was not personally involved in this issue, but some of my colleagues were and we had lively discussions about the relative merits of the options. Because the State Department had a deserved reputation as a staid institution, Congress decided that the wartime agencies would be more innovative and make quicker decisions if they continued to be independent.

I was assigned to a group working on another major problem confronting the State Department—the organization of the Foreign Service. The war had greatly expanded the role of the United States as a world power and it was obvious that the government's foreign operations had to be upgraded and modernized. Several bright young Foreign Service officers were asked to work on legislation revamping the Foreign Service and I worked with this group. Not having had any experience in diplomatic or consular affairs, I could contribute nothing substantive. Instead, I did research. Our work culminated in the adoption by Congress of the Foreign Service Act of 1946, which, among other things, established certain grades for Foreign Service officers, inaugurated the Foreign Service staff corps and set up the Foreign Service Institute to train personnel for overseas duty.

After passage of the Foreign Service Act, several associates and I were asked to prepare a form for an annual survey of the personnel needs of all of the embassies, legations and consulates throughout the world. We were to categorize the requirements by functions that the personnel performed, such as diplomatic work, political reporting, consular affairs and administration. The objective was to obtain statistical support for the department's budget requests to Congress. After we prepared a form, we compiled the information needed on a country-by-country, regional and international basis. Because of the sensitivity of the information we were to receive about the names and work assignments of State Department personnel, our requests for information were sent under the name of the secretary of state and were marked "confidential."

Aggregating the data was a mechanical exercise, but our first responsibility was to review the responses carefully to be sure that the information provided was consistent and accurate. It was a dull but demanding task. However, I learned important lessons that later proved useful to me in preparing budgets for the American Public Power Association.

One of the most interesting aspects of this assignment was reading the narrative material that accompanied the reports. These documents described in varying degrees of detail the issues facing the department's foreign outposts. The most literate, graphic and informative memos were those from remote consulates in China that described the living conditions and political issues confronting those who manned these outposts. Some of the reports were written by one or more Foreign Service officers who were later much maligned in the debate over the U.S. role in losing China to the Communists.

I compiled data for Africa, the Far East and the Near East. Fortunately, we did not have to add the numbers. An assistant, Jose´ Quintinella, had a mechanical calculator, which he used to add the figures for all regions. Without the benefit of computers, this was a massive job. When we faced a deadline for the completion of our report, Jose´ worked two full nights consecutively to finish our assignment.

Preparing material for the State Department budget taught me an important lesson about the relationship between Congress and executive department agencies. My colleagues and I spent an entire year compiling detailed figures on the department's needs and our work was reviewed by many others in the department and the Bureau of the Budget. Thousands of hours were devoted to this task. I naively assumed that our detailed supporting information presented an invincible case for the department's budget request. But after a short hearing, the House Appropriations Committee drastically slashed our budget proposal. My colleagues and I felt Congress acted in a cavalier manner. I had not learned that budgets were based on broadly defined political policies that sometimes led to arbitrary decisions and it was up to the departments to accommodate themselves to "top down" decision-making.

The background and interests of my colleagues at the State

Department were considerably different from those of the Office of Price Administration staff. At OPA, many of my colleagues were businessmen with no interest in career government service. They were merely biding time until they could return to their previous pursuits. Staff of the Foreign Service Planning Division were mostly well-educated, dedicated government employees whose interests more nearly paralleled my own. Jay Westcott was my immediate supervisor. A career civil servant who had graduated from the Maxwell School of Public Administration at Syracuse University, Jay was highly intelligent and had a good sense of humor. He and I became friends and our families socialized.

•

After we had settled into our new apartment, Sara got a job with the Cotrell News Bureau that covered Washington for a group of newspapers, including the *Nashville Banner* and others in North Carolina and South Carolina. The Cottrell bureau was named for its founder, Jesse Cottrell, a highly regarded newspaperman. The bureau concentrated on Washington news that pertained to the local interests of its client papers. Sara's job was to assist in covering the offices of senators and representatives from Tennessee. This assignment permitted her to continue her friendship with Kefauver and to become acquainted with other members of the Tennessee delegation. She fraternized with fellow journalists, especially several whose offices were on the same floor of the National Press Building as the Cottrell bureau.

One of Sara's most lasting friends was Virginia Reid, a reporter for the *Philadelphia Record*. Ginny was a dedicated liberal. She had been a staunch supporter of the Spanish Loyalists. Even though the Spanish Civil War had ended by the time we knew her, she continued to support its victims. Frequently, she would eat only a candy bar for lunch, so she could send money to the Loyalists. Ginny also was a strong supporter of organized labor and a member of the Newspaper Guild. When the Guild went on strike against the *Philadelphia Record*, she split with her boss, Bob Roth, head of the Washington bureau, and joined the strikers. She was especially disillusioned because the owner of the *Record* was a supporter of liberal causes. After the strike was settled, Ginny returned to the *Philadelphia Record*, but she never forgave the bureau chief for continuing to work during the strike and she subsequently left the *Record*. Much later, I hired her to work as a writer for the American Public Power Association.

Sara's assignments for the Cottrell News Bureau were more demanding than those for *The Chattanooga Times* and she enjoyed the excitement of covering Washington. I had not lost my fascination for newspaper reporting, so I reacted with vicarious pleasure (and envy) to daily accounts of her work and associations with fellow journalists.

In addition to friends that Sara and I made through our jobs, we also developed a social life around the professional people our age whom we came to know at Lee Gardens. After we returned to Washington, we resumed our friendship with the Davenports. Several Chattanooga couples who had moved to Washington also were in our circle of friends. These included the sister of Cecil Holland, who had been city editor of the *Chattanooga News* when I worked there one summer, and Travis Hedrick, former labor reporter for *The Chattanooga Times*, who had moved to Washington to join the Washington bureau of the *Federated Press*, a left-wing news bureau. Travis lived with his friend Millie (a labor organizer) without the sanctity of marriage—a lifestyle considered an aberration at that time.

•

Sara and I enjoyed life in Washington, but the political scene cast a menacing shadow over our lives. The uneasy friendship between the United States and the Soviet Union that developed during World War II began to fracture with the end of hostilities. The House Un-American Activities Committee became considerably more active and there was growing suspicion of the Soviet Union and its aggressive tendencies. The Communist takeover of China and the alliance between China and the Soviet Union exacerbated these concerns.

Because of fears of the spread of communism and allegations that Communists had infiltrated the U.S. government (especially the State Department), a number of political leaders clamored for the institution of a loyalty program, including the requirement that all government employees sign a loyalty oath. Sadly, President Truman succumbed to the pressure. He issued an executive order allowing investigations of all federal employees to determine whether they were loyal. Truman later conceded that the program had been a bad mistake.

I did not question the need for the government to protect itself from employees who were acting on behalf of a foreign power. However, I and many others opposed the loyalty program, especially in view of the witch hunt atmosphere that pervaded the process. Investigators would examine garbage disposed of by federal employees and FBI agents questioned friends and neighbors in their efforts to determine whether an employee was a "loyal American." Standards for determining loyalty were highly questionable. The term "disloyal" was not defined; individuals could be dismissed on the basis of "reasonable grounds," and the accused were unable to confront those making charges against them or even to know who they were or the nature of the charges. Organizations such as the Cooperative Bookstore, which I had joined in order to obtain discounts, were branded as Communist fronts and a government employee's subscriptions to certain publications were used to evaluate his or her loyalty.

I found the process repulsive and threatening. I had been a member of the Cooperative Bookstore and subscribed to several left-wing publications that were considered suspect. A number of our friends (such as Travis Hedrick) had connections that made them tainted by standards used to determine loyalty. Our next door neighbors, an older couple with extreme right-wing views, also were a problem. They were caught up in the anti-Communist hysteria and constantly taunted Sara and me to engage in arguments from which they doubtless concluded that we were part of the conspiracy. I felt certain that if they were interviewed by an FBI agent, they would accuse us of being Communist sympathizers.

Yielding to these threats, I cancelled my membership in the Cooperative Bookstore and Sara and I (largely at my insistence, I'm sorry to say) dropped our relationships with some of our friends—actions that I regret to this day.

•

Under the dark cloud of this atmosphere, Sara and I anticipated the birth of our first child. In those days, there was little preparation of parents—especially fathers—for parenthood. Sara, of course, saw an obstetrician regularly, and reported to me on her condition, but I had only the foggiest notion of the responsibilities of fatherhood. I was taking classes at George Washington University two or three evenings a week while continuing full-time work at the State Department. The classes, together with studying in the evenings and weekends, left me little time to contemplate parenthood. In the midst of my busy life, there were fleeting moments when I felt frightened and overwhelmed by what might lie ahead.

I accompanied Sara to buy a crib and other necessities for the baby. We had limited funds, so we shopped at a second-hand market in Georgetown for a chest of drawers. The chest was not in the best of condition, but looked respectable after I painted it white. Whatever equipment we needed was crowded into the relatively small bedroom of our apartment.

I accepted literally the date that Sara's obstetrician gave us for the baby's birth. We had no car, so we arranged with Sara's sister, Anna Jacobson, and her husband, Alec, who lived about a half-mile from us, to take Sara and me to the hospital when the appointed time arrived.

About 1 or 2 a.m. on the morning of February 24, 1947, Sara began having pains. This was about two weeks earlier than the date given for the baby's arrival. Furthermore, only a day or two earlier Sara and I had been traipsing through the snow in Lubber Run Park in Arlington. Surely, she could not be giving birth now. I told her to go back to sleep. However, the pains persisted and began coming with greater frequency. We called the doctor about 3 a.m. and he told us to report to the hospital as soon as possible. I called Anna and Alec and they drove us to George Washington University Hospital. Alec had business responsibilities and left shortly after we checked in at the hospital, but Anna remained with me in the visitors' lounge while Sara was in labor. Mercifully, we waited only a couple of hours before a doctor emerged about 6:30 a.m. with the news that I was the father of a $6^{1}/_{2}$-pound baby boy, who was in excellent condition, as was Sara. Anna and I were relieved and elated, but another half-hour or more elapsed before we could see Sara and the baby. We then went shopping in the neighborhood for a new robe for Sara.

After making calls to members of the family, we began preparing for the *bris* (circumcision), which was to be held at our apartment. By that time, my mother had married William Stahl from Chattanooga, and both came to the *bris*, as did Sara's parents. Unexpectedly, they were joined on the train ride to Washington by my brother Jake. He was then playing with the Baltimore Symphony Orchestra and was on tour in the South. By a happy coincidence, my mother, her new husband, and the Gordons were on the same train. Along with some members of the Baltimore Symphony Orchestra, they had a jolly time celebrating en route to Washington.

In addition to our family, other guests included Congressman Kefauver and Fats Everett. In the Jewish custom of naming children for revered deceased forebears, we named our boy Jay Jacob. Jay represented Joseph, my father, and Jacob was the name of my mother's father. It was a happy occasion.

After the festivities, Sara and I settled down to the mundane task of taking care of our son. Sara had quit her job and spent full time as a homemaker. The prevailing wisdom at that time was that formulas were better than mother's milk, so Sara did not attempt to breast-feed Jay. Every evening we went through the time-consuming ritual of mixing ingredients for a formula and sterilizing the bottles and nipples.

We alternated getting up at night to feed Jay. Disposable diapers were unheard of, so we washed a supply of cloth diapers regularly in a laundry room in the basement of an adjoining building. We had no car for six months or more after Jay was born, but fortunately a grocery store and other shops were within easy walking distance of our apartment.

As a present, Sara's mother and father made their housekeeper, Minnie, available to help us for about a week after Jay was born. Minnie slept on a couch in the living room. She was a small, wiry, take-charge person who was generally in a good humor. However, a crisis arose within a few days after she arrived when she had exhausted her quantity of snuff. She threatened to return to Chattanooga immediately if we could not replenish her supply. Snuff was not a commodity in big demand in the Washington area at that time, especially in the lily-white suburb where we lived. However, after a diligent search, I was able to find several tins— sufficient to keep Minnie with us for the remainder of her scheduled stay.

Chapter 10

Whitaker's Phone Call

By the summer of 1947, I was bored with the administrative work at the State Department. Without considerably more education, I would be ill-prepared to take the rigorous exams for entrance into the Foreign Service and, hence, had no prospect of participating in the substantive work of the department. I also was apprehensive about the impact on my mother if I left the United States for an extended period of time. By then her marriage with Stahl was falling apart.

My dissatisfaction was compounded by the demands for loyalty oaths and accusations about government employees. People I knew were accused—on the flimsiest grounds—of being Communist sympathizers. The air of fear and suspicion that pervaded government offices was repressive. I even felt I had to be furtive in buying the liberal newspaper *PM* and bringing it into the office.

I wanted to get out of government service, even though I felt strongly that government should play an important role in addressing problems facing American society. But this was not the time for me, as a government employee, to participate in advancing such an agenda.

What were my options? I had completed requirements for my bachelor's degree and had my credits at George Washington University transferred to the University of Chattanooga, which awarded me a B.A. in June 1947. Although I was conflicted about the decision, I applied and was admitted to the George Washington University law school. Some aspects of legal practice appealed to me, but I was turned off by the prospect of having to examine the minutia of laws. However, continuing my education would take time away from my family. Sara thus far had borne the brunt of taking care of Jay, because I worked full time and went to classes several nights a week. It was clear that my enrollment at law school would be a real burden on Sara. Nevertheless, I decided to go to law school and marched up the steps of the GW administration building to enroll. At the top of the steps I hesitated, turned around and walked down, aborting whatever career I might have had as a lawyer.

With hopes of returning to journalism, I applied for jobs at two well-regarded newspapers—the *Atlanta Constitution* and the *Louisville Courier-Journal*. The job market was highly competitive because of the large number of veterans returning from the war. Both newspapers turned me down. I also contacted the managing editor of *The Chattanooga Times*, who offered me a position as a reporter. However, I was not interested in returning to Chattanooga, especially in a job that represented no real advancement over the one I had before the war.

•

In November 1947 I received a surprise telephone call from Ken Whitaker, administrative assistant to the chairman of the Chattanooga Electric Power Board. He asked if I would be interested in working as Washington representative for the Tennessee Valley Public Power Association. Whitaker, his boss, L.J. Wilhoite, and S.R. Finley, manager of the Electric Power Board, had been instrumental in establishing TVPPA, an organization of the approximately 150 municipalities and rural electric cooperatives that bought wholesale power from the Tennessee Valley Authority and distributed it in all or parts of seven states. I had not known Whitaker, Wilhoite or Finley. Whitaker, the political operative for the group, had asked Jim Jarvis, managing editor of the *Times*, whether he knew someone from Chattanooga living in Washington who might be a candidate for this job. Jarvis gave him my name.

Whitaker explained that TVA was under severe attack from private power companies, which fought a continuing battle in Congress against appropriations to build and maintain the TVA power system. TVPPA's principal mission as a lobbying organization for the distributors was to support TVA's legislative interests. It therefore planned to hire a person in Washington to keep the organization informed about legislative developments affecting TVA and its distributors.

Without giving it a great deal of thought or learning more about the job, I said I would be interested and Whitaker arranged to meet with me in Washington to discuss the job in detail. The position appealed to me for several reasons. Foremost was that it would get me involved in a cause— public power—about which I felt enthusiastic. TVA and public power at that time were important elements of the New Deal and President Truman's Fair Deal and I wanted to be identified with these efforts.

From a personal standpoint, the opportunity to be associated with TVA was attractive. Having grown up in Chattanooga, I had seen first hand the benefits TVA brought to the region through low-cost power and river development. I also liked the idea of working with Congress and following its activities. I had no desire to run for public office, but was fascinated by the political scene.

My meeting with Whitaker reinforced my interest in this assignment. Whitaker asked me to meet with Carlton Nau, general manager of the American Public Power Association, a relatively new national organization of municipal and other local publicly owned electric utilities. TVPPA leaders thought they might want their representative physically located in the APPA offices in order to coordinate the activities of the national and regional groups.

After these interviews, I eagerly awaited a call from Whitaker to tell me whether I had been selected. Shortly before Thanksgiving 1947, Whitaker telephoned me at the State Department to say that his group had hired Sam O'Neal. I went home crestfallen. I had become especially eager to leave the State Department and Whitaker's call made me feel like I had received an indefinite sentence. However, I could understand why TVPPA had selected O'Neal. He was an older person who had a distinguished career as a reporter in the Washington bureau of the *St. Louis Post-Disptach*. He had become friendly with President Truman and a large autographed photo of Truman hung on the wall behind his desk. O'Neal also had been president of the prestigious National Press Club and was already well established as a lobbyist for a group of large postal users. Clearly, he had far better credentials than I.

•

A couple days after I got the bad news from Whitaker, I received a call from Nau, who asked me if I would be interested in working for APPA as his assistant. APPA was a fledgling organization; the staff consisted only of Nau and two secretaries. They occupied a two-room suite in an old converted apartment house on Vermont Avenue, near Thomas Circle. In its heyday, the building was considered elegant and was the address of prominent Washingtonians, but it was far past its prime by the time APPA moved there.

Although I had misgivings about the stability of the organization, I was so anxious to leave the State Department that I did not inquire in depth about the association's budget or financial stability. Nau assured me that APPA offered prospects for growth. Most important, the nature of the job appealed to me. I was to write for and edit most of a weekly newsletter and monthly magazine. I would cover Congress and the federal administrative agencies that affected public power. The position would get me back into writing and reporting and was more appealing than the State Department job.

As an inducement, Nau offered me an annual salary of about $6,000—a $500 raise over my State Department pay. After Sara and I discussed it, I decided to take the job. However, when I called the Gordons with the news, they were clearly dismayed, especially Wolf. He probably had visions of my becoming an ambassador or being promoted to some other high-ranking post in the State Department. He clearly thought it was foolhardy of me to give up a secure government position with a prestigious agency for a job with a small organization that faced an uncertain future.

When I told my boss at the State Department that I was leaving, he offered me various inducements to remain. The most appealing was a trip around the world to visit various embassies and legations so that I would have a better first-hand perspective on the issues I was dealing with. I had been working for more than two years with offices I had never seen and that I knew only in the abstract. But I was not tempted by the offer and stuck to my commitment to APPA.

On my final day at the State Department, my colleagues threw a lively party for me at a popular Greek restaurant in Chinatown, giving an international flavor to the end of my State Department career. I left the festivities with no regrets.

Chapter 11

Gestation of a New Organization

My first day of work at APPA in January 1948 introduced me to a dramatic change. At the State Department I was one of several thousand employees in large office buildings. My work revolved about world capitals and government agencies with far-flung international responsibilities. At APPA, my principal focus—besides the Tennessee Valley Authority—was the Department of the Interior, which marketed power produced at federal dams, and the Federal Power Commission, a regulatory agency. Compared with the State Department, these agencies had provincial, arcane responsibilities.

APPA's Vermont Avenue office suite had two rooms; one had desks for me and two secretaries (referred to in the parlance of the times as "the girls"), plus filing cabinets and a mimeograph machine. The bare walls were painted an antiseptic light green. Adjoining this room was Nau's private office, furnished modestly with second-hand furniture. The wood floors were covered with red rugs that Nau had purchased on sale at Hecht's department store. I had to remove a ring of red fuzz from my shoes every night when I came home.

When I went to work for APPA, I knew nothing about the origins of the organization. Bit by bit, I learned from Nau and others that APPA had been in gestation since the mid-1930s, before it was officially organized in September 1940.[1] Officials of municipally owned electric utilities formed APPA, but several well-known federal government officials also had a hand in creating it. These included Secretary of the Interior Harold Ickes, Federal Power Commission Chairman Leland

---

[1] The actual date of organization is unclear. Some APPA files refer to September 12, 1940 as the date when APPA was formed. The certificate of incorporation was filed on October 3, 1940.

Olds, TVA Chairman David Lilienthal and Rural Electrification Administrator Morris L. Cooke.

A confluence of circumstances made the time ripe for formation of a national organization of local publicly owned electric utilities. By the mid-1930s, about 2,500 cities and small communities throughout the United States had established municipally owned electric utilities. Cities began providing electric service when electricity was still a novelty. Its introduction into a community typically was celebrated with festivities. When streetlights were first turned on, people gaped with amazement at their brightness.

The first municipally owned utilities were formed as early as 1882, the year that Thomas Edison's Pearl Street Station in New York City inaugurated the concept of central station electricity. As electric service became more prevalent, some larger cities formed their own electric utilities, but most municipal utilities were located in smaller towns or villages. Private power companies passed over these communities and rural areas, concentrating instead on the more lucrative metropolitan centers. Some municipalities merely built distribution lines within the city and bought wholesale power from private utilities. Others installed their own generating plants.

Until the election of Franklin D. Roosevelt in 1932, public power was primarily the domain of municipal electric utilities. The federal government produced a modest amount of electricity at reclamation dams in the West. The New Deal introduced a radical change in the federal government's role in power development and gave impetus to the creation of a national public power organization.

To put people to work during the Great Depression, Roosevelt launched an ambitious program to build dams for flood control, navigation, irrigation and other purposes. The construction of dams, primarily for other purposes, made possible the installation of turbines that produced electricity and earned revenues to help pay for the water projects. Under congressional policy dating back to 1906, municipalities received preference in purchasing power at wholesale from the federal projects. This new supply of power was a boon to existing municipal electric utilities. It also encouraged formation of new municipal utilities.

As governor of New York in the 1920s, Roosevelt was a strong supporter of public power. His enthusiasm was enhanced by an extensive Federal Trade Commission investigation from 1928 to 1935, which revealed widespread abuses by large private power holding companies, notably those controlled by Samuel Insull.[2] Power companies were in public disfavor and became a target of the press and politicians. The scandals revealed in the FTC investigation were documented in *The Public Pays*, a book by Ernest Gruening, who later became the first elected U.S. senator from Alaska.

Roosevelt laid the foundation for his power policy in a speech in Portland, Oregon, on September 21, 1932, when he was campaigning for the presidency. He advocated government development of hydroelectric power on the St. Lawrence River in the Northeast, Muscle Shoals in the Southeast, Boulder Dam in the Southwest, and the Columbia River in the Northwest. Each of these hydroelectric power developments "will be forever a national yardstick to prevent extortion against the public and to encourage the wider use of that servant of the people—electric power," he said.

Roosevelt also strongly supported the establishment of municipal utilities. Where a community is not satisfied with the service or rates of a private utility, it has the "undeniable basic right," Roosevelt declared, to set up a governmentally owned and operated electric utility. No community served well by a private utility would seek to build and operate its own power facilities, he said. However, "the very fact that a community can, by vote of the electorate, create a yardstick of its own, will, in most cases, guarantee good service and low rates to its population. I might call the right of the people to own and operate their own utility something like this: a 'birch rod' in the cupboard to be taken out and used only when the 'child' gets beyond the point where a mere scolding does no good."

Once he became president, Roosevelt acted quickly to carry out his campaign promises. His reference to public power as a yardstick and a "birch rod in the cupboard" became a rallying cry for public power development. He used the Muscle Shoals project in Alabama as the keystone for formation of TVA. He strongly supported construction of Grand Coulee Dam and other federal power projects.

In the Tennessee Valley, the availability of federal hydro power triggered formation of municipal electric utilities and rural electric cooperatives to distribute power to their citizens. TVA directors, supported by Roosevelt, believed that the yardstick of public power

---

[2] The abuses were a primary factor in the enactment of the Public Utility Holding Company Act, one of the first major pieces of legislation adopted during the New Deal.

was not complete unless the TVA-produced power was transmitted and distributed to consumers through these public, nonprofit institutions.

Another New Deal agency, the Public Works Administration, promoted municipal utility ownership. To stimulate the economy during the Depression, the PWA made grants and loans to public agencies to build power facilities or other public works. It also advised numerous communities on the issuance of non-tax-supported bonds, now referred to as revenue bonds, to finance electric facilities.

New Deal programs stimulated development of state water resource and hydroelectric power projects, such as the Santee Cooper project in South Carolina and the Lower Colorado River Authority in Texas. Lyndon Baines Johnson, then a local political leader, played an important role in organizing LCRA.

•

Federal efforts to develop hydroelectric power met strong opposition from private power companies, which regarded public power as a threat to their existence and as an example of "creeping socialism." A national organization of publicly owned utilities could support appropriations for federal power development and disseminate information about the management of public enterprises.

Despite developments that encouraged formation of a national association, the gestation was long and difficult. Municipal utilities created before 1932 were formed without federal assistance. They relished their independence and many saw no need for a national organization that might be regarded as a front to promote federal programs.

As early as 1934, E.F. Scattergood, chief electrical engineer and general manager of the Los Angeles Bureau of Power and Light, tried to organize a National Municipal Utilities Association. He had strong support from Morris L. Cooke, the first administrator of the Rural Electrification Administration. REA was established in 1935, when only 10 percent of America's farms had electricity. To bring electricity to farms, REA was empowered to make low-interest loans to existing publicly and privately owned utilities and rural electric cooperatives. Existing utilities had largely ignored farms, because it was expensive to string distribution lines to sparsely settled areas.

Cooke and Roosevelt had been friends when the latter was governor of New York. Cooke believed a national association of municipal utilities would help his efforts to encourage municipal utilities to use REA loans to extend their lines into rural areas. In June 1935, he asked Boyd Fisher of his staff to work with farm organizations to help them set up rural electric cooperatives and bring power to farms. Existing farm organizations were available to serve as channels of communication, but reaching municipal utilities was more difficult because they had no national organization. Fisher decided to help form a national association. With Cooke's "hearty support," Fisher convened the first national convention of municipal utility managers in Kansas City on November 7, 1935. Those attending organized the National Association of Municipal Utilities and named Scattergood president.

Scattergood had an impeccable reputation as a supporter of public power. In 1911 he fought off efforts to get Los Angeles out of the power business by persuading business interests that a monopoly by Southern California Edison Company would result in higher rates and more uncertain service. He also was a major supporter of the construction of Boulder Dam (later renamed Hoover Dam). However, he was deeply involved in matters pertaining to Boulder Dam and other issues affecting the burgeoning city of Los Angeles and made little progress activating the National Association of Municipal Utilities after the Kansas City meeting.

In the fall of 1937 and the early months of 1938, Frank King, assistant superintendent of the Gas and Electric Department in Holyoke, Massachusetts, tried to infuse life into a national association. He wrote to public power supporters asking their opinion about "organizing municipal electric plants and other public power agencies."

•

An editorial in the July 1940 issue of *Midwest Municipal Utilities*, the magazine of the Kansas Association of Municipal Utilities, described the role of a national association. James D. Donovan, manager of production and distribution for the Bureau of Water and Power of Kansas City, Kansas, and editor of the magazine, wrote that the time for organizing a national association of publicly owned utilities "may not be far off." He wrote:

> Such an organization must recognize that its purposes and functions are those of the priest and not the prophet; those of the administrator and not the evangelist. Any effort to mix the two functions is to invite ineffectiveness and to duplicate the duties of existing organizations such as the National Popular

Government League[3] and the Public Ownership League of America.

[The journal of the organization must be directed] to the public administrators and utility managers of America, not to those whose thinking must be continually prodded with recital of the tremendous advantages of public, as contrasted with private, ownership of utilities. The essential emphasis of the organization must be better management and operation of those utilities we have, not more of them.

It is not meant, of course, that such an organization should fail to glory in the onward march of municipal and public ownership as one new city after another accepts the benefits of its own ability to serve itself, as one rural community after another forms its own electric cooperative. It is to say, however, that such should not be the essential function, the *raison d'etre*, of a national organization.

The time is ripe. Why wait longer?

When Donovan wrote that editorial, he undoubtedly knew that plans were under way to hold a meeting in Washington of officials of municipally owned electric utilities, TVA, Bonneville Power Administration and other federal agencies. The National Power Policy Committee, a federal inter-agency committee, called the meeting to discuss the role of public power utilities in defense production. An unstated purpose was to bring together municipal utility officials to form the American Public Power Association.

I have been told—and have no doubt that it is true—that Federal Power Commission Chairman Leland Olds was the guiding force behind the meeting. Olds had been secretary of the Power Authority of the State of New York when Roosevelt was governor of New York and had a strong influence on Roosevelt's views on public power.[4] Olds was an enthusiastic advocate of public power. He and Scattergood recognized that a government-sponsored meeting on national defense would give

---

3 The National Popular Government League was based in Washington. It was headed by Judson King, who was closely associated with Sen. George W. Norris of Nebraska in his advocacy of TVA.

4 Olds later became my mentor and a close personal friend. Because of vehement opposition from oil, gas and electric utilities, the Senate in 1949 rejected President Truman's reappointment of Olds to another term on the FPC. The story of Olds' unsuccessful battle for confirmation was said to be the basis for Alan Drury's book, *Advise and Consent*. A detailed account of the confirmation fight is contained in *The Years of Lyndon Johnson, Master of the Senate*, by Robert A. Caro.

municipal utility officials an occasion to meet separately to establish APPA. Boyd Fisher at REA also was involved in the effort.

Forty-one representatives of municipal utilities attended the meeting at the Department of the Interior. Interior Secretary Ickes, chairman of the National Power Policy Committee, opened the meeting and explained the need to address the adequacy of electricity supply for national defense. The National Power Policy Committee had met previously with officials of private power companies and called this meeting to obtain the advice of public power utilities and to inform them of federal resources available to help them.

Olds followed Ickes. He said that with the increased mechanization of the armed forces, more industrial and central station power would be needed than was used during World War I. Furthermore, development of aerial bombing called for decentralization of industries and the generating capacity to supply them. Since most municipal electric utilities were located in small towns away from large industrial concentrations, the municipal utilities were likely to receive a far larger proportion of defense loads than was the case immediately preceding and during World War I.

At a luncheon on September 11, 1940, 40 people at the national defense conference broke away and convened the first meeting of the American Public Power Association at the Lafayette Hotel, on the corner of 16th and I streets, N.W. Scattergood presided and attendees included officials of large municipal utilities (Los Angeles, Seattle, Memphis, Lansing, Michigan, and Cleveland, Ohio), as well as representatives of many smaller utilities, such as those in Muscatine, Iowa.; Wallingford, Connecticut; Wellsville, New York; and Alexandria, Louisiana. Also present were officials of state-owned utilities—the Lower Colorado River Authority in Texas, the Loup River Public Power District in Columbus, Nebraska, and the South Carolina Public Service Authority.

REA Administrator Harry Slattery and Boyd Fisher both attended. The Public Works Administration was represented by Clark Foreman, director of the power division, and Sewell Wingfield, chief project engineer.

James Donovan of Kansas City was elected president. Other officers were Scattergood, first vice president; and Frank King, then superintendent of utilities at Burlington, Vermont, executive vice president. Fisher was named secretary-manager, but remained on the REA payroll and was not paid for his work with APPA. He was negotiating an arrangement whereby funds would be collected for his salary, whereupon he would resign from REA and spend full time with APPA.

Northcutt Ely, for many years Washington counsel for the Los Angeles Department of Water and Power, was named general counsel. An assistant to Ray Lyman Wilbur, secretary of interior during the Hoover administration, Ely had been intimately involved with the Hoover Dam project and through that assignment was acquainted with Scattergood. Ely remained general counsel of APPA until 1981, when he moved to California.

•

The board of directors met in Donovan's office in Kansas City, Kansas, on October 28-29. The euphoria that surrounded the organization of APPA began to dissipate within a short time and friction developed between Fisher and Ely on issues related to the association's by-laws. Ely suggested changes to the by-laws without informing Fisher, who resented the fact that Ely reported directly to the board of directors rather than to him. There were philosophical differences, too. Ely, undoubtedly representing Scattergood's views, pressed for proportional voting based on a utility's revenues. Fisher did not entirely oppose such voting, but thought Ely's formula was skewed too much in favor of large utilities. Because of his work with rural electric cooperatives, I suspect he also was sympathetic to the cooperative principle of one member, one vote.

On December 20, 1940, Fisher wrote to Donovan declining the position of secretary-manager. He said prospects for coming up with a salary seemed unlikely and he expressed doubt that the board would meet during those troubled pre-war times. He also complained about the "method of organization, by which the attorney has been expressly set up as an agent independent of the management office," which, he said, "diminished and interfered with the functions of the secretary-manager." Fisher also expressed his misgivings about "the democracy of control of the association."

Loup River Public Power District in Nebraska then stepped into the breach and offered to lend its manager, Harold Kramer, to APPA to come to Washington for a short period to organize the association.

Chapter 12

APPA's Early Days

When Harold Kramer arrived in Washington, APPA had no funds, no office, no staff, no furniture, no telephones and no other trappings of a national organization. Loup River Public Power District had agreed to pay his salary and expenses for six months. (APPA repaid the district 10 years later.)

Kramer rented a room in the rear of the third floor of 734 Jackson Place, diagonally across the street from the White House. The small, dark room had one window and creaky, uncarpeted wooden floors.

A native of Columbus, Nebraska, and a veteran of World War I, Kramer was a businessman who had helped organize the Loup River Public Power District in 1932. He saw the district, which built a hydroelectric dam and transmission lines, as a means of stimulating economic development in a region hard hit by the Depression. He later became secretary-manager of the Loup River Public Power District and was serving in that capacity when he was loaned to APPA.

APPA made its bow to the public on February 25, 1942, when Kramer published the organization's first newsletter, called *Public Power*—a name later bestowed on the association's magazine. Under the headline, "HOW DO YOU DO!" Kramer wrote: "Coupled with the opening of modest offices recently of the American Public Power Association...comes this first bulletin, likewise thrifty and non-spectacular, befitting the expenditure of public funds." Kramer listed anticipated activities of the organization on the following page, but made it clear that his principal objective in the first few months was to build the organization's membership. Services would be limited to performing "specific errands" for members and prospective members in connection with wartime priorities.

By the time the second issue of the newsletter was published on March

25, 1942, the opening of APPA's office in Washington had attracted the attention of *Electrical World* magazine. Kramer reproduced the entire article on the front page of the APPA newsletter. It quoted Kramer as explaining that the association is:

> ...essentially a service rather than crusading organization— self-improvement by exchange of information and ideas is the underlying feature. But, make no mistake about it, we intend to defend against the onslaughts on public power on whatever front they may appear.
>
> Right now, of course, the publicly owned electric systems are straining to the utmost in their war efforts and our Washington office is giving all the cooperation we can to the various governmental power agencies, at the same time rendering service to the specific problems of our few members.
>
> Open for business barely a month, we are naturally but a faint voice in the wilderness. It is terribly unfortunate that the association was not started a year or five years ago so that we could now be functioning lustily, but we are nonetheless needed today and tomorrow and next year and from now on. We expect our membership will grow until we are serving a large proportion of the approximately 3,000 municipal plants, rural electrification co-ops and the various state and federal power authorities.

In addition to the allocation of scarce materials and supplies, another wartime issue confronting municipal utilities was the need to connect isolated municipal generating plants to a grid to make better use of excess capacity and to improve reliability. Some municipalities resisted interconnections. They feared that once their utilities were tied to a large private power company, the company would try to take over the municipal utility. Kramer addressed this problem:

> Despite the much vaunted boasts of certain private power company brass hats topped by glamorous advertisements in national magazines of the sufficiency of private power, the fact remains that the Power Division of the War Production Board is desperate for more capacity in order to fill the demands of war plants that must be constructed all over the country. One method of increasing both capacity and electric production is by interconnecting systems by transmission lines whenever it is feasible without the use of an excessive amount of critical material. You managers of public plants who swore you would never hook up with that soandso as long as a breath of fight was left in you are going to have to change your mind and we

know you are going to do it gladly for it is to win the war. The only thing is that you want to see that you are protected in the ways you want. First, the period shall be for the emergency and the purpose to further the war effort. You want a termination clause. You want the costs properly allocated and you want the proper sort of a connection both as to type and safety and you want a fair rate.

Kramer offered policy assistance to members considering an interconnection. He also provided information about War Production Board orders affecting municipal utilities.

•

Kramer was frustrated by his lack of progress in building the association's membership. When he left in the summer of 1942, only 12 municipal utilities had joined APPA. However, some supporters did not lose their enthusiasm. Foremost was the ebullient, fast-talking Frank King. During the early days of World War II, King was commissioned a lieutenant colonel in the Air Corps, and assigned to Washington to work in the War Production Board on the allocation of scarce materials and supplies to utilities. Probably through his dealings with the Rural Electrification Administration, he became friendly with Carl Nau, a tall, handsome, gregarious man who was assistant chief of REA's Applications and Loans Division.[1]

King was convinced that APPA had a bright future and imparted his enthusiasm to Nau. When Kramer departed Washington, King arranged for Nau to meet with APPA officers, who then hired him as general manager. Nau was making $5,600 a year at REA and was second in command of a 200-person division that dispensed millions of dollars of loan funds annually. His APPA pay would be half his REA salary, but Nau was attracted to the job because he foresaw the association's potential. He also did not want to be transferred to St. Louis, where REA was relocated

---

[1] Nau was one of the first persons hired by REA in 1935, and rose in the ranks as the organization grew. He was born in Littlestown, Pennsylvania, on August 15, 1908, but his family moved to nearby Gettysburg when he was two years old. His father for a while was a guide at the Gettysburg battlefields, but later operated a small grocery store that was put out of business by two large chain stores. Nau worked his way through college waiting on tables and playing trombone in a dance band. He graduated from college in 1931 and sold Fuller brushes in Hagerstown after graduation. His father was active in the Democratic Party and got a job for Carl with the local Congressman, Harry Haines, in 1932. While Nau worked for Haines, he went to George Washington Law School in Washington and earned his law degree.

early in the war.

Nau was enthusiastic about the prospects for *Public Power* magazine. Donovan was leery of having the association publish a magazine because of a previous experience with a libel suit. He also feared an APPA magazine would compete with *Midwest Municipal Utilities* magazine, published by the Kansas Association of Municipal Utilities. Consequently, Nau and King devised a scheme whereby a private company, the Modern Power Publishing Company, would be established to publish a magazine for the association. Nau and King put up a modest amount of capital for the magazine and agreed that Nau would act as editor and publisher while working for APPA as general manager. Profits, if any, from the publication of *Public Power* would accrue to the benefit of the owners, but APPA would pay all expenses of publication from advertising and subscription income. APPA agreed to purchase a limited amount of advertising to promote membership. (One ad pointed out that membership fees were "reasonable"—$25 a year for utilities with gross revenues up to $200,000, and $500 for systems having revenues of $4 million.)

•

Nau published his first APPA newsletter on June 24, 1942. Most news items concerned wartime activities, such as an order by the Federal Power Commission directing Florida Power & Light Company and the city of Jacksonville, Florida, municipal electric system to interconnect. Articles also warned of congressional consideration of a bill to tax the interest on bonds issued by municipal electric utilities.

By late summer 1942, the tax issue had become a major problem. In the August 31, 1942 newsletter, Nau reported that the Senate Finance Committee had voted 9-7 to tax the income from future issues of state and local bonds. On October 8, 1942, the Senate voted 52-34 against the bill. House and Senate hearings pointed out that the measure would have produced comparatively little revenue to the Treasury. Much of the congressional debate turned on the question of the constitutional immunity granted to local government securities and the principle of state sovereignty.

Other tax issues also arose. Private power companies proposed that the federal government tax the income cities received from their electric systems to support war needs. This proposal was shot down by the colorful New York City Mayor Fiorella LaGuardia, who told a congressional committee that the companies' proposal was aimed at thwarting the trend toward municipal ownership of electric utilities. LaGuardia wanted New York City to acquire the electric facilities of Staten Island Edison Corporation to create competitive pressure for the private power company serving New York. His proposal was later rejected by the City Council.

During his first year at APPA, Nau regularly trooped to the offices of war agencies, picked up copies of orders restricting the use of materials and other relevant subjects and sent bulletins to APPA members about these developments. By the end of 1942, he launched *Public Power* magazine. The cover of the 20-page issue featured Grand Coulee Dam. Superimposed over the photo was the caption, "Power for War—Grand Coulee Dam." Most articles in the first issue discussed War Production Board and Office of Price Administration orders.

Despite restrictions on travel and other war-related impediments, Nau increased APPA membership. However, by mid- or late-1943, he was called into service as a lieutenant junior grade in the Navy and was assigned as a contract officer with the Bureau of Ships in Washington. Because funds were limited, APPA officers decided not to hire a replacement. Instead, Nau worked the wartime schedule of six days a week at the Bureau of Ships and went to the APPA office nights and Sundays to keep the association going and to publish the magazine. A secretary took care of the office routine.

While he was in the Navy, Nau's salary for his part-time work with APPA was cut in half—to $1,800 a year—the same amount he received as a lieutenant junior grade. However, his APPA salary was somewhat academic. Salary checks were issued by the treasurer, C.E. Pray, manager of collections and accounts for the Kansas City, Kansas, Board of Public Utilities. Pray frequently called Nau and said, "Carl, we can't pay you. We can pay the rent and the girl, but I don't have enough to pay you."

By mid-summer 1944 it was apparent that the war was nearing an end and APPA members were considering post-war activities. Seattle City Light announced plans to expand its Skagit River hydro power project. Engaged in head-to-head competition within the city with Puget Sound Power and Light, Seattle City light also declared its intention to take over all service in the city when Puget's franchise expired in 1952.

Chafing under the limitations of conservation directives during the war, utilities and manufacturers began to work on promotion of new and expanded uses of electricity in the post-war era. The cover of the November 1944 issue of *Public Power* magazine offered a preview of a post-war electric kitchen and introduced the electric clothes dryer. General Electric Company announced plans for its "More Power to America" program. Representatives of TVA and other agencies began to tout the benefits of heating homes with electricity.

REA also planned a major expansion. In late 1944, the agency reported that only 40 percent of the nation's farms were electrified and about 3.5 million farms and 2.8 million other rural dwellings were still without electricity. It set a post-war objective of bringing electric service to all rural people, requiring an expenditure of $1 billion for line construction. Wiring premises, plumbing and electric appliances and equipment would require an additional $4.5 billion investment.

By July 1945 the government was so certain the war would end soon that WPB virtually lifted controls over utilities. Hostilities ceased in September 1945, and Nau returned to full-time duties at APPA.

•

The war gave a considerable boost to the federal power program and set the stage for further expansion in the post-war era. Construction of new dams and related hydro power facilities received a high priority because of the need for power for defense purposes, especially for production of aluminum and chemicals. However, it was not revealed until after atomic bombs were detonated over Hiroshima and Nagasaki that substantial power resources from TVA and BPA were used to produce plutonium needed to manufacture nuclear weapons.

The success of the federal power program and its general popularity with voters spurred the introduction of bills to authorize federal power projects in other regions. Sen. George Aiken, R-Vt., introduced a bill in the summer of 1944 to authorize construction of the St. Lawrence Seaway and Power Project. This project, first urged by President Calvin Coolidge in 1923, would produce more power than the TVA system in 1943 and as much as the "celebrated Dnieper Dam, the pride of Russia," Aiken said. Senators James E. Murray, D-Mont., and Guy Gillette, D-Iowa, introduced a bill to establish a Missouri Valley Authority. In 1945, Sen. Hugh Mitchell, D-Wash., sponsored a bill to create a Columbia Valley Authority and Rep. George Bender, R-Ohio, proposed an Ohio Valley Authority, which would serve most of Indiana, Ohio, Kentucky, West Virginia, and small portions of Pennsylvania, Tennessee and Illinois. Rep. John Rankin, D-Miss., outdid them all; he introduced a bill authorizing creation of nine river valley authorities.

Within a few months of taking office, President Truman urged Congress to approve development of the Columbia, Missouri and Arkansas rivers, and the Central Valley in California. Outside of Congress, Federal Power Commission Chairman Leland Olds was one of the most active supporters of the valley authority concept. In an April 1945 speech to the Washington Academy of Sciences, Olds said:

The approach to river basin development is in the direction of economic and social as well as political decentralization. In other words, it offers a way to preserve our traditional democracy by reversing the powerful trend of the past generation toward centralized control of the country's economic life by an all-powerful corporate bureaucracy. This trend has been steadily substituting great monopolies for the thousands of small community business units, which were truly characteristic of American free enterprise.

When Congress creates an authority on the TVA model, it actually sets up a regional development corporation with a wholly public purpose, which goes to work subject only to the annual check-up of its owners, the American people, through their representatives in Congress. The directors of the corporation, men in the field, are given the power of decision, and provision is made for the active participation of the people of the region through their local institutions.

The increasing support for federal development of the nation's hydro power potential as a part of flood control, navigation, irrigation and other programs met strong opposition from the power companies. They used newspaper ads and public relations tactics to brand public power as socialism. To circumvent the preference provisions of federal law, they also began to apply to the Federal Power Commission for licenses to install generators in federal dams, so they could obtain all of the power from these projects built with public funds. Power companies argued that flood control and power production were incompatible. One ad proclaimed, "You don't use a full pan to catch a leak. Would you use a full dam to catch a flood?" Certainly not, the ad responded, adding that hydro power and flood control are so opposed as to make multiple purpose dams impossible or uneconomic.

APPA responded to these attacks. At its annual meeting in Cleveland in May 1947, S.R. Finley, superintendent of the Chattanooga Electric Power Board, castigated the power companies for an ad comparing public power with Nazism. The association adopted a resolution urging federal appropriations for rural electrification, TVA, the Bureau of Reclamation, Bonneville Power Administration, the Southwestern Power Administration "and other public power projects as they may appear economically justified."

In September 1947 *Public Power* magazine published a full-page statement by E.F. Scattergood warning of private power company attacks on the federal power program. He called attention to efforts by the companies to order the federal government to turn over partially completed hydroelectric power projects to the companies. He also charged that the power companies were attempting to render federal regulation ineffective.

Scattergood's statement was followed by a "Call to Arms" published as a half-page ad in the November 1947 issue of *Public Power* magazine by the APPA Legislative Committee headed by Harold Kramer. The ad warned of actions of the 80th Congress—the Congress that was later the subject of a heated attack from Harry Truman when he won an upset victory over Thomas Dewey. The ad commented that actions of the 80th Congress "clearly indicated public power is due for some rough sailing. A good majority in both Houses have demonstrated their willingness to scuttle the power program—both by cutting off funds and by direct legislation." Even greater efforts, the ad said, could be expected next year.

The ad made an "urgent call" to all nonprofit power groups to tell their elected representatives:

> The facts of life…It's the only way the people's representatives can get both sides of the story. Don't let the high-handed high-riding utility lobby bottle up public power. Don't let them squirm out from under regulation.
> And don't let them tell you public power is a partisan issue. Beginning with Lincoln's protection of the public interest in the first land laws, other leaders such as Charles Evans Hughes and Theodore Roosevelt have opposed monopoly control of the nation's water and power resources.
> The fact that public power is exempt from federal taxation will be an issue. Tell your representatives why you don't pay Federal taxes and *WHY YOU SHOULDN'T.*"

This "Call to Arms" was an apt prelude to my reporting for work at APPA two months later.

Chapter 13

Federal Power Tug-of-War

Most of the issues Nau and I dealt with in 1948 revolved around the federal power program. New Deal initiatives and the need for additional energy during World War II led to substantial increases in generating facilities from 1933 to 1948. Much of the new capacity was hydro power built in the Tennessee Valley and the Pacific Northwest to provide energy for aluminum and nuclear weapons production. After the war, the Truman administration carried on Roosevelt's legacy by continuing to promote the development of river basins.

Although their conversion to public ownership had been planned for some years, several major new local public power utilities were established after World War II. Omaha Public Power District in Nebraska began operations in 1946. Sacramento Municipal Utility District in California began operating in 1947. Several public utility districts in the state of Washington—including one of the largest, the Snohomish County PUD—also initiated service in the late 1940s.

Rural electrification accelerated. As the number of distribution co-ops grew, some formed generation and transmission co-ops to provide power for the distribution systems.

Although they controlled 75 to 80 percent of the electric industry, private power companies were alarmed by public power expansion. The principal focus of their attack was the federal power program. The companies believed an increase in production of low-cost power by federal agencies would permit existing municipal utilities and rural electric cooperatives to flourish and would encourage creation of new public entities. They opposed appropriations for new federal power plants and transmission lines. Blocking construction of transmission lines was key to their efforts. They reasoned that their interests would not be threatened if the government lacked facilities to deliver electricity to public power customers, who had first rights of refusal to buy federal power. The private utilities also pushed for adoption of a policy to require sale of federal power at the bus bar, the point of generation. They recognized that most preference customers did not have the resources to build transmission lines to the dam sites. Consequently, restricting sales to the bus bar would bottle up the power at the dam, where only the power companies had the means to obtain it.

The political environment in Washington in 1948 appeared favorable for a change in direction in national power policies. The 80th Congress had taken office in 1947 and a large turnover in membership and a shift to Republican control were interpreted as a mandate to halt or redirect many policies of the Roosevelt and Truman administrations. Relations between Congress and the Truman administration were contentious. In the 1948 election, Truman ran against the 80th Congress, dubbing it the "Do Nothing Congress." But at the beginning of 1948, Congress was riding high and moved vigorously to overturn Roosevelt and Truman policies.

When I reported for work at APPA in January 1948, the major issue facing APPA was H.R. 3036, sponsored by the chairman of the House Public Works Committee, Rep. George Dondero, R-Mich. The bill would have required the government to sell power at the busbar, or dam site, where it would most likely be purchased by power companies. Hearings had been held on the bill in 1947, but it had not been reported out of committee. Nau showed how the Dondero bill would thwart efforts to bring the benefits of low-cost hydro power to consumers. He pointed out that Carolina Power and Light Company had purchased 210 million kilowatt-hours of federal power in 1946 at an average rate of 2.398 mills per kilowatt-hour. The company resold the power for 25.9 mills per kilowatt-hour, 11 times the purchase price.

Another Dondero bill would have ordered the Federal Power Commission to grant a license to the Savannah River Electric Company, a subsidiary of Georgia Power Company, to construct, own, operate and maintain the powerhouse at the Clark's Hill Reservoir project on the Savannah River between South Carolina and Georgia. The Army Corps of Engineers was building the project, but H.R. 3826 would turn over the installation's only revenue-producing function to the company, which would pay the government for falling water created by construction of the dam. The FPC had rejected the license application, so the company asked Congress to overturn the decision.

In the short session of an election year, Congress approved neither of the Dondero bills, but the philosophy behind them was advocated for many years.

Controversies over the Tennessee Valley Authority attracted national attention. Two issues were before Congress. Sen. Kenneth McKellar, D-Tenn., ranking member of the Senate Appropriations Committee, and TVA Chairman David Lilienthal disagreed sharply over the degree of congressional control of the agency. A master of patronage politics, McKellar resented having little or no influence over TVA's hiring practices. McKellar introduced a bill that would eliminate TVA's revolving fund and require the agency to operate entirely on appropriations. The bill triggered extensive hearings, but ultimately died.

TVA in 1948 also sought to build the Johnsonville steam generating plant. Until that time, TVA had produced virtually all of its power from hydroelectric dams. Power facilities were justified on the grounds that they were integral parts of multipurpose water resource projects. The Johnsonville steam plant presented a new and different issue. Until this proposal surfaced, TVA had built only one steam plant, Watts Bar, which was constructed during World War II to meet defense needs. It was not controversial. Johnsonville was the first steam plant funded and built by a federal agency during peacetime, primarily for civilian needs.

Private power companies considered Johnsonville the first step in a greatly expanded role of the federal government in the power business. The National Association of Electric Companies, led by Purcell L. Smith, launched an all-out attack against the appropriation. With an annual salary of $65,000, Smith was the highest paid lobbyist in Washington.

My work on this issue led to a close working relationship with three Chattanoogans who were TVPPA's principal political strategists: L.J. Wilhoite, chairman of the Chattanooga Electric Power Board and chairman of the Tennessee Valley Public Power Association's Power Distributors Information Committee; Ken Whitaker, secretary of the Distributors Information Committee; and S.R. Finley, superintendent of the Chattanooga Electric Power Board, who was then serving as TVPPA's first president.

Wilhoite, head of Southern Dairies, was a highly successful local businessman. He loved to dabble in politics and it was commonly said in Chattanooga that he could have been mayor had he chosen to run for that office. A New Deal Democrat, he was enthusiastic about public power and TVA. He was also a persuasive speaker and had a quick wit and a winning smile.

Finley's full name was States Rights Gist Finley. His father had been a congressman from South Carolina and was so dedicated to states rights that he gave his son that unusual name. (Friends generally called him "States.") Because of his father's position, Finley had spent some of his formative years in Washington, where he also acquired a taste for politics.

Finley had an engaging personality—gracious, articulate and understated. When he testified before a congressional committee, he invariably introduced himself by slowly intoning his full name. The invocation of states rights was enough to disarm even the most conservative member of Congress.

Like many southerners, Whitaker loved the game of politics and relished the opportunity to figure out ways to influence a member of Congress through friends or acquaintances. Even if there was a simple, easy way to go from A to D, he would choose to go by way of B and C.

At the first APPA annual meeting that I attended, in Colorado Springs in 1948, I spent a great deal of time with the Chattanooga triumvirate discussing how we could build congressional support for Johnsonville appropriations.

We were fighting tremendous odds. Indicative of the temper of the 80th Congress, Purcell Smith and his colleagues spent three hours behind closed doors before a subcommittee of the House Appropriations Committee, opposing Johnsonville funding. (In those days, most appropriations hearings were held in executive session.) Proponents were allotted 10 minutes for their testimony. Not surprisingly, the House Appropriations Committee deleted funds for Johnsonville, but TVA supporters took the issue to the House floor. They were led by Rep. Albert Gore, D-Tenn., father of former Vice President Al Gore and a staunch supporter of TVA and public power. However, the effort failed and Senate attempts to restore funding also were unsuccessful.

Elections brought a new Congress to Washington in 1949. President Truman's upset victory rejuvenated his power and when he requested funds for the Johnsonville steam plant, Congress quickly approved them. The success of this effort paved the way for succeeding appropriations for other steam plants needed to meet the pent-up demand for electricity after World War II.

•

Appropriations for federal hydro projects, especially in the West, also commanded APPA's attention in 1949. The Korean War, which broke out in June 1950, accelerated demand for electricity and in 1951 President Truman asked Congress for funds for seven new power projects for the defense program. These projects, together with the completion of additional generating units and transmission lines already authorized, were estimated to cost $1.5 billion, and would supply 3.9 million kilowatts of generating capacity. The new facilities and projects already completed would provide an ultimate capacity of 20 million kilowatts.

Several members of Congress renewed efforts to push for creation of TVA-like agencies in the Columbia and Missouri river valleys, but no bills won approval.

Appropriations battles also raged over money to construct transmission lines to integrate federal power plants and deliver energy to preference customers. The fiercest battles focused on the area served by the Southwestern Power Administration. In 1949, the Truman administration asked for $9 million to build transmission lines for SPA. Power companies—especially in Oklahoma—vigorously opposed the appropriation. Instead, they proposed a contract with SPA under which the companies would purchase power produced at federal dams and resell it, on a limited basis, to some preference customers. Municipal utilities would be excluded from the power sales and many restrictions would be placed on delivery of power to rural electric cooperatives.

At a hearing in the Capitol on this issue in June 1949, so many co-op and municipal officials attempted to crowd into the hearing room to voice their opposition that Capitol police had to post a standing-room-only sign one hour before the hearing was to begin.

Despite vitriolic opposition to the proposal, SPA Administrator Douglas Wright, a strong-minded, swashbuckling character, signed a contract the following year with the Oklahoma companies. APPA, the National Rural Electric Cooperative Association and members of both organizations protested so vehemently to Secretary of the Interior Oscar Chapman that he declined to approve the contract. As a result, the terms were subsequently revised so preference customers received more equitable treatment.

Nau was elated by Chapman's action. In a message to APPA members he thanked them and said, "the value of APPA was clearly demonstrated in this instance. We have turned the first thrust, but there will be more."

Although the revised contract provided more protection for preference customers, it also achieved the power companies' goal of blocking the construction of federal transmission lines and set a pattern for future wheeling contracts.

•

By 1949 there was so much activity in federal power development that APPA compiled its first comprehensive recommendations on federal power policy—an effort that consumed a great deal of attention from Nau, myself and APPA members for almost a year. Unveiled in November 1949, the statement pointed out that almost 17 million kilowatts of federally owned generating capacity were either operating, under construction or authorized, compared with only 226,000 kilowatts 20 years earlier. The secretary of the interior predicted that by 1960 an additional 30 million kilowatts of federal generating capacity would be installed.

"Since municipalities, cooperatives and other public agencies now have preference under the law in the disposition of this power, their stake in the policy followed becomes readily evident," the APPA statement declared.

"Accordingly, to protect their present interests, and to assure the economic feasibility and soundness of the program, the American Public Power Association has drafted these recommendations... Adoption of the statement...marks one of the most significant actions to be taken by APPA in its nine-year history."

The statement set the tone of the association's federal power policies for many years to come. It opened with a declaration that "every site for the generation of hydroelectric power should be developed if and when such development is economically feasible." It made these additional points:

- Because hydro power sites are natural resources of the people of the United States, preference should be given to public agencies in their development. Local public agencies should have preference in building facilities that fit into plans for maximum utilization of stream systems.

- "In every case in which the United States has, in effect, preempted a stream and/or precluded local development of hydroelectric power, or assumed the obligation to provide a power supply to an area, then it is the duty of the United States to develop power under an orderly program [that] will anticipate the potential power demands and meet those demands as they arise."

- "The United States should construct and own fuel-burning plants, integrated with its hydroelectric plants whenever necessary for the efficient economical operation of its hydroelectric plants."

- Public agencies and rural electric cooperatives should have preference in purchasing federal power and contracts with private companies should be of limited duration to protect the rights of preference customers.

- Federal power should be sold at the lowest possible rates "consistent with sound business principles."
- The United States should construct and own transmission lines necessary for the integration of its hydro or fuel-burning plants, and in every case where such construction and ownership is necessary to deliver power to its preference customers.
- Rural areas should be electrified as rapidly as possible and adequate funds should be provided to the Rural Electricification Administration for this purpose and to finance construction of generating plants and transmission lines.

The statement was reviewed extensively by APPA's board of directors, executive committee and members. In spite of the controversial nature of some of the recommendations, the statement received very little opposition from the membership.

•

Tax issues continued to demand attention. The National Association of Electric Companies filed a brief with the House Ways and Means Committee in February 1949 calling for three actions:

1. Taxing the net income of governmentally owned proprietary businesses;
2. Repealing provisions of the Internal Revenue Code that imposed a 3.33 percent federal excise tax on electric energy or, alternatively, removing the existing exemption of public bodies from this tax; and
3. Taxing income from municipal bonds issued in the future to finance public proprietary enterprises.

Treasury Secretary John W. Snyder, in testimony before the House Ways and Means Committee on February 5, 1951, advocated eliminating the federal tax exemption on interest earned on municipal bonds. He said the exemption was a "long-standing barrier to the achievement of equity in the distribution of the individual income tax burden." He acknowledged that the removal of the exemption would increase "to some degree" the cost of future state and local borrowing, but said a "reasonable basis" could be developed for the taxation of future issues without burdening states and localities excessively.

Snyder's proposal precipitated a firestorm of opposition from APPA and other organizations representing state and local governments. These included the American Municipal Association (predecessor to the National League of Cities), the U.S. Conference of Mayors, the Municipal Finance Officers Association, the Port Authority of New York, and the National Association of County Officials. Hearings on the proposal two weeks later demonstrated that the secretary's suggestion was doomed. Not a single witness appeared in its support. Witnesses, including mayors of several of the nation's largest cities, opposed the proposal.

APPA General Counsel Northcutt Ely joined the parade of witnesses. He told the committee that the right of states and political subdivisions to borrow money is an essential governmental power and that the proposed tax would constitute a direct and substantial burden on the power to borrow before it is exercised. According to U.S. Supreme Court decisions, the tax would be unconstitutional, Ely asserted.

Ely also demonstrated the effect of the cost of money on revenue-producing public works. For example, in the case of a turnpike, an investment of as much as $20 would be required to produce $1 of gross income. By contrast, one of the major chain stores showed that it collected about $6.50 of gross revenues for each $1 of invested capital. Accordingly, in a chain store with a high turnover, an increase of 1 percent in interest rates would only cause an increase of about 1/15 of 1 percent in the selling price. But a city would have to increase its taxes or its tax rate 20 percent for each 1 percent increase in the cost of money.

Referring to a $50 billion backlog of public works projects, Ely asked, "Which pattern of financing is best for the federal government: to encourage local governments to assume the financial responsibility for their normal part of these investments, or, by increasing their cost of money 50 percent by federal taxation, to force them to climb on the back of the federal Treasury if the necessary projects are to be built?"

Although Snyder's proposal was defeated, APPA was to be confronted with many similar challenges in the years ahead.

Chapter 14

The Public vs. Private Power Fight

National power policies and the controversy between public and private power were major national issues in the late 1940s. Platforms of both political parties contained planks on power policy and presidential candidates made speeches and were questioned by reporters on their views on building new hydro power projects or creation of a Missouri Valley Authority or a Columbia Valley Authority.

Rivalry between public and private power groups was intense. On the local level, managers of public and private electric utilities met to discuss operating problems, but on the national level, public power officials rarely, if ever, had face-to-face discussions with their counterparts in the private power industry. To the best of my knowledge, no public power official ever set foot in offices of the Edison Electric Institute or other power company organizations. This was enemy territory.

The climate was poisoned by the intensity of the campaign against public power. Power companies established at least four organizations dedicated to fighting public power. Leading the group was EEI, successor to the National Electric Light Association, which had been discredited in the utility scandals revealed in the 1930s. Headquartered in New York City, EEI ostensibly was a research organization, but it really coordinated the power companies' fight against public power. The National Association of Electric Companies, headed by Purcell Smith, handled Washington lobbying. The companies also formed the Electric Companies Advertising Program, which placed anti-public power ads in national publications, and the Public Information Program, which handled public relations.

In the confrontational environment created by these organizations, Nau and I looked for opportunities to demonstrate public power's strengths or to embarrass the opposition. APPA's most successful effort to create a positive image was publication of a booklet, *Public Power Pays!* This booklet had an interesting genesis. In the summer of 1948, Leland Olds asked Nau to meet with him in his office at the Federal Power Commission. Nau invited me to accompany him. This was my first meeting with an FPC commissioner and it was the beginning of a long personal and professional friendship with Olds. At the meeting, Olds told us the FPC had just completed its first compilation of statistics of Class A and B local public power utilities (those with gross annual electric revenues of $250,000 and more), making it possible to compare the operations of public and private utilities. He gave us a manuscript, which he said an associate had written, describing the comparisons. Olds suggested APPA publish the document, but under Nau's name, not the actual author's. If APPA decided to publish the document, he suggested that the association write a check for several hundred dollars to the author.

When Nau and I returned to our office and read the document, we immediately realized that it was a treasure. It revealed comparisons that were highly favorable to the publicly owned utilities, based on reliable data furnished by both segments of the industry and carefully compiled by the FPC. As a bonus, the writing style was excellent—concise and pithy. Nau and I were convinced that Olds, not his associate, was the author because it was obviously the product of a highly skilled professional writer—a career Olds had pursued for several years before his government service in New York and Washington.

•

Nau and I knew we were holding a bombshell and that we had to proceed carefully. He sent a copy to the association's officers for their careful appraisal. None found fault with the facts or arguments and the officers approved its publication with minor modifications designed to tone down some of the rhetoric.

Nau directed me to prepare the manuscript for publication. Because of its importance, I wanted it to be printed in an attractive, dignified manner, with charts and tables, so it would command serious attention. I had heard of a bright, imaginative group of artists and publication designers who had worked for the Office of Strategic Services, a predecessor to the CIA, during World War II, and who had started their own firm after their discharge from military service. They formed a company called Presentation, Inc., and I went to them for help. Thus began my long association with Hubert Leckie, a member of the firm, who subsequently designed almost all of APPA's publications during my tenure.

We titled the publication *Public Power Pays!* The name was an allusion to the book, *The Public Pays*, written by Ernest Gruening early in his career, before he became governor (and later, senator) of Alaska. Gruening's book was the story of the machinations of the power trust revealed in the Federal Trade Commission investigation of the 1930s.

The message of the 32-page *Public Power Pays!* was simple: local public power utilities not only charged lower rates than private power companies, they also paid proportionately more taxes and were managed more efficiently. In subsequent years, as new statistics became available from the FPC, we updated the material in an annual article in *Public Power* magazine titled "More Power at Lower Cost."

Public Power Pays! unabashedly extolled the virtues of public power. It dubbed publicly owned systems "service utilities," while the power companies were called "profit utilities." The booklet pointed out that the public utilities chalked up an excellent record despite the power companies' claimed efficiencies that supposedly resulted from their larger size and "business management." It showed that the average residential customer of the "profit utility" paid about 6 percent more and received about one-fourth less power than the customer of the "service utility."

"For each kilowatt-hour that he buys, the customer of the profit utility pays more than 40 percent more than he would if he were fortunate enough to be served by a service utility," the publication declared.

Commercial and industrial customers served by public power also paid less for electricity. The average commercial and industrial customer of local public power utilities was only about 80 percent as large as the average commercial and industrial customer of a private power company. However, the public power customer's average rate was 15 percent lower.

The study found relatively little difference in production, transmission and distribution costs, but a sharp divergence between the two sectors in costs for accounting and collecting, advertising and sales promotion, and administration. Noting that the accounting and collecting expenses per customer for the investor-owned companies were more than 30 percent higher than those of the publicly owned systems, *Public Power Pays!* boasted: "If the business-managed companies were as efficient as the service systems in this respect, they would save almost $30,000,000 per year."

Administrative costs of the publicly owned utilities were approximately $5.40 per $100 of revenue, compared to $6.60, or 22 percent more, for private utilities.

"If the private systems were administered with the same economy as the public systems, customers would be saved approximately

$60,000,000 each year," the report said.

•

The most controversial aspect of *Public Power Pays!* was its comments on the relative tax payments of the publicly and privately owned utilities. The study used Webster's definition of taxes—"to exact money for the support of government." Publicly owned utilities had a net investment in power facilities of $800 million—an amount that included materials and supplies and enough cash for working purposes. The report assumed that a 3 percent return would be required to support this investment. This amount would be enough to pay interest on the debt and return to the communities almost 20 percent on their actual cash investment.

"The income of the publicly owned utilities, however, exceeds this necessary return by a huge amount," the study declared. "Rather than the $24,000,000 necessary to pay an adequate return on the investment in facilities, the aggregate income of municipal utilities is $79,000,000, or $55,000,000 more than is required to provide service. This sum, plus the relatively small amount, $5,000,000 actually labeled as 'taxes,' gives an aggregate of $60,000,000 exacted for the support of government and as capital contributions to the public wealth."

The study concluded that more than 27 percent of the total electric revenues of the publicly owned utilities were supporting government— about 40 percent more than the 19 percent of private power revenues devoted to taxes.

As we expected, *Public Power Pays!* made quite a splash nationally, earning accolades from municipal officials, federal government executives, cabinet members, congressmen, rural electric cooperatives, newspapers and magazines. A first printing of 5,000 copies sold out quickly at $1 a copy and a second printing of 3,000 was ordered.

A column-long story in *The New York Times* of December 12, 1948 discussed the publication and revealed that the private power companies were "still smarting from an attack made by APPA." An EEI official quoted in the article said the organization was considering a broad public information program to "refute misinformation contained in biased utterances of many proponents of government ownership." After several weeks, EEI issued a response prepared by an "independent" consultant. Titled *Public Power Pays?,* the EEI response predictably challenged some of the rationale and figures used in the report, but it received relatively little attention.

•

About a year later, I obtained information on a clandestine basis from Charles Bartlett, Washington correspondent for *The Chattanooga Times.* I knew Bartlett because of my previous employment with the *Times* and also because Bartlett came to APPA as a source of news. Bartlett maintained good connections with private power organizations and APPA. Through his contacts with the investor-owned utilities, he obtained a brochure prepared for the Electric Companies Advertising Program that reported the results of a public opinion poll and recommended an advertising strategy for the companies. The booklet was intended only for the eyes of ECAP members, but Bartlett somehow obtained a copy and slipped it to me so APPA could publicize it. He could thereby use the APPA revelation as the basis for his stories, without revealing that he had obtained the document, which would have dried up his source of information.

The poll showed strong popular support for the Tennessee Valley Authority and public power. Sixty-three percent of the cross section of 3,000 people surveyed approved of TVA, while only 10 percent disapproved. Eighty-three percent of editors and educators approved of TVA, which also received a favorable rating of 55 percent of the Republicans (only 17 percent disapproved). A crowning blow to the companies was the finding that 45 percent of the private power company employees approved of TVA, while only 40 percent disapproved and 15 percent had no opinion.

In response to another question, 69 percent of those polled felt that socialism would be a bad thing for the United States, while only 10 percent felt it would be good for the country.

On the basis of these findings, ECAP declared, "it is apparent that to link our fight to the TVA question would run us into a lot of opposition, most of it based on lack of knowledge. But to link our fight to socialism is something else again. The people do not want socialism."

The July 1950 issue of *Public Power* magazine reported the survey results. We then distributed the information to the press, where it received a great deal of attention, to the embarrassment of the power companies. Nevertheless, they continued their advertising campaign, attempting to link public power with socialism. In one case, they used an ad showing a concentration camp and implied that public power would lead to a suppression of freedoms enjoyed by Americans.

The socialism theme was picked up on Capitol Hill. On March 30, 1949, Rep. Ben Jensen, R-Iowa, made a speech on the House floor accusing Dr. Paul Raver, administrator of the Bonneville Power Administration, of participating in a socialist plot to encroach on the "good private power utilities in the United States." Jensen alleged that

Raver was working with Guy Myers, a fiscal agent engaged by some Washington public utility districts to acquire private utility properties. Raver was vigorously defended by Rep. Henry M. ("Scoop") Jackson, D-Wash.

A year later the socialism charge against Dr. Raver was included in a *Reader's Digest* article by Leslie A. Miller, former governor of Wyoming and former chairman of the Natural Resources Committee of the Hoover Commission.[1] In an article attacking the Columbia Valley Authority, Miller referred to Raver as a socialist. Rep. Jackson again rose to Raver's defense and inserted in the *Congressional Record* an editorial appearing in the Portland *Oregonian* newspaper, which repeated a statement by Miller denying that he had written the portion of the article labeling Raver a socialist. Miller said he had no knowledge before the article was published of the reference to Raver as a socialist.

These public vs. private ideological battles continued, in one form or another and with varying degrees of intensity, for the remainder of my career in public power.

---

[1] The Hoover Commission was named for President Herbert Hoover, who was appointed by President Truman to head a panel to study reorganization of the federal government.

Chapter 15

Tested In My First Year

By early 1951, I still enjoyed my work at APPA, but was becoming a bit restless. Nau was a young man and I saw little opportunity for advancement. I sensed that Nau himself was becoming bored with the job and I occasionally had to prod him to undertake new initiatives.

My former boss at the State Department, Jay Westcott, told me about a job at the Bureau of the Budget (predecessor to the Office of Management and Budget) that involved examining proposed legislation to determine whether it conformed with the president's policies. I interviewed with the bureau's personnel chief and was offered the job. About the same time, Nau told me, much to my surprise, that he and his family were planning to move to Seattle. He had long wanted to live in the Northwest, the home of his wife, Mildred, but had remained in Washington because his aged father lived with them. But his father had recently died.

Nau had talked with S.R. Finley of Chattanooga, who was then APPA president, and Finley assured Nau that I would be named general manager. I was flattered by the offer, but I did not immediately accept it because I was considering the offer from the Bureau of the Budget. I also seriously questioned whether I wanted to become a manager. In my previous jobs, I worked under the direction of others. As a writer and editor, I conveyed the opinions of others, and did not initiate actions. I was uncertain whether I wanted to be out front making decisions and running an organization.

After a great deal of thought, I decided to stay at APPA as general manager. I felt the job would give me an opportunity to exercise imagination and initiative and concluded I would quickly become bored at the Bureau of the Budget. Spending all of my time analyzing the details of legislation was too akin to the work of a lawyer. I had earlier concluded that was not the career I wanted.

My promotion did not go smoothly. With the best of intentions, Finley, on the first day of the 1951 APPA convention in Chattanooga, told a reporter for *The Chattanooga Times* that I would be named general manager. Because I was a native Chattanoogan and a former reporter for the *Times*, the newspaper carried a story about my promotion at the top of the front page, together with my picture. It was the typical local-boy-makes-good story.

I presumed that before he made the announcement, Finley had discussed the matter with the officers or executive committee. However, the board of directors had not acted on my appointment. The outgoing board felt the new board should make the decision and deferred action to the following day. I spent a restless night worrying whether the new board would approve me. It did and about a month before my 30th birthday, I was designated head of the national organization. I never dreamed I would spend the next 35 years in that position—but I never doubted that I had made the right decision.

I would have had more trepidation about accepting the job if I had known that some of the most important battles in the history of public power were destined to take place during the 1950s. There were hints that momentous issues were about to emerge, but I had no inkling of the intensity of the ensuing debates or the national attention they would command.

During the 1950s, APPA played a major part in high-profile controversies involving federal construction and ownership of steam electric plants, the future of the Tennessee Valley Authority, construction and allocation of federal hydro power and development of atomic energy.

•

In late summer 1951, Chelan County Public Utility District invited me to attend groundbreaking ceremonies in Wenatchee, Washington, commemorating the enlargement of Rock Island Dam. That trip introduced me to the Pacific Northwest and had a lasting influence on my APPA career. It also set the stage for my first major test as general manager.

The first dam on the main stem of the Columbia River, Rock Island had been built 20 years earlier by Puget Sound Power and Light Company However, with the onset of the Depression, the dam was not completed to its full capacity. The PUD later acquired Puget

Sound's electrical distribution properties in Chelan County, leased the dam from the company and undertook to raise its height by 14 feet and install an additional 165 megawatts of generating capacity. Because vast quantities of low-cost electricity were needed to manufacture aluminum, the added capacity of the dam was an incentive for the Aluminum Company of America to build a plant near the dam site to produce 85,000 tons of aluminum pigs (metallic aluminum) from powdered aluminum oxide. It was a win/win arrangement for all parties and the PUD was rightly proud of its role in this venture.

By chance, I flew from Washington to Spokane on the same plane that carried then-Rep. Henry M. (Scoop) Jackson, D-Wash., who was to speak at the ceremony. We did not socialize during the trip because Jackson had a sleeping berth in the front compartment of the plane, while I sat up all night in tourist class. Once we were in Wenatchee, I talked with the congressman and began to form a friendship with him. I found him to be smart, personable, unassuming, knowledgeable and dedicated—attributes that later propelled him into national leadership.

On that trip, I also met Dr. Paul Raver, administrator of the Bonneville Power Administration, and many of his key staff. I was tremendously impressed by their enthusiasm, vitality and dedication. They brought to mind the best of the vibrant New Deal spirit. From them I gained a better appreciation of the tremendous potential for the power development of the Columbia River.

My visit to Chelan PUD was the beginning of my love affair with the Pacific Northwest—the people and the geography. I was impressed with the beauty of the region and the ability of humans to use irrigation to make the desert bloom. I was also attracted to the "down home" people of the area, especially the PUD commissioners, many of whom were rugged pioneers who had created beautiful orchards out of what were once wastelands.

•

The euphoria of my trip to the Pacific Northwest dissolved shortly after I returned to Washington. The House Public Works Committee held hearings on a bill introduced by Representative Jackson that called for federal construction of three steam plants and five gas turbine plants in the Pacific Northwest. A companion bill was sponsored by Sen. Warren Magnuson, D-Wash.

Although the federal government had constructed Grand Coulee and Bonneville dams in the Northwest, the Jackson-Magnuson bill marked the first time that the federal government was asked to build steam plants in the region. For several years there had been discussion of the need for new thermal capacity to back up the region's hydro power. By 1951, adverse water conditions and demand by defense industries for additional power had resulted in a shortage of electricity, spurring introduction of the proposed legislation.

The Jackson-Magnuson bill would authorize the Department of the Interior to build three 100-mw steam plants and five 20-mw gas turbine plants. The 400 mw of new electric generating capacity would cost $60 million. Bonneville Power Administration (then part of the Department of the Interior) would market power from the plants, just as it did with federal hydro power. In accordance with long established policies, public agencies and rural electric cooperatives would receive a preference in buying the power at wholesale.

Representative Jackson said two of the larger plants would be built in western Washington and could be completed in two and one-half years. Initially, they would burn oil and probably be converted later to pulverized coal. The five gas turbine plants could be completed in 18 months.

Coming in the wake of the Tennessee Valley Authority's incursion into the construction of thermal capacity, the Interior Department proposal was greeted with customary alarm by private power companies, especially those from other regions. They saw this move as one more significant step toward further involvement of the federal government in the power business.

The Northwest Public Power Association, Seattle City Light, Washington Public Utility Districts Association, and a number of individual PUDs supported the Jackson-Magnuson bill.

APPA's position was complicated by the fact that the president of the association, J. Frank Ward, was superintendent of the Light Division of the city of Tacoma, Washington. Tacoma Light Division had an application pending before the Federal Power Commission for a license to develop the hydro power resources of the Cowlitz River, a tributary of the Columbia River. Coincidentally, the capacity of the Cowlitz project was 460 mw—more than that of the proposed thermal plants.

Ward regarded the steam plants as a competitor for the Cowlitz project and felt that the city's hydro development should take precedence over federal steam plants. He also was in no mood to be friendly toward the Interior Department because the department had opposed the city's license application on the grounds that the project would have an adverse impact on fish.

When the hearings were announced, Ward told me he wanted to submit a statement as president of APPA, but that he could not attend the hearing. He asked me to present the statement on his behalf. He advised me of the position he wanted to take, but he did not ask for my input. I was merely to read his testimony to the committee and respond to questioning to the best of my ability.

I was disturbed by this turn of events. I could understand that Ward had a personal stake in this matter and wanted to protect the interests of the city of Tacoma. However, I felt his position did not reflect the views of the association's members, particularly those in the Northwest who were most directly affected. The major Northwest public power organizations had already gone on record in support of the Jackson-Magnuson bill. Surely, their viewpoint had to be taken into account. I felt that APPA should support the Jackson-Magnuson bill.

I also was hurt. I considered it a slight that I was to be merely a messenger who would not be consulted in the preparation of the substance of testimony affecting many members of the association. Ward seemed to regard me as not having the maturity or technical qualifications for the job as general manager. I did not relish the prospect of appearing before a congressional committee, on which Representative Jackson served, to oppose his bill. Nevertheless, I was in no position to challenge Ward. I decided to be as loyal as possible to Ward and to read his statement, but to make it clear that this was his statement.

•

I arrived at the Longworth House Office Building on Friday morning, September 29, 1951, to be the first witness of the day before the House Public Works Committee. The setting of a congressional hearing does not give confidence to a neophyte witness who is seated alone in front of an imposing wood-paneled, semicircular dais, from which committee members look down.

Ward's statement registered his objection to a provision of the bill that would have placed control of the rates to be charged for the steam-produced power solely in the hands of the Department of the Interior, without review by the Federal Power Commission. NWPPA, the PUD association and Seattle City Light all shared that view. Ward's statement then touched on the substantive issue of authorizing federal construction of the steam plants.

"The unanimous recommendation of the privately owned and pub-

licly owned utilities systems of the Northwest represented by the
Pacific Northwest Utilities Conference Committee[1]...has been that
second to prosecuting work on existing federal hydroelectric undertak-
ings more rapidly, the next step would be adequate support by Congress
and all federal agencies for non-federal construction of hydro plants,
some of which are proposed by publicly owned utilities, the principal one
being the 400,000-kilowatt Cowlitz power development of the city of
Tacoma," Ward stated.

"Following that, consideration should be given to construction of
steam turbine electric generating plants," he said, because non-federal
plants could be completed more rapidly. He also pointed out that demand
for steam turbines was so heavy that installation could not be completed
in less than four years, whereas orders for generators for hydro plants
were not so heavily booked.[2]

Ward also argued that only one coal field in Washington had output
sufficient to supply a 100-mw steam plant. Providing fuel for three such
plants would require turning to Wyoming and Utah fields or developing
new fields in Washington.

After I finished reading Ward's statement, committee members asked
whether the statement represented APPA's views or those of Ward personally. I said the statement was Ward's in his capacity as APPA president. That reply did not satisfy committee members. They wanted to
know whether APPA had passed a resolution on this subject or whether
the association's board of directors had approved this statement. My
answer to both questions was "no."[3] However, I pointed out that the board
of directors had adopted a federal power policy statement declaring that
hydroelectric resources should be developed wherever economically fea-

---

[1] I was rankled by Ward's invoking the action of the Pacific Northwest Utilities
Conference Committee to support his position. The committee was more closely aligned with
the power companies than with public power groups, even though some publicly owned
utilities were members of the organization. However, the chairman of the committee at that
time was Ward's boss, C.A. Erdahl, director of Tacoma's Department of Public Utilities.

[2] Later in the hearing, in response to a question, I testified, on the basis of information
given to me by Ward, that the Cowlitz project could be completed two years after FPC granted
a license. However, FPC's later award of a license was challenged before the U.S. Supreme
Court and power from the project did not go on line until 1963.

[3] When I returned to the office after the hearing, I called Ward and advised him of these
questions, and he told me that the executive committee had approved the statement. I so
advised the Public Works Committee by letter on the following day, and the letter was
inserted in the record of the hearing. It was not clear whether Ward had obtained such
approval before or after I testified.

sible and that public bodies should receive a preference in the development of such resources. Ward's position on the Cowlitz project therefore was consistent with APPA policy.

I failed to persuade some members of the committee. One of the sharpest exchanges I had came during interrogation by Congressman Clare Magee, D-Mo.

"So he [Ward] is only taking a selfish position in his present official capacity and not as president of the American Public Power Association? The facts bear that out certainly," Magee said to me.

"I would not impugn such motives to Mr. Ward," I responded.

"I do," Magee said.

Considerable skepticism about Ward's statement resulted from apparent differences between his position and that of the Northwest Public Power Association. Gus Norwood, executive secretary of NWPPA, had sent the committee a letter, which was inserted in the record, stating that the organization passed a motion at a membership meeting earlier that month supporting the Jackson bill. However, he said members of the association repeatedly made the point that "they would not wish for the construction of steam plants as an alternative to the much more desirable hydroelectric projects."

Implicit in the NWPPA position was the assumption that both the steam and hydro plants were needed. The distinction between their views and Ward's was that Ward opposed consideration of the steam plants until the Cowlitz project was built.

While I was testifying, I was handed a telegram from Owen Hurd, then general manager of the Benton County, Washington, Public Utility District and president of NWPPA. The telegram attempted to clarify NWPPA's position, and I was permitted to read it into the hearing record.

"Action by the Northwest Public Power Association in favoring the construction of federal steam plants should not be interpreted as a substitution for federal hydro projects [that] Northwest Public Power Association has gone on record as favoring or as a substitute for the Cowlitz or any other Northwest hydro plant now under construction or being planned by any private or public agency," Hurd said.

The telegram somewhat softened the differences between the NWPPA and Ward statements.

Jackson explained the position of most public power organizations on his bill, but he did not throw me hardball questions. During a break in the hearings, after I completed my testimony, I talked with Jackson and was relieved that he was not offended by my performance. He said he understood my predicament and thought I had handled myself well.

In early October, the House Public Works Committee approved the Jackson bill by a vote of 15 to 9, after striking a provision that would have given the Interior Department complete control over rates charged for thermal power. However, the impending adjournment of Congress prevented action on the floor of the House, and the Senate took no action during that Congress. For a variety of reasons, Jackson and Magnuson did not pursue this issue in future Congresses, but the question of the use of federally generated thermal power did not die. Intense controversy over this issue arose later in connection with the use of waste heat from the Hanford nuclear reactor to produce electrical energy. The Jackson-Magnuson bill also was a precursor of subsequent plans of local public agencies to build five nuclear plants under the aegis of the Washington Public Power Supply System.

•

Hearings on the steam plant marked the low point of my relationship with Ward, who was highly competent and dedicated, but rather humorless. However, as we worked together during the year, he gradually became friendlier toward me.

I credit my wife, Sara, for playing a part in his change of attitude. Ward was a very religious man and enjoyed talking about the Bible. Sara's knowledge about the Bible helped smooth my relationship with Ward. When we invited Ward to have dinner at our house, he and Sara had a lively discussion about the Bible, much to Ward's gratification. Her warm personality also loosened him up.

When Ward presided over the final meeting of the board of directors during his term as president, he acknowledged that he had begun the year with doubts about my qualifications for the job. However, he said that during this period he had gained respect and admiration for me and he concluded by giving me a warm endorsement. I admired his candor and sincerity and was gratified to have won his support. His remarks moved me to tears.

Chapter 16

Birth Of The ECIC

By the end of 1951, public power and rural electrification were under such strong attack from private power companies that supporters of these programs began to explore new means of countering the onslaught. Through their lobbying arm, the National Association of Electric Companies, the private power companies consistently ranked as the top spender for lobbying, which they backed up with a national advertising program. They wanted to stop appropriations for new federal hydro power projects and transmission lines. The companies also targeted appropriations for rural electrification loans, even though 15 percent of American farms still had not been electrified.

Early in 1952 Clyde Ellis, general manager of the National Rural Electric Cooperative Association, and I met with leaders of several farm, labor and cooperative organizations to discuss the need for a national conference to call attention to our problems and to form a coalition to coordinate our efforts.

Thus was born the Electric Consumers Conference, which spawned creation of the Electric Consumers Information Committee (ECIC). The committee played an important role for nearly two decades in defending public power and rural electrification. My association with the conference and ECIC made it possible for APPA to achieve objectives we could not have attained on our own. In calling the conference, the organizers stated its purposes as follows:

"The American consumer—laborer, farmer, housewife, manufacturer and merchant—has a fundamental interest in the production, distribution and utilization of the electric power resources of our nation. Among the factors instrumental in providing the widest possible use of electric power at the lowest possible cost is the prompt and orderly development of our nation's resources and the safeguarding of the benefits of such development for the American public, and not for exploitation by private interests. In order that the rights and interests of the American consumer will have a forum and an instrument of expression, the Electric Consumers Conference has been organized."

The conference was held May 26 and 27, 1952 at the Willard Hotel in Washington. More than 500 people attended and saw a star-studded cast of speakers, headed by President Harry S Truman. Other participants included Senators Lister Hill, D-Ala., George Aiken, R-Vt., and Wayne Morse, R-Ore.; Secretary of the Interior Oscar Chapman; Rep. Michael Kirwan, D-Ohio, chairman of the House Appropriations Subcommittee on the Interior; Walter Reuther, president of the United Automobile Workers; James Patton, president of the National Farmers Union; Henry Carstensen, master of the Washington State Grange; P.J. Donnelly, president of the North Dakota Farm Bureau Federation, and Ken Whitaker, administrative assistant to the Electric Power Board of Chattanooga and former deputy administrator of the Defense Electric Power Administration.

Murray Lincoln, who was well known for his work as president of the Ohio Farm Bureau Federation, the Farm Bureau Insurance Companies, CARE and the Cooperative League of the U.S.A., chaired the conference. The vice chair was Morris L. Cooke, first administrator of the Rural Electrification Administration, who more recently had headed President Truman's Water Resources Policy Commission. APPA was one of 17 sponsors. Others included NRECA, the Congress of Industrial Organizations, six other prominent labor unions, the Cooperative League of the U.S.A., the National Farmers Union, the Tennessee Valley and Northwest public power associations, and the Public Affairs Institute, a research organization that did work for labor and other groups.

Aware of the conservatism of the APPA board of directors, I had some apprehension about asking for approval of APPA's sponsorship of the conference. However, the board did so with the understanding that APPA would not endorse any action taken by the conference absent board approval.

•

The conference was exciting. Many of the speakers had an evangelical fervor characteristic of politicians in the pre-TV era. They whipped up the enthusiasm of the audience. President Truman addressed the first session and set the tone by attacking the advertising and public relations activities of the power companies.

"There is a terrible barrage of propaganda going around these days on behalf of the poor private power producers. The private power companies are spending millions and millions of dollars on their propaganda programs,"[1] Truman declared.

The campaign "is based on the old theory of scaring the people, of trying to frighten and confuse them instead of arguing on the basis of facts," Truman said. "There is no question that this is the theory of the power companies' vicious propaganda. They say so themselves in the literature they distribute privately among themselves...

"One of their advertising agencies actually boasted that their technique was so successful that ministers included some of this propaganda with their church notices, and some of their propaganda was posted on the bulletin boards of the Boy Scouts."

One of Truman's gestures reminded me of the famous moment when he gleefully waved before a crowd the front page of the *Chicago Tribune,* which erroneously declared Gov. Thomas Dewey the winner of the 1948 presidential race. In like manner, Truman held up a Wisconsin Power & Light Company advertisement calling for private redevelopment of Niagara Falls. Pointing to the ad, Truman declared, "You are paying for that. The tax collections of the government are not so great because they [the power companies] charge these off as expenses of operation. I think I will ask the attorney general...to take a look at this situation and see if the Corrupt Practices Act does not apply."

Other speakers also attacked the power companies' advertising and public relations campaign. Several denounced the ECAP study, first revealed by APPA, which advised the companies to equate public power with socialism, because a public opinion poll showed that a majority of people opposed socialism but favored public power.

Many speakers directed their remarks to specific projects that they felt were needed in order to develop the nation's natural resources and make the benefits available to the public through public power utilities and rural electric cooperatives.

Sen. Aiken spoke eloquently in favor of the St. Lawrence and Niagara

---

[1] After the conference, a spokesman for the Edison Electric Institute denied that the companies were spending "millions and millions of dollars" in their campaign against public power. He said the companies' annual bill for advertising and lobbying by EEI, the National Association of Electric Companies (the lobbying organization), the Electric Companies Advertising Program and the Public Information Program totaled "only" $3 million. However, this amount did not include power companies' local advertising or other expenses, such as travel, incurred by individual utilities in advertising and lobbying.

power projects. He accused investment bankers, the railroads and the power companies of attempting to block the St. Lawrence development.

Senator Morse condemned the power companies for their opposition to his bill to authorize construction of the Hells Canyon project on the Snake River. The power companies, he charged, were against his bill because it sought to prevent the development of monopolistic control of the Snake River by the Idaho Power Company The company "would prefer to have a private monopoly build a series of low-head dams that would not begin to develop the maximum power resources of that great river network," he said. "And unless you develop the maximum resources of that great river network, you...will limit the security possibilities of your nation in the great atomic era into which we are going."

Several speakers discussed specific national power policies—notably the preference clause and federal construction of transmission lines to deliver power to preference customers.

"Now just why are some of the [power] companies trying to destroy the policies [that] guide the federal government in marketing the people's share of our total power resources?" asked Secretary of the Interior Oscar Chapman. "The answer is quite simple," he said. "It is a policy establishing equality for consumers as against monopoly in the development of our public power resources. Its fundamental provisions have been embodied in a series of laws enacted by Congress over a period of more than 45 years.

"Congress has consistently written into every law governing federal marketing of hydroelectric power the provision that the people's power system, the public and cooperative power systems, should have a preferential right to distribute this power supply," Chapman continued. "Congress has also consistently authorized federal power marketing agencies to build the transmission lines necessary to deliver the power to points where the people's nonprofit systems could take it for distribution to their customers.

"This preference provision is the most effective antimonopoly provision to be found anywhere in federal law," he said. "It is one anti-monopoly provision [that]—when implemented by Congress with adequate appropriations for transmission lines—monopoly has found no way to circumvent, for it opens to consumers themselves an equal opportunity to secure economical power supply."

Other speakers called attention to power company attacks against regional power development in the Missouri River Basin, the Columbia River Basin and the Central Valley of California, and efforts to thwart public power in the Southwest and Southeast.

•

Several speakers delivered stirring remarks about more general concerns. Among them was Sen. Hubert Humphrey, D-Minn., who later was vice president under Lyndon B. Johnson.

"This is one of the first times for a long time that I've seen a group of people assembled in Washington that [was] truly interested in the public interest for a change," Humphrey said. "We've had many special groups that have come here and have been interested in some special interest. But thank God at last, the nation's capital is host to a group of people who again want to make America relive and make America reborn for the spirit of social progress and liberal democracy. That's what I see in this room. That is what America needs."

Besides Humphrey, the most spellbinding orator was labor leader Walter Reuther. Speaking without a text, he delivered a strong, lucid message in an intense, rapid-fire manner. Reuther placed the issue of public power in a broad context.

"The fight for public power is a part of a total fight of people to achieve abundance," he said. "And abundance takes on new and more significance in the world in which we live. We cannot hope to make freedom and peace secure in our world if we go on dividing up economic scarcity. Only economic abundance gives democracy the tools with which to build and expand and defend the basic values that we as a nation are dedicated to preserve and extend in the world.

"Peace and freedom are not possible in a world committed to the economics of monopoly and scarcity," Reuther said. "If you divide America between the have citizens and the have-not citizens, America cannot live at peace. And if you divide the world between the have nations and the have-not nations, the world cannot live at peace, because the forces of Communist tyranny will build their power out of injustice and they will ride the backs of those people who are the have-nots, and they will exploit the social dynamics and the emotional power of their struggle to achieve economic and social justice."

Reuther related his view of national and international issues to public power: "What are the power interests afraid of when we talk about public power? They are afraid of the whole basic concept of public power, which says that we ought to take our resources and utilize them to the fullest, applying our most advanced technology, so that the people can have the benefits of the highest possible volume of power at the lowest possible cost. That is the concept of abundance translated into practical achievement."

•

The high-level discussion of power policies and national politics was placed in a human perspective by a farm wife, Mrs. Raymond Ricketts of Fair Grove, Missouri. She vividly described the drudgery of farm life before rural electrification and how electricity had greatly lightened her burdens.

"I wonder how many of you know how to draw water with a bucket and rope and two hands," she said. "Before we installed our deep well pump, I learned another way and it might be well to pass it along to you. When I broke my arm about four years ago, I learned to draw it with one hand and one foot. Oh yes, I had to! Because I was at home with my three boys and they were thirsty and under six years of age. We had no telephone and I knew my husband would not be home until evening....Now, since the installation of our water system, my work has been lightened beyond description.

"No more dragging in that zinc wash tub for baths on Saturday night. I know it's supposed to be a joke, but it's also the truth. And of course, the whole family always had a bath in the same water, just adding a little to keep it warm, and leaving the dirtiest until the last."

Doing the family wash before rural electrification was especially burdensome, Mrs. Ricketts said. Drawing water was too much for her, so her husband had to get up 30 minutes earlier on washday to get the water she would need. Then they would carry it to the basement to be heated in a wood stove. Tests showed that before electrical equipment and running water were available, the average farm wife spent four hours doing the weekly laundry. She washed 116 pounds of wet clothes and carried 730 pounds of water to do the job.

•

After two days of speeches and discussions, conference attendees unanimously adopted a statement of principles, which included these recommendations:

- "There must be the best possible electric service to consumers everywhere—residential, agricultural, commercial or industrial—at the lowest rates consistent with sound business principles.
- "All feasible potential power resources of the nation, hydro or other, must be developed as rapidly as they can be soundly undertaken. Public and cooperative agencies must be permitted to build and operate fuel-burning generating plants and to integrate them with hydro power.
- "River basins should be developed not only for power production but

in accordance with comprehensive, basin-wide plans [that] will assure optimum soil and forest conservation, flood control, reclamation and irrigation of land, improvement of navigation, abatement of pollution, municipal and industrial water supply, protection of fish and wildlife, expansion of recreational and cultural facilities, salinity control, and other benefits. Such development can and must be done only by public agencies with widest practical participation of local public agencies and cooperatives....

- "Benefits of the development of the public's power resources must reach consumers undiminished by any unnecessary added costs. Wheeling contracts, exchange or rate arrangements violative of this principle must go. Public transmission facilities and aid to local agencies or cooperatives in the establishment and acquisition of distribution systems must be provided wherever and whenever need exists.
- "Electric power publicly produced belongs to the public. The public has first preference right to it as such owners. It should not be supplied to industries or private profit distributors 1) if needed by public agencies and consumers' cooperatives, or 2) without such control of resale rates and conditions of service by the producing agency as will assure that all publicly created benefits reach the public in the form of lowest possible rates.
- "The private power industry in America must be cleansed. Although its illegal, immoral and degrading activities were exposed and condemned only two decades ago [a reference to the Federal Trade Commission investigation], the unreformed and unrepentant industry given a privileged monopoly position to supply a necessity of our lives, is today again charging and expending rate-payers' money as operating expenses, to corrupt public sources of information, educational institutions, public agencies and the functioning of our democratic institutions....There must be immediate and continuous action to assure that benefits of tax concessions, accelerated amortization subsidies and similar windfalls to private companies reach consumers...."

The conference's final recommendation probably had the most lasting effect. It called for establishment of an Electric Consumers Information Committee in Washington composed of sponsors of the conference and others who wished to be associated with the group. ECIC would not lobby in its own name but would be a medium for exchanging information and coordinating activities of the sponsoring organizations in the electric power field.

This recommendation was implemented immediately. Clyde Ellis was elected chair of ECIC, I was chosen as vice chair, and Dewey Anderson, executive director of the Public Affairs Institute, was secretary-treasurer. Representatives of several labor unions, the National Farmers Unions and the Cooperative League of the U.S.A. were named directors. Ellis made Clay Cochran, an economist on the NRECA staff, available to serve as coordinator for the committee.

ECIC could not have been formed at a more opportune time. Within weeks the group was deeply involved in developing and coordinating strategy in connection with an array of national issues involving power policy. ECIC meetings generated a sense of excitement and urgency. We felt that we were wearing the "white hats," charging off to do battle with giants. Ellis and I generally took the lead in identifying issues, and rarely was there controversy over policies or strategy.

Despite our limited resources, this broad coalition of public power, rural electric cooperative, farm and labor groups gave ECIC the stature to command the attention of important public figures. Labor unions at that time were strong and politically influential and our alliance with them was especially important. ECIC representatives met privately with President Truman, Lyndon Johnson when he was majority leader of the Senate, President Kennedy, Mrs. Eleanor Roosevelt, and a host of senators, representatives and cabinet members. Our activities frequently were the subject of articles by nationally syndicated newspaper columnists. (In 1968, to broaden its base of support, ECIC helped organize and joined the Consumer Federation of America.)

One of our biggest battles came in 1954, when members of ECIC were deeply involved in congressional action to amend the Atomic Energy Act of 1946. Our active participation in this issue precipitated what was then the lengthiest continuous session ever held by the Senate—about 62 hours. Some referred to it as a filibuster. I and others affiliated with ECIC played a significant role in this debate. It was one of the most stimulating experiences of my life.

Chapter 17

The Great Nuclear Debate

Development of commercial nuclear power was one of the most difficult and contentious issues I dealt with during my career with APPA. Within a span of two decades I saw the euphoria about nuclear power (too cheap to meter) turn to disillusionment (utilities defaulting on their debt or facing bankruptcy because of investments in nuclear facilities).

APPA's early enthusiasm for nuclear power was rooted in the widely heralded belief that atomic energy was a virtually inexhaustible, non-polluting source of electricity. We hoped it would provide a new source of power as hydroelectric development options were exhausted. We also saw nuclear power as an effective competitor to coal, the dominant fuel used to generate electricity.

Our initial expectations were not dampened by concerns about the difficulties of handling or disposing of nuclear materials or by the complexities and expenses of building nuclear power stations. Warnings about these problems came later. The entire electric industry—public and private—was dazzled by nuclear power's prospects.

Public power groups feared they would be left behind in the development of this new source of energy. Power companies appeared before congressional committees and in other forums to demand that they be permitted to participate in the development of nuclear power. APPA wanted to be sure that its members had a piece of the action.

Unfortunately, we were so caught up in the euphoria that we ignored the advice of Admiral Hyman Rickover, the father of the nuclear submarine. Early on, he advised me that nuclear power was for "the big boys" and that we should not get involved.

Convinced that we were on the threshold of a new era in the electric industry, APPA began to follow nuclear power developments closely. An Ad Hoc Advisory Committee named by the Atomic Energy Commission said in a March 28, 1951 report that the prospects for nuclear power within the next decade were "robust enough to warrant a strong present and continuing interest on the part of the electric industry." The committee recommended assignment of electric industry personnel to the nuclear energy program and a greater exchange of information between the AEC and the industry. By the end of 1952, AEC recognized four teams of private utilities and industrial companies to study the feasibility of nuclear power.

Concerned that public power was being left behind, I arranged a meeting in February 1953 of 12 APPA members with AEC Chairman Gordon Dean to discuss local public agency participation in the atomic power program. APPA President Ralph Duvall, manager of production and distribution for the Kansas City, Kansas, Board of Public Utilities, headed the group, which included officials of larger APPA member utilities. APPA General Counsel Northcutt Ely and I also attended.

Dean advised that public power could participate in a study team that would work with the AEC. The commission believed that within a decade nuclear reactors would be producing power for seven mills per kilowatt-hour, he said. However, other AEC officials at the meeting declared that nuclear power plants would be economically feasible only with an installed capacity of more than 300 megawatts—a size that was out of reach for most APPA members.

Following that meeting, Duvall appointed a special APPA Atomic Power Policy Committee. There was speculation that the new Eisenhower administration and the congressional Joint Committee on Atomic Energy (JCAE) wanted to make major changes to the Atomic Energy Act of 1946. That law permitted only the federal government to own nuclear materials. Eisenhower and the new Republican-controlled JCAE favored private power company development of nuclear power plants. If APPA expected to be a player, it had to develop policies in this area.

Duvall wisely chose Samuel B. Morris, general manager and chief engineer of the Los Angeles Department of Water and Power and a former APPA president, to chair the committee. Morris was a highly respected leader with impeccable credentials. Before his appointment to the Los Angeles position, he was dean of engineering at Stanford University. He was self-effacing, and used his intellect and sincerity to persuade others.

Shortly after the APPA meeting with the AEC, the JCAE said hearings on amendments to the Atomic Energy Act would be announced by May 1. President Eisenhower was enthusiastic about releasing nuclear materials to private industry for non-military development. Rep. Sterling Cole,

R-N.Y., chairman of the JCAE, was equally enthusiastic and told news reporters the Atomic Energy Act of 1946 would have to be revised "in order to interest private industry in pushing ahead in this field."

APPA's Atomic Power Policy Committee agreed on policy principles at a March 8 meeting. The committee said it "approached the problem of government policy in the atomic energy field from the viewpoint of protecting the government's interest and of making available to the maximum number of people of the United States the benefits [that] may accrue from development of this new source of energy."

APPA endorsed the language of the Atomic Energy Act, which said that "development and utilization of atomic energy shall...be directed toward improving the public welfare, increasing the standard of living, strengthening free competition in private enterprise, and promoting world peace." Controls on the use of fissionable materials should not be lifted until adequate information was available on the use and development of atomic energy for industrial purposes and production of electric energy, APPA said, adding that a monopolistic advantage should not accrue to any private person or corporation. The association also called on the AEC to develop a pilot nuclear power plant. In addition, APPA supported research programs involving operation of pilot electric generating plants by utilities and urged that public power utilities be included in such efforts.

I transmitted APPA's recommendations to Chairman Dean. In response, he told me there was "no basis for apprehension" that publicly owned electric utilities would not be permitted to share in the application of atomic energy to electric power production. The commission wanted nuclear reactor development to be handled by public and private entities, he said. However, he added that for some time to come, the AEC would need to continue a vigorous research and development effort.

The JCAE on June 15 began two weeks of hearings on amendments to the Atomic Energy Act. Meanwhile, the AEC released a summary of its recommended amendments. The commission favored non-federal ownership and operation of nuclear power plants and believed private enterprise should be allowed to rent or buy fissionable material under "adequate security safeguards." The commission also recommended liberalization of patent rights and released summaries of reports it had received from the four private utility groups that had been studying nuclear power.

"All four groups concur in the belief that dual-purpose reactors are technically feasible and could be operated in such a fashion that the plutonium credit would reduce the cost of power," the commission reported.

"Conversely, all agree that no reactor could be constructed in the very near future that would be economic on the basis of power generation alone." All four groups wanted to continue with more detailed studies.

The Eisenhower administration's plans for amending the Atomic Energy Act met growing opposition. The most outspoken critic was Rep. Chet Holifield, D-Calif., an active, high-ranking member of the JCAE who had been a congressman since the New Deal. An outspoken liberal respected for his integrity and his thoughtful attention to legislation, Holifield later became chairman of the JCAE and was one of the most influential members of Congress in shaping the nation's nuclear policies.

In a major address on the floor of the House in early June 1953, Holifield bitterly attacked the proposed amendments to the Atomic Energy Act. He described plans for turning nuclear power development over to private power companies as "a giveaway program" and said the need for amending the Atomic Energy Act "has not yet arisen except in the minds of a few enterprising men who are maneuvering to get the atom-bomb business as a means of building privately owned atomic power plants with government subsidy. What the proponents of legislative change mainly are after is an opportunity to produce bomb-making materials as a private venture and to develop atomic power as a by-product of this very profitable occupation," he said.

Quoting scientists and engineers who had said that economic nuclear power was not yet at hand, Holifield said there was "no demonstrated need" for the proposed amendments to the law. He urged Congress to "proceed with care and caution and give searching scrutiny to any proposed changes."

•

In June and July 1953 the JCAE held a series of hearings on the AEC's proposals to open participation in the production of nuclear power to private enterprise. The hearings set the stage for enacting legislation the following year.

Holding public hearings on nuclear power was itself remarkable. The Cold War was raging and a great deal of secrecy surrounded the subject. Before the hearings were held, the JCAE conducted a dozen closed sessions with Eisenhower administration officials and private companies whose personnel had security clearances to participate in the nuclear power program.

Prior to the hearings, AEC Chairman Gordon Dean visited the JCAE behind locked doors guarded by uniformed personnel. To avoid security breaches at the public hearings, all witnesses were asked to assure in writing that no classified information would be discussed in the public hearings.

•

Samuel Morris testified before the committee on behalf of APPA on July 20. He urged that the federal government be authorized to build prototype nuclear power plants, with participation by private and public agencies. The government should not delegate this responsibility to private industry, he said. He warned that liberalization of patent rights would lead to greater secrecy in research.

Holifield complimented Morris on his testimony and noted that it was "quite different" from a number of statements made to the committee. Most of the testimony had called for allowing private industry to "come in and finish this job of research and development...but in return for that they have asked for subsidization in one form or another, either through the purchase of plutonium or through rapid amortization or through obtaining...restrictive patent rights."

The hearings were completed on July 31 after the JCAE heard 112 witnesses over 14 days. The hearings raised more questions than they answered. I posed some of the major issues affecting APPA members in an editorial I wrote for *Public Power* magazine of November 1953:

> If it is correct, as has been assumed heretofore, that 200,000-300,000 kw is the minimum size of an economically feasible nuclear power station, how are the benefits of this invaluable national asset to be made available to the relatively small, independently operated local public power systems and rural electric cooperatives? Will the construction of nuclear power stations in such large sizes mean that the smaller, independently operated utilities will be forced to purchase power from another utility in order to obtain the advantages of nuclear power? Or will other means be explored for making this power available to the small cities and rural areas which are urgently in need of new and lower-cost sources of power?
>
> Will developmental efforts be directed at the feasibility of installing atomic power plants for central station service of 3,000 to 5,000 kw of capacity? And how will the government's vast investment, first in developing nuclear fission and later in producing economically feasible nuclear power stations be passed along to all the citizens of the nation, who as taxpayers, have financed this development?

Early the next year, a national debate raged over nuclear power. In February 1954 President Eisenhower sent a special message to Congress proposing five amendments to the Atomic Energy Act that would:

- Relax statutory restrictions against ownership or lease of fissionable materials;
- Permit private manufacture, ownership and operation of atomic reactors;
- Authorize the AEC to establish minimum safety and security regulations to govern the use and possession of fissionable material;
- Permit the AEC to supply licensees special materials and services needed in the initial stages of the new industry; and
- Liberalize the patent provisions of the Atomic Energy Act.

Of the controversial patent question, the president said fairness dictated use of a mechanism to guard against monopoly until industrial use of atomic energy achieved a broader base. "I hope that participation in the development of atomic power will have broadened sufficiently in the next five years to remove the need for such provisions," he said.

In April identical bills on atomic energy were introduced by Chairman Cole of the JCAE and Sen. Bourke Hickenlooper, R-Iowa., ranking senator on the JCAE. The Cole-Hickenlooper bill constituted a complete rewrite of the Atomic Energy Act of 1946. Its provisions went far beyond Eisenhower's proposals.

APPA's concerns still focused largely on the patent issue. In May, Morris again appeared before the JCAE. Using uncharacteristically strong language, he charged that the patent provisions of the Cole-Hickenlooper bills would "afford opportunity for creation of a monopoly on a scale never before known in America." Pointing out that APPA had adopted a resolution the previous week at its annual conference opposing the patent provisions of the bill, Morris argued against "sweeping changes" in the law that would permit "private monopoly."

He said changes proposed in the bills should not be made in view of the $12 billion "previously expended by the people of the United States through their national government, as compared with a few million dollars by private industry."

In response to questioning by Sen. John O. Pastore, D-R.I., Morris gave an example of the dangers inherent in a patent monopoly. If a company held an exclusive patent on a device to produce atomic energy and wholesale power was selling in one area for a hypothetical price of seven mills per kwh, the company holding the patent would have to sell power for only six mills to be competitive, Morris said. Yet, it is possible that atomic power could be sold economically for three mills. But with monopoly control, the company would have no competitive pressure to reduce its price, he said.

•

APPA and the Electric Consumers Information Committee closely scrutinized the Cole-Hickenlooper bills. The more we examined them, the more deficiencies we discovered. There was no authorization for AEC to produce commercial nuclear-generated power, so the bills lacked the traditional preference clause for marketing federally produced power.

A group organized by ECIC met with Holifield and his staff to discuss our concerns. Fortuitously, the JCAE was preparing a report on the Cole-Hickenlooper bills and Holifield asked us to put our views in writing so he could incorporate them into his statement, which would be included in the committee report.

We asked Leland Olds to prepare the material for Holifield. He spent an entire weekend drafting report language. Holifield included our issues in the separate 33-page views that he and Rep. Melvin Price, D-Ill., filed on June 30, 1954. They noted that the bill did not permit AEC to produce commercial nuclear power and said: "If the nation is to realize the maximum power benefits from its investment in this new resource, a positive program of atomic power production by the federal government is essential." The power licensing provisions of the bill did not encourage public or cooperative distribution of nuclear power and did not assure that private power companies would sell nuclear power at the lowest possible rates, they declared.

Although the bill provided a preference in the location of nuclear power facilities to areas with high power costs, Holifield and Price noted that proposed legislation did not contain the usual preference to public bodies and cooperatives in marketing power from AEC installations. The congressmen proposed establishment of a Division of Civilian Power Application in the AEC, which would work with the Federal Power Commission "to apply substantially the same public interest safeguards in connection with the licensing of atomic power plants as are applied in licensing hydroelectric developments under the Federal Power Act."

Holifield and Price also criticized the patent provisions. Compulsory licensing of patents should be extended for 10 years, instead of five, they said. However, Chairman Cole opposed any compulsory licensing of atomic patents, saying it would be unconstitutional.

•

The Holifield-Price comments energized ECIC and we went all out to seek amendments to the Hickenlooper bill in the Senate. We focused on the Senate because we felt we had a better opportunity to succeed there than in the House. We asked members of the group to draft amendments and seek sponsors for them. We also sought support for a filibuster, which might cause the Senate to put the bill aside. I was assigned to ask Sen. Lister Hill, D-Ala., to lead the floor fight—or "extended discussion," as we euphemistically called the filibuster.

Senator Hill was highly respected and an accomplished orator. He had a stake in the bill because of his constituents' interest in the Dixon-Yates issue. Dixon-Yates referred to a power company scheme headed by Edgar H. Dixon of Middle South Utilities and Eugene Yates of Southern Company. The two proposed to build a 650,000-kw steam plant in West Memphis, Arkansas, across the Mississippi River from Memphis, Tennessee, to deliver power to the Tennessee Valley Authority at or near Memphis. Theoretically, this energy would help TVA serve an AEC production facility at Paducah, Kentucky, 200 miles distant. AEC would purchase power produced at the plant under a 25-year contract. The proposal, bitterly opposed by TVA supporters, was actually a convoluted scheme to prevent TVA from building a new steam plant. The Hickenlooper bill provided a vehicle for Dixon-Yates opponents to attach an amendment prohibiting the AEC from going forward with this arrangement.

Senator Hill readily agreed to lead the effort if ECIC would furnish the relevant speech material. ECIC members responded immediately. I volunteered to write material for Sen. Henry M. (Scoop) Jackson, D-Wash., about an amendment that would insert a public preference clause for marketing surplus power from any AEC plant.

•

As the Senate floor debate approached, ECIC prepared a number of amendments that were to be proposed for the 104-page, 19-chapter bill. I sent a letter to each member of the Senate urging adoption of the following amendments:

- a prohibition on the Dixon-Yates contract;
- substitution of the patent provisions of the Atomic Energy Act of 1946 for those in the Hickenlooper bill;
- permission for the federal government, where specifically authorized by Congress, to build nuclear power plants;
- a requirement that the AEC give preference to local public agencies and rural electric cooperatives in marketing power from federally owned nuclear power facilities;
- a stipulation that local public agencies and rural electric cooperatives would receive preference in obtaining licenses for nuclear power facilities, where there was a limitation on the availability of fissionable materials, and

- a provision bringing licensing provisions of the Atomic Energy Act
  in line with procedures established under the Federal Power Act.

I closed with this plea: "Depending upon the manner in which Congress acts upon the pending legislation, this energy source—holding such bright potentialities for the future—can either be developed for the benefit of all Americans, or it will become the province of a relatively few large corporations. Unless the amendments to which we have referred are adopted, we fear that the latter will be the result."

Extended debate on the bill began on Wednesday, July 21. As it proceeded, amendments were called up and we were encouraged by the results. ECIC members had zealously canvassed their constituents, urging them to contact their senators. The close working relationship established by APPA, NRECA, the National Farmers Union, international labor unions and other groups paid off. Although the amendment to prohibit the Dixon-Yates contract was defeated, the Senate adopted several of our amendments, including:

- an amendment by Sen. Edwin C. Johnson, D-Colo., authorizing AEC to generate electricity (power not used by AEC would be marketed by the secretary of the interior, with preference to public bodies and cooperatives);
- an amendment by Sen. Hubert H. Humphrey, D-Minn., requiring notification of all electric utilities within transmission distance of proposed nuclear power plants;
- another Humphrey amendment providing preference to public bodies and cooperatives for nuclear power licenses in cases of conflicting applications.

A third amendment by Senator Humphrey that would have created a new Division of Civilian Power Application in the AEC was tabled.

Because the Senate was meeting around the clock, the ECIC writers were hard pressed to provide speech material in a timely manner. We were determined that the debate would not contain irrelevant material, such as Bible readings—a tactic frequently used in filibusters.

I asked Ron Ross, editor of *Public Power* magazine, to help me prepare material for Senator Jackson. We began work on the speech in the early afternoon and, as we finished portions, we sent our copy to the senator's office by messenger. By early evening, Senator Jackson's chief of staff asked us to come to the senator's office and work at typewriters there. We worked in Jackson's office all night to keep the senator stocked with ammunition until he was relieved on the floor about 5 a.m., when we went home for an hour or two of sleep before returning to the office.

ECIC participants were bone weary, but hopeful that the debate could be continued. However, by Saturday, July 24, we began to hear rumors that Minority Leader Lyndon Johnson, D-Texas, was annoyed by the delay. Johnson won enough votes to limit the debate and the bill was passed on Tuesday night, July 27 on a roll call vote of 57–28.

The bill had to be approved by the House and differences between the two versions had to be reconciled. However, we knew from the outset that our only hope to make improvements would be in the Senate and we would need to retain our gains in conference.

As expected, the House adopted amendments which, for the most part, were diametrically opposed to those we had fought for in the Senate. Only two House amendments were consistent with our goals. One provided for preference in marketing power produced by AEC. A second required that utilities within transmission distance of proposed nuclear power projects be notified of license applications.

Faced with the sharply divergent positions of the Senate and House, conferees for the most part accepted the House version. The section on patents produced the sharpest conflict. Although the bill originally reported by the JCAE would subject atomic patents to compulsory licensing for five years, a House amendment would have deleted reference to compulsory patent-sharing. The Senate bill would have extended the five-year compulsory patent-sharing to 10 years. The conferees agreed on a compromise giving preference in issuance of commercial nuclear licenses to applicants who agreed to make their patents available to other licensees for five years.

Preference to public agencies and rural electric cooperatives in marketing power produced by the AEC and in the issuance of licenses for nuclear power stations was watered down in the conference report. It would be given only "insofar as practicable."

The federal nuclear power program was largely dropped in the conference report, which included Chairman Cole's House-approved amendment specifically barring AEC from producing electric power except as part of its research and development program. However, the AEC could build large facilities to demonstrate the practical value of nuclear power if specifically authorized by Congress.

The House quickly approved the conference report. The Senate, however, was so upset with the patent and preference provisions that it rejected them by a vote of 48–41. After the Senate vote, new conferees met and quickly reached agreement on the two controversial points. The new patent provision was the same as that contained in the bill originally reported to Congress by the JCAE. For about five years after passage of the bill, non-military patents would be subject to an elaborate licensing arrangement under which AEC would determine whether licensing of a patent was "of primary importance to effectuate the policies and purposes of the act." This extensive procedure contrasted sharply with similar provisions in the Atomic Energy Act of 1946, under which any patent declared by AEC "to be affected with the public interest" could be licensed.

The three little words limiting application of the power marketing preference only "insofar as practicable" were removed. The preference clause in the final version of the bill provided that energy produced at AEC installations could be sold by the commission with this proviso: AEC had to give preference to public bodies and cooperatives "or to privately owned utilities providing electric utility services to high-cost areas not being served by public bodies or cooperatives." Another section of the bill stated that in the case of conflicting applications for licenses for nuclear power facilities, "preferred consideration" must be given to applications by public or cooperative bodies.

With these changes, the Senate and House quickly approved the new bill and it was sent to the White House, where President Eisenhower signed it on August 30, 1954. The president noted the public-private power controversy over the bill and said he was confident the bill would "advance both public and private development of atomic energy."

"Debate on this legislation revealed some misunderstandings about the effect of certain of its provisions on public and private development of electrical power from the atom," Eisenhower said. "I want our people to know that these provisions are designed eventually to relieve the taxpayer of the enormous cost of the commercial aspects of the enterprise, while fully protecting the public interest in atomic energy. In fact, these provisions carry into effect the 1946 policy declaration of the original Atomic Energy Act, that free competition in private enterprise should be strengthened."

•

Thus ended the long, bitter battle over control of civilian development of nuclear power. Many more battles were yet to come, but enactment of the Atomic Energy Act of 1954 probably represented the high point of enthusiasm over the prospects for creating a new source of energy whose costs had been heralded as too cheap to meter.

Chapter 18

The Dixon-Yates Fiasco

Few battles over public power have commanded more national attention or generated more political heat than the Dixon-Yates affair in 1953.

At the center of the controversy was the Tennessee Valley Authority. In the early 1950s TVA had bitter opponents, but it was generally regarded as one of the prime accomplishments of the New Deal. It had given new hope to the people of the Tennessee Valley by enabling them to raise their standard of living. Many political leaders viewed TVA as an innovative model for what could be accomplished in river basins throughout the United States and other countries. Visitors flocked to the Tennessee Valley from all parts of the world to observe the progress sparked by TVA.

TVA had special significance for public power. In the minds of many observers, it was considered a model for successful public development of electric power. An independent federal agency with broad powers, TVA provided low-cost wholesale power for municipal electric utilities and rural electric cooperatives that distributed electricity to households and commercial and industrial establishments in all or parts of a seven-state region. The power distributors were governed by locally selected boards of directors.

Relationships between TVA and its municipal and rural electric cooperative distributors of power were cordial and interdependent. TVA generated the power, and the distributors supplied the market. The agency had assisted in the establishment of many of the distributors and continued to help them in their day-to-day management. The distributors were happy to accept TVA's responsibility for power supply, because they recognized that a large, integrated system was the most efficient means of providing electricity for the region. They also willingly acceded to TVA's authority to approve the retail rates charged by the distributors. TVA thereby could assure that consumers paid low rates and city officials did not use revenues from the electric systems for unrelated purposes.

But the private power companies continued to attack TVA. They smarted over the loss of their market in the seven states served by TVA. They were embarrassed by comparisons of TVA's low rates and their own substantially higher charges. The private utilities also feared that the TVA model would be replicated in other areas and threaten their continued existence. The power companies found allies among political leaders who opposed the New Deal and federal involvement in what they regarded as the domain of private enterprise.

The utilities and their supporters relentlessly sought to stop TVA's further development. When legal challenges aimed at halting TVA's authority to build steam electric generating plants failed, they employed political means to halt appropriations for new steam plants.

•

In 1952, TVA sought appropriations to build a new steam plant at Fulton, Tennessee, about 30 miles north of Memphis. The facility was needed to serve TVA's growing demand for power in Memphis and the western portion of the TVA system. After a bitter fight, Congress appropriated $150 million so TVA could build the plant. But the November elections that year changed the political dynamics. Gen. Dwight D. Eisenhower was elected president and Republicans captured control of the Senate. President Eisenhower's revised budget in 1953 eliminated funds for the Fulton plant.

TVA supporters were further alarmed when Eisenhower, at a press conference, cited TVA as an example of "creeping socialism." He charged that TVA's low-cost power, subsidized by the federal government, was luring industries from New England.

Within a fortnight after Eisenhower's comments, a delegation of more than 50 persons from the TVA area—including officials of municipal distribution systems, rural electric cooperatives, farm, labor and civic organizations—appeared before a subcommittee of the Senate Appropriations Committee. They made an urgent plea for funds to construct Fulton and other TVA steam generating units. Testifying on behalf of the people of Memphis and the distributors of TVA power, Maj. Thomas C. Allen, president of the municipally owned Memphis Light, Gas & Water Division, said the U.S. government, through TVA, had invited the people of the Tennessee Valley to buy all their power needs from the agency, and TVA agreed through contracts with the municipal and cooperative distributors to supply the power requirements of the area.

Major Allen (who had served as a major in the U.S. Army during World War I) said he did not believe the government would fail to fulfill these moral or legal obligations.

"It has been said that cities and cooperatives should build their own plants," Allen said. "This is not the economical answer. A great number of isolated, small plants cannot produce energy as cheaply as can large plants such as those being built by TVA....Large steam plants integrated with other plants of the TVA system reduce the necessary number of spare units and therefore idle capacity that would be needed."

Allen decried the suggestion that private power companies on the fringe of the TVA service area might provide the needed power. "To supply our needs for the future, these companies would have to build. We can build just as cheaply as they can build, and TVA can build cheaper than either of us."

After the hearing, Tennessee Gov. Frank Clement met for an hour with Eisenhower to discuss the matter, but failed to change the president's views.

By late 1953 the Bureau of the Budget had already initiated conversations with power company officials about an arrangement that became known as the Dixon-Yates proposal. The broad outlines of the deal were spelled out in the president's budget message to Congress on January 21, 1954:

> In order to provide, with appropriate operating reserves, for reasonable growth in industrial, municipal and cooperative power loads in the area through calendar year 1957, arrangements are being made to reduce, by the fall of 1957, existing commitments of the Tennessee Valley Authority to the Atomic Energy Commission by 500,000 to 600,000 kw. This would release the equivalent amount of Tennessee Valley Authority generating capacity to meet increased load requirements in the power system and at the same time eliminate the need for appropriating funds from the Treasury to finance additional generating units.

By mid-June, the other shoe dropped. At a hearing before the congressional Joint Committee on Atomic Energy (JCAE), the Atomic Energy Commission released a letter from Rowland Hughes, director of the Bureau of the Budget, to AEC Chairman Lewis L. Strauss announcing that the administration had ordered AEC to purchase 600 mw from the Dixon-Yates combine. It was revealed that Middle South Utilities (headed by Edgar H. Dixon) and the Southern Company (headed by Eugene A. Yates) wanted to form a new company,

Mississippi Valley Generating Company, which would build a 650-mw power plant at West Memphis, Arkansas. The new company would provide only $5.5 million of the estimated $107.3 million cost of the plant. The remaining amount would be financed through the sale of 30-year bonds to institutional investors. The 95-5 debt-to-equity ratio contrasted sharply with the 60-40 debt-to-equity ratio then required by the Securities and Exchange Commission. The federal government would pay all taxes incurred by the combine.

The Dixon-Yates plant ostensibly would be used to supply power to the AEC production facility at Paducah, Kentucky, which was served by TVA. In reality, the power would be delivered to TVA at Memphis, and used to displace power that TVA furnished to the Memphis area.

It was also revealed that three of the five AEC commissioners had voted not to accept the Dixon-Yates proposal. The dissenting commissioners said the proposal was none of AEC's business.

Witnesses at the hearing were sharply divided about the relative costs of the Fulton and Dixon-Yates plants. AEC staff said the annual cost to the commission under Dixon-Yates would be about $3.7 million greater than for TVA's Fulton plant. TVA Power Manager G.O. Wessenauer told the committee that TVA estimated the total annual cost difference at $5.6 million. The Bureau of the Budget, in its letter to AEC Chairman Strauss ordering the commission to enter into the Dixon-Yates plan, contended that the annual costs, excluding taxes, would be $18.6 million for the private power company plan, compared with $18 million for TVA.

•

News of the proposed contract precipitated an immediate storm of criticism that attracted nationwide attention. The General Accounting Office said the president and the AEC would have to invoke emergency powers in order to contract for power that would be pumped into the TVA system. Rep. Chet Holifield, D-Calif., asked the Securities and Exchange Commission to hold hearings on the matter. Sen. Estes Kefauver, D-Tenn., made a speech on the Senate floor charging that the president's directive was the "entering wedge" that the private utility lobby had been striving for "and on which it has been spending a tremendous slush fund in the nation's capital."

The Senate Judiciary Subcommittee on Anti-Trust and Monopoly Legislation held a hearing on the proposal. The Senate was controlled by Republicans. Fortuitously, the subcommittee chairman was Sen. William Langer, R-N.D., a populist maverick who was a strong supporter of public power and rural electrification. Sen. Kefauver was also on the subcommittee.

In a closed session, the subcommittee heard testimony about a proposal for another alternative to the TVA Fulton plant that had been rejected by the administration. This was a proposal by a banking syndicate headed by Walter Von Tresckow that would finance construction of a generating plant at Fulton. Under this proposal Von Tresckow would receive a fee of $4 million for financing construction of the plant, but ownership would transfer to the government after the investment had been amortized. Cost of power to the government would be lower under the Von Tresckow proposal than under the Dixon-Yates plan. Von Tresckow's attorney, Lucius Burch Jr., issued a statement charging that under Dixon-Yates the "economic loss to the people of the Tennessee Valley makes Teapot Dome look like a game of tiddlywinks."[1]

After initial hearings, the subcommittee concluded that the proposed Dixon-Yates contract might not be "the result of free and fair competition with competing groups" and that the plant might cost the government $90 million more than other options. The subcommittee adopted a resolution opposing implementation of the proposed contract until the full committee completed hearings and a report.

Asked at a press conference why he ordered the AEC to enter into the controversial contract, President Eisenhower charged that TVA had gone overboard in constructing steam plants to firm up water power development. Now, TVA was building plants on the periphery of its service area and might seek to expand its territory, he said. Eisenhower said he wanted to take a good look at the problem from every angle and tell the people what was the best future for that region and how far they could continue to build up the area at the expense of others. In view of the impending power shortage in the area, President Eisenhower said the Dixon-Yates contract would give the administration a chance to study the problem.

R. V. Taylor, president of the Tennessee Valley Public Power Association, promptly sent a letter to President Eisenhower charging that the Dixon-Yates proposal was "an effort to sell this area back to

---

[1] "Teapot Dome" referred to rich oil reserves owned by the United States in Wyoming. During the Harding administration, it was the subject of a scandal involving Secretary of the Interior Albert B. Fall, who negotiated the sale of the valuable reserves to a private party at a price that was considered a pittance of the worth of the reserves.

the power trust." The Dixon-Yates scheme "would place a plant at an uneconomical location; it would require an extra investment in transmission, extra cost of transportation of coal, and extra consumption of fuel, labor and materials to offset the energy lost in unnecessary longer transmission," Taylor said.

Meanwhile, controversy over Dixon-Yates was raging on several fronts. As part of the extended debate on amendments to the Atomic Energy Act of 1946, the Senate adopted an amendment authorizing the government to enter into the Dixon-Yates arrangement.

The Joint Committee on Atomic Energy was preparing to hold hearings on the contract. A major issue was whether the JCAE would waive a requirement that the contract should lie before the committee for 30 days, while Congress was in session, before it could be executed by AEC.

APPA, TVA distributors and the National Farmers Union called on the Securities and Exchange Commission to hold hearings on the contract. In a letter to the SEC, I said full public hearings were needed to explore whether the proposed stock issue would violate the Public Utility Holding Company Act of 1935.

•

In the midst of this furor, another bombshell burst. J.D. Stietenroth, secretary-treasurer of Mississippi Power & Light Company, which was part of Middle South Utilities, Inc., one of the two holding company partners of the Dixon-Yates combine, issued a statement charging that Middle South was dominated by "Wall Street" interests who had "coercively" forced rates that were costing MP&L customers millions of dollars annually. Stietenroth had been with the company for 26 years, had been secretary-treasurer for 17 years and was the utility's principal financial and accounting officer. His lengthy statement was printed in full under large, three-column headlines on the front page of the *Memphis Commercial Appeal.* Stietenroth charged that MP&L had at least two sets of books, the regular corporate books kept in Jackson, Mississippi, and tax books kept by Ebasco Services, Inc., a consulting firm engaged by Middle South Utilities.

"Mississippi Power & Light Company does not now and it never has in its entire history since 1927 prepared its own income tax returns." Stietenroth said. "As a matter of fact Mississippi Power & Light Company not only has never been permitted to employ competent persons to handle its income tax work, but even if it had competent people to do the work it would be absolutely impossible for us to prepare our income tax returns because we have never been able to get the tax books away from Ebasco

Services, Inc. or Electric Bond and Share Company"[2]

Stietenroth proposed that the officers and directors of the company "combine together and, with the help of God, the members of the organization, and the people of Mississippi, that we plead with said persons, sometimes referred to as 'Wall Street,' to permit us to exercise the powers and prerogatives and perform the duties of our respective offices and that, if said permission is not granted, we stand together and insist upon the right to do so, even if they discharge each and every one of us....

"This is my proposal and I pledge my support to it so long as I am an officer of the Mississippi Power & Light Company, which in all probability will not be for long."

Stietenroth's prediction about his tenure with the company quickly materialized. Hours after his statement was released to the news media, MP&L President R. Baxter Wilson announced that Stietenroth had been relieved of his duties. The secretary-treasurer had been fired because of "irreconcilable differences of opinion between himself and company management with respect to long established and accepted policies," Baxter said. The company's books and records were kept according to methods prescribed by the Federal Power Commission, and the company was subject to the jurisdiction of the SEC as well as FPC, he said.

•

The Stietenroth revelations were like manna from heaven for the Senate Judiciary Subcommittee on Monopoly and Antitrust Legislation. The panel quickly summoned Stietenroth to testify at hearings.

The *APPA Weekly Newsletter* described Stietenroth's testimony as "the most detailed revelations of big utility company financial maneuvers since the holding company investigations two decades ago."

Under questioning from subcommittee counsel Sidney Davis, Stietenroth said Middle South, Ebasco Services, Inc., and Reid & Priest, attorneys, (all of 2 Rector Street, New York, New York.) determined financial policies of MP&L, ordered improper transfers and records of company funds, contracted for major equipment, determined what facilities should be built, negotiated with the Bureau of Internal Revenue and Securities and Exchange Commission and simply presented MP&L directors with blank "signature pages" needed to complete financial transactions.

---

[2] Electric Bond and Share Company was the holding company for Middle South Utilities.

The *APPA Weekly Newsletter* of October 1, 1954 reported on the hearings:

During his 26 years with MP&L, Mr. Stietenroth said, Mississippi ratepayers paid 9 percent dividends to Middle South, not only on the holding company's original investment, but also on $3 million worth of stock dividends declared at the "suggestion" of the sole common stockholder, Middle South. "There is nothing so sure as death, taxes and tribute to Electric Bond and Share Company if you live in the 'Tri-state colonial empire,'" he said.

MP&L ratepayers, he said, "paid the bills" for two hunting lodges which cost "in the neighborhood of $200,000." The lodges, he said, are set up in the company's accounts as "Electric Plant in Service," and disbursements for operating cost, food and "miscellaneous merchandise" are "so well scattered throughout the records until I doubt if it would be possible to get them all together."...

Mr. Stietenroth said that although he was principal financial and accounting officer of MP&L, he had never prepared the company's tax return. He signed the returns as they were sent to him from New York, usually on the same day that they were to be turned in...

He said MP&L received an unexpected bonanza in the form of accelerated amortization allowances which brought about the problem of what to do with the funds, which would total $7 million to $8 million in deferred taxes. When he first read over the criteria for rapid amortization certificates, the official said, "I said what's this got to do with us? We can't possibly begin to qualify for this." Nevertheless, he later filed applications and "we began to pay less taxes as a result."

Mr. Stietenroth said he believed these funds should be held in a reserve fund since they represented a deferred liability—"certainly not profit." E.H. Dixon, president of Middle South, overruled the decision made by a group meeting in the "throne room," (Mr. Dixon's New York office) and insisted that the funds be carried into the surplus account, where they would be available for dividend purposes.

Stietenroth gave other examples of Middle South's domination of its operating companies. The holding company ordered major equipment direct from such suppliers as General Electric and Westinghouse for delivery to MP&L and other operating companies. As a result, MP&L had excess capacity, which had the effect of putting a mortgage on MP&L property for the sake of the Middle South system. Asked whether this meant ratepayers in Mississippi were subsidizing companies in other states, Stietenroth replied: "Our ratepayers pay our bills and that is bound to be the ultimate effect."

Although Stietenroth devoted most of his testimony to relationships between MP&L and Middle South Utilities, he recounted conversations he had at the New York headquarters of Middle South about Dixon-Yates. At one point, in discussing the Dixon-Yates contract with Paul Hallingby, Dixon's assistant, Stietenroth said he was advised that it was "all right. It is on the rails…and the rails are greased."

Arkansas Governor Sidney S. McMath, also a witness at the subcommittee's hearings, told about the political power exercised by Arkansas Power & Light Company another of the four Middle South operating companies.

Arthur E. McLean, president of the Commercial National Bank of Little Rock, called AP&L's recent application for a 15 percent rate increase "the most flagrant attempt to confuse a commission it has ever been my pleasure to observe." He said his sole purpose in testifying before the subcommittee was "to stop the greed of a few of the utilities that will destroy themselves. I do not want to see a return to some of the things that took place 20 years ago. I do not think these utilities can afford to see another debacle."

Former TVA Chairman Gordon Clapp testified that "the most important objection to the Dixon-Yates deal is that it represents the formation of a combine of two big holding companies who have a long record of determination to do anything that would cripple the TVA and thereby remove the salutary effects of the competition that TVA was giving them."

He said the proposal also was aimed at the 150 municipal electric distributors and rural electric cooperatives, which he called "full-fledged partners with the United States government through their contracts with TVA—a partnership set up long before we heard all the talk about partnership."

•

While the Langer subcommittee was holding hearings on the Dixon-Yates contract, the AEC announced it had approved the contract on October 5. The commission asked the JCAE to waive the requirement that the contract lie before the committee for a 30-day period while Congress was in session.

Announcement of the JCAE's intention to hold a hearing on the 30-day waiver triggered a vitriolic statement by Congressman Holifield, a member of the JCAE. He said his preliminary study of the contract had convinced him that it was "the most fantastic and obscurely worded government document" he had read in his 12 years in the Congress.

"This document is the brainchild of smart utility lawyers," Representative Holifield charged. "It is couched in legalistic double talk and technical jargon to conceal the naked fact that the government is obligating itself to pay the Dixon-Yates interests one-half billion dollars over the next 25 years.

"The contract is completely one-sided in favor of the company," he said. "Only token concessions have been obtained by the government. These concessions are for window-dressing purposes. The Atomic Energy Commission is trying hard to make this shabby deal look a little more presentable."

Representative Holifield's statement brought President Eisenhower into the act once again. At a press conference, he defended the Dixon-Yates contract, saying it had been approved by the FPC and TVA, and he felt the government was fully protected. It was later revealed at a JCAE hearing that there were dissenting votes on the TVA board and at the Federal Power Commission. Asked to comment on Stietenroth's testimony, the president was evasive. He said he knew of no one in the government whose common sense and business acumen he trusted more than AEC Chairman Lewis L. Strauss.

•

The Dixon-Yates battleground shifted to the JCAE, which opened hearings on the contract in early November 1954. The proposal to waive the 30-day waiting period assumed critical importance because Congress had adjourned, meaning the waiting period could not begin until the following year. In addition, the November elections handed control of the Senate back to the Democrats, who felt they would have the votes necessary to kill the contract when the new Congress convened.

Administration witnesses at the JCAE hearings wanted a waiver of the waiting period so construction could begin before adverse winter weather conditions set in. They said the contract had been amended to give the government the right to recapture the plant within three years after its effective date. Other amendments established a ceiling on the rate of return that the Dixon-Yates companies could make on their equity investment; required AEC approval of architect-engineers and the general contractor; and committed Middle South and Southern Company to provide 100 mw from their systems if the Dixon-Yates plant was not operating within 36 months after the effective date of the contract.

I was among the first of several opponents to testify. "Dixon-Yates is but the opening wedge in the crippling of TVA, and with the destruction of that agency the people of the nation will have lost one of their most effective allies in bringing lower electric rates and greater consumption of electricity to all of the homes, farms and industries of the nation," I said.

During the hearings, President Eisenhower sent a letter to JCAE

Chairman W. Sterling Cole, R-N.Y., arguing that "if the federal government assumes responsibility in perpetuity for providing the TVA area with all the power it can accept, generated by any means whatsoever, it has a similar responsibility with respect to every other area and region and corner of the United States."

•

As expected, the Republican-controlled JCAE voted 10-8 along party lines to waive the 30-day waiting period. Action then moved to the Securities and Exchange Commission, where a bitter new struggle took place, largely around the question of the amount of equity capital to be invested in the venture.

The Dixon-Yates combine had requested SEC approval only for the issuance of common stock, which represented 5 percent of the financing required for the plant. Tennessee and TVA power distributors asked the commission to extend the scope of the hearing to 11 additional issues. After hearing a number of witnesses over a period of several weeks, the SEC concluded its hearings on December 21, 1954, but was not expected to render a decision until late January 1955.

•

In February 1955 Major Allen said Memphis would build its own plant at Fulton, Tennessee. The move did not make economic sense, he said, because TVA could supply power more efficiently. But Memphis would build the plant to stop the Dixon-Yates deal.

Within a week after Allen's announcement, another bombshell was dropped. In a speech on the Senate floor, Sen. Lister Hill, D-Ala., charged that Adolphe H. Wenzell, a vice president and director of First Boston Corporation, secretly participated in early Dixon-Yates negotiations as a Bureau of the Budget consultant, at the same time that his firm was dealing with the Dixon-Yates combine for financing the proposed steam plant. The AEC previously had released what was purported to be a complete chronology of the Dixon-Yates affair, but Wenzell's role was not mentioned. His participation was uncovered by the state of Tennessee's attorney, Joe Volpe.

Further information about Wenzell's role came to light in June, when Governor Clement of Tennessee testified before the Tennessee Valley Authority-Atomic Energy Commission panel of the Senate Appropriations Committee. The governor said Wenzell "was serving two masters" and that Budget Bureau Director Rowland Hughes had "concealed the fact that Mr. Wenzell was working on the Dixon-Yates matter."

Governor Clement said "there was a deliberate attempt to withhold this information from the public," and that "many of the participants in the Dixon-Yates deal have been reckless with the truth, and I believe I am being charitable when I put it that way."

The Senate Judiciary Subcommittee on Antitrust and Monopoly Legislation held a hearing on the Wenzell matter on the evening of June 30, 1955. Democrats now controlled the Senate, and Senator Kefauver chaired the subcommittee. Minutes before the hearing was to begin, the White House announced that the president had asked the Bureau of the Budget to confer with TVA and AEC to determine "whether it is in the interest of the people of the area now to continue or cancel" the Dixon-Yates contract. The White House announcement was interpreted as a sign that the Dixon-Yates contract was to be scuttled soon. Upon receipt of news of the announcement, the subcommittee promptly postponed its hearings.

Nonetheless, Dixon-Yates opponents continued their pressure. A week later, Wenzell was called before the Kefauver subcommittee to answer questions about three meetings he had attended early in 1954 when he served as a Budget Bureau consultant while First Boston was the financial agent for the Dixon-Yates holding companies. No record of any of these meetings appeared in the AEC chronology. It was revealed that Wenzell had signed into the AEC as an official of First Boston when he attended a hitherto secret meeting arranged by Budget Director Hughes with AEC Chairman Strauss.

At his weekly press conference on July 6, 1955, President Eisenhower said he was "delighted" by Memphis' decision to build a steam plant. He hinted strongly at the cancellation of the government's contract with the Dixon-Yates combine, once the "complete feasibility" of the Memphis plant was established. In less than a week—on July 11, 1955—President Eisenhower finally ordered the cancellation of the Dixon-Yates contract, after conferring with Memphis officials on the city's plan to construct its own steam plant.

APPA President W.E. Hooper, general manager of Sheffield Utilities in Alabama, sent a telegram to Major Allen: "Your courageous and steadfast position against the forces which seek to destroy all public power shall long be remembered and honored by those who believe that our citizens have the right to be served by power systems of their own choosing. All of those who oppose domination in any form are indebted to you and your associates."

Chapter 19

TVA Gets New Access to Funds

The Dixon-Yates controversy stimulated action by the president, Congress and the Tennessee Valley Authority to consider legislation authorizing TVA to issue revenue bonds in the private financial market. Granting TVA such authority was not a new concept. As early as 1948, after TVA had experienced serious difficulty obtaining appropriations for the Johnsonville steam plant, the board directed the staff to study funding alternatives. One possibility was to issue bonds. However, the staff found so many problems with these concepts that no recommendations were made.

In the autumn of 1954, in the midst of the Dixon-Yates controversy, TVA again began studying bond financing. The TVA board recognized that bond financing would be more costly than appropriations, but felt there would be compensating advantages. Uncertainty over funding would be removed, planning could proceed on a more orderly basis and annual political fights over appropriations would be avoided.

President Eisenhower mentioned the TVA study in his budget message to Congress in January 1955. A month later the TVA board of directors unanimously recommended that TVA be permitted to issue revenue bonds. The board also recommended that bonds sold by TVA be secured solely by power revenues and not guaranteed by the U.S. Treasury. The bonds therefore would not be part of the national debt. Interest on the bonds would not be exempt from federal taxation and no ceiling would be placed on the amount of bonds that could be issued. In effect, the market would establish the limit on TVA's debt. TVA also would revise its procedures for repaying federal appropriations.

The proposals received a mixed reaction. S.R. Finley, general superintendent of the Chattanooga Electric Power Board and a former president of APPA, "heartily" approved the recommendations. Senators

Lister Hill, D-Ala., and Estes Kefauver, D-Tenn., tentatively praised the report, but Sen. Albert Gore Sr., D-Tenn., said the bond proposal would result in rate increases in the valley unless the bond issues were guaranteed directly or indirectly by the Treasury. Purcell L. Smith, the power companies' chief lobbyist in Washington, said the plan contained "loopholes you can drive a wagon through."

The Eisenhower administration sent its legislative proposal for revenue bond financing to Congress in late May 1955. The TVA board's proposal was changed drastically by 23 amendments proposed by the Bureau of the Budget, predecessor to the Office of Management and Budget.[1] The bureau's recommendations produced a split among TVA directors. Chairman Herbert D. Vogel, an Eisenhower appointee, said the bureau's proposals presented "no serious obstacles or restrictions in the operations of TVA." Board members Harry A. Curtis and Raymond R. Paty disagreed.

Differences between TVA and the Budget Bureau fueled a controversy that lasted the next four years. TVA directors Curtis and Paty disagreed with the Budget Bureau recommendation to limit TVA bonded indebtedness to $750 million. They also opposed including TVA revenue bonds in the federal budget and national debt, since the the Treasury Department did not guarantee the bonds. They objected to a proposal that TVA both amortize and pay interest on prior federal appropriations it had received for power facilities. They likewise opposed a proposal to give the secretary of the treasury authority over the timing, amounts and terms of TVA revenue bond issues.

APPA, the Tennessee Valley Public Power Association, the National Rural Electric Cooperative Association, Citizens for TVA, labor, farm and other organizations supported bills that generally followed the recommendations of the TVA board majority. Sen. Robert S. Kerr, D-Okla., chairman of the Public Works Subcommittee on Flood Control-Rivers and Harbors, introduced legislation that embodied the Curtis-Paty proposal. Representatives Clifford Davis, D-Tenn., chairman, and Robert E. Jones, D-Ala., member, of the Public Works Subcommittee on Flood Control, introduced companion legislation in the House.

In 1956, action on the revenue bond legislation was sidetracked as the president and Congress turned attention to other TVA issues, notably

---

[1] The Budget Bureau was long considered hostile to TVA. The bureau resented the fact that Congress, in an effort to give TVA greater flexibility, exempted TVA from certain bureau controls imposed on other federal agencies.

whether TVA could use its revenues to build additional power facilities and whether TVA should accelerate the repayment of its appropriated debt. TVA, which favored the first proposal and opposed the second, won both of these battles.

•

The tempo of activity on revenue bond legislation picked up in 1957, when extensive hearings were held in the House and Senate. In April, Rep. Howard Baker, R-Tenn.,[2] told a House Public Works subcommittee that "it is absolutely essential ...that a fair and workable financing bill be passed this session of Congress."

TVA Manager of Power G.O. Wessenauer was the principal witness at the House hearing. He spent four days on the witness stand, much of that time answering questions from Republican members of the subcommittee who opposed the bill's lack of a ceiling on the amount of bonds TVA could issue. Critics also complained that the bill placed no limitation on the TVA power system service area and would remove some of Congress' control of TVA's power program.

Wessenauer said the ceiling on TVA bonds would be set by the power requirements of the system. TVA's service area, he explained, was already limited by the TVA Act and there would be "an adverse effect" on areas outside the Tennessee Valley if the potential of TVA as a competitor were further walled in.[3]

On the question of congressional control, Wessenauer said TVA was a creature of Congress and was always subject to changes in the TVA Act. Under the proposed legislation, TVA would report to Congress before building new power plants and Congress would have time to veto any TVA proposal it considered undesirable, he said.

By summer 1957 supporters of the self-financing bill were optimistic that it could be passed during that Congress. In the first week of June, the Senate Public Works Committee held extensive hearings. By that time, three bills were before the committee: S.1855, by Senator Kerr, which generally followed the recommendations of the TVA board of directors;

---

[2] Baker subsequently was elected to the Senate, became Majority Leader, and during the Reagan Administration was named chief of staff to the President.

[3] Circumscribing TVA's service area was a sensitive issue for TVA and public power supporters. They did not envision major expansion of the TVA service area, but felt that if TVA's service area were defined by legislation, the threat of TVA as a viable competitor would be removed, to the detriment of consumers in the surrounding area. They were also concerned about several cities that had been attempting for many years to obtain TVA power and would be foreclosed from doing so if legislation banned them from such service.

S. 1855, by Sen. John Sherman Cooper, R-Ky., and S. 2145 by Sen. Edward Martin, R-Pa. Although Sen. Cooper was a strong supporter of TVA, his bill incorporated some of the recommendations of the Budget Bureau, such as the $750 million cap on outstanding bonds. However, he rejected the recommendation to give the bureau control over TVA financing. Senator Martin's bill went much further than Senator Cooper's. It would not only limit TVA's bonds to $750 million and establish a "wall" around TVA's service area; it also would impose other financial obligations on TVA. Senator Martin said an increase of "only 24 percent" in TVA's rates would "be ample to meet the requirements" of his bill.

William S. Peterson, general manager and chief engineer of the Los Angeles Department of Water & Power, who was then APPA president, testified against the $750 million ceiling, which would be "totally out of keeping with normal revenue bond procedures for a growing industry such as a power system," he said. He also opposed a territorial limitation.

In late June 1955, the Senate Public Works Committee approved the Kerr bill by a vote of 9 to 2, but amended it to include several Budget Bureau recommendations. The amended bill put a $750 million ceiling on TVA's outstanding bonds. TVA estimated it would need $150 million a year to build new generating capacity. After five years, TVA would need congressional approval to increase the debt ceiling. The bill required TVA to report its plans for new power plants to the president and Congress. Congress would have 60 days to disapprove proposed projects. TVA would be restricted to using bond proceeds for projects to serve counties that lay "in whole or in part" within the Tennessee River drainage basin or the then-existing TVA power service area, with a few specific exceptions.

Less than a month after the Senate Public Works Committee voted out the TVA bill, the House Public Works Committee approved the Davis-Jones bill without the bond cap or service area restrictions.

The full Senate adopted a series of amendments to the Kerr bill and passed it, 61 to 20, on August 9, 1957. However, supporters had to pay a price. The bill was amended to require TVA to pay $10 million annually into the U.S. Treasury. This would be in addition to TVA's "return on appropriation investment" payment, equal to the average interest rate payable by the Treasury on the government's outstanding debt. The Senate also limited expansion of TVA's then-existing service area. The only expansion permitted would be to accommodate growth in communities already receiving TVA power.

Although TVA supporters opposed these amendments, we agreed the advantages of bond financing would outweigh the new restrictions imposed on TVA.

The power companies and their allies felt the amendments did not go far enough. They succeeded in stalling action in the House. By late July 1958, largely as a result of pressure from the private power companies, the House Public Works Committee held hearings on the Senate-passed bill. The three-day session brought out a veritable who's-who of power company leaders.

The heat engendered by the issue was illustrated by an incident involving Senator Cooper, who was in the crowded hearing room waiting to testify in favor of the Senate bill. Senator Cooper exploded when his administrative assistant, Lee C. White, relayed a message from a coal company executive warning the senator against speaking in favor of the bill.

"You tell him he can go to hell," Senator Cooper declared in a clearly audible voice. "Those people needn't think they can tell me whether to be for or against a bill."

Senator Cooper told news reporters after the incident that he "just got so mad I blew up and shouted. After all, I've been working on this bill two years and this is the first time the coal people ever said anything to me about it. They have a right to present their views any time they want to, but they can't pressure me, they can't tell me when and what to testify."

Power company arguments generally followed the line that TVA did not need the bill, that TVA had embarked on a vast program of territorial expansion and that the bill would encourage further expansion.

Despite the strong opposition of the power companies, the United States Chamber of Commerce, the American Coal Sales Association, Associated General Contractors, National Society of Professional Engineers, and other organizations and individuals, the House Public Works Committee approved the Kerr bill by a party line vote of 19 to 15 on July 30, 1958.

By then, the odds for the bill's enactment seemed good. However, supporters did not count on the power of a single man—Rep. Howard W. Smith, D-Va., chairman of the House Rules Committee—to do mischief. Representative Smith was missing for a week and he did not call a committee meeting to vote on the bill. He resisted all efforts, including a plea from House Speaker Sam Rayburn, D-Texas, to get the Rules Committee to act. With the imminent adjournment of Congress, Smith successfully bottled up the bill by refusing to call a meeting of his committee. Supporters vowed to continue the fight in the next Congress.

Speaker Rayburn said he hoped "to get it up early next year. It is a good bill and I am strong for it."

•

Events moved rapidly as the first session of the 86th Congress opened in January 1959. President Eisenhower's budget message again urged Congress to "take action early in this session...in order that the authority may meet its needs for new generating facilities." Within a week, seven Congressmen from the Tennessee Valley introduced a bill identical to the one that had passed the Senate the previous year.

In March the House Public Works Committee once more held hearings on the bill. The principal focus was the power companies' insistence on erecting a tightly built "wall" around the TVA service area. Carrying the message for the companies was Rep. Carl Vinson, D-Ga., a powerful member of the House who headed the Armed Services Committee. Vinson said the proposed bill "contains a number of loopholes, ambiguities and exceptions, which could be used to expand TVA's existing service area virtually without limit." He submitted an amendment to freeze TVA's sales to the areas it served on July 1, 1957.

Chattanooga's Finley, president of the Tennessee Valley Public Power Association, challenged the need for a "wall" around TVA, pointing out that there had been no consequential change in the agency's service area for the past 12 years.

"Perhaps those who advocate a tight, non-elastic Chinese wall encirclement around the present TVA service area are much more interested in a tight Chinese wall encirclement around their own present rate structures," Finley declared. "If there is to be a boundary line of electric service it must have some elasticity on account of the unknown future physical changes in the area and the future unknown wishes of people who have a right to make certain decisions concerning their own problems."

A witness for the U.S. Chamber of Commerce opposed the bill as "unnecessary, unsound, and not in the public interest." However, if Congress were to proceed, he urged adoption of the service territory limitation; elimination of the sole-supplier clause in TVA's contracts with its wholesale customers; review of TVA wholesale rates by the Federal Power Commission and establishment of rates that "reflect all costs of producing the power." He also wanted TVA to make interest payments on the federal government's remaining capital investment in power facilities. Power company officials expressed similar views.

City Manager Lloyd Emergy of Paducah, Kentucky, sent the

committee a telegram noting that his city had been trying for 20 years to obtain power from TVA, but was frustrated by continuous legal challenges by the local utility.

"It would be most unjust to deny the city of Paducah, which is within 20 miles of the largest TVA dam and is on the banks of the Tennessee River, the right to acquire TVA power," Emergy told the committee.

The House Public Works Committee approved the bill in mid-March, after adopting the Vinson amendment to ban expansion of TVA's service territory. The bill moved to the House floor, where it was approved 245 to 170. TVA supporters felt they could not win a vote to delete the Vinson amendment, so made no effort to strike it.

The key vote in the House came on an amendment offered by Rep. William C. Cramer, R-Fla., which would have subjected any proposed bond issue to the veto of the Budget Bureau. The proposal was defeated, 129 to 170.

In mid-June 1959 the Senate Public Works Committee again took up the legislation. Harllee Branch Jr., president of the Southern Company, pleaded for "protection" from TVA for the power companies. To refute his assertion, I submitted a statement pointing out that Southern Company had increased its dividends for five consecutive years and had launched a half-billion dollar expansion program.

On June 19, the Senate Public Works Committee unanimously approved an amended version of H.R. 3460, which had been passed by the full House the previous month. The Senate version modified slightly the freeze on TVA's service area, increased TVA's cash payments to the Treasury and modified provisions on Treasury Department and Budget Bureau review of the TVA bond issues. Chairman Kerr called the measure "an excellent bill."

Nevertheless, stumbling blocks continued to confront the bill. Less than a week after the committee's action, Senator Kerr appeared on the Senate floor to ask that the bill be recommitted to the committee. He said "certain senators" asked to see the committee report after it was written to "offer suggestions or amendments or disagreeing views." This had not been done, Senator Kerr said.

Expansion of TVA's service area was the sticking point.. The bill approved by the committee would allow a maximum change of 2.5 percent in the TVA service area, but private power companies were not satisfied, and continued to lobby for a tighter restriction.

Coal companies supported the power companies. This became apparent when the committee's report was filed on July 2. It contained four-page supplemental views of Sen. Jennings Randolph, D-W.Va. Noting that the economy of West Virginia was vitally affected by the coal industry, Sen. Randolph said he was concerned not only about the "stability" of the private power companies, which were major customers of the coal companies, but he was also disturbed "by the size of TVA and the powerful bargaining position it has achieved with respect to its purchase of coal, as well as by the manner in which it has used that bargaining power." Senator Randolph complained that the amendment adopted by the committee would not prohibit a TVA wholesale customer from reselling power to another wholesale customer outside the wall.

The full Senate passed the bill 61 to 20, after supporters agreed to accept a more rigid territorial amendment proposed by Senator Randolph and Sen. Eugene Talmadge, D-Ga.

At that point only relatively minor differences separated the Senate and House versions. To speed passage, Rep. Clifford Davis, D-Tenn., author of the House bill, moved to have the House accept the Senate bill a week after the Senate vote. This would have made it unnecessary for the bill to be referred to a conference between the Senate and House. However, House Minority Leader Charles Halleck, R-Ind., blocked it. The Budget Bureau was unhappy because the Senate bill did not give the bureau veto power over TVA. President Eisenhower continued to make negative statements about the bill.

Finally, on July 23, the House agreed, by voice vote, to accept the Senate amendments, thus completing congressional action. However, there was uncertainty about whether President Eisenhower would sign it. He did so on August 6, after receiving assurances from congressional leaders that legislation would be passed swiftly to delete a provision that gave Congress, not the executive branch, effective review of TVA's power construction program. True to the word of its leaders, the Senate that afternoon approved a measure deleting the language the president objected to and the House followed suit the following week.

As finally signed into law, the bill gave TVA authority to issue bonds in the private money market, but set a $750 million ceiling on TVA's bonded indebtedness.[4] The legislation also put a wall around TVA, but allowed TVA the flexibility to add six cities in Kentucky and two each in Georgia and Tennessee to its service area. TVA was mandated to amortize its existing appropriated debt by a progressively higher annual payment to the Treasury

---

[4] Subsequently, Congress successively raised the ceiling to its current level of $30 billion.

until a total of $1 billion of the appropriated investment had been repaid.[5] TVA also was mandated to make an annual payment to the Treasury of interest on its outstanding appropriations investment. Considered as a "return on the appropriation investment," the payment was based on the average interest rate payable by the Treasury on its total marketable public obligations. However, TVA was not required to obtain Budget Bureau approval before issuing new debt within its ceiling.

The revenue bond legislation did not give TVA as much flexibility as some of its supporters had desired, but on balance they felt the bill represented a major gain for the agency's power program.

The TVA bond legislation remains unique. No other federal power agency has been given comparable authority.

---

[5] Payments were to begin at $10 million a year, and after 10 years would rise to $20 million a year. As of the end of fiscal year 1960, the appropriation investment in TVA's power program was approximately $1.2 billion. The amount that was not to be repaid, approximately $200 million, was to be considered as the government's equity in the system.

Chapter 20

The St. Lawrence Project Fight

The Northeastern United States had long been neglected in low-cost hydroelectric power development, despite its abundant resources. The region had the potential to develop 800 mw of capacity on the St. Lawrence River, and 2,400 mw through redevelopment of a site at Niagara Falls.

The potential for water power development in the international section of the St. Lawrence River was recognized as early as 1911, in a study released by Gen. W.H. Bixby, chief of the U.S. Army Corps of Engineers. He said up to five million horsepower of electrical energy could be developed between Ogdensburg, New York, and Montreal, Canada. Subsequent studies by the United States and Canada confirmed these prospects as well as the possibility for creating a seaway for ocean-going ships stretching almost 2,000 miles from Duluth, Minnesota, to the mouth of the St. Lawrence River in Quebec.

Franklin D. Roosevelt was an enthusiastic supporter of the St. Lawrence project. When he was governor of New York, the state Legislature in 1931 created the Power Authority of the State of New York (PASNY)[1] to improve the International Rapids Section of the St. Lawrence River near Massena, New York, in cooperation with U.S. and Canadian authorities.

A water-use treaty signed in 1950 between the United States and Canada cleared the way for additional power development at Niagara Falls. The original redevelopment plans called for construction of a new power plant with more than 1,300 mw of installed capacity. Niagara Mohawk Power Corporation's existing 360-mw Schoellkopf station, built in three sections between 1903 and 1924, and located about a mile

---

[1] PASNY's name was later changed to New York Power Authority.

below the falls, would remain.

Although both the St. Lawrence and Niagara projects had strong supporters, their construction was delayed for many years, largely because of their international scope. Private power companies opposed both projects, which they viewed as a threat to their near-monopoly position in the region. Railroads, some eastern ports and coal companies all opposed the projects too.

•

By the early 1950s, the impetus for the St. Lawrence Seaway and Power Project had accelerated and the International Joint Commission was considering the joint application of the governments of Canada and the United States to construct the power features. APPA's interests were directed primarily toward assuring that consumer-owned utilities—local public agencies and rural electric cooperatives—would receive preference in purchasing wholesale power from the St. Lawrence project.

We faced a difficult political situation. Although there were 125 municipal electric utilities in New York and New England, most were small and, in the aggregate, served only 300,000 customers. Consequently, they did not have a great deal of political clout. They also lacked experience in dealing with a controversial national issue requiring action by the president, the Congress and regulatory agencies.

On the other hand, public power supporters had important arguments in their favor. Power costs in the region were among the highest in the United States and a good case could be made for projects that would bring Northeast consumers the benefits of a large block of low-cost power. APPA and rural electric cooperatives formed an alliance with labor, farm and consumer groups to advocate public power development, with preference in marketing power to consumer-owned utilities.

If the IJC approved the project, the Power Authority of the State of New York would build it under license from the Federal Power Commission. Ontario Hydroelectric Power Commission, a public corporation created by the province of Ontario, would build the Canadian portion.

In a statement to the IJC, APPA pointed out that the municipal distribution systems in New York and New England paid wholesale power costs that were more than double those in areas with federal hydro power. The amount paid by residential customers for 100 kwh of electricity in New England or New York would buy almost 250 kwh in Tennessee or Washington, we noted.

Shortly after APPA filed its statement with the IJC, I was invited to speak at the annual meeting in Saranac, New York, of the Municipal Electric Utilities Association of New York. My wife, Sara, and I drove to the meeting and enjoyed the beauty of upstate New York during the fall. Managers and public officials of the municipal utilities in the Northeast had been subjected to power company campaigns against preference and a national advertising program that branded public power as "socialism." To counter these arguments, I devoted my speech to explaining the need for the preference clause and answering power companies' arguments against it. I explained that while APPA supported construction of the St. Lawrence project as quickly as possible, "it is equally important that the benefits of this project should be made available to the greatest number of consumers in accordance with long-established principles." I described the preference clause as an "equality clause" and pointed out that, without it, power from public projects would be sold almost exclusively to private utilities and the municipal and cooperative utilities would not get their fair share.

•

PASNY had filed an application with the Federal Power Commission to build the U.S. portion of the St. Lawrence power project. In mid-November 1952, the APPA board of directors authorized staff to intervene before the FPC to make the case for preference in marketing power from the St. Lawrence hydroelectric project. APPA General Counsel Northcutt Ely appeared before the commission in December. He said:

> There is at the threshold in this matter an issue of policy which may be of great historic interest in the development of the relationship of the publicly owned power systems of this nation to the United States and to the method of development by state agencies proposed here. Over a period of more than 40 years, there has developed in the federal statutes a very definite and certain policy for the protection of publicly owned and operated power systems referred to by the somewhat inaccurate title of the preference clause....If this project were developed by the United States, consequently, we know precisely what our protection would be under existing federal law. The project now before you is going forward as an alternate to a federal development in consequence of the application to the International Joint Commission...in which our government proposed that the power features be developed by an entity to be designated by the government of the United States.
>
> Our position briefly is that if the state of New York is designated as the entity to carry out this power development under that international agreement, we are entitled to the same protection from the projects developed by that agency as if it were developed by the principal, the United States.

The importance of our intervention was underscored during Ely's cross-examination of PASNY Chairman John Burton. Responding to Ely's interrogation, Burton declared that, although the state of New York was demanding a preference from FPC in obtaining a license for the project, the power authority did not feel it should pass this preference on to local public agencies in marketing the power at wholesale.

A week later, I testified before the FPC and cited the historical precedence of the preference provisions in national legislation. I described the benefits realized by ultimate consumers under public preference marketing and noted that public agency preference was consistent with the purposes of New York's Power Authority Act, which required that the St. Lawrence hydro development be primarily for the benefit of the people of the state as a whole, particularly rural and domestic consumers.

Sen. John F. Kennedy, D-Mass., asked the FPC to guarantee that a share of the St. Lawrence Project power would be allocated to New England and Massachusetts.

"Provision should also be made for assuring the availability of a fair share of the power for the municipally owned utilities in the region, of which there are 40 in Massachusetts, in a manner consistent with traditional American policies for the marketing of publicly developed hydroelectric power," Kennedy said.

Senator Kennedy's plea on behalf of the state's municipally owned utilities was in response to representations made to him by the indomitable Frank King, manager of the Gas & Electric Department of Holyoke, Massachusetts, and other municipal utility leaders in the state.

•

While the FPC was considering the power authority's application for a license, Congress debated legislation to authorize the St. Lawrence project. The principal bill was introduced by Sen. Alexander Wiley, R-Wis., chairman of the Senate Foreign Relations Committee. His bill would create a development corporation authorized to issue revenue bonds for the U.S. portion of the seaway project and would permit the power authority, under license from the FPC, to build the power project jointly with the Province of Ontario.

Another bill introduced by Sen. Herbert Lehman and Rep. Franklin D. Roosevelt Jr., both New York Democrats, would require the FPC to insert a preference provision for public agencies and rural electric cooperatives in any license issued for the construction of the power project.

When hearings were held in April 1953 on various St. Lawrence

Project bills, I testified that any bill the committee adopted should "contain adequate assurances that the municipal and other local public agencies and cooperatives receive a preference in the marketing of power from the project." Other public power witnesses took a similar position.

The need for a federal mandate for the preference clause became more apparent in July 1953, when the FPC issued a license to PASNY for the St. Lawrence project. The commission said it lacked authority to require a preference to public bodies and rural electric cooperatives. However, in a separate opinion, Commissioner Dale E. Doty disagreed.

"It is my view," Commissioner Doty said, "that only by the proposed preference condition can we be certain that the power developed by the St. Lawrence project will be marketed in such manner as to encourage the most widespread use thereof at the lowest possible rates to consumers."

Although the commission denied our principal demand, it made a bow in our direction. It ordered the power authority to "make a reasonable portion of the power capacity and a reasonable portion of the power available for use within the economic market area of neighboring states…" and to "cooperate with agencies in such states to insure compliance with this requirement."

•

Federal legislation was enacted subsequently and construction of the St. Lawrence Project began in August 1954. The dam was built jointly by PASNY and the Ontario Hydroelectric Power Commission. The U.S. and Canadian entities shared equally in the project's 1,600-mw capacity. The power authority issued $350 million of revenue bonds, which were not guaranteed by the state or federal government. The project produced its first power on July 1, 1958 and construction was completed by July 1959, two years ahead of the original seven-year schedule.

As the project was being constructed, battles of APPA and the New York municipals and rural cooperatives with the power authority entered a new, contentious phase as the authority revealed plans for contracting for the sale of power.

New York Gov. Thomas E. Dewey named Robert Moses chairman of the power authority. Moses had become legendary as a hard-driving builder noted for removing any obstacles to construction of large public works projects. In this case, his primary interest was to complete the project as quickly as possible. He was annoyed by the preference clause. He wanted to make contracts as expeditiously as possible for sale of large blocks of power to create a revenue stream to pay off the bonds. He announced plans for selling substantial quantities of power to large industries and power companies. Only after the municipal and cooperative utilities fought hard and resorted to legal action were they able to obtain a more equitable share of power from the project.

Although we lost the battle for a preference clause in the St. Lawrence Project, the struggle galvanized the municipal utilities in New York. It gave them the experience needed to make their case before the FPC and placed them in a better position to fight for Niagara Falls power.

Chapter 21

The Niagara Project Fight

During much of the time that APPA and consumer-owned utilities in the Northeast battled to secure power from the St. Lawrence Project, we also spent seven years pursuing legislation to authorize redevelopment of the power capacity of Niagara Falls.

In 1951, New York's Power Authority Act was amended to permit the state power authority to build and develop the additional power resources of the Niagara River. The power authority moved swiftly to pursue the project.

Congress faced three alternatives. Sen. Herbert Lehman, D-N.Y., and Rep. Franklin D. Roosevelt Jr., D-N.Y., wanted the Army Corps of Engineers to build the project and PASNY to operate it. They sponsored legislation that would transfer ownership of the project from the federal to the state government once construction was completed. New York Republicans Sen. Irving Ives and Rep. W. Sterling Cole sponsored a bill calling for construction by the power authority. A third bill introduced by Rep. William E. Miller, R-N.Y., and Sen. Homer Capehart, R-Ind., called for construction and ownership by power companies in the Northeast.

Only the Lehman-Roosevelt bill provided for a preference to local public agencies and rural electric cooperatives in marketing the power.

Availability of transmission was another major difference between the bills. Lehman-Roosevelt called for the power authority to construct or acquire transmission lines, while Ives-Cole stressed transmission by contracts.

Battles lines were clearly drawn in August 1951 when the Senate Public Works Committee held the first of many congressional hearings on the Niagara Project. PASNY Chairman John Burton testified against the preference provisions of the Lehman-Roosevelt bill, saying preference would "discourage integration of the separate power systems of the Northeast and restrict the availability of cheap hydro power to domestic and rural consumers not served publicly or cooperatively."

Rural Electrification Administrator Claude Wickard said the Ives-Cole bills would increase power supply, but offered few safeguards against continuing high rates and no assurance that consumer-owned utilities would obtain a fair share of power at the lowest practicable rates.

"The entire output of Niagara would be turned over to monopolistic utility companies who could simply meet increasing power loads on existing lines," Wickard said.

Despite the fact that most members of the municipal utility governing boards were Republicans, the Municipal Electric Utilities Association of New York endorsed the bill by Democrats Lehman and Roosevelt because of its inclusion of the preference clause. APPA, other public power groups, rural electric cooperatives and farm and labor organizations also supported the Lehman-Roosevelt bill.

In September 1953, I spoke at the annual meeting of the New York MEUA at Whiteface Inn, Whiteface, New York, at which Representative Roosevelt was the banquet speaker. I had worked with Roosevelt and his staff in connection with the Niagara legislation, and had gained a great deal of admiration and affection for him. He reminded me of his father, who was one of my heroes. I was interested in observing how this conservative, predominantly Republican audience would receive him.[1]

The response to Roosevelt was enthusiastic, not only because of the contents of his speech, but also because of Roosevelt's name and charisma. Tall, handsome, and with an engaging personality, Roosevelt captivated the audience. His voice and mannerisms were reminiscent of his father. After completing his address and receiving a standing ovation, Roosevelt "worked the room," shaking hands with the utility officials and guests in the audience. He then went to the back of the room to greet the waiters and waitresses, who had lined up to listen to him, more out of curiosity than from an interest in the content of his speech.[2]

•

When Congress convened in 1954, Lehman and Roosevelt introduced a new bill that narrowed the differences with previously introduced bills calling for state redevelopment. It dropped the provision calling for

---

[1] Roosevelt was already considering his candidacy for the governor of New York, and was pleased to have an opportunity to speak at a meeting in upstate New York.

[2] Roosevelt ran for governor in 1954, but was defeated by Averell Harriman in the Democratic primary. In the Kennedy administration, he was appointed Undersecretary of the Department of Commerce.

construction by the Corps of Engineers and instead authorized the Federal Power Commission to issue a license to New York state, with the stipulation that the license include a preference provision. The bill also provided for construction or acquisition of transmission facilities, and directed New York to negotiate with neighboring states to make available "a reasonable portion" of the output to other states within the "economic market area."

The Senate Public Works Committee held hearings again in 1954 and the irrepressible new chairman of the power authority, Robert Moses, did not wait to be called to testify. Almost immediately after he was appointed, he wrote a letter to Sen. Edward Martin, R-Pa., chairman of the Senate Public Works Committee, charging that the private power bills—one of which was introduced by Martin—were "robbery."

"The record shows that the worst possible procedure from the viewpoint of the public interest would be to turn over the waters of the Niagara to the five utility companies," Moses said. The companies' argument that Niagara power was "divinely preempted for private enterprise" was so much "chatter," Moses said. "As a conservative in every sense, I give you my considered conviction that any business interests of a political party which attempt to hand over the Niagara to the five private utility companies and the coal companies back of them will not survive long in our state," he said. "The political party which is responsible will create an issue on which it cannot win."

"If the majority in Congress is aching to revive the old charge of privilege, economic royalism and bourbonism, this is the golden opportunity to do so," Moses said. "No issue could be more conspicuous, dramatic and easily understood."

Responding to critics who charged that the state's plan was "socialism," Moses pointed out that the state would finance its proposed redevelopment of Niagara by selling its bonds to "prudent investors to whom unsound, socialistic schemes do not appeal."

Senator Capehart, sponsor of a bill to turn over Niagara redevelopment to five power companies, told the committee: "If Congress says to private enterprise that it can't build the project, then I'm ready to throw in the towel because we'll eventually go 100 percent socialistic in the United States as far as power generation is concerned."

Unhappily, as we were to learn later, Moses' enthusiasm for public development did not extend to the question of preference to public agencies in power marketing.

I was one of several witnesses representing public power, cooperative and labor organizations who testified before the Senate Public Works Committee in favor of the Lehman-Roosevelt bill. I pointed to the importance of marketing power with a preference to consumer-owned utilities.

Elwood Swisher, president of the United Gas, Coke, Chemical Workers of America, testified on behalf of the Congress of Industrial Organizations for the Lehman-Roosevelt bill. The bill "assures the greatest opportunity for low-cost industrial power and low retail rates through public development of Niagara," he said.

•

In June 1954, the Niagara issue came to a head in the Senate Public Works Committee in a stormy two-hour closed session. The committee voted 7-6 for a bill sponsored by Sen. Francis Case, R-S.D., and supported by President Eisenhower and New York Gov. Thomas E. Dewey. The Case bill would defer to the Federal Power Commission a decision on whether the project would be licensed to the state or a private power consortium. Since public agencies have preference under the Federal Power Act to licenses for hydroelectric power projects, it was expected that the Case bill would lead to a license for PASNY. However, based on APPA's experience with the St. Lawrence project, we concluded there would be no preference in power marketing to public agencies and rural electric cooperatives under the Case bill.

Fathers of a future president and vice president played important roles in the Senate committee's action. Sen. Albert Gore, D-Tenn., whose son became vice president of the United States in the 1990s, and Sen. Wayne Morse, I-Ore., led a strong but unsuccessful effort to amend the Case bill to include a preference provision. Sen. Prescott Bush, R-Conn., father of President George H.W. Bush and grandfather of President George W. Bush, voted against the preference amendment.

Although the House had passed a bill providing for private utility development and the Senate Public Works Committee had voted in favor of the Case bill, Congress adjourned without taking final action on Niagara redevelopment.

•

When a new Congress convened in January 1955, the political situation had changed. Democrats now controlled the Senate and House and Democrat Averell Harriman had replaced Republican Dewey as governor of New York.

APPA and allied organizations believed Harriman would be more sympathetic to our position than Dewey, and we quickly arranged to meet with him. I led a delegation of 14 representatives of public power, rural electric cooperative, labor and farm groups to a meeting with Harriman on February 3, 1955 in his office in an ornate room in the state capitol building in Albany. Perhaps the governor was not happy because we had challenged some PASNY decisions. Or perhaps he was not especially interested in electricity matters. In any event, it was a rather cold meeting. We made our case and received little response from the inscrutable governor.

But it may not have been entirely in vain. By June, Governor Harriman took what *Public Power* magazine described as "a firm stand on both sides of the question of a preference to municipal and rural electric cooperative systems in marketing of power from his state's two great hydroelectric projects—St. Lawrence and Niagara."

Probably in deference to Senator Lehman, a former governor and much-revered Democratic leader of New York, Governor Harriman announced his wholehearted support for Lehman's bill, which called for state development of the Niagara project, with marketing preference for consumer-owned utilities.

The legislative process continued throughout 1955. House and Senate committees held hearings. In May 1956 the Senate passed the Lehman bill, 48-39 after an unsuccessful effort by Sen. Prescott Bush to send the bill back to committee. Then in early June the legislative landscape changed dramatically.

In the late afternoon of June 7, 1956, what the APPA *Weekly Newsletter* described as the "most spectacular accident in the history of electric service" abruptly altered the outlook for redevelopment of Niagara Falls. A series of giant rockfalls sent two-thirds of Niagara Mohawk Power Corporation's large Schoellkopf hydroelectric plant crashing into the Niagara River gorge a half mile below Niagara Falls. The rockslide was caused by water seepage in rock crevices between the lip of the gorge and the hydraulic canal feeding into the station from above the falls.

Until the accident, it had been assumed that the Schoellkopf Station, with a capacity of 360 mw, would remain in operation after redevelopment of Niagara Falls. The new plant was to be constructed in Lewiston, N.Y., downstream from the Schoellkopf plant.

The accident added urgency to the need for redevelopment. It destroyed the argument of Niagara Mohawk Power Corporation and its four partners that the power companies were best suited to build the additional capacity at the Falls. The companies had pointed to the Schoellkopf Station as evidence that they should build the new plant. Ironically, Niagara Mohawk was forced to turn to the publicly owned Ontario Hydroelectric Power Commission to replace the capacity lost at Schoellkopf. Niagara Mohawk conceded that the 20,000 cubic feet per second (cfs) of water used at Schoellkopf could be utilized more efficiently if it were diverted downstream to the new plant. The higher head of the new plant would make it possible to add about 500 mw, compared with Schoellkopf's 360-mw capacity.

After the accident, Niagara Mohawk's position on redevelopment shifted dramatically. At a hearing June 26, 1956 before the House Public Works Committee, Lauman Martin, vice president and general counsel of Niagara Mohawk, testified that his company had taken "a calm, deliberate and careful look" at the legislative situation in light of the Schoellkopf accident and decided it would be best for the state to "carry forward promptly the development of Niagara."

However, Martin's endorsement of state development was qualified by three conditions: (1) assurance that Niagara Mohawk would receive the power output from the 20,000 cfs it had been using at the Schoellkopf plant; (2) elimination of the preference clause; and (3) assurance that PASNY would make in-lieu-of-tax payments to the city of Niagara Falls, where the Schoellkopf plant had been located.

Even with these caveats, the switch in the company's position shocked committee members who had staunchly supported the private power companies. Rep. Brady Gentry, D-Texas, declared that if the committee should reverse itself and vote for state development, it would be "the last stand of private enterprise insofar as electric power is concerned in this Congress." Rep. Alvin R. Bush, R-Pa., accused Niagara Mohawk of "putting every other private operation on the spot," and added: "There must be something more than you have stated to this committee that caused you to change your mind."

Martin responded that he was "an all-out advocate of the private enterprise bill," but that he was also "a pragmatic realist."

Asked by Rep. Robert E. Jones, D-Ala., whether he would prefer the Lehman bill as it passed the Senate, with a preference clause, to no bill, Martin said that question was like asking, "If you're going to be shot, which weapon do you prefer?"

The House Public Works Committee subsequently approved a bill sponsored by Rep. Charles A. Buckley, R-N.Y., authorizing PASNY to redevelop the Niagara River's hydroelectric project. However, the House Rules Committee failed to grant a rule permitting the bill to be brought to the floor of the House and Congress again adjourned without taking final action on the legislation.

•

Senator Lehman retired in 1956 and was replaced by Jacob Javits, a Republican who had been attorney general of New York state. Although Javits favored redevelopment of Niagara Falls by PASNY, he opposed the preference clause. He therefore teamed with the state's other Republican senator, Irving Ives, and with Rep. William E. Miller, R-N.Y. (who later became Barry Goldwater's running mate in the 1964 presidential election) in introducing a "compromise" bill endorsed by PASNY. The bill called for construction by the power authority, but with no preference in power marketing. Sen. Joseph S. Clark, D-Pa., and Representative Buckley sponsored a bill that included preference. Clark wanted a share of the power from the Niagara Project to be sold to preference customers in Pennsylvania.

At a hearing before the Senate Public Works Committee in April 1957, Chairman Robert S. Kerr, D-Okla., warned sponsors of the Javits "compromise" bill that Congress would not approve a bill that violated the principle of federal preference in power marketing. Senator Javits agreed to strengthen his bill by setting aside "a reasonable amount" of power for municipalities and rural electric cooperatives. The "compromise" bill also earmarked 445 mw for Niagara Mohawk Power Corporation in exchange for the company's transfer of 20,000 cfs of water to the power authority.

PASNY Chairman Moses, an advocate of the "compromise" bill, continued to oppose preference. Senator Kerr finally convinced him to accept "a reasonable statement" in the bill "with reference to a certain amount of power for municipalities and rural electric cooperatives within economic transmission distance" of Niagara Falls. Moses and Kerr reached agreement after a bitter clash. Senator Kerr told Moses that PASNY's cause would not be helped by "unwarranted arrogance on your part."

By early July 1957 the Senate Public Works Committee approved a bill to allow PASNY to build the Niagara project, with a requirement that half of the power output be sold under preference conditions. The bill also stipulated that a maximum of 20 percent of the preference share be allocated to public bodies and cooperatives within "reasonable" economic transmission distance in Pennsylvania and Ohio. Efforts in the committee to raise the allocation to the neighboring states were unsuccessful.

By mid-July the House Public Works Committee adopted a bill identical to the Senate committee bill and on August 1 the House passed the bill, without amendment, by a vote of 313–75. Two weeks later, the

Senate approved the bill, after defeating four amendments designed to increase the share of Niagara power allocated to Pennsylvania and Ohio.

The legislation permitted PASNY to build the $600 million project upon receiving a license from FPC. The fight for preference was not entirely successful, but the reservation of 50 percent of the power for preference customers was a vast improvement over the St. Lawrence power marketing provisions. Niagara Mohawk Power Corporation obtained an allocation of 445 mw, more power than it could have generated at Schoellkopf.

•

My satisfaction over the generally favorable outcome of the fight for the Niagara Project was marred by a personally painful incident that occurred during the concluding months of this battle. The APPA board of directors wanted to invite retired Senator Lehman to be keynote speaker at APPA's 1957 annual convention, which was to be held at the Lake Placid Club in Lake Placid, New York.

Shortly after sending a letter of invitation to Lehman, I received a telephone call from Julius Edelstein, his administrative assistant, who said the senator wanted to speak at our convention, but that the club did not admit Jews. When Lehman was governor of New York, he refused to address a meeting of the National Association of Manufacturers at the club because of its record of discriminating against Jews. Lehman could not accept our invitation unless it was clear that the club no longer had such a policy, Edelstein said.

I wrote to the club to inquire about the policy on February 12, 1957. I received a two-paragraph response from Charles W. Holt saying that when group meetings were booked at the club, "all of the members of the group, as well as such honored guests and speakers as they may wish to invite, are received and entertained without discrimination of any kind."

I discussed this situation with William S. Peterson, general manager of the Los Angeles Department of Water & Power, who was serving as APPA president, and sent him a copy of Holt's letter. Peterson and I concluded that Holt's letter was an admission that the club practiced discrimination. However, we did not wish to draw an incorrect conclusion, so Peterson called Holt to discuss the matter. Holt told Peterson there was nothing in the club's by-laws to prohibit Jews from joining, but confirmed that no Jews were members. Peterson asked me to arrange a conference call of the APPA Executive Committee to discuss what action should be taken.

While we were addressing the discrimination matter, I began to have other concerns about the location of the convention, principally related to transportation to Lake Placid. Only one airline served Lake Placid with one flight each day from New York City. I asked a member of the APPA staff to see if suitable hotel space was available in New York City and found that arrangements could be made.

In advance of the conference call, I sent a four-page memo to the Executive Committee explaining the facts. "This question, of course, is a moral one of some importance, and has other implications of a serious nature insofar as the reputation of APPA is concerned," I said. "For example, the association undoubtedly would lose a certain amount of respect among its friends in the Congress if it were generally known that the association held its annual convention at a place which has such a policy."

My memorandum concluded: "I would like to make one other important point clear. For those of you who may not already be aware of the fact, I am Jewish myself. However, as I told Mr. Peterson when I discussed this with him last week, I do not wish this fact to enter into your consideration to any degree whatsoever. I mention this fact only so that the record may be clear. I will be happy to abide by your decision, whatever it may be, and know that your judgment will be a good one.

"So that you can discuss this question quite freely and without any inhibitions, I propose to excuse myself from the conference call after I have answered any questions you might have."

At its conference call on March 5, the Executive Committee voted unanimously to move the meeting to New York City. I was never asked to excuse myself from the call.

A few days later, I wrote to the Lake Placid Club advising them of the committee's decision and the reasons for its action. The general manager of the club sent a long telegram to all members of the Executive Committee and to APPA General Counsel Northcutt Ely. No copy of the telegram was sent to me. The telegram said:

> The suggestion of cancellation at this late date by an organization of the high standing and integrity of the American Public Power Association in view of the firm agreement which we have entered into is unprecedented. We cannot believe that you and your associates on the Executive Committee, being experienced and honorable businessmen, can condone such unethical and cavalier treatment, which, if carried out, would place you and your association in an untenable position with respect to ethical and responsible business conduct. We cannot accept the cancellation at this late date...In view of the circumstances, we believe that you as a member

of the Executive Committee should press for an immediate full-scale investigation by the Executive Committee and delay final action until such investigation has been concluded.

I had some anxious moments after the telegram arrived, but the Executive Committee held firm. The club did not file a lawsuit, as I had feared.

The resolution of this issue was a huge relief for me. I had always felt a sense of unease about being Jewish, especially in an organization in which probably 99 percent of the members were not Jewish. The transportation difficulties we encountered made the cancellation decision somewhat easier, but I doubt that we would have changed the location of the convention if Senator Lehman had not questioned the club's policy of religious discrimination.

The meeting in New York was successful, except for two matters. The weather in New York was unseasonably and uncomfortably hot and many of the rooms at the Biltmore Hotel (then considered one of New York's best), were not air conditioned. However, there were few complaints from members, since air conditioning was not universally provided at that time. A second problem was that Senator Lehman could not speak at the meeting after all.

Chapter 22

Hells Canyon: Not "Who" but "What"

The tumultuous 1950s were also marked by competing public and private proposals to develop the Hells Canyon site on the Snake River, between Oregon and Idaho.

APPA and its members in the Pacific Northwest were interested in the site because of its tremendous potential for hydroelectric power production. But Hells Canyon development also was important for flood control, navigation and irrigation.

The Hells Canyon site was spectacular; it was the deepest gorge on the continent—2,000 feet deeper than the Grand Canyon of the Colorado River. The dam, proposed by the U.S. Bureau of Reclamation, was to be 722 feet high, only four feet lower than Hoover Dam. The Snake River is a principal tributary of the Columbia River and any development there would have a major beneficial impact on downstream projects on the Columbia River.

A high dam at Hells Canyon was considered ideal for flood control. Its reservoir would flood little, if any, land then in use and it would provide one-seventh of the water storage planned for the 1960–1970 phase of the master control plan for the Columbia Basin. Water storage at Hells Canyon also was critical for developing the 500-mile inland navigation system contemplated in the comprehensive plan for the Columbia Basin. Although Hells Canyon would not provide water for irrigation, power revenues from the dam could help finance important new irrigation areas.

Idaho Power Company filed an application at the Federal Power Commission for a license to build three smaller dams on the Snake as an alternative to the high Hells Canyon Dam. Public power supporters said the Idaho Power Company plan would not develop the full power production and water storage potential of that stretch of the river. The federal high dam would provide 688 megawatts of power at the site and would have made possible the addition of 436 mw of power at downstream federal dams, for total electric production capacity of 1,124 mw. The three smaller Idaho Power Company dams would add 577 mw at the site and 103 mw to downstream dams.

New sources of power were urgently needed during the 1950s and power from the high Hells Canyon Dam was to be marketed throughout the Northwest by the Bonneville Power Administration. If Idaho Power developed the Snake River sites, power would go chiefly to the company's customers.

Power prices and water storage were key issues in the debate. Electricity could be produced at high Hells Canyon for about 2.7 mills per kilowatt-hour, compared to 6.69 mills (according to FPC staff estimates) at the Idaho Power dams. The high Hells Canyon Dam would store 4.4 million acre-feet of water; 3.8 million acre-feet were regarded as usable storage. The three Idaho Power dams would have a useful storage of only one million acre-feet.

In our campaign to win approval for high Hells Canyon Dam, APPA argued that the issue at stake was not "who" but "what." We pointed out that Idaho Power's plan would reverse a trend begun nearly half a century earlier when President Theodore Roosevelt advocated comprehensive development of the nation's water resources.

•

The Bureau of Reclamation disclosed its plan for the high Hells Canyon Dam reclamation project in 1946. Controversy erupted the following year, when Idaho Power applied to the Federal Power Commission for a preliminary permit to build Oxbow Dam in the stretch of the Snake River that would be occupied by Hells Canyon Dam. The interior secretary protested and nothing happened until December 1950, when the company applied for a license for Oxbow Dam, which would be the first of five low dams in its plan for "comprehensive" development of the Hells Canyon reach of the Snake River. After FPC field hearings in 1952, the company amended its application to provide for a new three-dam "comprehensive" plan. The three dams would have more electric generating capacity than the five dams.

Meanwhile, in late 1951, Rep. John Murdock, D- Ariz., introduced a bill to authorize construction of the initial phases of the high Hells Canyon Dam. An identical bill was introduced by Wayne Morse (then a Republican senator from Oregon who later became an Independent and finally a Democrat). The battle was joined.

For the next seven years, activity proceeded concurrently on two tracks: congressional consideration of legislation to authorize high Hells Canyon Dam and FPC action on Idaho Power Company's application for a license to build three dams.

President Truman endorsed the federal project in his 1952 budget message to Congress. Two months later the House Interior and Insular Affairs Subcommittee on Irrigation and Reclamation held hearings on Murdock's bill. Witnesses included Interior Secretary Oscar Chapman and businessmen and landowners from Idaho, who supported the federal project and complained that Idaho Power had forced three rural electric cooperatives out of operation.

Opponents of high Hells Canyon Dam argued that the development of that stretch of the river should be carried out by private enterprise, without government funding.

•

By mid-summer 1953, Hells Canyon had mushroomed into a major national political issue, largely because of the 1952 election of Dwight Eisenhower as president. Under President Truman, the Interior Department had opposed Idaho Power's license application. The company's plan would not maximize development of that stretch of the Snake River, the department said. DOI had urged the commission to reject the company's application and instead recommend that Congress authorize the federal plan. The department planned to provide the principal technical witnesses against the power company's proposal.

FPC hearings were set to begin July 7, 1953, but on May 5 President Eisenhower's new Secretary of the Interior, Douglas McKay, former governor of Oregon, dropped a bombshell with his announcement that the Interior Department was withdrawing its opposition to the company's plans. He insisted that FPC, not Interior, had jurisdiction and he felt Interior should not insert itself into the commission's provinces. The Interior Department's action was consistent with the administration's "partnership" policy, which placed reliance on non-federal funding of major water resource projects, McKay said.

Supporters of the high Hells Canyon Dam in the Northwest quickly formed the National Hells Canyon Association, consisting of labor, farm and public power groups, to supplement the work of small regional groups that had been working for the high dam. At the urging of Ken Billington, executive director of the Washington Public Utility Districts' Association, eight PUDs in the state provided substantial

financing for the legal effort.[1] They should support the high dam not
only because of the low-cost power it would produce, but also because
of the flood protection it would provide, Billington said. Many PUD
commissioners still had vivid memories of the tremendous flood
damage in 1948 at Vanport, Washington, on the lower Columbia River.

The Interior Department's withdrawal as an intervenor placed a
cloud over the position of any department employee who was called as
a witness. Undersecretary of Interior Ralph Tudor said Interior
Department witnesses who testified at the FPC hearings would be
"entirely free to testify as to the facts in the matter as they understand
them and to further testify as to their own conclusions regarding these
facts without restraint."

The National Hells Canyon Association's lead attorney was C. Girard
Davidson (better known as "Jebby"), an assistant secretary of the Interior
Department during the Truman administration. Davidson was a lively,
aggressive public power advocate. One of his principal assignments as
assistant secretary had been to advocate legislation to create the Columbia
Valley Administration, modeled after TVA.

Davidson was assisted primarily by Evelyn Cooper, a former Interior
Department attorney, who conducted most of the day-to-day work on the
FPC proceeding. Cooper was strong-willed, dedicated and adept at
delivering a sharp barb in a quiet voice, sometimes tinged with sarcasm.
Cooper and one or two other lawyers faced a battery of power company
attorneys in the FPC proceeding.

The commission hearings opened in a packed hearing room on July 7,
1953 before FPC Presiding Examiner William J. Costello. Davidson
promptly moved for a 90-day continuance. He felt the delay was
necessary to permit high Hells Canyon Dam proponents to prepare to take
on the burden dropped two months earlier by the interior secretary.
Numerous requests for delays had been granted in the six years since the
company first applied for a preliminary permit for a project on the Snake
River, Davidson noted. The Interior Department had been a leading
opponent of the company's proposals until May 5 and the company's
current application for a three-dam development—which Davidson
described as "a little plan for a big river"—had not been filed until May

---

[1] The eight PUDs were Lewis County PUD, PUD No. 1 of Klickitat County, Benton
County PUD, Clark County PUD, PUD No. 1 of Skamania County, PUD No. 2 of Pacific
County, PUD No. 3 of Mason County, and Franklin County PUD.

15. Davidson's motion was denied.

"We feel this is a substantial miscarriage of justice and we can reach but one conclusion: the commission does not want an adversary proceeding; the commission does not want a full hearing on the relative merits of a high Hells Canyon dam and three small dams on the Snake River," Davidson charged. "This commission does not want the public interest represented."

Costello also denied a motion by the National Hells Canyon Association to order the company to amend and complete its application in accordance with FPC rules. Davidson charged that Idaho Power's applications contained "deficiencies so basic as to raise doubts about the good faith of the company in pressing the applications to hearing in their present incomplete form."

But Costello and FPC staff attorney John Mason said the commission's rules routinely were not followed and the commission planned to rewrite them.

The Interior Department's withdrawal from the case and the FPC's handling of the case prompted Senators Warren G. Magnuson, D-Wash., and Wayne Morse to introduce a resolution calling for an investigation.

•

Despite objections from NHCA and criticism from Congress, Costello proceeded with hearings on the company's application. Early in June 1954, I testified that if the company's plan were approved by FPC, it could "mark the initiation of a policy in which we content ourselves with only partial development of our resources, with the benefits being channeled into the hands of a fewer rather than a larger number of people." Urging the FPC to recommend construction of the high dam, I said:

> The high Hells Canyon project has been regarded, not as an isolated structure, separate and apart from other projects on the river, serving only a restricted area, but as another stone in the structure of the interlocking projects operated as a unit with the end in view that the water resources of the entire basin can be harmoniously intertied to bring to the citizens of the area all the gifts of the river, the utmost in power development, flood control, navigation, recreation, irrigation, and fish and wildlife.

In late November 1954, FPC attorney Mason filed a brief with the hearing examiner supporting the power company's application for the three-dam plan. Mason acknowledged that the company's plan would deprive the Pacific Northwest "of a block of power equivalent to the output of the Bonneville Dam," but he said that the federal government "need not" develop the Hells Canyon site as proposed by the Bureau of Reclamation. Referring to the Eisenhower administration's "partnership" plan for river basin development, Mason commented:

> The utilization of non-federal agencies to accomplish public objectives is still a major aim of the government, as is evidenced by the many major hydroelectric projects now under construction or constructed under FPC licenses in the last few years.

NHCA, eight Washington state PUDs, and the National Rural Electric Cooperative Association filed a brief comparing the company's low-dam proposal with the plans of Washington Water Power Company to construct a low-power dam at the Kettle Falls site on the Columbia River several decades earlier. The FPC in 1933 rejected the Kettle Falls application. Today that site is under the waters of Lake Roosevelt, the reservoir formed by Grand Coulee Dam.

Idaho Power's application for low dams "affords the commission much the same opportunity as in the historic choice between high Grand Coulee and low Kettle Falls," the brief said.

•

As the FPC proceedings continued, activity picked up in Congress. In early March 1955, identical bills were introduced in the Senate and House to authorize federal construction of the high Hells Canyon Dam. Senator Morse, who by then was a Democrat, was the lead sponsor of the Senate bill, which had 29 cosponsors. House bills were introduced by Representatives Gracie Pfost, D-Idaho; Edith Green, D-Ore.; Don Magnuson, D-Wash.; and Lee Metcalf, D-Mont.

Hells Canyon supporters wanted Congress to trump the action of the FPC. Federal construction of the high dam would moot FPC's licensing of the three-dam plan. We were clearly in a race for time. If the FPC issued a license and the company began constructing one of the projects, Congress would be unlikely to authorize the high dam.

Pointing to the greater power production potential of high Hells Canyon Dam, Senator Morse said the high dam would have a "tremendous business-stimulating" effect. The new large block of power and the revenues it would produce also would aid irrigation and "would have an economic impact on the region that would be felt for decades, yes for centuries to come."

Sen. Richard Neuberger, D-Ore., called high Hells Canyon Dam "the keystone in the arch of resources out in the great Pacific Northwest" and added that "if Hells Canyon is given to private monopoly for far-less-than-full development, other resources will likewise pass from the hands of the people."

•

In May 1955 action shifted back to FPC. Presiding Examiner Costello dumped the case into the laps of the full commission with his unenthusiastic opinion recommending a license for Brownlee, the only one of the company's proposed three dams that would provide flood control and navigation benefits, as well as power. He rejected the Oxbow Dam and the low-head Hells Canyon Dam, saying the company had no market for their power output in its service area.

Costello had no sympathy for intervenors' pleas to urge construction of the high Hells Canyon Dam. Such a recommendation "would be a completely useless act" because "there is no reason to assume...that development of these major water resources would be undertaken by the United States within a reasonable time," he said.

Nevertheless, his opinion provided ammunition for supporters of the high dam. "The facts seem to point to the inescapable conclusion that with the marked and substantial advantage of the government's credit, the high dam would be dollar for dollar the better investment and the more nearly ideal development of the Middle Snake," he said.

Costello admitted that any of the company dams would eliminate a single dam "of heroic proportions" that would store three times as much water as the dams proposed by Idaho Power and that was originally proposed by the U.S. Army as "one of the key projects for flood control regulation in the Columbia Basin."

•

In late July, the commission overruled Costello's recommendation to reject Oxbow and the low Hells Canyon Dam and approved the company's entire proposal on the grounds that the benefit-cost ratio of the three-dam plan was greater than that of the one-dam plan.

The commission's decision was announced shortly after Congress had adjourned. Although they were caught in the post-adjournment rush for home, congressional supporters of the high dam reacted angrily. Senator Morse said that the Hells Canyon fight "is far from over" and vowed that "the people's interest will prevail."

Sen. Robert S. Kerr, D-Okla., chairman of the Senate Public Works Committee, said the Idaho Power license would end "in the same junk pile where the remains of Dixon-Yates are now corroding."

I issued a statement predicting that "those legions in the Pacific Northwest and throughout the nation who believe in sound development of our natural resources will not stand idly by in the face of this myopic decision on Hells Canyon. If this decision is permitted to stand, it will constitute the most serious threat in the past half-century to the sound principles under which we have sought nothing less than maximum development of our valuable water resources."

NHCA Attorney Evelyn Cooper said the FPC "has bulled through a political decision." It had taken two years and a 20,000-page record to get the Hells Canyon case to the commissioners, who then reached their decision in a matter of days, she said.

In its unanimous decision, the commissioners brushed aside the argument that the cost of power would be lower under federal development. The Federal Power Act does not require "that we recommend federal development for the sole purpose of making power available at costs lower than would be possible if the same water resources were developed by a private entity under a license," the FPC said. The opinion continued:

> Needless to say, if the supplying of power at the lower costs resulting from federal development should be considered as a decisive factor, there would be few cases involving major power projects where private development would be licensed under the [Federal Power] Act because of the substantial difference in annual cost of investment money in favor of federal over private financing and because of the much higher annual cost of taxes paid under private development as compared with the freedom from taxes under federal development, or, in some few instances, the minor annual payments by some federal projects in lieu of state taxes.

In comparing the power capacity of the high dam versus the three-dam plan, the commission ignored the downstream power benefits that would be provided by the high dam. The commission described the high dam as having installed generating capacity of 800 mw, with provision for an additional 100-mw unit and referred to the power company plan as having a capacity of 783 mw. The commission did not mention that the downstream benefits of the greater storage capacity of the high dam would make possible a total of 1,122 mw, which would include capacity at Hells Canyon and downstream projects.

The commission admitted that the 1.1 million acre-feet of storage under the three-dam plan would fall short of the 3.8 million acre-feet of useful storage contemplated for the high Hells Canyon Dam. Although the high dam would provide storage adequate to control the maximum flood of record at The Dalles on the Columbia River, the FPC said the three-dam plan "would be adequate to control the Snake River runoff for the second greatest flood of record." The FPC also suggested developing other sites for added flood protection.

•

A week after the commission's decision, I testified before the House Government Relations Subcommittee on Water Resources and Power, which was conducting hearings on problems facing consumer-owned utilities. I asked the subcommittee to investigate three aspects of the FPC decision on the Idaho Power Company application:

1. Considering the fact that the written record of the examiner's hearing on the Hells Canyon case consumed more than 20,000 pages and lasted more than a year, how much time did the commission actually give to consideration of its decision? [The commission's 24-page opinion and 15-page order were adopted three weeks after the commission held oral argument.]
2. Why was the announcement of the commission [decision] delayed for eight days—until after the adjournment of Congress?
3. Was work started on the preparation of the decision before oral argument was held?

Meanwhile, Sen. James E. Murray, D-Mont., chairman of the Senate Interior Committee, said his committee would investigate the FPC order. Sen. Estes Kefauver, chairman of a Senate Judiciary subcommittee investigating the Dixon-Yates deal, said his group, too, might look into the circumstances surrounding the FPC decision.

In May 1956, attorneys for the National Hells Canyon Association appeared before a three-judge panel of the U.S. Court of Appeals to ask that the court set aside the FPC order granting a license to Idaho Power. But Congress was the principal focus of activity in 1956. In the latter part of that year, the Senate Interior Committee approved the Hells Canyon bill in a voice vote and a week later the House Interior and Insular Affairs Committee voted 15–13 in favor of the bill.

Supporters of high Hells Canyon Dam were guardedly optimistic because Democrats, who generally supported public power, controlled the Congress. However, they were not unmindful of President Eisenhower's opposition to the federal dam. They recognized that Eisenhower would likely veto a Hells Canyon bill. Advocates of the high dam also were aware that their support was stronger in the Senate than in the House.

To obtain as many votes as possible for the bill, officers of the Electric Consumers Information Committee, of which I was vice chairman, arranged a meeting with Majority Leader Lyndon Johnson. Senator Johnson had rejected our earlier efforts to kill or amend the 1954 Atomic Energy Act, but he was entirely supportive of the Hells Canyon legislation. As a result of his efforts to develop the Lower Colorado River in Texas, Johnson was knowledgeable about and supportive of water resource projects and he appreciated their importance in bringing low-cost electricity to rural areas. He also had a good relationship with members of our group from labor and rural electric cooperatives.

The majority leader quickly took command of the meeting and assigned us to work on senators whose votes were uncertain. We left his office with renewed enthusiasm and were gratified after the meeting when Senator Johnson announced that the Hells Canyon bill was on his list of "must" legislation for that Congress. He also said the bill had been cleared by the majority policy committee to come up on the Senate floor at any time.

The Hells Canyon bill reached the Senate floor on July 17, 1956 but after two days of highly charged political debate, it was defeated by a vote of 51 to 41. Proponents cast the issue in terms of comprehensive versus limited resource development. Instead, amid reports of the administration's pressures to defeat the bill, debate frequently degenerated into partisan political bickering.

In the House, the Interior and Insular Affairs Committee had approved a companion bill, but it was not brought to the floor before Congress adjourned and it died with that session of Congress.

In September the U.S. Court of Appeals for the District of Columbia Circuit handed down a unanimous decision affirming the FPC's award of a license to Idaho Power to build the three low dams. The court emphasized the discretion granted the FPC under the Federal Power Act and commented that "it may be the commission could properly have concluded that the high dam project was appropriate for federal development. But the decision was for the commission, not for us."

Despite these setbacks, elections in the fall of 1956 gave hope to supporters of the high dam. Several newly elected Democratic members of Congress were strong advocates. These included Frank Church, elected to the Senate from Idaho, and Representatives Al Ullman and Charles Porter of Oregon. Ullman was closely identified with Hells Canyon, having served as executive director of the Idaho-Oregon Hells Canyon Association before his election to Congress.

In addition to the appeals of these new congressional supporters, Democrats who replaced Republicans as governors of Oregon and Washington urged Congress to pass the Hells Canyon legislation.

Four other events placed the Hells Canyon issue in a new light. Spring floods in 1957 washed out cofferdams that had been constructed to enable work to begin on the core of Idaho Power's Brownlee Dam. The washout simplified the problem of abandoning that site in favor of Hells Canyon. Second, an appeal pending before the U.S. Supreme Court placed a cloud over the FPC license to Idaho Power. Third, the administration announced that it was studying a high dam at Pleasant Valley, downstream from Hells Canyon, thereby calling into question overall plans for development of the Snake River. Finally, the Northwest Public Power Association floated a proposal to increase the capacity of the high Hells Canyon Dam by using it for peaking capacity. The greater capacity would change the revenue and feasibility figures for the project.

With growing public support for the high Hells Canyon Dam and new questions about the viability of the company's license, congressional supporters introduced new bills. In early March 1957 Senate and House committees held hearings.

NWPPA Executive Secretary Gus Norwood, in testimony before Senate and House committees, suggested turning high Hells Canyon Dam into a peaking plant. The original design of the Hells Canyon Dam "was tightly circumscribed by the assumption that the project would be measured in terms of prime power as part of an all-hydro or predominantly hydro power system," Norwood said. "That concept is now obsolete."

Norwood said it would be desirable to increase generating capacity at storage dams on projects such as Hells Canyon "in order to utilize the project for producing the type of power [that] commands the highest premium price in the marketplace." He said his analysis of stream flow indicated that the range of ultimate capacity at Hells Canyon Dam could be from 1,200 to 1,600 mw.

A month after the congressional hearings, the U.S. Supreme Court declined to review the lower court decision upholding the FPC license to Idaho Power Company Hells Canyon supporters were undeterred. They recognized that their only recourse now was for congressional action and proceeded to make their case there.

Reacting to the Supreme Court decision, I issued a statement saying "the fight for high Hells Canyon Dam must and shall be continued. ...High Hells Canyon Dam still means at least 444,000 kW of additional power capacity—the equivalent of Bonneville Dam—and 3.8 million acre-feet more flood storage than would be available at the three lower dams proposed by Idaho Power Company." Comparing the battle for a high Hells Canyon Dam with the 20-year campaign by Sen. George W. Norris that led to creation of TVA, I said, "no lesser a principle is involved in the Hells Canyon issue and no lesser a struggle should be made."

•

Three weeks after the Supreme Court's decision, the Office of Defense Mobilization approved Idaho Power's application for fast tax write-off certificates for two of its three proposed dams.[2] Idaho Power had applied for the fast tax write-offs more than a year earlier. I opposed granting such certificates. In a letter to ODM, I pointed out that the certificates could bring subsidies to the company about equal to the cost of the high Hells Canyon Dam:

> The essential difference, however, is that if the government were to build high Hells Canyon Dam (instead of subsidizing Idaho Power Company's low dam), all of the government's investment in power facilities would be repaid in full, with interest, and the people would receive the benefit of almost 3 million acre-feet of *additional* usable flood storage and 444,000 kilowatts of *additional* power than would be provided by the company's three low dams. To say, therefore, that the issuance of these tax subsidies to Idaho Power Company compounds a travesty is to describe the situation mildly.

Award of the certificates to Idaho Power made a mockery of the company's claim that it was building the dams without subsidy and supporters of Hells Canyon Dam were quick to pounce on the ODM decision. Senator Morse called the ODM action a "shocking betrayal of the public interest," and a "tremendous handout."

---

[2] Certificates granted by ODM would permit Idaho Power Company to write off in five years, for tax purposes, 65 percent of the estimated $67 million cost of Brownlee Dam and 60 percent of the estimated $35.9 million cost of Oxbow Dam. Computation of the benefits of the certificates showed that they would cover $43.6 million of the cost of Brownlee and $21.6 million of the cost of Oxbow, or $65.2 million of the cost of construction. Assuming that the projects otherwise would be depreciated over the 50-year term of the license, the total interest-free loan would be $30.5 million, which, invested at 6 percent interest, would bring the total subsidy over 50 years to $329.3 million. Cost of the Hells Canyon Dam was estimated at $354 million

In early May, former President Truman spoke out against the tax certificates. At a meeting of the Electric Consumers Information Committee, Truman said he hoped it would "bring about such a wave of revulsion that the whole scheme for giving away Hells Canyon will be upset." He expressed hope that Congress would pass the Hells Canyon bill "as a lesson to those who would plunder the great natural resources that belong to the people of the country."

The following week NHCA filed a supplement to its petition for rehearing before the Supreme Court. It cited the grant of a fast tax write-off certificate to Idaho Power Company as "an intervening circumstance of substantial effect" in view of the FPC opinion "that the three-dam project licensed by the commission order would be constructed at no cost to the United States."

Sen. Harry F. Byrd, D-Va., chairman of the Finance Committee, asked ODM Director Gordon Gray whether the Idaho Power Company dams would aid any defense installations and whether any study had been made to determine that power was needed for defense purposes in the company's service area.

"It was not justifiable under the law to make this concession" to Idaho Power Company, Senator Byrd said, adding, "this construction has been going on for six months...what contention did they make that they were entitled to this subsidy?"

Gray said the certificates were not a subsidy. He added that the program "has been progressively narrowed" until only eight expansion goals remain open, of which five are under study with a view toward closing them "relatively soon."

The Antitrust and Monopoly Subcommittee of the Senate Judiciary Committee got into the act later that month and uncovered new information that created a sensation. At a subcommittee hearing, it was revealed that Secretary of the Interior Fred Seaton had opposed granting the tax certificates to Idaho Power Company—a fact that had previously been concealed from the subcommittee.

ODM Director Gray said Interior had recommended the certificate in October 1955. He did not disclose that his predecessor, former ODM Director Arthur S. Flemming, had received a sharply worded letter from Seaton urging that the Idaho Power application be denied.

In view of the FPC declaration that the company's three dams would be built "at no cost to the United States," it would be "most inequitable for the federal government now to assume any portion of the cost of those licensed projects," Seaton said. He added that testimony before the FPC "appears to establish clearly the company made its case before the FPC on the basis that it would not need accelerated tax amortization in order to justify granting the license to the company."

Subcommittee Chairman Kefauver produced the letter after announcing that it had turned up in an Interior Department file. ODM files provided to the subcommittee did not include the Seaton letter, Senator Kefauver said.

ODM Director Gray said he had withheld the Seaton letter on the grounds that it might be a privileged communication. Shortly before the meeting convened, the letter was given to the subcommittee, he said.

Senator Kefauver charged that ODM produced the letter only after learning that Interior had provided a copy to the subcommittee. Gray later maintained that the Seaton letter did not relate to criteria by which applications for write-offs are judged, but instead involved broader policy issues.

Disclosures at the hearing led Senator Morse to charge in a Senate speech that the Seaton letter "was suppressed, just as facts were suppressed in the Dixon-Yates case."

The Washington Post published an editorial June 9, 1957 asserting that Gray's disclosures before the Kefuaver subcommittee were "wrested from him by Senator Kefauver's persistent, knowledgeable and skillful questioning," The *Post* declared that two conclusions were inescapable:

...one, that the Federal Power Commission's issuance of a license to the Idaho Power Company for the construction of dams on the Snake River was based on a mistaken premise; and, two, that Mr. Gray, as director of the Office of Defense Mobilization, acted on extremely dubious grounds in issuing certificates of rapid tax amortization for construction of these dams.

Pointing out that the grant of the fast tax write-offs to Idaho Power Company would "entail a very appreciable expense to the United States" and would in effect constitute an interest-free loan, the editorial called on Congress "to step in and preserve Hells Canyon, the choicest dam site on the North American continent, for full development by a multiple-purpose high dam that will give the Northwest the power resources it needs."

In the week following publication of the editorial, Senator Kefauver held another hearing on the case, this time calling before his subcommittee Idaho Power President T.E. Roach and Counsel R.P. Parry. Senator Kefauver said there was "a serious question" in his mind "as to whether the tax certificates were obtained by misrepresentations." The

FPC had licensed the company to build the dams on the premise that the projects would be constructed "without cost to the United States," he said.

Roach and Parry countered that the government was not giving Idaho Power Company any money for construction of the dams. They challenged the "astronomical figures" presented by the FPC's chief accountant as the value of the tax write-offs.[3]

"I don't agree for a single minute that the rapid amortization certificate takes a single solitary penny away from the federal government," Roach said. The inquiry into the company's fast tax write-off certificates is "persecution of the worst sort, intended to discredit Idaho Power Company in the eyes of the public," he said.

But Sen. Joseph O'Mahoney, D-Wyo., a member of the subcommittee, noted that FPC Chairman Jerome K. Kuykendall had testified that the commission granted Idaho Power Company a license to build the dams in the belief that they would cost the government nothing. Roach countered that the company would save the government "up to a billion dollars" in initial outlay in the Hells Canyon reach of the river. Moreover, the company would pay $300 million in federal, state and local taxes and would supply "free of cost" flood control, worth $1 million a year, he said.

Senator Kefauver responded dryly that Idaho Power Company customers would pay all of these costs.

On Thursday night, June 20, as the Senate was debating the Hells Canyon legislation, Idaho Power President Roach announced the company would reject the tax write-off certificates. He took this unusual step "to eliminate further beclouding of the real issues" in the Hells Canyon controversy, he said.

The company's action was immediately characterized in the Senate debate as an "obvious attempt" to influence the vote on the Hells Canyon bill. Senator Magnuson said the announcement "reminded me of the fellow who was caught outside the chicken house with a bag of chickens" and said, "I will give them back." Senator Neuberger called it "deathbed repentance," while Senator Jackson accused the company of "trying to amortize a few votes" by returning the certificates.

Senator Kefauver was more cynical. Roach could change his mind before January 1, 1958 about giving up the certificates or he might be forced to do so at the demand of stockholders, he said, adding:

---

[3] Russell C. Rainweater, chief accountant of the FPC, had testified that the certificates would cost the federal government $83.5 million in interest and that the value of the certificates to the company, as interest free loans, would be $339.3 million.

> Certainly no officer of the company, even if he were acting in good faith and not merely for the purpose of trying to obtain votes for the passage of the bill, has a right to give away something of great value—almost as valuable as the property of the Idaho Power Company—without the consent of the stockholders or, at the very least, the consent of the board of directors.

The next day, June 21, the Senate passed the Hells Canyon bill by a vote of 45 to 38. Visitors in the packed Senate gallery burst into loud applause as the vote was announced. Vice President Richard Nixon, who was presiding, reminded them that demonstrations of approval or disapproval were not permitted in the gallery.

Ten days after the Senate vote, the euphoria of supporters was dampened when the House Interior and Insular Affairs Subcommittee on Irrigation and Reclamation voted 15 to 12 to strike the bill's enacting clause—an action that killed the bill. Thirteen Republicans and two Democrats—Representatives James Haley of Florida and George Shuford of North Carolina—voted to kill the bill.

Despite the fact that membership of the full committee was almost identical to that of the subcommittee, Hells Canyon supporters maintained a lingering hope that the action of the subcommittee would be overturned by the full committee. Maneuvering in the committee continued through the remainder of 1957 and into spring of 1958.

The denouement came in June 1958 on Representative Pfost's motion in the subcommittee to report her bill, which was identical to the Senate-passed measure. It was defeated by a vote of 15-13.

Congress adjourned on August 24. A few days later, Idaho Power Company announced that Brownlee Dam, the first of the company's three dams, was generating electricity, thus ending all hope to build high Hells Canyon Dam.

Chapter 23

Visiting the Soviet Union

In 1959, a thaw in the Cold War between the United States and the Soviet Union gave me an opportunity to take part in the most exciting trip of my life—a 31-day, 12,500-mile inspection tour of hydroelectric power projects in the Soviet Union. Sen. James E. Murray, D-Mont., chairman of the Senate Interior and Insular Affairs Committee, asked me to serve as a consultant to three senators representing the interior committee and the Public Works Committee.

Joseph Stalin's death in 1953 and his succession by Nikita Khrushchev led to a January 27, 1958 agreement between the United States and the Soviet Union providing for cultural and scientific exchanges. The Soviets' successful launch of Sputnik I in 1957 intensified U.S.-Soviet competition for preeminence in scientific and economic development.

One manifestation of economic rivalry was the Soviet Union's progress building hydroelectric projects. On December 27, 1957, Senator Murray sent a report to his committee and the Public Works Committee summarizing Soviet progress in hydro power. The report was based primarily on findings of Michael W. Strauss, former U.S. commissioner of reclamation. The Soviets were building new hydroelectric capacity faster than the United States. They were constructing longer and higher voltage transmission lines and they were building four hydroelectric stations, any one of which would exceed the capacity of Grand Coulee Dam, then the largest hydro power plant in the United States.

The Soviet Union's hydro power development stood in sharp contrast with that in the United States. Largely due to its ideological antipathy toward federal power development (arguments against "creeping socialism" were rampant), the Eisenhower administration had imposed a "no new starts" policy for federal hydroelectric projects.

At a Senate hearing in early 1958, Maj. Gen. E.C. Itschner, chief of engineers of the U.S. Army, said just five hydroelectric plants under construction in Siberia would have a combined capacity half again as great as the total capacity of all federal hydro projects in the United States, including those of the Corps of Engineers, Bureau of Reclamation and Tennessee Valley Authority.

Sen. Henry M. Jackson, D-Wash., said the Soviets were developing their hydroelectric base "to make good their boast to catch up with us industrially in the next 20 years."

On July 28, 1958, the Senate unanimously adopted Senate Resolution 248 calling on the Interior and Insular Affairs and Public Works committees to recommend ways to accelerate development of U.S. natural resources.

•

Against this background, the two Senate committees proposed sending a delegation to study Russian water resource development. Three Democratic senators—Ernest Gruening of Alaska, Edmund Muskie of Maine and Frank E. (Ted) Moss of Utah—were tapped to make the trip.

Senator Gruening's interest stemmed primarily from his proposal to build a huge hydroelectric power project at Rampart Canyon on the Yukon River in Alaska. The 5,000-mw project would have capacity more than twice that of Grand Coulee Dam, but in a climate similar to that of Siberia.

Senator Muskie wanted to join the trip primarily because of his advocacy of the Passamaquoddy tidal project and other water resource development in Maine. Elected to the Senate after serving as governor of Maine, Muskie believed water resource projects would stimulate economic development in his state. During the Roosevelt administration, work had started, but later was abandoned, on the Passamaquoddy project. But the planned tidal project at La Rance, France, had renewed interest in Passamaquoddy. He wanted the group to visit Paris on its return trip to learn about the La Rance project.

As a westerner from an arid state, Senator Moss was interested in reclamation projects. He believed the trip would boost support for building new water resource projects in the West.

Clyde Ellis, general manager of the National Rural Electric Cooperative Association, also was invited. He and I wanted to learn about Russian advances in water resource development to determine whether some of their methods could be used in the United States. We felt publicity about the trip would stimulate interest in federal hydroelectric power development in the United States.

Our delegation included two other unpaid consultants—Harry Kuljian, president of the Kuljian Corporation, an international engineering consulting firm headquartered in Philadelphia, and Harvey McPhail, former assistant commissioner of reclamation and manager of Kuljian's Hydroelectric Division. Also in the delegation were Vic Reinemer, executive secretary to Senator Murray; Michael Strauss, a consultant to the Senate interior committee; Milton C. Mapes of the interior committee staff, and Theo W. Sneed of the Public Works Committee staff.

The State Department arranged the six-week trip. Working out details took a year and a half. In addition to four weeks in the Soviet Union, we were to stop in Copenhagen and Helsinki en route to Moscow for briefings. After visiting the Soviet Union, we were to stop in Warsaw, Paris, Anchorage and Fairbanks.

Never having been to Europe, I was excited but also had trepidation about the trip. I would be away from my wife and two small children, who were 12 and 7 years old. Moreover, my wife and I had bought a new house and settlement and moving were scheduled to take place while I was to be in the Soviet Union. Nevertheless, Sara encouraged me to take the trip, recognizing it was an opportunity of a lifetime.

At about 10:30 a.m. on Tuesday, September 15, 1959, our delegation met at National Airport in Washington for the first leg of the trip to Idlewild Airport in New York (now John F. Kennedy Airport). We traveled by SAS from New York to Copenhagen. While waiting in the SAS lounge at Idlewild, we watched on television as Nikita Khruschev arrived at Andrews Air Force Base outside of Washington for his first visit to the United States. Symbolizing the warmer relations between the two nations, Khruschev was to be in the United States for several days. Our group had more than a passing interest in his well-being while he was here. If he met harm, our delegation would be likely hostages.

Shortly after Khruschev's plane touched down, we departed for Copenhagen. We spent a day or more each in Copenhagen and Helsinki, where we had briefings from U.S. Embassy staffs, meetings with officials of local utilities and sightseeing.

Thinking about how far away I was from home and worried about my family, I had difficulty sleeping Thursday night, September 17, in anticipation of our departure the next day for Moscow.

On Friday afternoon, September 18, we boarded a small propeller-driven plane in Helsinki for the flight to Moscow. With butterflies in my stomach, we touched down at 9 p.m. A uniformed man checked our passports before we disembarked. We were cleared through Customs by a stony-faced official and went outside to three large black limousines, already loaded with our luggage. Ellis, Sneed and I shared a limousine and had our first glimpse of Moscow. The area around the airport was dark and had little housing or other activity, but after a few miles we entered a wide boulevard flanked with large apartment houses, each about eight stories tall. They were impressive, but monotonous in their uniformity. Finally, we turned a corner and I saw the Kremlin, the tomb of Lenin and Stalin and St. Basil's Cathedral. It was about 11 p.m., and the vast Red Square was empty. It left me with an eerie, surreal feeling.

After more driving along nondescript, austere streets, we arrived at the Sovietskaya Hotel, a relatively new luxury hotel built primarily to house foreigners and distinguished visitors. The marble lobby was elaborate and ostentatious, but it did not prepare me for my room.

I was dumfounded when I was ushered into my spacious suite. It consisted of an entrance hall, a living room, a bedroom and two baths. The large living room was furnished with a piano, television set, radio, dining room table and cabinet containing bric-a-brac. The furniture was heavy and highly polished. Walls were painted light green, except for an alcove where there was a built-in couch. That corner was covered with silk or brocade fabric. The commodious bedroom was furnished with twin beds covered with pink bedspreads and bulky pink bolsters. Lamps had ornate silk shades. The entire suite seemed ominous and not at all welcoming. Albeit on a much grander scale, it reminded me of the type of furniture my parents had selected for their apartment over our grocery store in Chattanooga. I did not sleep well that night, either.

The next morning we assembled for breakfast in a large dining room that was normally used as a ballroom. We were the only patrons. We learned later that it was customary to order room service for breakfast. Although the waiters were friendly, they knew little English, and we had difficulty ordering. Several of us asked for two eggs, either fried or boiled. Ellis received two omelets, Kuljian was served egg salad and McPhail and I were presented with four eggs each.

•

Thus began our 31 days in the Soviet Union. We traveled more than 12,500 miles—from Leningrad (now St. Petersburg) in the West to Irkutsk and Bratsk in Siberia. We journeyed as far south as Sochi on the Black Sea. Most of the trip was by air, but we traveled approximately 1,000 miles by car, 360 miles by boat on the Volga and Don rivers and the Volga-Don Canal, and 340 miles by train. We inspected 11 dams (four under construction) on eight rivers, four hydroelectric institutes, four construction towns, a generator manufacturing plant, a thermal power station, a power substation, transmission lines, Lake Baikal (a natural reservoir in Siberia that stores more water than all five of the Great Lakes combined), a collective farm, and a state farm. We visited several art museums (the most impressive of which was the world-famous Hermitage in Leningrad) and attended three operas and one ballet. We visited churches, schools and scenic and historical sites, notably the Kremlin. We saw countless statues of Lenin and Stalin.

We learned much about the Soviet Union's hydroelectric power program and other aspects of its water resources development, including navigation, flood control, irrigation and recreation. The USSR's progress in building and operating hydro power projects was impressive. Although the United States had more installed hydroelectric capacity, the Soviets had surpassed us in terms of the size of the dams and powerhouses then being built and in the magnitude of ongoing programs. A report issued by the Senate delegation after the trip[1] stated the group's conclusion succinctly:

> The Soviet power program has produced the largest hydroelectric stations in the world, yielding the greatest project volumes of electricity from the largest generators connected by the longest transmission lines operating at highest voltage.

The Senate report warned that the Soviet Union was catching up with the United States in electric power production. The senators acknowledged that the United States was still far ahead, with 142 million kilowatts of installed capacity at the beginning of 1959, compared with 53 million kw in the Soviet Union. However, the Russians could overtake the United States in 1975—in 15 years—"unless we speed up or they slow down," the report said.

The Soviet Union allocated four-fifths of its power to industry, while the United States used a far smaller share for industrial production, the report noted. The Soviets could surpass the United States in the amount of power allocated to industry in 1973.

We were impressed by the Russians' recognition that power could be produced from hydroelectric power stations at a lower cost than other sources and that their river systems were one of their greatest

---

[1] "Relative Water and Power Resource Development in the U.S.S.R. and the U.S.A," 86th Congress, 2nd Session, January 4, 1960.

inexhaustible resources. Consequently, the proportion of their total power produced from hydroelectric resources had risen from less than 2 percent in 1925 to approximately 20 percent in 1958. The Soviet Union intended to maintain the ratio of 20 percent production from hydro power and 80 percent from thermal sources. However, the Senate report noted that in the United States, the proportion of hydroelectric power would drop from 35 percent in 1946 to an estimated 15 percent by 1970, and that the proportion was expected to drop to 12–14 percent by 1980. These figures, of course, were relevant to our goal of emphasizing the need to accelerate the U.S. hydro power program.

I was often asked about the quality of the Russians' construction. Not being an engineer, I could not judge, but Kuljian and McPhail—both engineers—said the construction was excellent. However, they felt the dams and powerhouses lacked the amenities of U.S. projects and the housekeeping was not as spic and span as in the United States. Virtually all of the equipment was made in the Soviet Union, with the exception of large gantry cranes, which were imported from East Germany.

•

The Russians revealed to us, in our final meeting with the Ministry of Power Station Construction, that they had devised new construction techniques to speed completion of dams and reduce their construction costs. I.T. Novikov, the minister, proudly showed us a model of a dam that he said would "revolutionize" the art of building dams.

They planned to use preformed concrete blocks to build a 1,000-mw hydroelectric project on the Volga River. They had used such blocks for several years, but said they had refined them to save considerable time and money. In the model we saw, the Russians had standardized six types of concrete blocks that would be used to build 65 percent of the structure. The only monolithic concrete in the dam would be a pad or footings for the blocks. Using the blocks would simplify concrete pouring and, more importantly, eliminate the need to build wooden forms for concrete. Use of the blocks also would permit telescoping of some of the construction. The blocks could be manufactured without waiting for completion of other work that normally would have to be done before concrete was poured.

By using this technique, the Russians expected to cut construction time on the dam from five to three years. Cost savings were expected to amount to 30 percent.

After showing us this model, Minister Novikov turned to Senator Moss and said, "Now do you see how anxious we are to catch up with you?"

Novikov's comment epitomized the sentiments we encountered throughout our trip. In an article I wrote after our trip for the North American Newspaper Alliance, I said:

In a gravel pit where workers were excavating rock for use in building a dam, in numerous conferences with Soviet engineers, in conversations with a director of a collective farm our group visited, we were repeatedly told that the primary objective of the Russian people is to beat the United States in the production race, and to do so at the earliest possible time...

Everywhere one is confronted with charts showing the goals of the current seven-year program, and exhorting the people to fulfill the program in six years. And always the charts show the lines going upward at a steep incline.

Although the Soviets' principal objective was to surpass the United States in economic development, they also were clearly counting on their economic power to extend their influence to other countries. This was especially true with China. We saw many Chinese, in their blue Mao uniforms, in the streets, hotel lobbies and theaters. The gift store at our hotel displayed books and other publications printed in Chinese.

Hydroelectric power was one avenue used by the Russians to strengthen their ties with China. Some engineers we met had worked closely with the Chinese. According to the Russian engineers, China had 255 dams under construction and their goal was to have 70,000 mw of hydroelectric capacity by 1970. Even though China was the most populous country in the world, the Russians said it was experiencing labor shortages. Lacking mechanical construction equipment, the Chinese were using human labor to perform work that would be accomplished by machines in industrialized countries.

The most dramatic example of Soviet-Chinese cooperation in hydroelectric power development was their joint efforts in planning what was to be the world's largest dam. The dam would be built at the Itchang Gorge on China's Yangtze River and its capacity was to be 25,000 mw, or nearly 13 times that of Grand Coulee Dam. Russian engineers said the dam's ultimate capacity would be 40,000 mw. (Almost 40 years later, in September 1997, my wife and I visited the site of this dam, which was under construction. It was then referred to as the Three Gorges Dam and we were told its capacity would be 18,000 mw, smaller than projected in 1959, but still by far the largest hydro power plant in the world.)

Although the Russians were concentrating on China, they also used their leadership in hydro power development to strengthen ties with other countries. At the Electrosila Works in Leningrad, where large generators were manufactured, we were told the plant was supplying equipment to 23 countries—both "peoples democracies and capitalist countries." The director said the "capitalist" countries were India, Burma, Finland and Egypt.

The various design institutes for hydroelectric projects also were working with other countries. At one institute we saw work on the Aswan Dam in Egypt, a project at the center of considerable controversy when U.S. aid was withdrawn and replaced by assistance from the Soviet Union.

•

We had a kaleidoscopic view of many aspects of Russian life, although we did not get an objective impression of life in the Soviet Union. We had little time to wander the cities or countryside and most of the people we spoke with were selected for us by our hosts. Nonetheless, some of the less desirable features of Russian life could not be obscured. We saw long lines of people waiting to buy simple necessities. When we did a modest amount of shopping, we were aware of shortages. Shopping also gave us a taste of Soviet bureaucracy. A customer would select an item, pay for it, then take a receipt to a clerk to obtain the article. Traveling through major cities revealed many unpaved side streets with poor housing.

Women were more prevalent in the Soviet work force than in the United States and held more physically demanding jobs. We saw women working as street sweepers, watchpersons at railroad crossings and hod carriers. They sorted bricks, drove railroad spikes, unloaded coal barges and performed physically taxing jobs at dam construction sites. We encountered few women working as engineers or in other professional positions at water resource projects. However, when a member of our group needed medical attention, he was treated by a female physician.

Private automobiles were rare. Only three models were produced, and their price was prohibitive for the vast majority of Russians. As in the United States, young people craved automobiles. While we were seated on a plane, one of our young guides, Alex Neznanov, asked me how many weeks or months a person of average means would have to work in the United States to earn enough money to buy a car. It was the only question any Russian guide asked me about living conditions in the United States.

Despite the lack of consumer goods, there was intense building activity. Construction cranes abounded, especially in Moscow. We concluded that if one were to select a symbol of Russian society, it would be the crane. Much of the construction was for new apartments. We were told the goal was to build 700,000 apartments in Moscow alone.

We could not judge the sufficiency of food for Russians, because all of our meals were furnished to us and they were sumptuous. At the guest house where we stayed while visiting Kremenchug Dam, breakfast offerings included fish, baked apples, duck, soft boiled eggs, ham, carrots, beets, onions, salami, pickles, cheese, yogurt, tomatoes, apricot juice, grapes, fresh apples, coffee and tea.

On Sunday, September 27, we had an unforgettable experience on a drive from Tbilisi, in Georgia, to the Khrami power station. We came upon an open-air market, a flashback to lifestyles in existence for generations. We saw unshaven men wearing muddy boots and baggy pants; women with shawls draped over their heads or shoulders; people selling or bartering sheep, pigs, chickens, vegetables and other items; and beautiful oriental rugs displayed for sale on a wall. We passed shepherds leading herds of sheep from summer pasture in the mountains. Some shepherds, wearing tall sheepskin hats, rode horseback; others walked or drove teams of oxen. In the hills, ancient castles stood at commanding heights.

There was a sharp distinction between Soviet advances in technology in some spheres and the primitive state of development in others. The launch of Sputnik I entailed sophisticated technology, as did building dams, power plants and transmission lines. The contrast was most evident during a two-day trip on the Volga and Don rivers, when we traveled on a 250-passenger ship that stopped at a number of villages. This allowed us to observe many aspects of Soviet life. People came aboard carrying live geese or chickens. When we disembarked or viewed a village from the ship, we could see horse-drawn wagons filling water tanks by backing the tanks into the river. People carried bricks or other building materials in what we would regard as a wheelbarrow, but without a wheel. Instead, two people carried the contraption by long wooden poles that extended from each side.

A walk through the village of Kalach was especially memorable. I imagined that I was in the *shtetl* where my father grew up. The streets were unpaved. All of the modest single-family houses were built of wood and had low roofs and windows covered with shutters. Several men drove horse-drawn carts (perhaps like my grandfather, the "handler" who loaded his wagon with produce and other merchandise from his *shtetl* and took it to Minsk to sell). Women wore dark shawls, black quilted coats, skirts and boots. Two women sawed wood; another carried a table over her shoulder. Boys wandering the streets were friendly until Sen. Moss tried to give them pennies as souvenirs. The father of one of the boys then shoved them away when some of us began to take pictures.

As we left Kalach, we saw a sign comparing the percentage growth in the gross national products of the Soviet Union, the United States and England. A line showed that the Soviet Union was forging ahead of the two "capitalist" countries.

When we disembarked at Stalingrad (now known as Volgograd), our luggage was loaded on wooden racks strapped on the backs of elderly porters, who carried their heavy loads in a stooped position.

•

In the spirit of friendship, every formal meal with our Russian hosts (usually one or two each day) began with toasts, which continued throughout the meal. Since each of the three senators and some of the consultants responded or proposed toasts on their own initiative, a meal could easily consist of a dozen or more toasts.

During our first formal dinner, the Russians insisted each toast of vodka be "bottoms up," implying it would be impolite if we did not consume all of the vodka after each toast. Not wishing to create an international incident, I and the other Americans at first abided by this custom, until we experienced the consequences. On future occasions, most of us took only a sip after each toast, even at the risk of offending our hosts.

All the toasts expressed our mutual desire for friendship and the opportunity for Americans and Russians to become better acquainted. Only once was there a sour note during a social occasion. It was at a dinner on October 6 during a visit to what was then known as the Lenin Dam near Kuibishev. Earlier in the day, Michael Sarkisov, the chief operating engineer, had given us a warm welcome and provided a lucid briefing about the dam's construction. However, he took umbrage at a toast by Senator Gruening, who eloquently extolled Americans' freedoms of press, speech, assembly, religion and travel.

Sarkisov said Russians had complete freedom, but their primary aim was to raise the standard of living of their people. He asked how Americans could enjoy freedom of the press when the U.S. media told so many lies about Russia and the Cold War.

Senator Muskie said the U.S. government could not control what the press said, but the right of the people and the press to free speech was respected, even if individuals disagreed with some of the sentiments.

The evening ended on a cordial note when Mike Strauss made a toast to engineers and dam builders who, he said, had learned the same secret—that water runs downhill in Russia, just as it does in the United States. There had never been a cold war or a hot war between engineers, he said.

•

There were other strains. Even after we arrived in Moscow, negotiations continued between the State Department and the Soviet government about our itinerary. The Russians were arranging trips for their own delegations to the United States and they used our requests as bargaining chips to obtain permission to visit certain installations in the United States. In the end, we visited all the places we wanted to see, except Krasnayarsk Dam in Siberia.

We were warned our hotel rooms and telephones were probably bugged, so we should be discreet in our conversations. We were also told our guides and interpreters might be KGB agents. We felt uneasy about relying solely on Russians for translations and wanted someone from the U.S. embassy to accompany us as a translator.

The Russians balked at this request. At that time, U.S. embassy personnel were permitted to travel only within a 50-mile radius of Moscow and the United States imposed a similar restriction on travel by Russian embassy personnel in the United States. We began our trip with Russian interpreters. However, while at our first stop outside of Moscow, the Russians relented and permitted George Winters of the embassy to join us and act as our interpreter, along with the Russian guides. We were told Winters was an economic counselor.

Having been confined to Moscow, Winters was delighted to travel with us, especially to Siberia, where the Russians were said to have nuclear installations. Winters was an avid observer and interpreter.

Several months after our return, newspapers reported that Winters had been expelled from the Soviet Union on the charge that he was a CIA agent. When his mother, who lived in Florida, was informed of this incident, she told a newspaper reporter she had known all along that he worked for the CIA.

We were not allowed to take pictures of airports, railroad stations or the Volga-Don canal. When we inquired about the limitation on picture taking on the canal, we were told that the United States would not allow photography in the Panama Canal.

•

One of the highlights of the trip was our visit to Siberia. I had pictured this region as a cold, desolate area noted mostly for its prison camps. We were not shown any prison camps, of course, although we suspected that gangs we saw working along a highway were prisoners. However, the climate, vegetation and people were anything but desolate.

We took off for Bratsk and Irkutsk at 3 a.m. on Friday, October 9 in a TV-104 jet aircraft. Jets had not yet been introduced into commercial service in the United States, so we were excited about the aircraft. We stopped at Novosobirsk at 7:30 a.m. and were greeted by many red flags and large pictures of Khrushchev. The city was preparing to welcome him soon on his way from Moscow to Peking (now known as Beijing).

The weather was considerably warmer than in Moscow. The area between the tarmac and the terminal building was nicely landscaped with dwarf marigolds and snapdragons, which were still blooming. Young trees had not yet shed their leaves.

We landed at Irkutsk at 5 p.m., had a one-hour layover before taking a smaller aircraft to Bratsk. The landscape reminded me of the terrain and vegetation in the Upper Peninsula of Michigan or upstate New York. We reached Bratsk at 7:30 p.m. and rode limousines to the construction camp, where we were divided into two groups, one staying at a guesthouse where Khrushchev had stayed only two days earlier. The other group stayed at a guesthouse across the street. Senator Gruening insisted on sleeping in the same bed used by Khrushchev.

Mike Strauss called our visit to Bratsk Dam, then under construction, the "summit" of our trip. It confirmed Senator Gruening's views about the feasibility of constructing a hydroelectric project in a harsh climate. Russians worked on the dam throughout the year. They took advantage of winter weather by using the frozen river as a roadbed for construction vehicles and poured concrete by using heated forms.

•

We saw some of Russia's historical and cultural attractions. In Moscow, we walked inside the grounds of the Kremlin and visited the Kremlin museum. Most art exhibited there was produced during oppressive czarist reigns. As we marveled at the craftsmanship of objects in the museum, our guide said the Russian people did not approve of the czars, but they honored the skill of the Russian workers who had produced these objects.

Immediately outside of the Kremlin walls, we visited the tomb of

---

[2] Stalin's body was later removed from the mausoleum, and buried inside the Kremlin grounds. When we were in Moscow, an embassy wag referred to the tomb as "The Gruesome Twosome, the Only Air Conditioned Show in Moscow."

Lenin and Stalin.[2] Hundreds of somber people had lined up for several blocks, waiting patiently in the rain, to go through the tomb, but as foreign visitors we were placed at the head of the line. I noted in my diary that I had a "great sense of anticipation" as we prepared to enter the marble structure. Even after entering the mausoleum, we had to walk through a long, dark corridor before descending steps into the tomb, where Lenin and Stalin were enclosed in a glass case. Lenin was dressed in a dark suit, wearing a polka dot bow tie; Stalin was in uniform. Their facial expressions were serene. It was a moving experience to see two men whose thoughts and actions had such an impact on the history of the world.

The outstanding cultural event for me was a performance of one of my favorite operas, Mussorgsky's *Boris Godounov*, in Moscow's famous Bolshoi Theater. The Bolshoi has five balconies, and glitters with gold gilt. The singing, staging and orchestra were superb. At the end of the second act, exuberant patrons in box seats threw flowers on the stage for the bass who sang the role of Boris.

Although we saw much of the splendor of Russian arts, we also observed the ravages of battles the Russians had endured during World War II. This was especially true in Stalingrad, the scene of a six-month siege in 1942 that was the turning point of the German invasion of the Soviet Union. Large sections of the city destroyed in the war had been rebuilt by 1958, but the Russians had deliberately left standing a shell-pocked flour mill that was the site of the Russians' stubborn resistance that ultimately turned back the Nazi advance.

We also visited an impressive memorial to the Russian soldiers who had been killed in the battle for Stalingrad. About one million Germans and Russians were killed in the siege of Stalingrad and eight million Russian soldiers were killed in the entire war, according to our guides.[3] We were also told 2.5 million people were left homeless after the war, and 1,700 cities were destroyed.

•

After a final conference with officials of the Power Ministry and a farewell luncheon on October 19, our journey to the Soviet Union ended.

We left Moscow on a Polish airliner, en route to Warsaw, with a stop at Vilnius in what was then the Soviet satellite state of Lithuania. We were

---

[3] Other estimates place the number of Russian soldiers killed in the war at seven million. Civilian dead has been estimated at 20 million.

not allowed to disembark in Vilnius.

Although the trip through the Soviet Union was stimulating and informative, we were glad to leave. An oppressive atmosphere permeated the country. With a few notable exceptions, especially in Leningrad, the buildings and streets were drab. And despite the good sense of humor of many Russians, most of the people were unsmiling.

On our arrival in Warsaw, we were struck with the lighter atmosphere. Although Poland was part of the Soviet bloc, the Poles were beginning to express their independence. The people wore more colorful clothing and the officialdom did not seem as heavy-handed as in the Soviet Union.

We stayed only briefly in Warsaw, then departed for Paris, where, because of Senator Muskie's interests, we met with officials of Electricite de France to learn about the La Rance tidal power project, planned for the northwest coast of France.

From Paris we stopped briefly in Copenhagen before flying for 15 hours over the polar route to Anchorage. Senator Gruening was a local hero and we were feted with luncheons and other festivities, but the principal event was a flight in a small chartered plane over the site of the proposed Rampart Canyon Dam on the Yukon River. I experienced the much-heralded daring of Alaskan bush pilots. To get a good view of the site, the pilots flew close to the walls of the canyon—too close for my comfort. Nonetheless, the excitement was a fitting conclusion to an exhilarating journey.

The trip attracted considerable press attention and upon my return I wrote a series of newspaper articles and spoke at a number of meetings about our observations. Other participants also addressed audiences and the report to the Senate received considerable public attention. Although the trip did not have an immediate impact on power policy, our emphasis on the need for additional water resource development became an issue in the 1960 national elections and influenced policies of the Kennedy administration, which came into power in 1961.

Chapter 24

Suburbia in the 1950s

Aside from my professional career, the 1950s were eventful from a personal standpoint. With one small child, we found our one-bedroom apartment in Arlington, Virginia, inadequate. We also were thinking of having another child. Consequently, in 1950, Sara and I purchased a home in Hollin Hills, a unique new community under development about five miles south of Alexandria, Virginia. The move introduced us to suburbia—a new phenomenon of post-war America. It also was destined to change my life in many ways.

We were introduced to Hollin Hills by Bob Davenport, a lively, imaginative person who had been my boss when I worked for the Office of Price Administration in Washington during World War II. I kept in touch with Bob while I was in the Army and we renewed our friendship when I returned to Washington after the war. Although he was a career civil servant, Bob became interested in home building immediately prior to the war, when he became involved on a part-time basis in the construction of a cooperative housing development, Tauxemont, south of Alexandria. After the war, Bob left the federal government and devoted himself exclusively to completion of Tauxemont. Subsequently, he directed his considerable energies and talents to building nearby Hollin Hills.

Bob defied the conventions of that era, when developers of moderately priced homes customarily bulldozed the trees and leveled the ground to build tract houses, many of which were identical and situated in neat rows facing the street. Bob and his architect, Charles Goodman, were determined to preserve the trees and the natural landscape. Roads were to be built on the high ground and drainage areas were to be used as community parks.

Goodman grew up in Chicago and was influenced by the noted

architect Frank Lloyd Wright, who had designed a number of homes in the Chicago area. Goodman's plans called for houses that were unpretentious, with clean, simple lines and an open floor plan. They were built on a cement slab—a radical concept at the time. The homes were distinguished by large floor-to-ceiling windows. Window walls generally faced south so each home could take maximum advantage of the winter sunlight.

The designs were easily adaptable to additions, which proved exceptionally practical as families grew in size and affluence. As they needed larger homes to accommodate expanded families, most residents chose to remain in their existing homes by adding wings, whose design had to be approved by an architectural review committee.

Most importantly, the houses were affordable, especially with the 4 percent mortgage to which I was entitled as a World War II veteran. Our house, including a breezeway that connected the home to a storage unit, cost about $17,000. It probably had no more than 1,200 square feet. Larger, more luxurious split-level homes priced at $25,000 to $30,000 were considered to be on the "gold coast." (Today, some of the homes, with additions, have sold for $300,000 to $400,000 or more.)

Instead of providing a minimum of foundation planting, Bob furnished each homeowner with a landscape plan designed by Dan Kiley, a nationally recognized landscape architect and one of his associates. The relatively large lots of about half an acre made the landscape plans especially desirable. Each plan was designed to blend into that of the neighboring yards to create a park-like setting throughout the community. To enhance the casual, somewhat rural atmosphere, streets had no sidewalks—a mixed blessing. Today, more than half a century later, Hollin Hills consists of about 450 homes and is renowned for its architecture and site planning.

•

Hollin Hills attracted a homogeneous group of young, idealistic, politically active families, the vast majority of whom were liberal Democrats. Most residents were well-educated professionals involved with the federal government, law firms, the media, educational institutions, or nonprofit organizations. Because Hollin Hills was relatively isolated and residents had similar interests, social life was largely limited to the community. Politics and government programs were favorite discussion topics. As the decade drew to a close and the Kennedy administration took office in 1961, some Hollin Hills residents were appointed to important positions in the new administration.

Sara and I flourished in this environment. The conviviality of an active social life with people of similar interests was intellectually stimulating. The floor-to-ceiling windows, looking into the woods or gardens, brought us close to nature.

Drawing upon her skills as a newspaper reporter, Sara began publishing a community newsletter. She enlisted help from other residents, some of whom were also professional writers. Hilda Thorpe, a resident who later became a nationally recognized artist, did the artwork.

Sara also got involved in interior decoration and landscaping. She had no formal training in these fields, but had an innate sense of design and neighbors sought her advice on furnishings. She learned the rudiments of landscaping from Barney Voigt, who worked with Kiley in designing the plans for Hollin Hills.

Although living in the community was idyllic in many ways, it was not paradise. Some attributes that made Hollin Hills attractive also bred occasional friction—professional jealousy about jobs, or parents boasting about their children's academic and athletic accomplishments. Social life also had its strains; some residents felt slighted if they were not invited to certain parties. A degree of snobbery or elitism, frequently directed toward more conventional communities, was also evident. Despite these occasional tensions, life was good in Hollin Hills. Not inappropriately, it was sometimes called Happy Hills.

About 15 months after we moved to Hollin Hills, our second son, William Gordon (Bill), was born at George Washington University Hospital in Washington on March 25, 1952. We celebrated this joyous occasion with our friends while Sara was still in the hospital. In violation of the hospital's rules, some well wishers brought a flask of martinis to the hospital and drank toasts to our new son in Sara's room. After Sara and Bill were released from the hospital, we celebrated again at a *bris* (the traditional Jewish circumcision ceremony for newborn males) at our home, with members of the family and friends present.

Bill and our older son, Jay, enjoyed growing up in Hollin Hills. There were many children in the community and they moved freely from house to house. Mothers were generally home and houses were never locked. The open space in the outdoors left ample room for play and children walked to the nearby grammar school through trails in the parkland.

•

The Hollin Hills environment stimulated a great deal of activity on both the local and national political scene. Few, if any, residents were natives of the area. Consequently, we were held in disdain by Virginia's old-timers, who viewed us as interlopers at best or, worse, as possible Communists.

The Byrd machine, dominated by long-term Sen. Harry F. Byrd, ruled Virginia politics. Although he was a Democrat, Byrd was in the conservative wing of the party and his views were diametrically opposed to those of most residents of Hollin Hills. Byrd's control extended to local and state positions and our congressional district was represented by one of his close allies, Howard W. Smith, chairman of the powerful House Rules Committee.

Hollin Hills residents became actively involved in opposing Byrd, Smith and county officials allied with the Byrd machine. We were about as welcome in Virginia Democratic politics as the proverbial skunk at a garden party. Nevertheless, we persisted and, as more outsiders moved into Northern Virginia, we made modest gains.

Sara was actively involved in fund-raising for the Democrats. Through Hubert Leckie, who designed APPA publications, we met Charlie Byrd, a popular classical and jazz guitarist. Sara persuaded Charlie to perform at various Democratic events.[1] Joe Glazer, an official of the United Rubber Workers of America,[2] whom we met through a mutual friend, was well known for his recordings and performances of folk and labor songs and he, too, occasionally played at fund-raisers organized by Sara.

The most memorable event Sara staged was a 1956 fund-raiser for Adlai Stevenson and Estes Kefauver, the Democratic nominees for president and vice president. Sara had known Kefauver since he was a congressman from Chattanooga, when she covered his activities for *The Chattanooga Times*. When we moved to Washington, she again covered him for the Cottrell News Bureau. In the course of working with him, Sara became friendly with his charming wife, Nancy. Sara became actively involved in the 1956 campaign and invited Nancy to appear at a large fund-raising cocktail party at our home. In addition to greeting people, Nancy officiated at a raffle of art objects donated for the occasion. The party attracted a large group and was a resounding success.

Hollin Hills gave me an opportunity to know people who had important positions in government and the news media. Lively discussions with neighbors sharpened my knowledge of public affairs.

---

[1] Byrd later became nationally recognized, perhaps best known for his popularization of bossa nova music in the United States.

[2] During the Kennedy administration, Glazer was labor attaché at the U.S. Embassy in Mexico City.

Probably the most intense conversations were held in an essential Hollin Hills institution—the carpool. Most families could not afford two automobiles. However, most mothers stayed home with their children and needed an automobile to run errands and transport children to various activities. Since public transportation was virtually nonexistent, carpools were a necessity for the husbands. Carpools usually had five members, each of whom drove one day a week. Even with this schedule, it could be inconvenient for a person to deprive his family of a car even one day a week.

Our carpool hit upon the idea of purchasing a cheap, old car that could be used exclusively for the carpool. We found an ad for a vintage black Cadillac that had literally been owned by an elderly lady who used it principally for Sunday outings. Although it was at least 10 years old, the car appeared to be in good condition, had been driven only about 45,000 miles and seemed to be a steal for the asking price of $375. Clay Cochran, economist for the National Rural Electric Cooperative Association and a member of the carpool, said that as the son of a poor Texas farmer, he had always aspired to own a Cadillac. Now, for his $75 share, Clay could not resist. Others were likewise enthusiastic. So we purchased the car and Cochran proposed we buy a black cap for the designated driver of the day, so it would appear we had a chauffeur.

Alas, the car turned out not to be a bargain. Repairing its frequent mechanical problems cost more than we had paid for the vehicle. Restoring malfunctioning window wipers, for example, was a major undertaking, requiring removal of all of the apparatus behind the dashboard. After about six months we abandoned the Cadillac, with a better understanding of why Cadillacs were meant for the wealthy.

•

In 1959, after Sara and I had built three additions to our modest home, it still did not fulfill our needs. When we learned that a larger, more elegant, beautifully landscaped Hollin Hills house was available, we quickly made an offer on it. It commanded a bucolic view of a dairy farm and surrounding countryside and proved to be an excellent locale for the increased entertaining we were to do during the Kennedy administration, which took office a little more than a year after we moved into the home.

Chapter 25

Introduction to the Kennedy Years

In the 35 years I was executive director, APPA reached the zenith of its influence during the presidencies of John F. Kennedy and Lyndon B. Johnson.

Kennedy did not begin his political career with an interest in public power, nor was he actively involved in the issue when he served in Congress. This was not surprising, since there is no federal power program in the Northeast and the Boston congressional district he represented was served by a private power company.

Kennedy was elected to the House in 1946. The first mention of him in an APPA publication was in the *Weekly Newsletter* of July 20, 1951. An item headed "IMPORTANT LATE FLASH!" reported the House had adopted an amendment sponsored by Kennedy to extend jurisdiction of the Office of Price Stabilization over rates of municipal and cooperative utilities. Rates of most cooperative and public power utilities are locally regulated.

The Senate and House Banking and Currency committees had previously killed similar measures. When Kennedy introduced his amendment, he was the only Congressman who spoke in its favor. Nevertheless, it was approved on a voice vote. Because no similar provision was contained in a companion bill already passed by the Senate, the issue was referred to a Senate-House conference committee.

In a letter to members of the conference committee, I said the amendment would bring more than 3,000 nonprofit electric utilities, which account for only 25 percent of the nation's electric business, under federal rate control, while 850 private power companies selling 75 percent of retail electricity would be subject to state control. The amendment would do little to hold down the cost of living and "would add immeasurably to the workload of OPS, with little commensurate return," I said.

A week later, the conferees killed the Kennedy amendment, and it was not offered again.

•

Less than a year later, the *APPA Weekly Newsletter* reported that Rep. Bob Jones, D-Ala., made a House floor speech responding to Kennedy's allegations that the Tennessee Valley Authority's low power rates were luring the shoe and textile industries from New England—a complaint commonly made by power companies and congressmen from the Northeast. Jones accused Kennedy of "sectionalism" and said power rates were not a controlling factor in the total operating costs of either the textile or shoe manufacturing industries. He pointed out an estimated $180 million had been spent in the TVA area during the previous year for electrical appliances, almost all of which were manufactured in the East.

In the congressional elections of 1952, Kennedy won a seat in the Senate and within a year his views on public power had changed. Two people influenced this reversal, Theodore (Ted) Sorensen, a member of Kennedy's staff, and Charles Bartlett, Washington correspondent for *The Chattanooga Times* and a longtime personal friend of Kennedy's.

Sorensen was from Nebraska and his father was an attorney who represented rural power districts in that all-public power state. Sorensen had learned about public power from his father. Early in his career with Kennedy, he invited me and my wife to dinner at his home. He told me that as a youth, he would visit his father's office and read *Public Power* magazine, copies of which were displayed in his father's reception room.

TVA held prime importance in the Tennessee Valley and was the subject of much news coverage. Hence, Bartlett's interest in TVA. He was an unusual reporter who influenced as well as reported on government policies and he sought to change Kennedy's views on TVA. As part of this effort, he invited me to have lunch with him and Kennedy while Kennedy was in the House, but preparing to run for the Senate. Bartlett asked me to brief the congressman on the importance of public power, its significance as a yardstick for electric rates and the role of the preference clause in power policy.

At our luncheon in the House dining room in the Capitol, Kennedy was cordial but businesslike. He listened intently and asked searching questions, but he obviously did not have strong interest in public power.

Sorensen's and Bartlett's influence became evident in early December 1953, when Kennedy, then a senator, addressed a meeting of the Chattanooga Chamber of Commerce. Bartlett had arranged the invitation and Sorensen drafted his speech. Kennedy acknowledged that TVA's power rates were one of several reasons some New England industry was moving south, then he said, in language that clearly bore Sorensen's stamp:[1]

> It is my position, a position not shared by all segments of opinion in New England, that our answer to your power advantage in the struggle for industry should not be attempted dilution of power development in Tennessee; but instead the development of our resources in Massachusetts and New England. The TVA is not "creeping socialism" because it attracts industry which might otherwise locate, remain or expand in New England. It is a challenge to us to seek further utilization of our own natural resources. I do not want to see your electric bills for industrial power go up; I want to see our bills go down.[2]

•

After his visit to Tennessee, Kennedy was not active in power issues until he began his campaign for the presidency in 1960. Meanwhile, interest in natural resources and energy development was heating up because of criticism of President Eisenhower's policy of "no new starts" on federal hydroelectric power projects. Eisenhower also came under fire for the actions of the Federal Power Commission, which was charged with favoring natural gas and electric power interests to the detriment of consumers. The FPC issue came to a head in May 1960, when Eisenhower refused to reappoint Commissioner William R. Connole because he had become "identified with one particular point of view"— interests of the consumer.

During the 1960 presidential election campaign, which pitted Kennedy against Vice President Richard Nixon, APPA submitted statements to both the Democratic and Republican platform committees. Among other things, we advocated:

- retention and enforcement of the preference clause;
- comprehensive river basin development;

---

[1] After his election as president, Kennedy appointed Sorensen as his special counsel. Sorensen was one of Kennedy's chief speech writers, noted for his eloquent style.

[2] In the audience at that luncheon was another person who was to play an influential role in national power policy—Lee C. White, a former classmate of Sorensen at the University of Nebraska law school. At the time of the Chattanooga luncheon, White was an attorney for TVA, but had been hired by Kennedy and was to report for duty the following month to work on power issues, among others. After Kennedy's election to the presidency, Sorensen named White as assistant special counsel. President Johnson later appointed White chairman of the Federal Power Commission.

- construction of federal transmission lines "wherever they are economically necessary for the proper integration of federal power plants";
- establishment of a Northeastern Power Administration to plan for and coordinate maximum development of northeastern rivers;
- a dynamic federal program for construction and operation of developmental nuclear power reactors, in addition to projects proposed by the utility industry, and
- adoption of a federal capital budget for financing federal loans, hydroelectric installations and other "productive, self-liquidating capital investments."

Both political parties adopted platform planks calling for specific policies in natural resources and power development. The Democratic plank said a new Democratic administration would "foster the development of efficient regional giant power systems from all sources, including water, tidal and nuclear, to supply low-cost electricity to all retail electric systems, public, private and cooperative." The platform also pledged to:

> continue to develop "yardsticks" for measuring the rates of private utility systems. This means meeting the needs of rural electric cooperatives for low-interest loans for distribution, transmission and generation facilities; federal transmission facilities, where appropriate, to provide efficient low-cost power supply; and strict enforcement of the public-preference clause in power marketing.

Two weeks later, the Republicans adopted natural resource and power planks in their platform. Although not as detailed as the Democratic provisions, the Republicans, too, pledged to "observe the preference clause in marketing federal power" and to support "the basic principles of reclamation."

The Republican natural resources policy called for continued "teamwork between federal, state and private entities," which has "resulted in sustained conservation and resource development programs on a scale unmatched in our history."

The previous seven years of Republican leadership "have seen the development of more power capacity, flood control, irrigation, fish and wildlife projects, recreational facilities, and associated multipurpose benefits than during any previous administration in history," the

Republicans said.

In its only mention of nuclear power, the GOP platform recommended "continued expansion of the Eisenhower-Nixon atoms-for-peace program."

By mid-September 1960 the campaign was in full swing. In early September, both candidates made speeches in the West calling for expanded resource development.

In Boise, Idaho, Vice President Nixon said the time had come to "put greater emphasis on new starts for sound multiple-purpose projects in the field of reclamation and power development and flood control.

"Since 1953, under the leadership of the Eisenhower administration, Congress has authorized 53 new projects or units" with construction started on 44, Nixon said. "In five of the last six years, Democratic Congresses have appropriated less than the administration has requested for reclamation," Nixon said.

Democratic Vice Presidential Candidate Lyndon Johnson called Nixon's speech a "repudiation" of the no new starts policy and "a pretty late start."

In a speech the same week in Redding, California, Kennedy said his first step in the resources field, if elected, would be to "reverse the defeatist policy of no new starts and move ahead with full development of our natural resources..."

Kennedy pointed out that by 1975 there would be more than 230 million Americans, and:

> their need for electric power in all-electric homes, all-electric factories, all-electric farms, will be three times as great as it is today....We must expand our generating capacity to meet the need. We have the potential—an estimated potential of 117 million kilowatts [of hydro power capacity]. But we have developed only 26.5 million kilowatts—only a fraction of our most powerful resource.

The highlight of the campaign for public power was Kennedy's speech before the Western States Water and Power Consumers Conference in Billings, Montana, on September 22, 1960. The conference was held biennially during the years of congressional elections. The conference was supported by many of the same groups that comprised the Electric Consumers Information Committee but its sponsorship was augmented by a number of western organizations. Directors and employees of rural electric cooperatives comprised the largest group of participants.

Representatives of public power utilities, labor organizations, the National Farmers Union and other consumer-oriented groups also attended.

Presidential or vice presidential candidates of both political parties were always invited to speak. In 1960, because of the emergence of public power and rural electrification as major issues, Clyde Ellis and I worked hard to get Nixon and Kennedy to speak to the group. The invitation was more appealing to the Democratic candidate because of the policies advocated by the Western States Water and Power Consumers Conference. Sen. "Scoop" Jackson of Washington was chairman of the Democratic National Committee and I urged him to do what he could to persuade Kennedy to accept our invitation.

Kennedy agreed to speak but Nixon had a conflict and could not attend. Residents of the Billings area as well as conference delegates were invited and the meeting was moved to the Shrine Auditorium. About 6,000 people packed into the standing-room-only auditorium.

Ellis and I, along with James Patton, president of the National Farmers Union, and Pat Greathouse, vice president of the United Auto Workers Union, met Kennedy at the airport and escorted him to the auditorium. His private campaign plane, the Caroline (named for his daughter), was due to arrive at about 7 p.m., but Kennedy was running about two hours behind schedule—understandable because he had made six speeches in Iowa and North and South Dakota before arriving in Billings.

Kennedy's plane finally touched down about 9 p.m. Despite the long day, he seemed fresh, eager and energetic.

Taking note of the Cold War rivalry between the United States and the Soviet Union, and referring to a United Nations conference then being held in New York, at which Khrushchev was present, Kennedy declared:[3]

> Mr. Khrushchev confronts us at the United Nations with arrogant confidence because he believes that the economy of the Soviet Union and the Communist bloc is growing at a faster relative rate than is ours. He feels that he is rapidly closing the gap between Russian and American economic strength, and he knows and we know that last year the United States had the lowest rate of economic increase of any major industrialized society in the world...

---

[3] Quotations from Kennedy's speech were taken from the actual transcript, as published in The Speeches of Senator John F. Kennedy Presidential Campaign of 1960 on September 13, 1961 by the U.S. Government Printing Office for the Committee on Commerce, United States Senate.

Mr. Khrushchev is not impressed by words....Mr. Khrushchev is going
to be impressed by one thing and so is the world community, and that is
the power of the United States, and that includes not only military power;
it includes industrial power, atomic power, water power and electric power
of every kind...

Kennedy laid out a nine-point program for resource development:

First, we will reverse the policy of no new starts...And we are going to
move ahead under that program on comprehensive plans for multi-purpose
river development.

Second, we will devote the benefits of public resources to the public
good. That includes adherence to the preference clause in carrying out the
principles of Theodore Roosevelt and Franklin Roosevelt. We will not
stand by and permit our resources to be wasted or taken for partial
development for the benefit of special interests. We will not stand by, for
example, and permit another Hells Canyon blunder in the Clark Fork
Basin...

Third, we will appoint to the Federal Power Commission, to the
Department of the Interior, to the Rural Electrification Administration, and
to every other agency, men who will put the public interest first...

Fourth, we will establish a Council of Resources and Conservation
Advisors in the Office of the President, to coordinate planning in this
field...

We need a rational schedule of action, instead of the hit-or-miss
development that depends upon annual political or budgetary pressures.
We need a national as well as a local and regional view, planning, for
example, how we might profitably link the power systems of the Columbia
and the Missouri rivers, and deciding where public and cooperative power
systems require steam as well as hydro plants...

Fifth, we shall, I hope, develop more businesslike budget practices for
the natural resources development, practices which distinguished between
capital investments and operating expenditures, instead of a system which
treats capital invested in a wholly self-liquidating power project, the same
as an expenditure which cannot ever be recovered...

Sixth, we will restore REA to its former role of preeminence, bringing
it from...concern over political interference, higher rates of interest and
budgetary starvation and enabling that remarkable American institution to
get on with its work of providing low-cost electricity and telephones for
every American farm family.

Seventh, we will step up the fight against water pollution. I can imagine
nothing more wasteful than to pollute our rivers and permit valuable water
to flow to the sea in conditions where other people cannot use it...

Eighth, we will restore America's leadership in atomic development and protect the public's tremendous investment in this source of energy which must be tapped for the public good.

Ninth, and finally, we will apply to the development of our resources the same scientific talent and energies which we have applied to the development of our national defense, inquiring into methods of preventing evaporation, of controlling weather, above all, of converting salt water to fresh water, for whichever nation wins that race, to develop an economical way of using our seas for plants and human consumption will have done more to win the friendship of people who live in deserts around great oceans than all the sputniks in outer space.

Kennedy's 20-minute speech was interrupted by applause 20 times and at the conclusion he received a standing ovation.

Ken Holum, executive director of Midwest Electric Consumers Association, joined Ellis, Patton, Greathouse and me in escorting Kennedy back to his plane. On the return to the airport, we had a conversation that was to have long-term impact. We told Kennedy it was essential to have people in his administration who understood and were sympathetic to the need for natural resources and power development. We said we would like to meet with him after the election to advise him on appointees to some key positions in the administration. He agreed to our request.

The Billings speech was a landmark. It was frequently cited during his administration and in the Johnson administration as the basis for natural resource and power development.

•

Although the Billings speech remained Kennedy's most comprehensive statement on natural resources and power policy, he discussed the issue at a number of campaign events. Concern that the United States was falling behind Russia in building large hydro power stations was consistent with a major theme of the campaign—the reputed "missile gap" between the United States and the Soviet Union.

In October, Kennedy raised the power issue during his first televised debate with Nixon. His comments were based on the report of the three senators who had visited Soviet hydro developments in 1959. He said he was not satisfied with the nation's progress "when we are failing to develop the natural resources of the United States to the fullest." He added:

Here in the United States, which developed the Tennessee Valley and which built the Grand Coulee and the other dams in the Northwest United States, at the present rate of hydro power production—and that is the hallmark of an industrialized society—the Soviet Union by 1975 will be producing more power than we are.

Nixon responded by declaring:

We have developed more hydroelectric power in these seven and a half years [of the Eisenhower administration] than was developed in any previous administration in history.

In a subsequent speech, Nixon again disputed Kennedy's assertion that the Soviet Union would surpass the United States in hydro power capacity by 1975. He said the Russians would have to build eight Grand Coulee Dams a year from then until 1977 "just to catch up with U. S. capacity."

The debate on the relative rate of expansion of hydro power capacity continued. In a speech in St. Louis, Kennedy repeated his earlier charge that the Soviet Union would catch up with the United States in power production by 1975 and added:

It would not take eight Grand Coulees a year to bridge this gap by 1975. It would not even take three.

And the facts of the matter are that this year the Soviets are building three dams larger than Grand Coulee, two of which are more than twice as large.

Kennedy also challenged Nixon's assertion in the televised debate that the Eisenhower-Nixon administration had "developed more hydroelectric power in seven and a half years than was developed in any previous administration in history." Kennedy responded:

Ask your local REA director about what has happened on generation and transmission facilities. Ask the people who live in the great river valleys whether our rate of power expansion increased as fast as it did before. Ask the Army engineers to list all the projects Mr. Nixon talks about and you find out, contrary to his implication, they are not power projects; they are not public projects and they were not initiated by the Republican Party. It's time to get moving again on power development.

Campaigning in the Tennessee Valley, both candidates praised TVA. At Bowling Green, Kentucky, Kennedy called TVA "one of the Democratic

Party's proudest achievements." Nixon, speaking in West Memphis, Arkansas, said TVA and Grand Coulee Dam were examples of big programs in which the federal government must take the lead, because individuals and localities could not carry them out without federal assistance.

•

After the election, the five people who met with Kennedy in Billings quickly asked to meet with the president-elect to discuss policies and appointments. Our primary interests were the chairman of the Federal Power Commission, the undersecretary and assistant secretary for water and power of the Department of Interior and the administrator of the Rural Electrification Administration. The assistant secretary's position was especially important because the person holding this post had jurisdiction over the Bureau of Reclamation and the federal power marketing agencies, such as Bonneville, Southwestern and Southeastern power administrations.

To get an appointment with Kennedy, I sought Senator Jackson's assistance. About a month after the election—early in the week of December—I was in Omaha to speak at the annual meeting of the Mid-West Electric Consumers Association when I received a call from my secretary, Elaine Shinn. Evelyn Lincoln, secretary to the president-elect, had called to say our group would meet the following afternoon with Kennedy at his home in Georgetown.

Ken Holum was also at the Omaha meeting. We returned to Washington that night. The only flight we could get brought us to Baltimore, where we arrived about midnight.

In anticipation of the meeting, we had already prepared briefing materials to leave with Kennedy, but we got together the morning of our appointment to make last-minute decisions about our conference with the president-elect. We then took taxis to the Kennedys' home.

The Kennedys lived on N Street in a vintage row house that fronted directly onto the sidewalk in the fashionable Georgetown section, where many prominent government officials lived. A double living room was separated by doors. The room nearest the front of the house was used as a reception area; Kennedy met with visitors in an adjoining room in the rear.

About 15 minutes after our arrival, we were called into the room Kennedy used for his meetings. We reiterated our support for acceleration of hydroelectric power development and the need for high-voltage inter-regional transmission lines, especially between the Pacific Northwest and the Pacific Southwest. We gave him two memos. One covered general policies and water and power projects we felt should be initiated. A second listed names of people we recommended for appointments to key administration positions.

The press was staked out in front of the Kennedy home on a 24-hour basis and the president-elect warned we would be interviewed after the meeting. He cautioned us to be general in our responses, advised us on the approach we might use and escorted us to the door.

As spokesperson for the group, I told the press that we had primarily discussed policy issues related to natural resource development. Neither I nor others in the group mentioned that we had suggested the names of possible appointees. To have done so would have betrayed the confidentiality of our discussions and would have been the kiss of death for anyone on our list.

We did not wait long for the announcement of appointees. During that week, Kennedy named Rep. Stewart Udall, D-Ariz.. to be secretary of interior. We felt good about this appointment. We knew him to be friendly to our cause (the NRECA voting record gave him a 100 percent score for rural electrification and public power). *The Wall Street Journal* described him as an "advocate of public power development," but added that he would "not try to freeze private enterprise out of power development." The *Journal* said under Udall there would be a drive "slow at first—to construct a number of hydroelectric plants on the Grand Coulee scale. Most likely sites for priority treatment: The Columbia, Colorado and Missouri rivers."

•

One of the most sensitive positions to be filled was the chairmanship of the Federal Power Commission. The agency had authority to regulate wholesale rates of private power companies but it never had taken this responsibility seriously. There were periods—notably during Leland Olds' chairmanship—when the commission had a consumer orientation in carrying out its other responsibilities, especially with regulation of natural gas companies. However, during the period immediately preceding the 1960 elections, the FPC was regarded by consumer and public power advocates as little more than a rubber stamp for the industries it regulated.

During the election campaign, Kennedy asked James M. Landis to study the performance of regulatory agencies. Landis was a former dean of the Harvard Law School and a former chairman of the Securities and Exchange Commission and the Civil Aeronautics Board. In an 87-page report submitted to the president-elect in mid-December 1960, Landis excoriated the regulatory agencies. He singled out the Federal Power Commission as "the outstanding example in the federal government of the breakdown of the administrative process." The FPC should get preference in an extensive reorganization of the regulatory agencies because it was one of four agencies (including the Federal Communications Commission, the Interstate Commerce Commission and the Civil Aeronautics Board) "in the worst situation." FPC "appears to have refrained from any real effort to deal with its docket" of natural gas cases in the expectation that legislation would be passed to free gas producers from federal regulation, Landis said. The regulatory agencies suffer from "industry orientation," and "the regulated have become the regulators," Landis said.

When our group met with Kennedy, we avoided recommending someone closely identified with public power because such a person might be regarded as biased against the private power companies and would likely not be appointed. However, after release of the Landis report, I received a telephone call from Adam Yarmolinsky, who was vetting appointments for Kennedy. Yarmolinsky said we had not suggested anyone who was tough enough to fill the FPC chairmanship and asked us to propose additional names.

I was surprised but pleased by Yarmolinsky's request and immediately consulted with Jim Grahl, J.D. Brown and Larry Hobart of my staff. We agreed upon Joe Swidler, former general counsel of TVA. After consulting with the other four members of our ad hoc committee, I called Yarmolinsky to recommend Swidler. Much to our delight, Kennedy accepted our suggestion.

In early January, Kennedy announced the appointment of two others whom we had recommended for key positions in the Department of the Interior. James K. Carr, assistant general manager of the Sacramento Municipal Utility District, was named undersecretary and Ken Holum of Mid-West Electric Consumers Association was appointed assistant secretary for water and power.

•

Kennedy followed up quickly on his campaign commitments to accelerate development of water resources. In his State of the Union message to Congress in January 1961, he said he would propose measures to "increase the development of our natural resources." In February, in his economic message to Congress, he called for a long-range energy resource development program "and accelerated programs for economical production of energy from nuclear sources, including nuclear fusion."

The message pointed out that the economic growth of the United States "has been favored by an abundant supply of natural resources of almost every sort. But resource needs and supplies are not static. As our needs mount, as past reserves are depleted, and as technological requirements change, we must constantly develop new supplies if growth is not to be inhibited."

Secretary Udall also announced plans for resource and power development. In February 1961 he released a policy memorandum outlining the direction he expected the new administration to follow. Production of electricity by the federal government was to be regarded by his department as a great asset to the nation or, as he described it, a "necessary good." The Eisenhower administration, he said:

> regarded public power as something of a necessary evil. We regard it as a necessary good. We're not—as they did—going to go out searching for ways to let private industry have access to hydroelectric sites and falling water at dams built with federal funds.

Udall asked Interior Department staff to give immediate attention to plans for early interconnection of areas served by the power marketing agencies with common-carrier transmission lines and to "enlarging regional cooperative pooling of generation and transmission facilities."

On February 23, 1961 President Kennedy highlighted the importance he attached to natural resources and power development by sending a special message to Congress on the subject. The president rejected the "no new starts" policy of the Eisenhower administration and said he had asked the Bureau of the Budget to "schedule a progressive, orderly program of new projects to meet accumulated demands." Kennedy also directed the interior secretary "to develop plans for early interconnection of areas served by the department's marketing agencies with adequate common carrier transmission lines; to plan for further national cooperative pooling of electric power, both public and private, and to enlarge such pooling as now exists."

The president said his administration would adhere to these principles in marketing power produced by the federal government:

- Preference in power sales shall be given public agencies and cooperatives.

- Domestic and rural consumers shall have priority over other consumers in the disposal of power.
- Power shall be sold at the lowest possible rates consistent with sound business principles.
- Power disposal shall be such as to encourage widespread use and to prevent monopolization.

These policies paralleled those advocated by APPA. We were, of course, delighted.

The first year of the Kennedy presidency gave indications of the major federal power issues that were to develop during his first term: reinvigoration of the FPC, initiation of new starts in hydro projects, approval of a Pacific Northwest-Pacific Southwest intertie, authorization of power production at the New Production Reactor at Hanford, Washington, and construction of federal transmission lines for the Colorado River Storage Project. Some of these issues were resolved during the Kennedy presidency; others did not reach fruition until the Johnson administration.

The early Kennedy years were heady ones for me. I attended frequent meetings in the offices of Udall, Carr and Holum and was gratified by the trust they placed in me and the APPA staff. I had known most of the top appointees in the energy field before they joined the administration and enjoyed a cordial relationship that was deepened by social as well as professional contacts during the Kennedy administration. My wife Sara and I frequently entertained them and their spouses in our home, along with members of Congress with whom I worked. Neither before nor after the Kennedy and Johnson administrations did I have such access to so many high-ranking officials in the government.

Chapter 26

Crossing Swords with the Kennedy Administration

In the 34 months he served in the White House, President Kennedy saw a number of his administration's federal power initiatives come to fruition.

Public power and rural electrification advocates generally supported the president's efforts, but a serious rift occurred in 1962. Secretary of the Interior Stewart Udall triggered the dispute with a controversial decision on construction of transmission lines for the Colorado River Storage Project.

The issue—ownership of transmission lines to deliver power from federal power projects to the government's wholesale customers—reached to the heart of conflicts between public and private power. Under federal law dating back to 1906, municipal electric utilities (and later rural electric cooperatives) had a preference in purchasing low-cost power from the government's hydroelectric power facilities. Preference was an anti-monopoly provision that assured benefits of a public resource flowed directly to consumers through nonprofit institutions and promoted competition in the electric industry. However, preference would be meaningless if the government did not own transmission lines to deliver power to its customers. Because most preference customers were small entities, they did not have the resources to build the necessary transmission lines.

The power companies devised strategies to thwart the government's efforts to deliver power to consumer-owned utilities. They offered to build the transmission lines themselves. Ignoring the fact that the cost of the government's transmission lines would be repaid in full, with interest, by users, the companies said no appropriation would be needed if they built the lines. At the same time, the government would be foreclosed from making a further intrusion into the electric business. Federal regulation of transmission rates was virtually nonexistent at that time and the power companies could impose transmission rates that would make the federal power too costly for preference customers. That would enable the power companies to buy the power at a bargain price.

•

Seeds of the problem surrounding transmission of Colorado River Storage Project power were sown late in 1958. Utah Power & Light Company and Arizona Public Service Company announced plans to construct a $23 million, 230-kilovolt transmission line that would connect the two companies and the 1,356-megawatt federal power plant at Glen Canyon Dam, under construction in northern Arizona and scheduled to begin producing power in June 1964. It was a key element of the CRSP, which also included Flaming Gorge Dam in Utah (152 mw), scheduled to go on line in June 1963, and Curecanti Dam in Colorado (135 mw), slated to begin operation in 1966.

The power companies' proposed transmission line would reach from Mexico to Canada, crossing Arizona, Utah, New Mexico, Colorado, Wyoming, Idaho and Montana.

The possibility of linking the northern terminal of this line with the federal hydroelectric system of the Missouri Basin to the east and the Bonneville Power Administration system to the west was not advertised by the power companies. However, the logic of such a move led to speculation that the proposed line would become a major leg in a private utility inter-regional grid linking large federal hydro systems in the West.

Consumer-owned utilities feared the private utilities' transmission grid would become an unavoidable toll gate for electricity. Cooperative and municipal electric utilities and irrigation power districts in the region formed Colorado River Basin Consumers Power, Inc. (CRBCP) to study alternative plans for transmission.[1]

The consumer-owned utilities estimated they could use all of the firm power from the Upper Colorado River storage plants by 1970. They did not want to become beholden to two companies with a long record of vigorous opposition to public power and rural electrification.

CRBCP hired the Kuljian Corporation, consulting engineers of Philadelphia, Pa., to draw up plans for a federal transmission grid that would meet the needs of preference customers. Harvey McPhail, a former assistant commissioner of the Bureau of Reclamation, headed the effort

---

[1] CRBC was the predecessor to the Colorado River Energy Distributors Association (CREDA) which currently represents consumer-owned utilities that distribute power from the Colorado River Storage Project.

for Kuljian. The Bureau of Reclamation had been studying a plan for federal transmission lines, but had not disclosed its proposal.

McPhail presented his report to the Bureau of Reclamation in March 1960. He proposed federal construction of a transmission grid that would cost between $155 million and $165 million and recommended that funds be sought for fiscal 1961 to begin immediate construction of lines from Glen Canyon to Curecanti and from Flaming Gorge to Oak Creek, Colorado. He also recommended an interconnection between the federal grid and the western division of the Missouri Basin project. Integration of the federal projects would reduce costs for consumers and boost government revenues. He also proposed an interconnection between the CRSP and the downstream Colorado River dams, including the Hoover, Parker and Davis projects.

McPhail estimated private utility charges for wheeling power over their lines would add more than $60 million to preference customer power costs over the life of the CRSP. Further, the private utility plan would not permit the federal government to take advantage of diversity of load or to share reserve capabilities. The companies' plan would give ultimate control over Upper Colorado River power to the private utilities, McPhail said.

In December 1960 CRBCP told the Bureau of Reclamation the private utility plan would reduce the federal government's capital investment, but wheeling charges would add $492 million to the cost over the project's 100-year amortization period. The federal grid proposal, through interchanges of energy and displacement of power, would result in economies "not only for the Storage Project but for all systems [that] its transmission lines interconnect," CRBCP said.

•

In the final week of the Eisenhower administration, Secretary of the Interior Fred Seaton, a Nebraska Republican, approved a plan for an all-federal transmission system to carry CRSP power to preference customers. He announced an average power rate of 6 mills per kilowatt-hour for firm energy, 2.5 mills per kwh for non-firm energy, and $15 per kilowatt-year for peaking capacity would be sufficient to meet project payout requirements. Seaton approved Reclamation Commissioner Floyd E. Dominy's recommendation to reject a private utility plan for construction of major Upper Colorado transmission lines. The private utilities' average firm power rate would have to be at least 6.57 mills per kwh, Dominy said. That would increase costs for preference customers by $2.9 million annually, or $253 million over 86 years.

Two weeks after the Kennedy administration took office, Secretary Udall announced his support for construction of an all-federal transmission grid for the CRSP and said he would expedite the project. The president asked Congress to appropriate $13.7 million for fiscal 1962 for the project, including $5.8 million to begin building the controversial lines the private power companies wanted to build. Both the private companies and preference customers supported "non-controversial" backbone transmission facilities that were already under construction by the Bureau of Reclamation.

The Kennedy administration's announcement set off a flurry of activity. Five companies—Pacific Power & Light, Utah Power & Light, Public Service Company of Colorado, Public Service Company of New Mexico, and Arizona Public Service Company—launched a vigorous campaign to oppose federal appropriations. They proposed to build a majority of the lines themselves as part of a "combination" system.

Feverish lobbying of Congress was aimed initially at influencing hearings on the appropriations, scheduled for June 1961 by the House Appropriations Subcommittee on Public Works. Eighty-one representatives of consumer-owned electric utilities from 11 states came to Washington to support federal funds. Six members of the group testified before the subcommittee.

During the hearings, Sen. Frank E. Moss, D-Utah, said wheeling arrangements such as those proposed by the private utilities would encourage creation of interconnected monopolies of private companies.

"The efforts of the government should be directed toward curtailing and curbing monopolies—not toward fostering and encouraging them by placing a strangling toll gate on this great federal reclamation project," Moss said.

Colorado River Basin Consumers Power, Inc. President Marion Wilson said the private utilities, by constructing segments of the transmission system, would control "the entire billion-dollar Colorado River Storage Project with an investment equal to only 10 percent of the project's cost."

The five power companies launched a major public relations campaign and argued that the bureau's comparison of the companies' plan with an all-federal transmission system was the result of a flawed analysis. A fair appraisal, they said, would show power could be delivered to preference customers at the same rate projected by the bureau. They claimed their plan would save taxpayers $136 million in transmission line construction costs and produce new federal, state and local tax revenues of more than $3 million annually.

Lobbying activity on the all-federal transmission lines continued at a frantic pace from June until September, when the Appropriations Committee and the full House were to take up the issue. Veteran congressmen described the private utility campaign against the federal transmission lines as the most intensive they had ever experienced.

To counteract the private utility campaign, CRBCP set up a command post in the Congressional Hotel, located across the street from the Cannon House Office Building. The 81 people who came to Washington in June for the House subcommittee hearing reported each day on their contacts with members of their delegations. After the hearing, relays from the region continued to travel to Washington to meet with congressmen and senators. Les Alexander of the Salt River Project, assisted by other CRBCP representatives and members of the APPA and National Rural Electric Cooperative Association staffs, manned the command post. One of the most effective speakers in behalf of federal transmission lines was R.J. McMullin, SRP general manager then serving as APPA president.

The fight over transmission lines attracted national attention. *The Washington Post* published a cartoon by its award-winning cartoonist, Herblock, showing a large circus tent under a sign reading, "U.S. PUBLIC POWER PROJECTS." Two men labled "Private Transmission Lines" were shown erecting a ticket booth with the sign, "Pay Here" in front of the tent. The caption read, "All We Want To Do Is Set Up This Little Stand."

•

In early September the House Appropriations Committee approved the full $13.7 million requested by the president, including $5.8 million to begin construction of the controversial lines that the power companies wanted to build. A week later the full House took up the appropriation bill. A bitter debate ensued over an amendment proposed by Rep. Ben Jensen, R-Iowa, to eliminate funding for the federal transmission lines.

Speaking against the appropriation, Rep. Frank Becker, R-N.Y., said the fight was a "private-public fight and one of much greater magnitude than meets the eye." The proposed federal system would not deliver power to all the preference customers, he said. The Bureau of Reclamation then would require millions of additional tax dollars to extend the proposed system or the rural electric cooperatives would have to borrow "additional millions of dollars from the government at 2 percent interest to build lines to the federal system. After all of this is done, then the bureau will be back for millions of additional tax dollars to tie the all-federal Colorado River project system in with other federal systems."

Speaking in defense of the appropriation, Rep. Clarence Cannon, D-Mo., chairman of the House Appropriations Committee, said that

> the investor-owned companies are attempting to muscle in—"reaping where they have not sown and gathering where they have not strawed." They are interested in dividends—the highest rates obtainable to provide high returns on their stock...What we insist on is that there should be sufficient public power to keep rates reasonable, to have a yardstick, to have a policeman on the corner, to have enough competition to control predatory rates and services.

Private utilities "are trying to put up a tollgate on a necessity of life that is as indispensable to the average family as are air, water and sunlight," Cannon said. "Today every family must have electricity and congressmen must see that they get it at as reasonable a rate as can be provided."

At the height of the debate, President Kennedy issued a statement supporting federal construction of the controversial lines, which he called "fundamental to a sound power policy" and necessary "to insure that the federal investment in these projects will benefit the general public."

Persistent efforts of CRBCP and their allies bore fruit. After a bitter floor fight, the House killed the amendment to eliminate funding, by a vote of 224 to 182. The Senate approved the appropriation in late September. While the House voted the funds without qualification, the Senate tied the appropriation to a new study of wheeling prospects by the secretary of the interior. The Senate directed the secretary to report back to Congress before starting construction.

Senate-House conferees did not support the Senate position. They agreed that constructiion of transmission lines should proceed "unless the secretary of the interior finds it practicable and in the national interest to enter into wheeling agreements with the private power interests."

We viewed the result as a victory. After final congressional action, Udall said he would proceed immediately to construct the basic back-bone transmission lines needed to market Colorado River Storage Project power. Because of Udall's previous commitment to an all-federal transmission system, we did not take sufficient heed to another part of Udall's statement in which he promised to negotiate interconnection and wheeling agreements with all power suppliers that were "in the national interest and provide mutual advantage to all parties concerned."

•

Supporters of the all-federal transmission system were shocked in February 1962 when Udall announced plans for a combination federal-private power company transmission system. He described the new plan, based on letters of intent submitted by the companies, as a "middle way" approach to transmission planning.

Preference customers, who would use all of the power output from the CRSP, "have received the fullest possible protection" under the plan, Udall said. Asked whether preference customers would be permitted to use the lines to transmit power from their own generating plants, the secretary said the arrangement could best be called a "limited common carrier" principle. Capacity would be available only to the extent that federal capacity would have been available under an all-federal system, he said.

Under the agreement, some sections in the original all-federal proposal would be eliminated while construction of others would be delayed, Udall said. Acceptance of the utilities' proposal would mean a $27 million reduction in the federal investment for the CRSP transmission grid and would add $77 million to the Colorado Basin Fund by the year 2042, when the 87-year payout period would be completed.

Udall's announcement met an immediate storm of protest from consumer-owned power groups. I had a good relationship with Udall, so my initial public comments about his action were restrained in tone. I called the secretary's announcement a "sharp disappointment" to those who had supported the all-federal transmission system. Clyde Ellis, general manager of National Rural Electric Cooperative Association, and I sent a joint telegram to Udall urging him to reaffirm his earlier position. Later, I made these additional comments:

> The fight for the federal transmission lines in the Colorado River Storage Project was one of the few major victories for public power during the last session of the Congress. To find now that some of the most important of these hard-won gains have been bargained away is indeed a bitter pill to swallow.

> What makes the situation even more distressing is that the federal lines have been traded off on the basis of mere letters of intent by the power companies, and many of these letters are vague and indefinite in their commitments.

There was no mention of "common carrier" in any of the letters of intent and in four of five cases the offer was specifically limited to delivery of CRSP or other federally generated hydro power. The letters of intent contained no commitment to transmit power produced by preference customers, as contemplated in an all-federal system.

I disagreed with Udall's statement that "monopoly control over transmission was prevented." A permanent statewide wheeling arrangement with Utah Power & Light Company—which had repeatedly opposed federal and preference customer power programs—would ensure the company's continued dominance over the power supply of municipal and cooperative electric utilities in Utah.

"Our experience over the years with the private power companies in the Colorado River Basin has taught us to be very wary of their proposals," said Marion Wilson, president of the CRBCP. "They are not our friends. They do not believe in our continued existence."

In early May 1962, the Department of the Interior announced the first contract for transmission from CRSP had been signed with Public Service Company of New Mexico. Udall called the contract's "common carrier" language a "significant breakthrough for electric power consumers in the West."

The contract ignored plans by preference customers to build two large steam plants to tie in with CRSP—a proposal that had been generally recognized as highly beneficial to the basin fund. Nor did it provide for termination of existing contracts for wholesale power between the power company and preference customers. We had requested these provisions.

In late May, the department signed contracts with Public Service Company of Colorado, Pacific Power & Light Company and Utah Power & Light Company. Udall said the common carrier principle had been written into all of the contracts. On June 28, Udall announced he had signed contracts with Colorado-Ute Electric Association and the Salt River Project in Arizona, which would permit interconnection of systems and exchange of energy between the two utilities and CRSP. Colorado-Ute and the Salt River Project planned construction of a steam plant near Hayden, Colorado, and a possible second powerplant near Shiprock, New Mexico. The two thermal generating plants would have capacity of 600 mw.

•

As a result of the contractual arrangements for transmission of CRSP power, some 900 miles of the previously scheduled 3,000-mile federal transmission grid were eliminated and an additional 350 miles were postponed for future construction.

In testimony in May 1962 before a Senate appropriations subcommittee, I said the all-federal transmission system would have provided more benefits to the purchasers of CRSP power than a combination of federal transmission and power company wheeling. I acknowledged that some common carrier service would be available under most of the wheeling contracts, but added:

> We do not believe it is possible, through contractual arrangements, to provide the same degree of flexibility of service, interchange of power among preference customers, or potentialities for future power supplies as would be possible under federal ownership of the lines.

"We are not yet convinced that our requirements will be fully met by these contracts," said CRBCP President Wilson. He showed the subcommittee a chart showing that the power companies' proposed "rock bottom" wheeling charges over the 86-year payout period of the project had shrunk from more than $600 million in 1959 to about $60 million in 1962. This dramatic reduction was clear evidence that a viable competitive proposal by the federal government—and the strong support of such a proposal—paid big dividends to the government and its customers, he said.

•

I and others involved in this effort often wondered why Udall backed away from the all-federal transmission system. Ken Holum, assistant secretary for water and power, was a long-time friend of mine. Knowing his commitment to public power and rural electrification, I am sure he did not personally favor this move. On several occasions I tried to get the full story from Ken, but he was unfailing in his loyalty to Udall and would not give me even a hint as to why Udall reversed himself. I can only speculate that the tremendous political pressure on members of Congress by the power companies had induced Udall to make private concessions. It may be significant that at least one powerful Senate Democrat—Clinton Anderson of New Mexico, a member of the Interior and Insular Affairs Committee—was quick to laud Udall's announcement of the "middle way" approach.

Interior's execution of the agreements with the companies did not end the controversy. In March 1963, McPhail, addressing a CRBCP meeting, said he disagreed that the small prospective savings warranted the "middle way" plan, and added:

Subsequent events, particularly in Utah, have tended to firm my convictions. Thus far, there is no indication that an honest endeavor is being made to carry out the spirit and intent of providing all the benefits that would have been available to the consumer-owned utilities from an all-federal system.

McPhail said Udall had accused the two companies of "bad faith and selfishness" in their efforts to block construction of the cooperatives' Hayden plant. He cited an article in the *Denver Post* that quoted Udall.

"Now had I known that the Utah Light and Power subsidiary [Western] and Public Service would take such a position of blind obstructionism, that might have made a great deal of difference in the agreements we made with them at that time," Udall said. "They got their part of the agreement and then they move over and try to block an essential part of the overall plan. I say that is an element of bad faith and selfishness."

Chapter 27

Winning the Battle at Hanford

APPA worked successfully with the Kennedy administration on the controversial issue of using waste heat from the Atomic Energy Commission's New Production Reactor (NPR) at Hanford, Washington, to generate electricity. Like the Colorado River Storage Project transmission lines issue, the Hanford matter had its origins during the previous administration, but came to a head after Kennedy became president.

APPA got involved when Sen. Henry M. (Scoop) Jackson, D-Wash., spoke at the association's annual conference in Seattle in May 1959. For an additional cost of $100 million, the $145 million NPR, then under construction, could be modified to produce electricity as well as plutonium, the senator told APPA members. Waste heat from the plutonium manufacturing process could support 700 megawatts of electric generating capacity.

Electricity generated at the Hanford facility would be "the lowest cost nuclear power we presently know how to produce," and would provide an opportunity for training both public and private power personnel in the Northwest, Senator Jackson said. Large-scale federal funding would continue to be needed for construction of prototype plants and only the government had the resources to support such programs, he said. He asked APPA to endorse "the kind of nuclear power program that will put competitive atomic power on the line at the earliest possible time."

President Kennedy was quick to advocate conversion of the NPR to a dual-purpose reactor. In late March 1961, only two months after he was inaugurated, the president asked Congress to appropriate $60 million to add electric generating capability to the plutonium production facility.

The NPR would be the world's largest power-producing reactor. Total cost of the power production facilities and reactor modifications was estimated at $95 million. The $60 million appropriation request was needed for engineering and to purchase the turbine generators and heat exchangers.

President Kennedy's request for funds touched off a bitter two-year battle. Largely because of the influence of Senators Jackson and Clint Anderson, D-N.M., an influential member of the Joint Committee on Atomic Energy (JCAE), the proposal received strong support in the Senate. Advocates said the project was primarily a conservation measure that would permit use of an otherwise wasted resource. Without the electric generating facilities, heat from the plutonium production process would be released into the Columbia River, raising the river's temperature. The Cold War was also an important factor in the debate. Most Soviet reactors were dual-purpose, giving the Russians a propaganda and technological advantage because they could argue they were committed to peaceful applications of nuclear power.

The dual-purpose reactor was regarded as a hedge against the possibility that a future disarmament agreement could obviate the need for producing plutonium, resulting in millions of dollars of unproductive investment. A dual-purpose reactor would retain some value in these facilities. In addition, the Northwest region needed power. Firm power produced at Hanford would enhance the value of Bonneville Power Administration's non-firm hydroelectric capacity.

These arguments were overshadowed in the House by opposition from coal and private utility interests. Coal companies feared the advance of nuclear energy would reduce the market for coal. The dual-purpose reactor would represent the first federal involvement in commercial production of nuclear energy. Hence, the private power companies feared the conversion of Bonneville Power Administration into a Tennessee Valley Authority-type organization that would generate electricity from sources other than water power.

Responding to coal interests, important constituents in his congressional district, Rep. James E. VanZandt, R-Pa., a member of the JCAE, led the fight in the House against funds to convert the NPR into a dual-purpose reactor.

Rep. Chet Holifield, D-Calif., chairman of the JCAE, spearheaded the effort in support of the NPR. Having grown up as a poor farm boy in Arkansas, Representative Holifield was penurious when it came to use of government resources. He was deeply troubled by the prospective waste of heat from the NPR if it were not also used in a reactor.

In May 1961, Representative Holifield spoke at APPA's annual conference in San Antonio and urged support for conversion of the NPR to a dual-purpose reactor. He said President Kennedy's request for funds for the project showed "a new and bolder spirit in the executive branch" toward development of nuclear power. APPA members at the conference adopted a resolution in favor of the project.

•

Strong support for the project was evident at JCAE hearings in June 1961. Dr. Glenn Seaborg, a 1951 Nobel laureate and chairman of the Atomic Energy Commission, testified that installation of generating facilities with a capacity of 700 to 800 mw was "economically feasible and would result in substantial benefits." AEC studies showed that revenues from the dual-purpose NPR would cover the capital investment of $95 million in power facilities, all power operating costs, interest on the investment and even a hypothetical insurance cost of $750,000 per year, Seaborg said. He emphasized the value of the dual-purpose reactor from the national security standpoint if the United States and the Soviet Union reached a disarmament agreement. The Hanford plant could continue to operate to produce power, yet could switch to plutonium production within a few days if such an agreement were to break down.

Bonneville Power Administrator Charles Luce told the committee conversion of the Hanford reactor would add 750 mw of salable power to the Pacific Northwest. Even with no large new industrial loads, Luce said, there was a possible deficiency of supply in 1965–66 that the NPR would more than cover. BPA would market the electricity at standard Bonneville rates and would repay the Treasury to cover the cost of the NPR power facilities.

The Edison Electric Institute opposed the project. "Building and operating of any thermal plant for the production of power for the sale to the public by the federal government is contrary to the public interest and American principles," EEI said.

On July 13, 1961, the House approved, by a vote of 176 to 140, an amendment by Representative VanZandt to block funding for the conversion. VandZandt did not want the AEC to "take its place alongside the Department of Interior and TVA as a major power producer of government-generated electric power." The plant threatened "a dangerous precedent for further encroachment of the government into the power business," he said.

Despite the setback, Senate proponents hoped to pass the bill and send it to a Senate-House conference, where it could be revived. Senator Jackson called the House vote "a victory for the private utility and coal industries," and added: "The losers were the American people."

•

A week after the House vote, the Senate approved an appropriation for the project, rejecting an amendment to strike the funding by a vote of 54-to-36.

Parliamentary maneuvers in the House delayed the Senate-House conference for about a month. Power companies used this time to step up their negative campaign. Their tactics infuriated New Mexico's Senator Anderson, a former chairman of the JCAE. On August 4, he made a blistering statement accusing the private utilities of using "outrageous" lobbying tactics.

"I happen to come from a state which is not known as a public power state, nor am I known as a proponent of public power, as such," Anderson said. "But I hope and believe I have a sense of fair play and I must say that this Hanford project is being made the victim of one of the most outrageous lobbying efforts that I have ever witnessed. I am glad to say that this effort has not proved very effective in this body."

Senator Anderson threatened to hold up federal funding for nuclear power development partnership projects with private utilities.

A week later, in early August, the House, after acrimonious debate, voted 235-to-164 to instruct its conferees not to accept the Hanford power project in any compromise with the Senate.

Leading the fight against the motion to instruct the House conferees, Rep. Holifield described private utility lobbying as "a real demonstration of greed and irresponsibility." He added:

> At this point, I believe it is necessary to describe the advantageous position of the privately owned electric utilities. They are the first to yell "private enterprise" in describing their industry. They are the first to yell "socialism" against the rural electric utilities, the great federal, regional, and municipally owned utilities...Any time the people of a city or region decide to bond themselves to produce their own electricity, they—the private utilities—are the first to yell "socialism" or "tax evaders."
>
> Let's look at their operation and compare it to real competitive private enterprise: First, they operate in defined areas on the basis of a monopolistic franchise. In most instances no competition is permitted; second, they are allowed to amortize their capital plant investment on either regular or accelerated formulas of amortization...; third, all of their costs of doing business are allowed in computing their rate levels. This includes high salaries for their executives and top officers and lobbyists...; fourth, their monopolistic franchises have the effect of creating captive customers...; fifth, they are guaranteed a specific profit on their

operations.

I warn the privately owned utilities to guard their luscious bone of captive customers, noncompetitive franchises, guaranteed profits, and rapid amortization. In their dog-in-the-manger selfishness they might start a train of events which could result in the loss of the luscious bone they now have.

When the Senate-House conferees finally met, they compromised on a single 400-mw unit, but all of the power would be used exclusively by the AEC to operate its Hanford facilities. However, even this watered down version was rejected decisively by the House. Shortly thereafter, the Senate, in order to provide funding for AEC for the fiscal year, approved an appropriations bill with no provision for the Hanford power project. The vote ended efforts in that session of Congress to proceed with the dual-purpose reactor.

•

Following the defeat, officials of BPA, AEC and the state of Washington met in October 1961 and agreed to study the feasibility of the state financing and constructing the project. The group was spurred on by BPA Administrator Luce. He reported that the region was expected to fall about 120 mw short of its needs by 1965-66 and the reactor project was the only known source of low-cost power that could come on line in time to avert a shortage.

Within a week after the BPA-AEC-Washington state meeting, the executive committee of the Washington Public Power Supply System authorized Managing Director Owen Hurd to offer WPPSS' services in financing construction of the Hanford power facilities.

WPPSS, a municipal corporation, could issue revenue bonds and therefore offered a means for obtaining low-cost financing, an important factor in determining the project's feasibility. The Supply System had studied the possibility of operating the project for several years. Now it was ready to consider construction as well as operation.

By December 1961 WPPSS submitted a preliminary proposal to AEC and BPA to finance, construct and operate Hanford's power production facilities. During the period of dual-purpose operation, AEC would make available to WPPSS the site for the plant and would sell WPPSS the steam to generate electricity. After the period of dual-purpose operation, AEC would lease the reactor facilities to the Supply System. BPA would purchase the power, integrate it with the federal power system and reimburse WPPSS for its costs.

The government could acquire the facilities at its option and at no cost, at the expiration of the proposed agreement or when all bonds or other obligations incurred by WPPSS were retired.

WPPSS had supported federal development of the power facilities at Hanford, Hurd said, "and we are prepared to do so again. However, we have submitted this proposal because it now appears that non-federal authorization was necessary to get the job done."

AEC and BPA had contended that, since no federal funds would be required, congressional authorization would not be needed to proceed with WPPSS financing and construction. However, on July 6, 1962, Assistant Comptroller General Frank H. Weitzel sent a letter to AEC Chairman Seaborg contending otherwise. Weitzel said the proposed agreement with the Supply System would materially change the nature of the Hanford project from that authorized by Congress and would therefore require specific authorization by Congress. Weitzel's letter returned the issue to Congress.

Responding quickly to the comptroller general, Senator Jackson proposed an amendment to an AEC authorizing bill that would specifically permit construction of the power facilities by WPPSS, but would reserve one-half of the power for private power companies.

Senator Jackson offered his amendment, which was approved with only one dissenting vote—that of Sen. Albert Gore Sr., D-Tenn., who thought the reservation of 50 percent of the power for private utilities would dilute the federal preference clause, which grants rights of first refusal in sale of federal power to consumer-owned utilities.

•

Supporters of the project thought the offer of non-federal financing and reserving half of the power for the companies would mollify opponents. The compromise would allow the government to recoup $25 million already spent on dual-purpose features of the reactor and would make it possible for the government to receive between $31 million and $125 million for steam that otherwise would be wasted.

Any illusions advocates had about the new plan were quickly dispelled. The ink was hardly dry on the JCAE amendment when the battle began on the House floor. Rep. John Saylor, R-Pa., a long-time fierce public power opponent from a coal-mining district, jumped into the fray. In a speech on the House floor, he said Congress already "expressed its will in no uncertain terms when the administration attempted to foist the multimillion-dollar Hanford electric steam plant boondoggle on the American public." Now, he said, although a non-federal agency proposed to build the plant, "it must be apparent that Bonneville is actually the real party of interest and, in fact, stands to be stuck with the bill."

The offer of 50 percent of the power to the private utilities did not satisfy the companies. Through the Edison Electric Institute, they waged an intense campaign against the amendment. Because of strong regional political advocacy for the NPR, power companies in the Northwest did not openly oppose the proposal. However, EEI President Edwin Vennard told me he had personally contacted the presidents of the power companies in the Northwest and they assured him they supported EEI's position.

President Kennedy endorsed the WPPSS plan, stating that it "provides a highly satisfactory arrangement for insuring the maximum utilization of the facility, demonstrates national leadership in resource development, and will aid in achieving national defense objectives."

An important new ally was Rep. Craig Hosmer, R-Calif., a high-ranking and respected member of the JCAE, who previously had opposed the dual-purpose reactor. Representative Hosmer generally supported the private power companies, but he was won over by the proposals for non-federal financing and the reservation of 50 percent of the power for the companies.

Many newspapers in the Northwest and around the country also gave editorial endorsements. The publisher of the *Tri-City Herald*, Glenn Lee, and the newspaper's managing editor, Don Pugnetti, not only gave the issue strong editorial support; they also came to Washington, D.C., to lobby for the project. ("Tri-City" refers to Richland, Pasco and Kennewick, Wash. The Hanford plant is in Richland.)

Despite these efforts, the House on July 17, 1962 voted 232 to 163 in favor of an amendment by Representative VanZandt prohibiting AEC from entering into any arrangements for the construction or operation of electric generating and transmission facilities at the NPR.

Less than two weeks after the House action, the Senate approved the NPR by a voice vote. Washington State Democratic Senators Jackson and Warren G. Magnuson easily shepherded the bill through the Senate. However, the bill had to be referred to a conference committee to resolve differences between the House and Senate. If the conferees approved a compromise allowing WPPSS to build the project, the conference report would have to be approved by the House and Senate. Prospects for House acquiescence appeared dim.

Even Representative Holifield was pessimistic. Larry Hobart of the APPA staff and I visited with Holifield about future action in the House, but he had little appetite for another battle. However, after we assured him of an all-out national and regional effort, he responded with the instincts of a valiant warrior. We talked about inserting new language in the conference report that might be reassuring to the House. Characteristically, Holifield pulled out a yellow pad from his desk and began working with us on language to incorporate in the report.

•

The Senate action triggered an intense lobbying campaign. Ken Billington of the Washington Public Utility Districts' Association, and Hurd virtually camped in D.C. for the next six weeks. They brought in relays of supporters from other regions. Lee and Pugnetti of the *Tri-City Herald* also spent a great deal of time in Washington, calling on members of Congress and groups that might support the effort. Lee was an intense, energetic person who made no secret of the fact that he was a Republican and had been a strong supporter of the private power companies. However, he felt betrayed by the Northwest power companies' adamant opposition to the project.

As the date for another showdown vote approached, Representative Hosmer bombarded his colleagues with unique, attention-getting communications. Members of Congress were accustomed to receiving formal, somewhat staid "Dear Colleague" letters from other members, spelling out the reasons for their positions on legislation. But Representative Hosmer personally prepared hand-lettered pamphlets, some with drawings, spelling out his position. His messages were simple, emphasizing that the new Hanford proposal would not require federal appropriations and customers of both private and public utilities would receive low-cost power produced at Hanford.

The 11 Democrats and eight Republicans in the Northwest congressional delegation, Washington's Democratic Governor Albert Rosellini and Oregon's Republican Governor Mark Hatfield all supported the project. APPA and the National Rural Electric Cooperative Association worked closely with their members in the Northwest to elicit support from other regions. Directly and through the Electric Consumers Information Committee, we garnered support from labor, farm and consumer groups.

These efforts climaxed on August 29, 1962 when the House took up Representative VanZandt's amendment to instruct House conferees to reject any proposal that would sanction the Supply System's construction of the power facilities at Hanford. The intense activity of the previous six weeks bore fruit. In a dramatic reversal of its action six weeks earlier, the House rejected the VanZandt amendment by a vote of 232–163.

Although the supporters' activity had a decisive impact on the House's reversal, an unrelated political event also affected the outcome. Republican leader Charles Halleck of Indiana was angry with 19 Republicans, including VanZandt and most opponents of Hanford, because they had voted earlier the same day for the president's accelerated public works bill, which Halleck opposed. Allegedly with Halleck's approval, 65 Republicans voted against the VanZandt motion, twice the number who had taken this position in July.

The House defeat of the VanZandt motion broke the logjam. Now conferees supporting the NPR could fashion a compromise acceptable to both chambers. They prepared a conference report making it clear that WPPSS would buy the steam from the AEC and pay all costs of building an 800-mw electric generating facility that would convert the steam to electricity. The report also stipulated that WPPSS would offer 50 percent of the power output to private power companies. Electricity produced at the NPR would be delivered to BPA under an exchange arrangement under which BPA would take all of the power into its system and exchange it for a blend of power that would be delivered by BPA to utilities that had contracted for the Hanford energy.

•

In late September, both the Senate and House quickly approved the conference report, but not before Representative VanZandt made a final effort to recommit the authorizing bill to the conference committee with instructions to House members not to accept the Hanford provision. This motion lost by a vote of 186–150.

President Kennedy signed the bill at a White House ceremony on September 26. At the ceremony, the president said the Hanford steam plant would be four times larger than any other such project in the world and would "give the United States a freer margin for superiority in the peacetime use of atomic energy. I think it will benefit, in that way, the entire country, North and South and West." He congratulated Representative Holifield and Senator Jackson for their efforts, and added:

It is a source of great satisfaction to me that a way has now been opened for the efficient utilization of this energy resource for the benefit of this growing region. To have permitted this resource to be wasted would have been in conflict with all the principles of resource conservation and utilization to which we are committed.

Owen Hurd was a guest at the signing ceremony and received one of the pens the president used to sign the bill. I was invited to represent APPA, but had a previous commitment. Larry Hobart of the APPA staff attended, which was fitting because Larry had done a great deal of excellent work on this project.

A year to the day later, on September 26, 1963, I attended the ground-breaking for the Hanford power project. President Kennedy arrived at the ceremony by helicopter. It was a thrill to watch the president's helicopter land on the dusty site of the project and see the smiling president emerge.

In keeping with the nature of the occasion, Kennedy waved a uranium-tipped "atomic wand" over a radiation counter, which activated an automated crane to break ground for the project. After paying tribute to a number of people, including Owen Hurd, the president talked about resource development. He advocated an aggressive program of developing hydroelectric and nuclear power and new means of making coal more competitive for generation of electricity. He also urged the construction of efficient inter-regional interties. Finally, the president said:

> We must not allow this technology [nuclear power] to lead to monopolization, either by the federal government or large combines of private utilities. We should realize the economies of size without jeopardizing the rights of our citizens to be served by the type of electric utility they prefer and also to encourage competition.

The fight for Hanford was a boost to the morale of public power advocates and taught us lessons we could use in the future. It also raised the visibility and prestige of the Supply System, which was a relatively new, untried agency at that time. In a sense, the victory may have had mixed blessings, because it prepared the way for the system later to embark upon an ill-fated program to build five additional nuclear power plants.

Chapter 28

A Key Link in Giant Power

Pennsylvania Gov. Gifford Pinchot triggered public power enthusiasm for high-voltage interconnections in 1925 when he issued his Giant Power study. Inter-regional transmission lines could save both energy and money. Utilities could take advantage of diversities between time and climate zones. Power could be moved between the East and West to meet peak demands during the day and between North and South to meet changing seasonal requirements. Large interconnections would reduce the need to build new generating stations and enable utilities to substitute renewable, non-polluting hydroelectric power for electricity generated at coal- or oil-burning plants.

The use of direct current instead of alternating current for long distance transmission offered further potential savings. Although the initial cost of constructing dc lines was higher than for ac lines, lower line losses of dc transmission more than compensated for the larger initial investment.

Public power utilities wanted the federal government to construct high-voltage lines linking existing federal systems, such as those in the Pacific Northwest, the Pacific Southwest and the Missouri Basin. The lines would pay for themselves, conserve resources and could be interconnected with those of private power companies to the advantage of all utilities.

By the end of the 1950s, the Pacific Northwest and the Pacific Southwest were prime candidates for a major high-voltage inter-regional intertie. Bonneville Power Administration was losing the opportunity to earn millions of dollars because it had no way to reach a potential market for all the power it could generate in the spring, when melting snow packs produced an abundance of water that could not be stored behind the Columbia River dams. BPA could avert a rate increase if it could sell surplus energy. At the same time, companies in California were a ready market for the Northwest's low-cost hydro power, especially for irrigation pumping. An intertie between the regions that would permit BPA to sell its surplus in the spring to California also could be useful in the winter, when surplus power in California could be sent to the Northwest to help meet the increased needs for heating.

A five-year political battle on the issue of a Northwest-Southwest intertie began with relatively little fanfare in April 1959 with a Senate interior committee hearing on a proposed contract between BPA and two California power companies—Pacific Gas & Electric Company and California Oregon Power Company. The proposal called for sale of surplus BPA energy to the California utilities over a privately built transmission line.

Members of Congress, public power groups and governors of the affected states opposed the proposal because the line would not permit the full utilization of the potential of an inter-regional interconnection. Public power utilities also objected because the private utility line would be used solely by the companies, thereby precluding California's public power utilities from purchasing surplus power from BPA.

After the hearing, the committee directed BPA to study the issue. In a draft report released in December 1959, BPA endorsed a privately owned interconnection between the two regions, a conclusion consistent with the Eisenhower administration's unsympathetic attitude toward public power. The draft report said that the best use of surplus BPA energy would be as replacement for power produced by fossil-fired steam plants in California. Little or no benefits were foreseen from coordination between the federal power system in the Northwest and the government's Central Valley Project in California.

The report raised the sensitive issue of regional preference. Anxious to use the Northwest's vast hydroelectric resources to develop the region's economy, political leaders felt that Northwest consumers served by private as well as publicly owned electric utilities should have preferential access to low-cost hydro power produced in the region, before it was shipped outside of the region.

The concept of a regional preference created considerable controversy within APPA. Public power utilities that were preference customers in California, the Southwest and Midwest challenged the concept. They felt publicly owned utilities within transmission distance of federal projects should have preference to government-produced power, regardless of regional boundaries. A regional preference could lead to further dillution of public preference, a foundation stone of public power.

APPA's Northwest and California members fought over the issue in the association's Legislative and Resolutions Committee. Northwest utilities refused to support an intertie unless it was accompanied by a regional preference. California interests were equally insistent in opposing the concept. After many long and acrimonious debates, Gilmore Tillman, counsel for the Los Angeles Department of Water and Power, the most obstinate opponent of regional preference, acknowledged that the intertie would not be built without regional preference. He recognized the inevitable and acquiesced to the Northwest's position.

"There are times when one has to rise above principle," he said.

•

Responding to growing interest in a Northwest-Southwest intertie, a subcommittee of the Senate Interior Committee held a hearing on the subject in April 1960. Bonneville Administrator William A. Pearl and Assistant Secretary of the Interior Fred G. Aandahl testified that there would be a surplus of 10 billion kwhs of electricity in the Northwest. Ample supplies would be available for preference customers in California, provided they could take delivery. However, Pearl and Aandahl offered no suggestions as to how the California public power utilities might avail themselves of the Northwest's surplus.

At a Senate hearing, Aandahl told Sen. Henry M. Jackson, D-Wash., there was enough surplus secondary energy "to justify several lines, fully loaded" into California. There was nothing to prevent public agencies from building lines up to Bonneville, he said.

"Why have a series of duplicating lines when you can have one line serving all customers?" Senator Jackson asked. Aandahl said the proposed PG&E-Copco contract "would in no way conflict" with the interests of preference customers, but was merely a plan to help the federal Treasury by disposing of surplus energy.

Reacting to the opposition, Aandahl in May 1960 told the Senate Interior Committee he would not sign a contract for the private utility intertie unless the committee asked him to do so.

•

Aware that pressures were building for action on the BPA-power company proposal, Northwestern and California public power utilities met in Seattle in June 1960 to plan their strategy. They were determined to press for construction of a high-capacity, extra high-voltage transmission line between the two regions. Preliminary findings of a new study undertaken by the state of California anticipated surpluses of 20 billion kwh annually of secondary energy in a favorable water year. This amount was more than 20 times the energy that could be transmitted through the smaller BPA-power company line.

In mid-June 1960 the state of California gave the Senate interior committee preliminary results of the study it had commissioned by H. Zinder & Associates of Seattle. Sol Schulz, manager of the Zinder firm and a former chief engineer of BPA, said a double-circuit, 500-kv transmission line extending from BPA as far south as Bakersfield, California, would provide "overwhelming" benefits to the Pacific Coast states. He told the subcommittee a major intertie would provide up to 2,000 mw of hydroelectric peaking capacity to California. It would also increase by 180 mw the supply of low-cost power in the Northwest and give West Coast utilities the benefit of at least 500 mw in peak load diversity.

Senator Jackson, who presided at the hearings, said Congress "should provide legislative assurances in unequivocal language" that would spell out the prior rights of customers in the Northwest states before any power was sold to California.

The Zinder report was confined primarily to the question of a major interconnection between Bonneville and California, but Schulz had an expansive view of the intertie's potential. He saw additional benefits by enlarging the coordination to include southwestern Canada, the Colorado River Basin and other adjacent areas.

PG&E Executive Vice President Robert Gerdes was not impressed with Schulz's vision of the intertie's potential. He said his company's proposed contract with Bonneville "means very little to PG&E." The surplus Bonneville power would be used only for fuel replacement on the PG&E system and the utility's costs of generation were very close to the cost of BPA's energy, he said. In a magnanimous gesture, he added, "We are ready to save the government some money if the government wants us to."

After the Zinder report hearing, the Senate interior committee adopted a resolution calling on the secretary of interior to suspend negotiations for sale of BPA energy to California until the Zinder study could be completed. The resolution succeeded in stalling action on the BPA-power company contract for the remainder of 1960. Meanwhile, Zinder released more detailed studies of intertie potentials in November 1960 and February 1961. The new studies showed that a 500-kv transmission line between the Pacific Northwest and Southern California could pay for itself within 10 years and provide an additional average net benefit of $12 million per year.

In March 1961 Secretary of the Interior Udall named a five-person task force, headed by BPA Administrator Charles Luce, to study the feasibility of an extra-high-voltage common carrier transmission line between the Pacific Northwest and the Pacific Southwest. He asked the task force to recommend legal safeguards to assure that each region would have a permanent priority in the use of electricity generated on its rivers.

That December, Luce's task force formally recommended construction of one or more extra high-voltage common carrier transmission lines between the Pacific Northwest and the Pacific Southwest. Udall promptly endorsed the recommendation and said he would ask for planning funds for the intertie in the department's budget for the next fiscal year.

•

Although the power companies as late as December 1961 had publicly expressed little interest in the proposed federal intertie, by February 1962 four major California private utilities met in Portland with representatives of BPA and the Bureau of Reclamation to discuss their possible participation in the venture. Luce said the meeting was "cordial and constructive" and the utilities were interested in the intertie. However, most of the discussion dealt with the utilities' own plans for enlarging pooling arrangements among themselves and how these plans could be coordinated with those for an extra high-voltage interconnection between the two regions, Luce said.

In late May 1962, Gerdes testified against the president's request for $500,000 for the intertie at a Senate appropriations hearing. The funds were unnecessary because private power companies on the West Coast were already moving ahead with an inter-regional intertie of not less than 500 kv, he said. The proposed federal intertie:

> would constitute a new invasion by the federal government into the electric power business. There is no need for federal construction of facilities where the electric utility industry does, can and will provide them at a saving of hundreds of millions of dollars to federal taxpayers.

PG&E, San Diego Gas and Electric Company, California Power Company and Southern California Edison Company planned to form the California Power Pool, which would build a transmission line of "not less than 500 kv" from Round Mountain, in northern California, to the Los Angeles area when Northwest power became available upon "reasonable terms," Gerdes said.

Gus Norwood of the Northwest Public Power Association said the intertie would be like "a valve with cash registers on each side." If the power companies built the intertie, the government would be at the mercy of the utilities, he said.

Congress cut the administration's budget request of $500,000 to $300,000 and said money could be spent only for preliminary engineering, reconnaissance surveys, economic analyses and negotiations with public and private utilities on a coordinated plan for power interchanges between the two regions.

•

At the beginning of a new Congress in 1963, President Kennedy escalated the administration's plans for the Northwest-Southwest intertie. His budget requested $24.5 million to build an extra-high-voltage intertie between the two regions. The budget request contemplated an all-federal 750-kv dc transmission line from the Columbia River to Los Angeles and an all-federal 500-kv ac connection from the Columbia River to the California-Oregon border.

In June 1963 Udall testified before the Senate Appropriations Committee in favor of the $24.5 million appropriation requested by the president. A week later spokesmen for four California private utilities opposed the appropriation. Gerdes called the proposal "an unprecedented, unauthorized undertaking by the federal government." It was "the start of a federal extra-high-voltage grid system that would spread across the country, the ultimate cost of which would be many billions of dollars," he said.

The following week I had my turn before the Senate Appropriations Committee. I supported the federal appropriations for both lines. However, I said that the 500-kv "half" line from the Bonneville system to California that would be terminated at the California-Oregon border should be extended further south to Tracy, so that it could serve the publicly owned utilities in northern California. I continued:

> These local publicly owned electric systems are concerned because the proposed 500-kv line...will be controlled by the private power companies, who proposed to purchase all BPA power entering that state and who would be the sole channel for non-federal power [that] might become available in California markets....[W]e believe that the Congress has a unique opportunity [in appropriating funds for the federal intertie] to obtain the largest return from its previous investments, provide the greatest benefits to all power consumers of the regions affected, prevent monopoly control of valuable resources, and make a significant advance in American technology.

During the last week of June 1963, a number of witnesses from California—including a representative of the governor, Sen. Claire Engle, D-Calif., and officials of California public power systems—testified before the Senate Appropriations Committee in favor of extending the 500-kv line to Tracy. "Whoever controls the store ought to control the cash register," Senator Engle said.

•

On November 22, 1963, President Kennedy was assassinated and Lyndon B. Johnson became president.

Within a few weeks after Johnson took office, Secretary Udall announced that the new president supported appropriations for the Northwest-Southwest interties and by early December Congress voted to appropriate $7 million for the project in fiscal 1964. Funds were provided to initiate construction of two transmission lines to interconnect the BPA system, the Central Valley Project at Tracy, California, and the Colorado River Storage Project. The Senate-House conference report said at least one of the lines would be for dc transmission. It continued:

> One of them may connect with a non-federal power system at the northern California border and be terminated at that point. If it is determined that only one line shall be constructed at this time, it shall be a direct current line to accomplish the interconnection of the Bonneville system, the Central Valley of California, and the Hoover Dam power plant.

The battle over the intertie reached its final phase in 1964. By that time, 11 non-federal entities had expressed interest in building all or part of the interties. To evaluate these proposals, Assistant Secretary of the Interior Ken Holum outlined a federal "yardstick" system for interconnecting the power systems of the Northwest and the Southwest, against which all non-federal proposals were to be measured. The 11 entities were invited to submit firm written proposals to the department.

The federal "yardstick" plan called for construction of two transmission lines. The first would be a 785-mile, 750-kv dc line from The Dalles, Oregon, to Grapevine, California, 30 miles south of Bakersfield, and 50 miles north of Los Angeles. The second line would be a 500-kv alternating current line with a tap in northern California and another near San Francisco. Its first leg from John Day Dam, upriver from The Dalles, to Tracy, California, would be about 590 miles long. The second leg from Tracy to Grapevine would be about 290 miles long. Lines running from Grapevine would tie the southern terminal facility to Hoover Dam and Phoenix, Arizona, thus integrating the BPA system with the Bureau of Reclamation's Colorado River projects. The federal plan envisioned one 500-kv line from Grapevine to Hoover, and two 345-kv lines from Hoover Dam to Phoenix.

Holum challenged the non-federal entities "to demonstrate that they can build these lines and move the power better than the federal government and at comparable costs." After the proposals were received and evaluated, the department would submit its recommendations to Congress, Holum said.

On June 24, 1964, Udall sent Congress a detailed plan for four major lines and three interconnecting lines to link the power systems of the Northwest and the Southwest. The plan called for a mixture of entities that would build the facilities, including federal agencies, the Los Angeles Department of Water and Power, and private power companies.

Udall said his report complied with a congressional directive to negotiate with non-federal parties interested in building all or part of the interconnection. He added that 251 preference customers in 11 western states would benefit from the interties, either through lower cost power or an increased supply of power or both. The proposed federal investment would be $280 million out of a total investment of $697 million.

•

Part of Udall's proposal called for the California portion of a 500-kv line to be built by power companies. This was a serious sticking point for the northern California congressional delegation and public power utilities in that area.

Senator Engle called the intertie package "a surrender of control of the most lucrative power market in the West to a combine of six private utility companies." He said "all service in northern California would be at the will and whim of the Pacific Gas and Electric Company, which would own and operate both the intertie lines proposed for that territory."

Speaking for himself and 22 other California congressmen, Rep. John Moss, D-Calif., said they were unable to support the plan because it "does not protect the public interest in several important respects."

Public power witnesses in the Northwest and Southwest testified in favor of the plan, but controversy persisted. Udall made several concessions to the northern California congressmen, but he did not change the aspect of the plan calling for construction of two 500-kv lines in California by private power companies.

As the end of the congressional session loomed in an election year, intertie supporters recognized they had to break the congressional deadlock before Congress adjourned. Three Democratic California congressmen—Moss, Harold Johnson and Bernie Sisk—arranged for a meeting with President Johnson and Udall. Although Representative Holifield had not been actively involved in the controversy, the others invited him to join them at the meeting with the president. They knew Holifield had been a long-time friend of Johnson's; in fact, Holifield had supported Johnson over Kennedy in the 1960 Democratic convention. Holifield's presence at the White House meeting proved to be a crucial factor in the future of the intertie legislation.

The meeting was described as follows in a biography of Holifield published in 1996:[1]

> At the meeting, Holifield was a silent observer as the three congressmen made their case. The discussion in the Oval Office went back and forth. According to Holifield, Johnson discovered that there were disagreements both among the congressmen and between them and Udall. Holifield recalled that Johnson suddenly interrupted the discussion and said, "You're all friends of mine. But you apparently have different viewpoints. If you think I am going to get in a position of being shot down by both sides, you are mistaken." Then, turning to Holifield, the president pointed his finger at him and said: "Chet, I am appointing you as chairman of an ad hoc committee composed of all interested senators and representatives and other involved entities. Get everybody together and develop a unified position by all of the parties. I want you to report back to me in 30 days." Johnson added for emphasis: "Let me know if there is a unified position. If not, I want you to report back to me and tell me why and *who* is responsible for any lack of unity."

Holifield reportedly was startled by the president's request and told Johnson he was not an expert in this field.

"You have had a lot of experience in holding hearings and negotiating compromises and I have confidence in you," the president replied.

Holifield immediately became deeply immersed in the president's assignment. After amassing a great deal of background material, he held a series of informal meetings with House and Senate members from five affected states and with utilities. By the end of July, the congressional delegation had agreed that one of the two 500-kv alternating current lines

---

[1] *Chet Holifield - Master Legislator & Nuclear Statesman*, by Richard W. Dyke and Francis X. Cannon, published by University Press of America

running from the BPA system to northern California would be all-federal. This line would run south to Round Mountain, California, where it would connect with a new 230-kv federally owned tie to Cottonwood, California.

Holifield also worked out an agreement on the regional preference issue, addressed in separate legislation. An amendment to the preference bill, sponsored by Rep. Jack Westland, R-Wash., would have required congressional authorization for the intertie. The Interior Department argued that existing law already granted it authority to build the intertie. The groups convened by Holifield agreed the Northwest-Southwest intertie would not require congressional authorization.

Although the Holifield compromise was generally accepted, PG&E continued to object. During an extensive long-distance telephone conversation, Holifield invited Gerdes to meet with him. Gerdes took an overnight flight to Washington and met with Holifield for 40 minutes the following day. He finally agreed to the compromise, if he could win assurance that he would not be asked for any further concessions. Holifield said he could not commit others in the ad hoc group, but he invited Gerdes to meet personally with the committee, at which time Gerdes was given an opportunity to poll each member of the group, and was assured that no further concessions would be requested. A triumphant Holifield then reported on the agreement to the president.

President Johnson promptly asked Congress to appropriate $45.5 million to begin work on the federal portions of the intertie. Four north-south extra high voltage lines were involved in the intertie plan endorsed by the president. Total cost of the entire system was estimated at $700 million, with the federal share set at $300 million.

Presidential press secretary George Reedy announced the president's action at a press conference. He said Mr. Johnson regarded the plan as "the launching of a new era of cooperation between private power and public power in the United States, both working in partnership, in supplementing each other to provide for the consumers efficiently and economically."

By mid-August Congress voted to provide $45 million to begin construction of three of the four proposed Northwest-Southwest tie lines during the 1965 fiscal year, which began July 1, 1965. The fourth line—from The Dalles Dam to Hoover Dam—was to be constructed only after the secretary of the interior reviewed load potentials and found the project economically feasible. The president signed the bill August 31 at his ranch in Johnson City, Texas.

The separate bill giving the Northwest priority over the sale of power from the region was enacted into law shortly thereafter.

An editorial in the August 1964 issue of *Public Power* magazine hailed the intertie "as one of the most significant developments in the electric industry of this decade," and said it promised "to open a new era of electric service to the American people."

The editorial gave special mention to Holifield for handling "the latter stages of this controversy skillfully and constructively." It noted that the Department of the Interior deserved "great credit for initiating studies and making plans for the intertie for almost four years," and observed that the intertie studies were one of the first projects undertaken by Secretary Udall.

The Los Angeles Department of Water and Power also received a kudo. The editorial commented that the department would now build a 570-mile direct current line between the Oregon border and the Los Angeles area. Having designed and constructed the 230-kv line from Hoover Dam to Los Angeles in the 1930s, the department would be carrying forward the department's long tradition as a pioneer in developing high voltage transmission of power.

Begun in 1966 and completed in 1970, the intertie was the largest transmission program that had been undertaken at that time in the United States.

Chapter 29

Golden Years at the FPC

One of the most far-reaching changes in energy policy wrought by the Kennedy administration was the transformation of the role of the Federal Power Commission.

Prior to taking office, President Kennedy asked James M. Landis to study the regulatory agencies. A former chairman of the Securities and Exchange Commission and the Civil Aeronautics Board and former Harvard Law School dean, Landis was well versed in regulatory affairs.

In a report to Kennedy in December 1960, Landis singled out the Federal Power Commission as "the outstanding example in the federal government of the breakdown of the administrative process." Shortly after taking office, President Kennedy appointed three strong regulators to the FPC—Joe Swidler as chairman and Howard Morgan and Charles Ross as commissioners. With these appointments, Kennedy transformed the commission from a moribund agency into an effective regulatory force.

After Swidler took office, I met with him frequently and repeatedly discussed the need for FPC to regulate wholesale rates. Swidler was receptive to my plea. Because of his experience as general counsel of the Tennessee Valley Authority, he was familiar with municipal electric utilities and sympathetic to their plight. He was also a strong manager, intent upon exercising the FPC's full legal authority.

The new commissioners instituted meaningful regulation of wholesale electric rates. Although the Federal Power Act gave the agency authority to regulate wholesale electricity sales, it had not exercised this power. More than 900 municipally owned electric utilities were captive wholesale power customers of the private companies. The power companies did not compete for wholesale business and most municipal utilities were too small to build their own large generating plants.

The wholesale suppliers also served retail customers in areas adjacent to municipal utilities so they were not eager to provide low-cost wholesale power to these small competitors. The municipal utilities desperately needed effective regulation of wholesale rates.

During his five years on the commission, Swidler initiated vigorous regulation of wholesale electric rates, led efforts to bring about a more rational organization of the industry, induced electric utilities to spend more money for research, and completed a national power survey.

•

Swidler's nomination as chairman of the FPC was stalled in the Senate for several months after Kennedy took office, but by late 1962, he had taken full command of the agency. In the summer of 1963, the FPC published a list of 189 power companies defined as "public utilities" under the Federal Power Act and therefore subject to FPC regulation. Utilities on the list were ordered to file all wholesale rate schedules with the FPC and to obtain commission approval for rate changes.

Most municipal utilities were unfamiliar with the rate case process and were intimidated about dealing with a distant federal agency. To encourage the association's members to take advantage of this opportunity, APPA staff provided information about FPC procedures, recommended attorneys and consultants who could help and assured them that prospective savings would more than compensate for their time and expense of contesting rate increases. Merely filing a rate case could result in a five-month suspension of a proposed increase. Savings during the suspension frequently covered the cost of the proceeding.

To their credit, a number of managers and boards of small municipal utilities ventured into these uncharted waters, risking protracted, costly legal actions fraught with uncertainty.

Six Wisconsin cities—Kaukauna, New London, Oconto Falls, Shawano, Florence and Clintonville—were one of the first groups to seek relief from FPC. The cities contested a rate increase proposed by Wisconsin Michigan Power Company Instead of increasing its rates by $213,000—representing a 14.7 percent increase—the company should have cut them by $87,800, the cities contended. The commission found that the proposed rate increase was excessive and ordered a refund

The municipal utility in Shrewsbury, Massachusetts, challenged New England Power Company and its subsidiary, Massachusetts Electric Company. The city complained that it was required to buy power from the subsidiary even though NEPCO's lines were only 20 feet away from those of Massachusetts Electric. The city said it could save $50,000 a year if it bought power directly from the parent company.

George Spiegel was Shrewsbury's Washington attorney. Spiegel liked to take up the cause of the underdog and relished cases that pitted small organizations against very large corporate interests. He understood that small utilities had limited financial resources and knew he would have to go for the jugular if his clients were to prevail. Frequently, that entailed allegations of anti-competitive behavior.

Spiegel told the commission that "NEPCO transmission lines run right through town, but when Shrewsbury asks for service NEPCO says, 'you have to buy from this subsidiary over here.'" The rate question was only part of Shrewsbury's case, Spiegel said. The city wanted to get clear of its "entanglement with Massachusetts Electric." The 20-foot gap in a substation between the NEPCO and Shrewsbury systems cost the municipal utility one mill per kwh, since the intermediary company obtained a middleman's profit for the 20-foot facility.

The commission unanimously ordered NEPCO to sell wholesale electricity to the city at its standard rate. Direct sales "will be of benefit to Shrewsbury and its consumers and will not burden either Nepco or Massachusetts Electric," Swidler said. "The rate savings to Shrewsbury will be large and of growing importance."

•

Power companies attacked the FPC's new activities on legal and political battlefields. From a precedent-setting standpoint, the most important legal challenge to the commission's jurisdiction came in a proceeding involving the city of Colton, California. State regulators had approved a wholesale rate increase for Southern California Edison Company. Colton filed a complaint at the FPC, which ruled the increase was invalid. FPC claimed jurisdiction on grounds that out-of-state energy produced at the federally owned Hoover, Parker and Davis hydroelectric projects was included in the sales to Colton by Southern California Edison Company. Subsequently, the Ninth Circuit U.S. Court of Appeals, in a divided opinion, set aside the FPC order and the U.S. Supreme Court agreed to review the case.

APPA filed a friend-of-the-court brief in August 1963 in support of Colton. In the brief, APPA General Counsel Northcutt Ely said the Appeals Court's decision would recognize FPC's jurisdiction over wholesale power transactions only after finding each transaction to have a "national interest." Ely said:

> Such a test would be totally unworkable; for it would create confusion and doubt in the regulation of many hundreds of wholesale sales to publicly owned electric utilities, would in many instances result in wholesale sales

without regulation by either a federal or state commission and would ignore the factors in the development of the electric power industry which increasingly demand uniform federal regulation.

At least 130 private power companies made wholesale sales to at least 967 municipalities. If the test of the Appeals Court were to stand, "it would be years before these hundreds of municipalities would know the appropriate forum to contest the reasonableness of wholesale rates and service," Ely said. Many state commissions lacked both authority and resources to regulate wholesale sales. Moreover, the fast-growing trend toward interconnections of the nation's electric utilities made state regulation infeasible, Ely said.

The Supreme Court unanimously overturned the lower court ruling in March 1964. Over the years, the court said, its decisions "have squarely rejected the view of the Court of Appeals that the scope of FPC jurisdiction over interstate sales of gas or electricity at wholesale is to be determined by a case-by-case analysis of the impact of state regulation upon the national interest. The court declared:

> Rather, Congress meant to draw a bright line, easily ascertained, between state and federal jurisdiction, making unnecessary such case-by-case analysis. This was done in the Power Act by making FPC jurisdiction plenary and extending it to all wholesale sales in interstate commerce except those which Congress has made explicitly subject to regulation by the states. There is no such exemption covering the Edison-Colton case.

I promptly hailed the court's action as a "landmark decision that has tremendously far-reaching implications for those municipal utilities and other local agencies [that] purchase power at wholesale from private power companies." There had been mounting evidence that many municipally owned electric utilities had been paying excessive charges for wholesale power, and were subjected to unreasonable purchase conditions.

Within six months, another 71 power companies filed wholesale rates with the commission and within a year the FPC's wholesale rate regulation activities were in full swing. Speaking at APPA's annual conference in May 1964 in Jacksonville, Florida, Swidler said wholesale rate cases under way at FPC involved power companies in 20 states. He told APPA members the commission had undertaken a "thoroughgoing review" of all electric rate schedules then on file with FPC "with a view toward eliminating excessive or discriminatory rates and unreasonable provisions in these rate schedules."

•

The power companies launched a legislative effort to overturn the Colton decision and lobbied against appropriations for the commission. In a speech to the American Power Conference in April 1964, Swidler warned the companies that their resistance could backfire. If consumer-owned utilities were denied access to regulation of wholesale rates, they would seek greater development of federal power and form joint action agencies to provide power supply, he said. He urged the companies to cooperate with the commission and seek to increase their own share of wholesale sales.

Swidler's entreaties fell on deaf ears. The companies instigated introduction of legislation, S. 218, to strip the FPC of authority to regulate most wholesale sales. The bill was introduced by two powerful senators—Florida Democrats Spessard L. Holland and George Smathers.

The Senate Commerce Committee held a hearing on the bill in May 1965. Shortly before the hearings began, we were dismayed to learn that state utility commissioners and the power companies had formed an alliance to seek passage of S. 218.

Mrs. Esther Peterson, special assistant to the president for consumer affairs, who was highly regarded in Washington, told the committee the question raised by the bill was "*effective* regulation versus *no* regulation."

Swidler said survival of the nation's smaller electric utilities was the key issue before Congress. Provisions of S. 218 "would substantially repeal the commission's regulatory authority over interstate power companies and bring to an end the system of responsible regulation of electric utility systems which Congress initiated with the public utility holding company legislation of 1935," he said.

In my testimony, I said many small local public power utilities were paying wholesale rates equal to or higher than retail charges for the companies' large industrial customers. I also pointed out that the commission had pending 35 cases involving 647 wholesale customers and power bills in excess of $100 million annually. FPC wholesale rate regulation, I said, was more important than ever before.

John R. Kelly, director of utilities in Gainesville, Florida, testified that 11 municipal utilities in Florida purchased wholesale power from the Florida Power Corporation in 1963 for an average of 11.75 mills per kilowatt-hour while rural electric cooperatives purchased power from the same company for an average cost of 9.61 mills per kwh.

Robert T. Person, president of Public Service Company of Colorado and president-elect of the Edison Electric Institute, said the basic question before Congress was not "how far the federal government can go in regulating the electric industry under the commerce clause, but how far it should go." The primary issue was whether Congress wished to authorize a federal agency "to concern itself with matters that are primarily local in nature and which do not affect the citizens of other states," he said. Person declared that FPC should not regulate a utility that operated entirely within one state, even though it was interconnected with another utility that operated across state lines.

Edwin L. Mason, chairman of the Florida Public Service Commission, said municipal utilities would be better off without federal regulation.

"The best regulation is little or no regulation," Mason said.

On June 30, 1965, the Senate Commerce Committee, in a closed session, rejected S.218 by a one-vote margin. Supporters of the bill turned their attention to the House, but their efforts were unsuccessful.

•

Aside from energizing FPC's jurisdiction over wholesale sales, Swidler brought new insights into the electric industry by initiating a National Power Survey. In late January 1962 he announced the commission would undertake a survey to determine how the nation's electric industry could best be coordinated to assure the lowest possible cost to consumers and the largest possible market to utilities. The objective of the survey was to suggest in broad outlines how the nation's 3,800 electric systems could look beyond their local areas and key future expansion to a national scale.

Swidler estimated electric utilities would spend $100 billion for new facilities during the following 20 years and it was important that this money be spent with a view of overall economy and the national well being. He was cognizant of the growing interest in building extra-high-voltage interties such as the proposed lines between the Pacific Northwest and California. Great technological strides in generating electricity had occurred during the past 20 years, but "there has not been equal development on the transmission side" where "the opportunities for savings are even more dramatic," he said.

The United States was "the only civilized country" without a coordinated national power system, Swidler declared. The FPC survey would attempt to show "where capacity should be located to meet projected loads and how that capacity should be tied together." Savings in production costs for a fully coordinated power supply system could be "enormous," he said. Improved efficiency of only 5 percent from a fully coordinated system could reduce generating costs by $300 million a year and reduced reserve requirements should save more than $3 billion by 1980, he pointed out.

Although APPA was generally supportive of the survey's goals, we had reservations about the outcome. The commission's work on the survey was to be guided by an Executive Advisory Committee whose composition, reflecting the relative size of each industry segment, meant large power companies dominated the committee. On the other hand, power company officials feared the survey would lead to federal government planning for the industry.

Swidler addressed some of these issues in a speech at the American Power Conference in Chicago in March 1963. The nation should have a power supply network planned, built and operated by all 3,600 electric systems as though they were one, "but without sacrificing the benefits of the stimulation and invigoration [that] come from a multiplicity of management organizations, diverse in structure, each with special responsibilities to particular communities or regions," he said.

One of the most serious obstacles to reaching this goal, he added, was "the bitterness that has developed in the relations between the public and cooperative segments of the industry, on the one hand, and the privately owned companies, on the other." He continued:

> It is not the purpose of the National Power Survey to prefer one kind of power enterprise over another or to disturb the status quo. Neither, may I say, do we consider it our function to entrench the status quo. Rather, we think that the survey should be an instrument for bringing together all of the segments of the industry for planning on a voluntary basis to make the best possible use of our electric power resources in the national interest.

Reducing the number of small and inefficient generating units in the industry offered a major opportunitiy to trim overall costs, he said. "We need more of the large efficient units. They will be installed as the many power systems are interconnected and integrated in large regional power pools and ultimately in a nationwide pool tied together by [extra-high-voltage] lines."

Economies of scale so important in generation and transmission "did not apply in the distribution of electricity," the chairman said. It must be possible in the future "for small distribution systems as well as large to share in the benefits of such large-scale generation and transmission." To obtain such benefits, access must be provided on fair terms that ensure power purchased from a neighboring utility

> will not be used by the seller as a club to destroy the buyer. As part of the
> bargain for power supply, the small distributor has the right to expect that
> the seller will recognize the buyer's right to exist, will not compete for
> retail customers by invading the buyer's own territory, will share fairly the
> economies of low-cost power sources, and will provide security for
> meeting growth in loads over the long term.

•

In mid-December 1964 FPC published its 296-page *National Power
Survey*. The utility industry stood at the threshold of a new era of low-cost
power for all sections of the country, the report said, pointing out that
technological tools were available to bring consumers savings of $11
billion a year by 1980. The commission suggested an industry target for
1980 of approximately 1.2 cents per kilowatt-hour as the combined
average retail price for all residential, commercial and industrial sales of
electricity throughout the nation. That target represented a 27 percent
reduction from the comparable figure in 1962, which was 1.68 cents. In
1940, it was 2.1 cents. Achieving this would require:

- Participation in "fully coordinated power networks covering broad
  areas of the country"—ultimately the interconnection of all electric
  systems in the nation into a single network;
- Long-range planning of all generation and transmission facilities,
  "whether owned by private, cooperative, federal or other public
  agencies" as part of large coordinated power networks to achieve the
  lowest cost of bulk power supply;
- A large increase in per capita use of electricity.

"The key to the future is growth," the report said. "We are projecting
that power demands in the 1980s will require the production of 2.8 trillion
kilowatt-hours of electricity or more than $2\frac{1}{2}$ times the estimated
production of 1.1 trillion kilowatt-hours in 1964."

"We are aware that many controversial areas of public policy are
related in one way or another to the industry's success in lowering power
costs," the report said. Disputes involved service territories, "the
usefulness of public power programs as a yardstick to supplement
regulation of privately owned systems," variations in tax, financing and
earnings requirements of individual utilities, relationships between large
and small utilities, the propriety of the preference clause in federal power

marketing, and the proper scope of regulation.

President Johnson praised the report and said the experience of the United States in the past few decades "demonstrates conclusively how the standard of living of American citizens has continued to rise as we have developed greater supplies of electrical energy."

The study "points the way to achievement of more electricity at lower cost for all Americans," I commented in a public statement. But I cautioned that "the ultimate test of the value of new technology and techniques will be whether or not the benefits are passed on to consumers in their electric bills."

•

As Swidler's term neared its end in 1965, speculation was rife as to whether he would be reappointed. Newspaper and trade press reports led observers to believe President Johnson would not reappoint Swidler, who had incurred the enmity of the oil and gas industries as well as the private electric utilities. As a senator from Texas, Johnson had been partial to oil and gas companies and there was reason to believe he did not approve of some of Swidler's actions.

Johnson also had been advised by his close friend, Donald Cook, president of American Electric Power Company, against reappointment of Swidler. On November 18, 1964, Johnson had a telephone conversation with Cook on a wide range of issues, including appointment of new commissioners and whether incumbent commissioners should be asked to submit their resignations, pro forma. Cook mentioned that Swidler's term would expire in June 1965, and he described Swidler as "one of the most dangerous fellows you got in your administration. He has no principle and no loyalty."

"I think that's about right," Johnson responded, but he asked Cook whether he should be allowed to continue as chairman for the remainder of his term.

Cook: "Oh, I would let him go on as chairman, particularly this fellow. If you displace him the newspapers are going to immediately say that you got rid of him because of his attitude on natural gas."

Johnson: "Oh yeah, the newspapers would burn my tail."[1]

Lee White, who had responsibility on the White House staff for natural resources and energy matters during the Kennedy years and the first Johnson administration, told me that Johnson was inclined to reappoint

---

[1] A recording of this conversation was made available to the author by the Lyndon B. Johnson Library in Austin, Texas.

Swidler to refute allegations that he was beholden to the oil and gas industry. For political reasons, Johnson also desired to retain Kennedy appointees. However, Johnson was a strong-willed, vain man and he wanted Swidler to ask for reappointment—a request that did not materialize.

Swidler, too, had a strong ego. Lacking a signal from the White House, he did not ask for reappointment for fear that he would be rejected. In this stalemate, a frustrated Swidler finally sent word to the president that he was not interested in being renamed, thereby taking Johnson off the hook.

Nevertheless, when the Northeast blackout occurred in November 1965, Johnson quickly asked Swidler to lead an investigation of the blackout, even though his term had expired and he was serving on the commission only until his successor was confirmed. Swidler at first demurred, because he and Dave Freeman, his assistant, had already decided to open a law practice together and had rented office space. However, Johnson was so eager to have Swidler lead the investigation that he arranged to compensate him for the expenses incurred to start the law firm.

Swidler acceded to the president's request and launched enthusiastically into this task—so much so that he virtually excluded other members of the commission from the investigation, much to their annoyance. Upon completion of the report, Swidler and FPC's chief engineer, Stewart Brown, flew to the president's ranch in Texas to deliver the report personally.

•

When Swidler left the commission in November 1965, he was honored at a dinner in Washington sponsored by the Electric Consumers Information Committee and attended by 200 high level government officials and representatives of consumer, labor, farm, cooperative, and rural electric cooperative groups.

A message from President Johnson, read by Presidential Counsel Lee White, called the testimonial dinner "a well-earned salute to your unstinting efforts to ensure the well-being of America's energy producers and the protection of her consuming public."

As chairman of ECIC, I presented Swidler a certificate expressing "deep gratitude and appreciation" of electric consumers for his "progressive leadership," for his "vision in stimulating the electric industry to think creatively about the problems of the future, for his keen interest in advancing the cause of more power at lower cost for all Americans and for lighting the path for other regulators to follow."

Consumer groups were not alone in their praise. As the chairman's term was nearing completion, *Electrical World* magazine, generally sympathetic to the private companies, published an editorial giving Swidler high marks. The editorial complained about the chairman's "expansion tendencies," but concluded that:

> weighing Swidler's contributions to the industry against his inclination to intrude unwarrantedly, we believe he has achieved an outstanding record as a regulator and public servant. From our point of view, he stands head and shoulders above most of the men who have occupied the chairs of the Federal Power Commission over the past 20 years.

Chapter 30

From New Frontier to Great Society

The Kennedy years were exhilarating. The president's charisma enchanted much of the nation and his New Frontier programs stimulated the interests of many people, young and old, to participate in government. The Kennedy era reminded me of the excitement of President Franklin D. Roosevelt's New Deal and President Harry S Truman's Marshall Plan for rebuilding war-torn Europe. These programs energized people already serving in the government and attracted many eager, idealistic newcomers to Washington.

The sense of excitement was palpable, but my personal situation was far different during the Kennedy administration than in the Roosevelt and Truman periods, when I held lowly jobs in the bureaucracy. Thanks to my position with APPA, I had met with Kennedy when he was a senator, a presidential candidate and president-elect. I had ready access to many members of the president's staff as well as key figures in Congress.

President Kennedy became involved in public power and water resource development issues because they were raised during the election campaign and grass roots agitation for new projects continued after his election. The president's swing through the West in August 1962 was indicative of his interest in water and power resource development and his recognition of its political importance. He spoke at the dedication of the Oahe Dam, near Pierre, South Dakota; visited the site of the Fryingpan-Arkansas project in Colorado shortly after signing authorizing legislation for this project, and participated in ground-breaking ceremonies for the San Luis project in California.

Although I had little to do with Oahe Dam, I was invited to attend its dedication, largely through the efforts of my good friend and colleague, Ken Holum, assistant interior secretary for water and power. Ken arranged for me to sit on the platform, along with himself, Interior

Secretary Stewart Udall, the governor of South Dakota, representatives of the U.S. Army Corps of Engineers, other high-ranking government officials, and representatives of water resource development organizations.

Pomp and ceremony accompanied the entrance of the president at public occasions. Guests were seated well before the president's arrival, and eagerly awaited his appearance, which was heralded by the bustling arrival of the press corps, the entrance of the military honor guard, followed by the playing of "Hail to the Chief." There was a rustle of excitement as the smiling president entered, accompanied by a coterie of Secret Service agents.

At the Oahe Dam dedication, the president referred to the gains made in electrifying the West in one generation. He told of battles his administration faced in achieving energy and water resource development goals:

> We cannot permit railroads to prevent coal slurry pipelines from conveying the resources of our mines.[1] We cannot permit the mining industry to say there shall be no nuclear energy because it may affect them adversely. We cannot permit, as a country, public and private power interests to veto each other's projects, or one region to say another region shall not develop. If we do that, we shall stand still and forget the lesson history has taught us.

•

President Kennedy's interests in water and power matters were not limited to the West. On May 18, 1963 he spoke at Muscle Shoals, Ala., on the 30th anniversary of the Tennessee Valley Authority Act. The president recalled that many regarded TVA "with doubt, some with scorn, some with outright hostility. Some said it could be done, some said it should be done, some said it wouldn't be done, but today, 30 years later, it has been done."

Despite its record of success, TVA still had its skeptics and critics, the president said:

> There are still those who call it creeping socialism and we recently saw an advertising campaign which implied that the TVA and public power were comparable to the Berlin Wall and East Berlin police as threats to our freedom.

---

[1] This was a reference to a fight in Congress over legislation to authorize a pipeline that would transport coal by slurry from western coal fields to the site of a coal-burning steam electric generating plant.

But the tremendous economic growth of this region, its private industry, its private income, make it clear to all that TVA is a fitting answer to socialism, and it is not creeping, nor will it in the future.

•

Public power supporters had good working relationships with the Kennedy administration, but Clyde Ellis, general manager of the National Rural Electric Cooperative Association, and I wanted to meet personally with the president to express our support of ongoing programs and to urge the adoption of new initiatives. We knew the president might be receptive to a meeting because another election campaign would begin soon. Working primarily through Ken Holum and Lee White, assistant special counsel to the president, we arranged a meeting with the president in the Oval Office on September 23, 1963. Ellis and I, along with officers of APPA[2] and NRECA, met with President Kennedy and two cabinet officers, Udall and Secretary of Agriculture Orville Freeman, whose department included the Rural Electrification Administration. Holum and White also were present.

Because of the size of our group (11 persons) and the limited time allotted to us, we stood for the entire meeting before the fireplace. I was lead spokesman for the group and began by thanking the president for his support of public power during the previous election.

"It didn't do me much good in the West," President Kennedy quipped, with a smile. Everybody laughed, but I had no good comeback; indeed, the president had not carried many western states.

After Ellis and I made brief presentations, we gave the president detailed briefing papers and expressed support for authorization of five hydroelectric power projects proposed by the administration, which Congress had not acted upon. We asked for the president's endorsement of the five million-kw Rampart Canyon Dam on the Yukon River in Alaska, which, if completed, would be the largest hydro power project in the Free World. We expressed appreciation for the administration's support of the Passamaquoddy tidal power project and the St. John River development in Maine.

Citing the growing trend toward large power pools, we advocated

---

[2] APPA officers participating in the meeting were president J. Dillon Kennedy, commissioner of utilities, Jacksonville, Florida; first vice president R. J. McMullin, general manager of the Salt River Project, Phoenix, Arizona, and second vice president Frank H. King, manager, Gas and Electric Department, Holyoke, Massachusetts

development of a nationwide power grid. Although we supported FPC's efforts to reduce the cost of electricity through more effective regulation, we opposed the commission's attempt to assert jurisdiction over the rural electric cooperatives, which we regarded as a conflict with the authority of the Rural Electrification Administration.

We left the meeting in a buoyant mood. None of us could have imagined the tragedy that was to befall President Kennedy and the nation barely two months later.

•

About 2 p.m. on November 22, 1963, I returned to the office from a luncheon with a representative of General Electric Company and was greeted by the APPA receptionist with the shocking news that President Kennedy had been shot while riding in a motorcade in Dallas. Members of the staff were anxiously huddled around a radio while we waited for further news. First reports indicated the seriousness of the incident, but it was not until 2:38 p.m. that we received the tragic report that the president had died. We listened for a while, but gradually it became apparent that the entire city of Washington—indeed, the entire country—was so traumatized that it was no longer possible for us to work. Government offices were shut down and for the next few days my family and I were glued to a television set watching the incredible events: the swearing in of President Johnson on Air Force One, in the presence of Jacqueline Kennedy, who was still wearing a blood-stained suit; the arrival of President Kennedy's body in Washington, accompanied by members of his family; Jack Ruby shooting the accused assassin, Lee Harvey Oswald—shown live on television; the funeral procession in Washington; the lighting of the eternal flame at Arlington National Cemetery; and President Johnson's meeting with world leaders who were in Washington to attend the funeral.

In tribute, the front page of the next issue of the APPA newsletter contained excerpts from one of President Kennedy's last speeches on water and power development. He had made the speech October 3 at the dedication of Greer's Ferry Dam on the Little Red River at Heber Springs, Arkansas.

This is a great country that was given to us and a great land. It is our job, it seems to me, to make the most of it, to make sure that we in our time plant our forests, use our water, develop our power, provide recreation for our people, to do in our time to the extent that we can what Franklin Roosevelt did in his time and, before him, what Theodore Roosevelt did in his time—to use this great country, which in the short space of 30 years ago had only 130 million people within its borders and, by the year 2,000 will have 350 million people, to make sure that we take those steps now which will make it possible for those who come after us to have a better life.

•

Although the scars to the individual and the national psyches over President Kennedy's assassination lingered for many years, life in Washington gradually resumed a more familiar pace as Lyndon Johnson took command of the presidency.

President Johnson was a strong public power supporter. NRECA's voting records showed Johnson had cast 38 Senate votes favorable to public power and rural electrification and only seven unfavorable. His first vote in the Senate supported appropriations for the Tennessee Valley Authority's controversial New Johnsonville steam plant. He worked actively for authorization of the Hells Canyon project, regarded by some as a litmus test of support for public power.

Because Johnson was sympathetic to public power, the APPA officers and staff thought his ambitious Great Society program offered opportunities for initiating new public power ventures to stimulate the economy. We wanted the APPA Executive Committee to meet with the president to outline a comprehensive public power program that could become an integral part of the Great Society. Lee White arranged a meeting for us for July 8, 1964.

Our seven-member Executive Committee, headed by President R.J. McMullin of the Salt River Project in Phoenix, arrived early in the morning at the West Wing of the White House.[3] We were ushered into a lower floor and then directed to the cabinet room to wait for the president. A tall, commanding figure, President Johnson soon arrived. He greeted us graciously and almost immediately launched into a detailed recounting of his role with public power and rural electrification in Texas. He described his part in founding the Pedernales Electric Cooperative in Johnson City, Texas, and in serving as a member of the co-op's first board of directors. He said he had been involved in establishing a number of municipal electric utilities in Texas. He described in detail his role in the formation

---

[3] Other members of the Executive Committee were first vice president Frank King, second vice president Kirby Billingsley, manager, Chelan County Public Utility District, Wenatchee, Washington; Ivan L. Bateman, assistant general manager and chief engineer, Los Angeles Department of Water and Power; J. Dillon Kennedy, Jacksonville, Florida; John B. Preston, general manager, Loup Power District, Columbus, Nebraska, and B.G. Adkins, superintendent, Electric Department, Danville, Virginia.

of the Lower Colorado River Authority, a state agency that constructed several dams in Texas. He was obviously proud of his involvement with these public power and rural electric cooperative activities and was knowledgeable about their operation.

Mindful of the imminence of the election campaign, McMullin pointed out that APPA represented the interests of more than 2,000 cities throughout the country. He offered the assistance of the local publicly owned electric utilities in meeting the president's goals of a "Great Society" and emphasized the importance of providing an abundance of low-cost electricity to advance the nation's economic growth and prosperity.

Initiation of the Pacific Northwest-Pacific Southwest intertie was hotly debated in Congress at that time and this was the first item on our shopping list. I said the intertie offered the Johnson administration an unprecedented opportunity to bring about one of the most far-reaching and constructive developments ever achieved in the United States in the transmission of electric power and integration of regional power systems.

The president never lost an opportunity to give assignments to those who asked him for help. He urged us to redouble our efforts to build support in the Congress for the intertie and to attempt to resolve some of the differences that had arisen in connection with this issue.

With deference to APPA Vice President Frank King of Holyoke, Massachusetts, we made a strong plea for continued support of the Passamaquoddy and St. John River hydro power project in Maine, then being debated in Congress. We pointed out that these projects could "break the cycle of high rates and low electric use which hampers the economic progress of the area."

We also asked the president to support authorization and appropriations for other water resource projects and to promote more research on combination power and water desalting plants. We urged him to continue President Kennedy's policy of appointing "top-flight professional people" to the FPC and other regulatory commissions and to support adequate appropriations for the commissions to strengthen federal regulation of the electric industry.

Recognizing that President Johnson idolized President Franklin D. Roosevelt, we quoted Roosevelt on public power's role as a "birch rod in the closet" that could be used to spur competition in the electric industry. However, we added that if the competitive force of public power was to be maintained, the federal government would have to exercise leadership as a steward of the nation's energy resources and assure regulation in the public interest.

We were pleased with the results of the meeting. It demonstrated to friends and opponents our access to the highest office in the land and helped cement our relationship with Secretary Udall and other government officials. Although forces in addition to ours were at work, our meeting with the president must have helped build White House support for projects we endorsed. Johnson enthusaistically endorsed building the Pacific Northwest-Pacific Southwest intertie. Later, he was instrumental in breaking a legislative deadlock on the issue.

•

Public power became an issue in the 1964 campaign and President Johnson rose to our defense. In November 1963, Sen. Barry Goldwater, R-Ariz, who later became the Republican presidential nominee, called for sale of the Tennessee Valley Authority. His statement was alarming not only because TVA was such an important icon of public power, but also because the Arizona senator had voted against public power projects on numerous occasions. A notable exception was his support of the Central Arizona Project, a $1 billion federal reclamation and power project that benefited his state.

Former President Dwight D. Eisenhower publicly disagreed with Senator Goldwater, but the senator stuck to his position. The American people did not share Senator Goldwater's view. Pollster Louis Harris reported in *The Washington Post* that Goldwater's proposal was the senator's most unpopular domestic stand. Polling showed it was opposed by a 2-1 margin nationally; 4-1 in the South. Only slightly more than a majority of conservatives agreed with the proposal.

Senator Goldwater and his vice presidential running mate, Rep. William E. Miller, R-N.Y., both had voting records unfavorable to public power. Senator Goldwater in his 10 years in the Senate cast only three votes supporting public power, while 44 were unfavorable, according to National Rural Electric Cooperative Association voting records.[4] Representative Miller, in his 14 years in the House, supported public power six times and opposed it 42 times.

In spite of widespread opposition to his stand, Senator Goldwater continued to advocate the sale of TVA. In September, during a campaign

---

[4] Sen. Goldwater's position on TVA was consistent with his record before he became a senator. Prior to his service in the Senate, he was a member of the Phoenix City Council and opposed a municipal parking lot, arguing "that the parking facilities should be privately operated and that city ownership would be socialism."

tour that included speeches in Knoxville and Memphis, he elaborated on his position. He favored the sale of TVA's fertilizer and steam generating plants to private companies, but said the remainder of TVA's operations might be sold to a quasi-public corporation because it was too big to sell to a single private customer.

In mid-October, speaking at a rally in Nashville, President Johnson responded to Goldwater's proposal, saying TVA is "part of the blood and bone of Tennessee and of the greatness of America and it is not for sale." The Johnson administration will not sell the nation's rivers, he said.

The Republican platform did not advocate sale of TVA, but the platforms of each party expressed markedly different views on power and resource issues. Although both professed support for comprehensive water resource development, the Republican platform called for a more limited role for the federal government and less regulation. A key provision of the Republican platform favored a "continual examination and the reduction of government competition with private business, consistent with the recommendations of the second Hoover Commission."[5] These recommendations, made in 1955, proposed "that private enterprise be offered the opportunity to provide the capital for the electrical component of multiple-purpose dams and dispose of the power through their own systems."

The Democratic platform pledged to continue "the quickened pace of comprehensive development of the river basins in every section of the country" and to "promote the development of new and improved methods of generating electric power, such as the recent important gains in the field of atomic energy and the Passamaquoddy tidal power." The platform also vowed to "preserve the TVA."

The Democratic platform credited President Johnson for his leadership in developing a plan for interconnecting the electric power systems of the Pacific Northwest and the Pacific Southwest. It also pointed out that, under the Democratic administration, federal hydro power capacity had increased by 2,600 mw and work had started on the dual-purpose reactor in Hanford, Wash.

At APPA, we were disappointed that neither of the party platforms expressed support for the federal preference clause, which gives consumer-owned utilities preferential access to federal hydro power.

---

[5] The Hoover Commission referred to a presidential commission headed by former President Herbert Hoover that was charged with making recommendations on the structure of the federal government.

Previous platforms of both parties had endorsed preference.

Sen. Hubert Humphrey, D-Minn., the vice presidential candidate, laid out his views on public power at the Western States Water and Power Consumers Conference at Bismark, North Dakota. This was the same forum used four years earlier by then-candidate John F. Kennedy to make a major speech about public power and water resource development. Humphrey expressed hope that "the publicly owned electric systems, which serve some 2,000 local communities in the United States" would "grow and prosper." He added that Americans also should continue "to have the right to decide for themselves whether they wish to provide electricity for themselves or contract for service for their cities and towns with private power companies."

Senator Humphrey called for "firm federal leadership in the comprehensive development of our water resources," implementing the "letter and spirit" of the preference clause, promoting use of advanced technology in the power industry, and carrying forward research and development to give America "a healthy atomic energy industry."

As a non-partisan organization, APPA could not endorse either candidate, but our publications gave extensive coverage to the views of both the Democratic and Republican standard bearers. However, I had personal and professional reasons to favor President Johnson. I was a life-long Democrat bred on the political philosophy of Franklin D. Roosevelt and I believed President Johnson carried forward Roosevelt's goals. In view of Senator Goldwater's strong opposition to public power and President Johnson's staunch support, there was no question which candidate would best serve APPA's interests. I had many personal ties to Johnson administration officials, so was elated by the Johnson-Humphrey victory.

I was also pleased with the results of the congressional elections. Several die-hard opponents of public power were defeated and a number of strong supporters were brought to office or reelected. Tom Foley of Washington state was elected to Congress in 1964. I had known him previously as a special counsel to the Senate Interior and Insular Affairs Committee. A protégé of Sen. Scoop Jackson, Foley climbed steadily in the ranks of the House and later became speaker.

After President Johnson's election, one of our principal concerns was the reappointment of Joe Swidler as chairman of the Federal Power Commission. As time passed, it seemed Swidler would not be reappointed and by late 1965 he said he would not seek another term. We were relieved when the president tapped Lee White to replace Swidler. This was a logical appointment, but the manner in which it was made provided interesting insights into President Johnson's personality and *modus operandi.*

White was well qualified professionally and politically. He was both an engineer and attorney, had been a member of the legal staff of TVA, and had worked for Sen. John Sherman Cooper, R-Ky., and for John F. Kennedy when he was a senator and president. On the White House staff, White was responsible for a broad portfolio of subjects, including natural resources, energy and civil rights.

After Kennedy died, Johnson retained White. Although President Johnson had a reputation as a strong-willed person who could be harsh with his staff, the president admired White because he was forthright but diplomatic in expressing his opinions, even when their views differed. White also appealed to Johnson because, as White put it, he wore an invisible badge that said, "former member of the Kennedy administration." Because of the aura that surrounded the martyred president, it behooved Johnson to retain former Kennedy appointees.

But there was a hitch. White had already planned to leave the White House at the end of 1965 and had committed to join a prominent Washington law firm. He advised a member of the president's staff of his decision, whereupon the president called White into his office. As their meeting began, Johnson pulled out of his coat pocket a copy of a letter he had written to Abe Fortas after Fortas had turned down a seat on the U.S. Supreme Court. Johnson's letter said he had just signed an order sending 75,000 troops to Viet Nam and that he had not given those troops the opportunity to say no. The president told Fortas he should not have such a privilege, either. White capitulated.[6]

Commenting upon White's appointment, *The New York Times* said that he "can be expected to carry forward Mr. Swidler's policy of vigilance and fairness," and *The Wall Street Journal* declared that White "is considered solidly pro-consumer" and his "judicial approach...should assure electric utilities, oil and gas companies that FPC regulations aren't in danger of being drastically reshaped."

A shrewd, knowledgeable person of integrity, White carried on the policies pursued by Swidler, but was less confrontational and did not arouse the strong antagonism Swidler had engendered. I was delighted about his appointment. I had a close personal relationship with him which has continued to this day.

---

[6] In recounting this episode, White said he thought Johnson always kept a copy of the letter to Fortas in his pocket so he could pull it out whenever it was appropriate.

Chapter 31

Sara's Death

By 1964 I had spent 16 years with the American Public Power Association, almost 13 as executive director. I was gratified with the progress of the organization and my role in its development.

Throughout this period, my wife, Sara, had played an important part in the association. At a time when APPA had limited staff and funds, she worked in the office and at the registration desk during annual conferences. Her charm, unpretentious nature and interest in others endeared her to APPA members and staff. She was an excellent hostess at the association's social functions and quickly developed friendships with members and staff.

More important, she provided stability and gratification in my personal life. Her unquestioned love gave me a sense of security that was important in the development of my career. She was the mother of our two sons, who enriched our lives and gave us much pleasure. She opened my eyes to art and aesthetic considerations. Her gregarious nature introduced me to an active, stimulating social life.

Sara had changed considerably since we were married in 1942, when she was 19 and I was 21. As a young woman she was attractive, lively and made friends easily. As she matured, these qualities were strengthened, and others blossomed.

Perhaps her most important characteristic was her sensitivity to the feelings of others. Friends—or those whom she had known only casually—easily confided in her and sought her counsel on personal matters.

She was not perfect. Her moods tended to be mercurial and when she was depressed, she was not easy to live with. But when she was in a cheerful frame of mind, one quickly forgot unpleasant incidents. She had strong convictions and was not reluctant to express them. She could become combative—sometimes to my embarrassment. But after a heated argument, she often had charmed those with whom she had debated and they parted as friends.

She provided an excellent counterbalance to my temperament. Her daring and exuberance pulled me out of my shell .

Although APPA was an important part of her life, she maintained other interests and pursued her own career. After our sons Jay and Bill were born, she wanted to be home when they were not in school. Nevertheless, she found time to write a weekly newsletter for a Tennessee Congressman (from the district that included Chattanooga), and she started a community newsletter. People admired her taste and sense of design in furnishing and landscaping our home and frequently sought her advice. She began to do interior decoration and landscaping professionally, although she had no formal training in these areas.

She also became deeply involved in local politics and worked assiduously for candidates for the county board of supervisors. Later, she became involved in the campaign of Sen. Estes Kefauver, D- Tenn., the vice presidential candidate during Adlai Stevenson's 1956 unsuccessful race for the presidency. She had known Kefauver as a newspaper reporter in Chattanooga and later in Washington.

•

Early in 1964, Sara began to experience pains in her abdomen. Her doctor had difficulty making a diagnosis, but thought she might have a hiatal hernia. An examination showed this not to be the case. This information disturbed Sara because the hernia condition could have been treated relatively easily.

Unable to find a physical cause for Sara's pains, her doctor thought she might be depressed. He prescribed a mild anti-depressant and recommended she see a therapist. She did so and for a short time felt somewhat better.

In May, Sara and I went to Jacksonville, Florida, to attend the APPA annual conference, an event that was normally stimulating to her. We engaged someone to stay with our children and for a few days Sara led a carefree life taken up with parties, sightseeing and social engagements.

Although not her usual exuberant self at the beginning of the trip, Sara became more animated as the conference progressed. In those days of unabashed male chauvinism, APPA arranged a ladies program for wives of conference delegates, virtually all of whom were male. In 1964 the principal speaker at the "ladies luncheon" was Sara's personal friend, Frances Lewin, an Associated Press White House correspondent who covered Lady Bird Johnson. Sara and Frances had a great time together. Sara was also energized by other conference events. By the end of the meeting, she was experiencing little pain and returned home in a positive frame of mind. Both of us were relieved.

Gradually, however, her pain returned and became more intense. She had little appetite, and began to lose weight. By early July she consulted another doctor, who recommended she have an exploratory operation. The doctor gave no intimation of the possible cause of her discomfort.

On the morning of the operation at George Washington University Hospital, I held Sara's hand as she smiled faintly and kissed her as she was wheeled out of her room on a gurney. I was only mildly concerned. I thought the operation would lead to a diagnosis of a condition that could be remedied. Sara was only 41 years old and it did not occur to me that she might have a terminal illness.

I waited in Sara's hospital room during the operation. After about an hour or less, a surgeon came into the room. I was seated in a chair; he sat on the bed, and quickly gave me the news. Without any warning of the catastrophic message that he was about to deliver, he said bluntly that Sara had cancer of the pancreas, an incurable and inoperable condition. She could be expected to live two to four months. During that time she would undergo chemotherapy, but this was not a cure. It might alleviate the condition slightly, but it would be administered primarily to give Sara hope. We were not to tell Sara about the gravity of her situation. We were merely to say that she had cancer and that some of it was removed, but it was impossible for all of it to be taken out. The remainder would be treated by chemotherapy.

The doctor advised me that nothing could have been done earlier to save her. By the time pancreatic cancer is discovered, it is too late to remove it. To ease her pain, he would prescribe a more powerful painkiller, thorazine, and sleeping pills. He felt her pain could be controlled. As her condition worsened, morphine would be administered in carefully measured doses so it would not lose its effectiveness before her death.

I was devastated by the doctor's report and dropped to my knees and wept. The doctor quickly departed and I was left alone to confront this calamitous, shattering news.

Sara was to be brought back from the recovery room in about an hour. I had these 60 minutes to inform Sara's sister and my brother and to regain my composure. I went to a drugstore across the street from the hospital and used a public telephone to call our relatives. I cautioned them that Sara was not to be told the full story. Sara's sister, Anna, who lived in Washington, agreed that, for the time being, Sara's mother and brother, who lived in Chattanooga, were not to be informed of her terminal condition. My brother and I felt our mother, who lived in Baltimore, also should not be advised of the extent of Sara's illness.

•

An immediate problem was what to do about informing our children. Our older son, Jay, was 17 and I decided initially to give him the same story I was to convey to Sara. Our 12-year-old son, Bill, was away at summer camp and would not return for about a week. I had told Bill when I visited him at camp that Sara was not feeling well, but said nothing about her impending operation.

In the interim before Bill's return, I consulted a therapist with whom Sara and I had been working. She said Jay was old enough to learn the truth immediately and he and I should experience together the tragic unfolding of events. However, the therapist felt Bill was too young to be burdened with the knowledge of his mother's impending death and I should shield him from the news until the virtual end.

I did as the therapist recommended. Going through this experience—tragic as it was—strengthened my relationship with Jay. Many years later I learned that Bill—after the fact—deeply resented the therapist's advice. He felt he had been deprived of an opportunity to say a final good-bye to his mother and that he had been unfairly denied information entrusted to his older brother.

•

After telephoning relatives and the APPA staff (I gave them the same story I was to tell Sara), I rushed back to the hospital. When Sara was wheeled back into the room, her doctor had already told her she had cancer, that some of it had been removed, and the remainder would be treated with chemotherapy. He did not tell her that her condition was terminal.

I repeated this story to Sara, but she was not deceived. The mere mention of the word "cancer" was enough to send her into a deep depression. I tried to reassure her, but to no avail. Meanwhile, I had to prepare for her return home and plan for an entirely new regimen in our lives. It was obvious that Sara could no longer be responsible for running a household. Sara's sister, Anna, persuaded a former household employee, Katherine Eley, to begin full-time work for us as a housekeeper. Cheerful, level-headed, resourceful and responsible, Katherine played a critical role in our home in the months ahead. She relieved me of chores and made it possible for me to continue my professional routine as best I could under trying conditions.

Sara's doctor asked me to fill prescriptions for thorazine and sleeping pills prior to her return home. I did so and brought the pills back to Sara's hospital room. I told her I would take them home.

"Why don't you leave them here?" Sara said. "I'll pack them with my things and bring them home with me." It seemed an innocent request, so I left the pills with her. Sara was in a more cheerful mood as I left the hospital. I was to pick her up the next morning.

About 6 a.m. the following day, I received a call from the hospital informing me that I should come there as soon as possible. During the night Sara had overdosed on sleeping pills, but the incident had been discovered and her stomach was promptly pumped. Her condition was not life-threatening.

Without telling Jay what had happened, I rushed to the hospital. She was still groggy and somewhat chagrined when I arrived. She did not want to discuss the matter and I tried to comfort her.

Later, I learned more details from one of the attending nurses. During the preceding night, before Sara went to bed, she had engaged the nurse in a discussion about Marilyn Monroe, who had recently died from an overdose of sleeping pills. During the conversation, Sara casually asked how many sleeping pills Monroe had taken before her death. The nurse gave her an approximation, apparently without knowing Sara had sleeping pills in her room.

Sara recuperated quickly from the overdose. When she was released from the hospital the following day, I kept the sleeping pills in my possession and gave them to her only when necessary.

•

About a week after Sara came home, Bill was to return from summer camp, and I had to anticipate the agonizing experience of telling him about Sara's situation. Bill's train was late and I spent an hour or more walking around the grounds near the Capitol to prepare for my meeting with him. He and Sara were very close, but he took the news stoically. I tried not to drop any hints about the extent of the problem.

The next few months were the most painful, agonizing ones of my life as I watched Sara's condition deteriorate and her level of pain increase. Despite her doctor's assurances that her discomfort could be kept reasonably under control, she was frequently racked with pain before going to sleep. After she had taken a sleeping pill and thorazine before bedtime, I frequently held her in my arms in bed before the pain subsided and she quietly went to sleep. I could feel her body gradually relax as the pills took effect. Once, as I held her, she said, "Do you suppose we will ever again...?" and her voice trailed off.

With the help of Katherine, friends and neighbors, we managed to maintain a relatively normal routine. After a while, I could no longer keep up any pretense, and confided to J.D. Brown and Larry Hobart of the APPA staff about Sara's condition. They and other members of the staff were magnificent in the support they gave me. They relieved me of many responsibilities so I could spend as much time as possible with Sara and our children. More than that, their compassion and friendship were a great source of comfort.

R.J. McMullin, general manager of the Salt River Project, Phoenix, Arizona, was president of APPA, and I also told him about Sara's condition. He and other members of the board of directors were understanding and compassionate.

Other colleagues, too, were helpful. Joe Swidler, chairman of the Federal Power Commission, was especially sensitive. He was very fond of Sara. She had been supportive of him in the past and he felt close to her. He periodically invited me to lunch with him at the commission; his demonstration of concern was comforting. (After Swidler left the commission, I differed seriously with him on some of the positions he took, but my feelings were always tempered by recollections of his concern for Sara and me during a critical period in our lives.)

In the period after Sara's operation, I discontinued all out-of-town trips except one to the fall meeting of the board of directors in New York City. The most poignant experience during that trip came one evening, when Raphael Urrutia, executive director of the Puerto Rico Water Resources Authority, visited me in my room. Sara loved Puerto Rico and we had become friendly with Urrutia and his family, who had entertained us in their home in San Juan. Urrutia had come to my room to express his concern and as we talked about Sara both of us wept and embraced.

Even toward the end, Sara wanted to keep her ties with APPA. On one of the few occasions she left home after her surgery, she visited the APPA office to attend a luncheon with the staff.

•

The hard times were leavened somewhat by a constant stream of visitors. Sara frequently did not want to see anyone, but when she agreed, she usually perked up and took part in lively conversations. One of the most refreshing and sustaining visitors was Sara's closest friend, Virginia (Ginny) Selin, a former neighbor who had moved to Marquette,

Michigan. After Sara was released from the hospital, Ginny spent almost a week with us. She took over cooking and other household responsibilities. Mainly, though, their close friendship opened the door to intimate conversations that were reassuring to Sara. Her visit was also helpful to Jay, Bill and me. She was an upbeat person, and for a short time, she provided an air of normalcy to our household. Her visit brought back memories of happier times, when Ginny lived in our neighborhood and her family and ours were frequently together.

One evening during her visit, a friend who was a psychiatrist dropped in for what turned out to be a hilarious occasion. He was a clever raconteur and he regaled us with humorous (and sometimes poignant) stories about some of his patients. His behavior was unprofessional, but for one evening he made us forget about Sara's predicament.

•

In late October, about three months after the exploratory operation, I left home about 9 a.m. for the office. Sara would be alone for a half hour or less. About 9:45 a.m., Katherine called and told me Sara had again tried to kill herself. Somehow, she had hoarded a few sleeping pills and had taken them after I left, then tied a plastic bag over her head. Fortunately, Sara's brother-in-law, Alec Jacobson (Anna's husband) arrived for a visit shortly thereafter, discovered what had happened and quickly removed the plastic. Sara was asleep and still breathing. Meanwhile, Katherine arrived and called me immediately.

I called a doctor and rushed home. The doctor arrived shortly after I returned and said Sara had reached the stage where she would have to be given morphine injections regularly to control her pain. He recommended she be taken by ambulance to a nursing home near Dupont Circle in downtown Washington so she could have continuous care and monitoring.

Sara was still asleep when she was moved to the nursing home. I was with her when she awoke. She was remorseful about the turn of events, but I was relieved she could now have around-the-clock attention in pleasant surroundings and would obtain medication that would ease her pain.

At this point, there was no longer any pretense about the gravity of her situation, and she and I could talk frankly about her prognosis, about ourselves, our lives together and how much we meant to each other. Fortunately, the APPA office was within easy walking distance of the nursing home, and I visited her two or three times a day. Sara also had visits from a number of friends, one of whom, Audrey Keir (who was divorced and living alone) spent many evenings with Sara when I was home with Jay and Bill. Audrey had a good sense of humor and her visits were cheerful. Sara's sister, brother-in-law and mother also visited regularly, as did my mother, brother and sister-in-law. One of her friends later told me, after visiting Sara, that "she knew how to live and how to die."

Even in the nursing home, Sara did not lose interest in what was happening in the world. She felt strongly about the heated presidential race between Lyndon Johnson and Barry Goldwater and insisted I cast her absentee ballot in support of Johnson. She discussed plans for Bill's *bar mitzvah*, which was to occur the following March and made a list of people to be invited.

She also thought about her friends. She asked me to bring her all of her jewelry. She placed various pieces in bags with labels that bore the names of friends, and requested that I deliver them after her death. Two prized possessions—a gold choker, a pearl necklace and matching earrings, gifts from her parents—were to be given to the wives of Jay and Bill when they were married.

Shortly after her illness was diagnosed as cancer, Sara began knitting an intricately designed sweater for her close friend, Ginny Selin. She managed to finish the sweater in the nursing home, and asked me to present it to Ginny after her death.

Although Sara was proud to be a Jew and was a loyal Zionist, she did not actively participate in organized religious activities. When our rabbi asked whether he could visit her, she declined. She regarded him as somewhat pompous and said she did not want him to deliver a eulogy at her funeral.

As the days passed, Sara was reasonably comfortable, but under the influence of morphine she slept a great deal. Nonetheless, it was an excruciating experience for both of us. She knew she was dying and was in the process of withdrawal. Visits from Jay and Bill were painful for all of us.

I wanted to be with Sara, but also tried to spend as much time as possible with our sons, and attempted to maintain the household in as normal a manner as possible. I did not want to neglect APPA, either. Trying to carry out these responsibilities was a tremendous strain physically and emotionally. As much as I loved Sara, I could not at times escape an occasional feeling of regret that her last suicide attempt was not successful. Whenever I could, I found solace and courage in music, especially in listening to a spiritual whose principal lyrics were, "We

must walk this lonesome valley; we have to walk it by ourselves. Oh
nobody else can walk it for us; we have to walk it by ourselves."

Despite the agony in seeing Sara deteriorate and waiting for the
inevitable, I treasured the times that Sara and I were able to talk and
express our love for each. Those occasions gave us a chance to say a
proper farewell.

On the evening of November 19, 1964, Jean Barnett, a neighbor, was
visiting Sara at the nursing home when I left to go home to have dinner
with Jay and Bill. I kissed Sara and told her good-bye. As I walked to the
door, I turned around. She smiled and waived. That was her last gesture
to me.

At about 4 a.m. the following morning, I received a call from the
nursing home informing me that Sara had lapsed into a coma and that I
should come there as soon as possible. I awakened Jay, told him what was
happening and quickly drove into Washington. When I arrived, I called
Anna and she and her husband arrived at about 6 a.m. Sara's doctor came
shortly thereafter. The doctor said Sara was not likely to survive, but we
should be careful what we said in her presence, because it was not known
how much a person in a comma might comprehend.

All day Anna and I stood vigil and in the late afternoon Sara's mother,
stepfather and brother arrived from Chattanooga. About 6 p.m., Anna
encouraged me to go home to have dinner with Jay and Bill. I had called
them during the day to report on the situation and when I came home for
dinner I told them their mother was not likely to survive.

When I returned to the hospital, Anna and Sara's mother were standing
in the corridor outside of Sara's room. They told me Sara had just died.
They left me so that I could spend a few minutes alone with her. I sat at
her bedside, held her hand, and cried. It was a Friday evening and our
rabbi was about to begin the Friday services. I telephoned him at the
temple, told him Sara had died and arranged to have the funeral on
Sunday afternoon. Then I went home to convey the news to Jay and Bill
and tried to comfort them.

As I made arrangements the following day for the funeral, I was
reminded of the impact that my father's funeral had on me as a 10-year-
old. I could not forget the foreboding sight of the black hearse and large
black limousine that took our family to the cemetery. I could not spare my
children the agony of a similar occasion, but I wanted them to feel that
life would go on. I therefore asked the funeral home to supply a white
hearse and limousine for our family, as a sign of hope.

The rabbi conducted a short, traditional service the following day at the temple, which was crowded with Sara's family and friends. I could not hold back tears when her casket was rolled into the synagogue and I had to say the *Kaddish*, the traditional prayer for the departed.

Mindful of Sara's admonition that she did not want the rabbi to deliver a eulogy, I wrote a tribute to Sara a few days before her death, and asked the rabbi to read it. This is what I wrote:

> The noted English poet John Donne wrote, "And therefore never send to know for whom the bell tolls; it tolls for thee."
>
> With the passing of Sara, the bell tolls loudly and clearly for a multitude of people here and throughout the land, because with her passing some part of all of us died.
>
> The bell tolls loudest and clearest for her immediate family. For it was they who knew best her unique capacity to love and be loved; it was they whose hearts were set aglow by her warmth; it was they who shared her delight in beauty and creativeness; it was they whose characters were enriched by her honesty with herself and with others, and her disdain for sham and pretense.
>
> But the bell that tolls so loudly for her immediate family likewise tolls for hundreds of others who knew her and treasured her friendship. Because Sara had the rarely given capacity to bestow her love and her compassion upon many others—close friends as well as casual acquaintances. When friends were in grief, she wept with them; when they were joyous, she laughed. And when others were dejected or felt alone or helpless, Sara could comfort them and nurture their spirits in a way very few mortals could.
>
> Sara bestowed her love and compassion upon those in all stations of life—be they senators or seamstresses, artists or maids. All had value and meaning for her.
>
> She had an innate sense of beauty that left its mark on many gardens and homes and the beauty she brought to others will be enjoyed by them for many years to come.
>
> Despite the gravity of her illness, of which she herself was only too painfully aware, her courage and her lack of fear were a comfort to others. Even in the final days of her life those who visited her at the hospital left with that rare feeling of warmth, vitality of spirit and cheerfulness that she had such a rare capacity to impart to others.
>
> Little wonder that so many were so deeply moved by the great tragedy of her illness.
>
> There can be no real consolation in the passing of one so young, so vibrant, so loving and so much loved, and possessed of such an incisive understanding for the feelings of others.
>
> There is some solace, however, in the fact that during her all-too-brief lifetime on this planet she gave generously to many the most precious, the most meaningful and the rarest of gifts—love, compassion, warmth, wit and beauty. Those who had the good fortune to be recipients of these gifts

have been enriched and ennobled beyond the power of words to describe. Such gifts can never be taken away and they will be treasured for ever and ever.

After the service, a long motorcade wound its way through Northern Virginia suburbs to the burial at King David Memorial Cemetery in Falls Church, Virginia, which was reserved for deceased of the Jewish faith. King David is maintained in a park-like setting, with fountains and statuary by a noted Swedish sculptor, Carl Milles. All headstones are small, level to the ground, and contain only the names and dates of birth and death of the deceased. The unpretentious, aesthetic quality of the cemetery seemed to be a fitting place for Sara's final resting place.

I wanted to set an example for my children to be confident of the future. During this ordeal, my mother told me repeatedly, in Yiddish, *zeit shtark* (be strong). After the brief service at the gravesite, I took the arms of Jay and Bill, looked straight ahead, and walked erectly and briskly with them to the limousine.

When we returned home, friends and relatives had arranged a reception. It was an eerie experience. In many ways, it was like the parties that Sara had hosted, except that a central figure was not physically present. Yet her presence could be felt everywhere in a home that was so infused with her spirit. After the reception, when everyone had left, the stark, quiet reality of loneliness and grief hit me.

Chapter 32

The Northeast Blackout

In a report to President Johnson in December 1965, the Federal Power Commission gave this account of one of the most important events in the annals of the electric industry:

> Beginning at approximately 5:16 p.m. on November 9, 1965, most of the northeastern United States experienced the largest power failure in history. The outage lasted from a few minutes in some locations to more than a half day in others. It encompassed 80,000 square miles and directly affected an estimated 30 million people in the United States and Canada. Occurring during a time of day in which there is maximum need for power in this area of great population density, it offered the greatest potential for havoc.

The matter-of-fact tone of the commission's 95-page report failed to reveal the dramatic impact of the blackout. A pilot coming into Boston's Logan Airport at 5:21 p.m. watched the lights of the entire city go out as he landed. Lights sparkling in New York City skyscrapers went dark and three million people were without electricity for as long as $13^{1}/_2$ hours. A front-page *New York Times* headline the following morning declared, "800,000 ARE CAUGHT IN SUBWAYS HERE; AUTOS TIED UP, CITY GROPES IN DARK."

The blackout was a stark demonstration of the dependence of the U.S. economy and lifestyle on electricity. It crippled transportation— planes, trains, elevators, buses, taxis and private vehicles. Businesses were disrupted. Millions of dollars in financial and insurance transactions were halted because computers were inoperable. Many of the 850 hospitals without commercial service ran their own generators, but some generators would not work and others ran out of fuel during the long night. Medical experiments demanding a controlled environment were ruined with a change of light or temperature. Television was completely cut off, newspapers were not printed and theater performances were cancelled.

President Johnson immediately directed the Federal Power Commission to investigate the cause of the blackout and recommend steps to prevent a recurrence. FPC Chairman Joe Swidler was slated to leave the commission November 15, but the president asked him to remain until the report was completed. The Federal Bureau of Investigation and other federal agencies also investigated.

When the blackout occurred, Congress and the administration already were considering legislation to address reliability. Foremost was a proposal to give FPC authority to approve utility plans to build extra-high-voltage transmission lines.

The blackout called attention to the superior reliability of the region's municipal electric utilities. Only a few miles from Manhattan, the municipal electric utility in Rockville Centre, New York, with approximately 9,000 customers, kept the lights on for all but a two-minute period when it sent emergency power to a private utility. Holyoke, Massachusetts, Gas and Electric Department used its generating facilities to maintain service during the blackout. Holyoke supplied power to the CONVEX pool, consisting of four power companies in Connecticut and Massachusetts, even though Holyoke Gas & Electric had been excluded from the pool.

•

APPA President Frank King, manager of the Holyoke Gas & Electric Department, told the press the Northeast power failure forcibly pointed to the need for more comprehensive long-range planning and full development of power resources by both private and public utilities.

"Up to now, development of a power grid system in this region has been too much on a temporary, short-range basis with insufficient coordinated long-range planning," King said. He suggested the Northeast follow the pattern of the West Coast, with extra-high-voltage interconnections and adequate development of power resources.

Further study might indicate a need for a regulatory authority to oversee huge electrical grid development, King said. If so, it would be logical to grant such authority to the FPC, he said.

I appointed a five-person staff task force, headed by Legislative Director Larry Hobart, to study the blackout and its consequences. The task force screened more than 4,000 newspaper clippings, analyzed the results of a survey of public power utilities in the Northeast, reviewed the FPC report, and interviewed experts on problems associated with the outage.

In its report, issued December 6, 1965, the FPC offered its explanation of the cause of the blackout:

> At 5:16 PM, a backup protective relay on one of the five 230-kv transmission lines taking power north from the Beck plant of Ontario to the Toronto area operated and caused the circuit breaker to disconnect the line. The flow of power on the disconnected line was thus shifted to the remaining four lines going north from the Beck plant, each of which was then loaded beyond the level at which its protective relay was set to operate. They tripped out successively in a similar manner in a total of about $2^1/_2$ seconds.

Investigations showed the relay had been set in 1963 to operate at 375,000 kw, but loadings on the line had grown heavier since then, and operating personnel were unaware of the 1963 setting. The commission placed responsibility for the start of the blackout on Ontario Hydro's relay, but said New York City's blackout might have been prevented if Consolidated Edison's operator on duty had shed loads or severed ties with other systems.

The commission made 19 specific recommendations. Many dealt with system planning and operations, such as building stronger transmission networks within each system and stronger interconnections between systems; establishing unified planning and operating groups, and checking relay settings when circumstances changed. The FPC recommended utilities review the adequacy of their reserves in generating and transmission, and procedures and equipment used for dispatching during emergencies. It advocated installation of auxiliary power supply sources for civilian services that could not tolerate interruptions, such as hospitals, airports and tunnels, and called for development of plans for evacuating subways and elevators.

The commission also said it was actively considering the need for legislation to give it jurisdiction over reliability.

•

FPC's failure to recommend a role for itself in reliability reflected an intense struggle that had been going on for almost a year.

In April 1965, the commission sent Congress two draft bills, subsequently introduced as H.R. 7788 and H.R. 7791. With one vacancy on the commission, its membership was split evenly between the two bills. Commissioners David S. Black and Charles R. Ross favored H.R. 7791, requiring FPC certification and licensing of interstate transmission lines. Chairman Swidler and Commissioner Lawrence J. O'Conner supported the less stringent bill, H.R. 7788, which provided for FPC consultation with private utilities in transmission planning, with opportunity for public hearings if doubts arose.

About two weeks before the FPC issued its report, Swidler told Congress the 2-2 deadlock had been broken by the commission's newest member, Carl E. Bagge, who had been sponsored by the Senate's Republican leader, Sen. Everett Dirksen of Illinois. Bagge opposed the mandatory licensing bill.

Swidler told Congress the commission's proposals were developed before the November 9 blackout and the FPC was "studying the circumstances of that failure with the aid of experts drawn from its staff, other agencies, and from the electric utility systems." He added: "We are not yet in a position to decide whether the experience of the November 9 failure calls for additional proposals."

•

On December 9, 1965—three days after the FPC issued its report on the blackout—APPA published its own report on this subject. APPA's publication designer, Hubert Leckie, prepared a clever, eye-catching cover, which was entirely in black. The title of the report was printed in letters slightly less black than the background. The report, written by Larry Hobart and the staff task force, was distributed widely and attracted much favorable attention.

The APPA report described the response to the blackout by municipal utilities and power companies. It assessed the impact of the blackout on military, civil defense, economic and social matters. It discussed legal questions and reactions by government, people and newspapers. The conclusions and recommendations incorporated suggestions by the APPA Executive Committee and board of directors. The blackout "proved that the impact of electricity upon the lives of all citizens is even more far-reaching than anyone had supposed," APPA said. "Within 15 minutes the vast megalopolis of the Eastern Seaboard was immobilized." The report continued:

> Many millions of Americans suddenly were made aware that they had given over control of this critically important element in their daily lives—electricity—to a group of men calling themselves the electric utility industry. The power thus delegated is as great as many of the powers given to government, yet it carries no provision for referendum or recall. With respect to reliability of service, it is a power subject to no effective control at the federal level, to limited state control, and to virtually no control at the local level...

When a private utility is given an exclusive franchise to provide electric power to a community, it automatically accepts a legal obligation to provide the best service possible. It is evident that while consumers in the Northeast pay rates among the highest in the nation, they receive something less than the best service possible. With few exceptions, municipal utilities dependent upon the private systems for wholesale power were unable to provide service. Municipals with their own generation continued to serve the public. This indicates that dependability of service must be considered, along with reasonable rates, to be a major goal of the local public power systems—and, in fact, all utility systems.

An obvious conclusion that can be drawn from the blackout is that power systems in the United States are regional entities, whether or not they accept the notion. When a broken relay in Canada can put out the lights in Rhode Island, the contention of the nine Northeast utilities still claiming to be intra-state, and not subject to federal jurisdiction, is effectively demolished....

The electric power industry is a public business, whether operated by private companies or public agencies. It is affected with the public interest and it must be subject to public control to assure reliability of service as well as reasonable rates.

The APPA report recommended enactment of legislation giving the FPC authority to establish and enforce minimum standards for design and operation of interconnected electric systems. It called for federal assistance in providing emergency electrical facilities, stronger transmission ties, expanded use of direct current transmission lines and development of new generating resources in the Northeast.

Municipal utilities in the Northeast with their own generating stations maintained electric service during the blackout, but maintenance of 100 percent standby facilities would be expensive and inefficient, APPA said. The report recommended municipal utilities give increasing attention to interconnections with other utilities and those utilities wholly or partially dependent upon private companies for wholesale power should consider providing more of their own power requirements if Congress did not grant FPC authority to oversee reliability.

•

Criticized by the press for its less-than-informative statements following the blackout, Consolidated Edison Company held a press conference to tell "all" to the local press. *New York Herald Tribune* Columnist Jimmy Breslin said it went something like this:

> *Reporter:* Would you please tell us how you could tell there was trouble with the lighting system?

Con Edison Official: Because the lights in my office went out.
Reporter: Well, perhaps your operating man could help us.
Con Edison Power Station Boss: I'd be glad to.
Reporter: You were on duty at the main switchboard in the West Side Power Station. When did your dials and other equipment first show you that something was wrong?
Con Edison Power Station Boss: I didn't know when the dials first indicated that there was trouble. After all the lights went out, I couldn't see the dials.

The blackout also precipitated speculation about what people did while the lights were out. *The New York Times* had an answer. It said that several large metropolitan hospitals reported sharp increases in births nine months after the blackout. Hospitals in areas where lights were restored in two to three hours reported normal birth rates. But where electric service was not restored until the following morning, some hospitals reported increases in birth rates of more than 100 percent.

•

The blackout forced FPC, Congress and the utility industry to focus on reliability legislation. In its initial report on the blackout, the commission voted 3-2 to support a voluntary approach favored by Chairman Swidler. However, in 1966 Lee White replaced Swidler as chairman. He led a majority favoring a more comprehensive plan to give FPC authority to regulate high-voltage transmission lines.

In July 1966 a subcommittee of the Senate Commerce Committee held hearings on bills that took two approaches to FPC jurisdiction over transmission lines. One would give FPC licensing authority; the other would grant the commission "consultative review."

Chairman White said the entire commission felt legislation was needed to promote the construction of new extra-high-voltage lines. Four of the five commissioners favored the bill granting licensing authority to the FPC.

APPA Legislative Director Larry Hobart testified in favor of mandatory action. By providing a mechanism for comprehensive planning, all electric utilities—regardless of ownership or size—could insure their transmission needs received full consideration, he said. "And instead of the possibility of a number of lines built to satisfy the requirements of separate systems, a single facility might be created to serve a number of utilities on an equitable basis," he said.

•

In 1967, pressure for reliability legislation escalated. In a special message to Congress on consumer protection, President Johnson said the nation needed "greater coordination" among electric utilities to provide more reliable and economical power service. Chairman White sent the administration's proposals to Congress in June, three days after a major regional blackout had swept across four mid-Atlantic states, affecting 13 million people in a 15,000-square-mile area that included portions of New Jersey, Pennsylvania, Delaware and Maryland.[1] The new proposal was more comprehensive than previous bills. It called for:

- Formation of regional planning organizations, comprising all segments of the industry, to plan for adequate bulk power supply;
- FPC establishment of standards for reliability, planning and operation of EHV transmission lines;
- FPC review and approval of EHV transmission lines exceeding 200 kv;
- FPC authority to order construction of lines, if needed.

Recognizing that power companies would be hostile to the proposed legislation, the Johnson administration attempted to sweeten the package for them. The FPC would be authorized to grant limited antitrust immunity to utilities once a regional planning council developed an acceptable transmission plan.

Chairman White told the Senate Commerce Committee the regional councils would be "the key to improved coordination." Every utility in a region would be represented on the regional council, which would formulate plans for regional reliability, he said. FPC would have non-voting representation on the regional councils and "would pass on their basic organization to insure fairness," White said.

•

Introduction of the administration's Electric Reliability Act stirred up controversy and stimulated introduction of other bills. Some members of Congress—notably Rep. John Moss, D-Calif.—felt the administration's bill did not go far enough. Representative Moss introduced a bill that would not grant antitrust immunity to utilities. It also would have made EHV lines "true public utilities" by giving any electric utility the right to increase the capacity of lines (regardless of ownership) at its own expense, subject to FPC regulation.

Private power companies vehemently opposed the proposed

---

[1] As in the November 1965 blackout, service in the affected area was maintained only by municipal electric utilities with their own generation.

legislation. They spearheaded an effort to establish a voluntary national utility council to promote reliability. They also criticized the proposal to permit smaller utilities to participate in regional planning councils. At a National Power Conference in Washington in October 1967, Donald C. Cook, president of American Electric Power System, said the majority of the nation's electric systems should be eliminated because they were "obsolete, wasteful and an expensive anachronism." Small utilities should not be included in regional planning councils because "they have no real contributions to make" to the problems of reliability, which were limited to major power producers, he said.

Although APPA had endorsed the bill in principle, members and staff examined the proposal in greater detail and began to have reservations about some aspects. We felt the current FPC was fair, but we recognized the composition of commissions would change and a future commission might be unsympathetic to public power. Some APPA members felt the bill would shift too much authority from utility management to a federal agency that lacked adequate resources to make such important decisions involving the industry. APPA members also believed small public power utilities would be overshadowed and outvoted in the regional councils. We feared that putting publicly, cooperatively and privately owned utilities together in the regional councils would lead to a homogenization of the industry and reduce the healthy effects of competition.

Other APPA members supported the bill, believing continued growth in demand for electricity and the need to build larger generating stations and higher voltage transmission lines required coordination between all segments of the industry. These utilities cited instances when they had been excluded from power supply planning in their respective areas. The regional planning councils could provide a mechanism to allow all public power utilities to demand to be included in regional planning.

The APPA Legislative and Resolutions Committee in January 1968 recommended major amendments to the bill. The committee's resolution advocated establishment of voluntary regional councils to coordinate utility generation and transmission plans. However, participation in the councils would be open to all utilities and each council's plans would be available for public inspection. It would be illegal to exclude a utility from a council.

The resolution said the federal government should be empowered to set guidelines for proper planning, including comprehensive development and reliability standards. Continued failure of utilities in any region to initiate and implement planning consistent with national goals would constitute grounds for federal intervention.

All transmission lines 200 kv and above were to be consistent with a comprehensive plan adopted by the regional councils, APPA's resolution said. To the extent feasible, planning for every extra-high-voltage facility should take into account all capacity needs within the affected areas and reasonable provision should be made for expansion. Any extra-high-voltage line not consistent with an approved regional plan could not be constructed without FPC certification.

•

To forestall the growing pressure of federal legislation, power companies formed their own national reliability organization. Previously, utilities had organized 12 regional groups, which acted primarily as power pools and planning organizations. However, the groups acted independently and there was no national organization. Consequently, in the summer of 1968 the regional groups formed the National Electric Reliability Council.[2]

The council was to be administered by an executive board with representatives from each regional organization. However, despite that promise, many public power utilities were excluded. Missouri Basin Systems Group, representing 125 municipal and rural electric cooperative systems in the Midwest, protested its exclusion from membership in Mid-Continent Area Power Pool, one of NERC's 12 regional councils.

Floyd L. Goss, chief engineer and assistant general manager of the Los Angeles Department of Water and Power, was elected the first chairman of NERC. After his election, he told the press the formation of NERC did not represent an effort to circumvent federal reliability legislation, but it would remove the need for legislated controls over electric utilities.

The formation of NERC, the national elections and the preoccupation of the American public with the Vietnam War put reliability legislation on the back burner in 1968. However, by February 1969 the fourth major blackout in the Boston area since Christmas renewed interest in reliability. A bipartisan group of 41 members of Congress—led by Representatives John Moss, D-Calif., Richard Ottinger, D-N.Y., and Torbert Macdonald, D-Mass., in the House and Sen. Edward Kennedy, D-Mass., in the Senate—introduced similar bills to prevent blackouts and to provide new consumer and environmental protections.

In March 1969 a subcommittee of the House Interstate and Foreign

---

[2] The name of the organization subsequently was changed to the North American Electric Reliability Council, reflecting participation by Canadian and Mexican utilities.

Commerce Committee held hearings on reliability legislation. Chairman White did not take a position on the new bills, saying they were still under study by the commission. Goss, who testified on behalf of the Los Angeles Department of Water and Power, the Western Systems Coordinating Council and NERC, said there was no need for reliability legislation. Reliability was already "the primary concern of electric utilities" and proposed legislation "would, in fact, adversely affect reliability rather than enhance it."

Joseph Talley Jr., general counsel of ElectriCities of North Carolina, testified in favor of the new bills. The bills "would achieve, for the first time in our history and for the last chance we may have, reliability and rationality and responsibility in our largest industry," he said.

Robert Cowden, city manager of Redding, California, and secretary of the Northern California Power Agency, testified that the proposals offered "substantial assistance to relatively small systems, like our members, in obtaining the benefit of low-cost power generation."

Edison Electric Institute President Robert Gerdes, chairman of Pacific Gas & Electric Company, said reliability legislation was "neither necessary or desirable...and would have an adverse effect on industry's efforts to achieve and maintain reliability."

•

The House hearings in 1969 were the last hurrah for reliability legislation. With the inauguration of Richard Nixon as president in January 1969, White resigned from the FPC and the president appointed John Nassikas, a Manchester, New Hampshire, lawyer, as the new chairman. Nassikas opposed reliability legislation. The legislation would mean "an enormous increase in personnel" for the FPC and the possibility of massive power failures such as the Northeast blackout has been greatly reduced because the utilities have "vastly improved the reliability of their systems," he said.

Nevertheless, concern about reliability and the organization of transmission systems persisted. The Energy Policy Act enacted in 1992 provided for the voluntary formation of regional transmission organizations, and legislative proposals in the late 20th and early 21st centuries for restructuring the electric industry contained important provisions endowing NERC with greater responsibility for reliability.

Chapter 33

Environmental Protection
Takes on New Dimensions

The emergence of environmental concerns in the 1960s presented some of the most difficult policy questions APPA members and staff had faced.

Some of public power's most cherished principles and objectives were challenged, and new standards were established. Environmentalists opposed building new hydroelectric dams, which public power had long regarded as an inexpensive, non-polluting, renewable source of electricity. Environmentalists criticized electric rates that encouraged electricity consumption and other efforts to promote use of electricity. These objections made it more difficult for utilities to find acceptable sites for new facilities, especially transmission lines and large generating stations. Utilities were blamed for not spending enough money on research. Responding to public concerns, the federal government instituted measures to control pollution from power plants, adding to the cost of producing electricity. Citizens demanded that utilities place power lines underground and give more attention to aesthetics.

Initially, public power advocates felt pressures to protect the environment were an extension of the conservation movement promoted by Presidents Theodore Roosevelt and Franklin D Roosevelt. Public power was closely identified with that movement, especially its emphasis on comprehensive development of the nation's water resources and protection of these resources from monopoly control.

In the 1960s, the conservation movement took a new direction, hearalded by the publication of Rachel Carson's best-selling book, *Silent Spring*. Carson's warning that fewer species of birds would be singing each spring if pesticide poisoning was not curtailed alerted the public to dangers lurking in the food they ate, the water they drank and the air they breathed. Her book awakened public consciousness to the need to take difficult steps to reduce environmental pollution.

For the most part, public power leaders failed to give sufficient recognition to the potentially far-reaching impact of the Carson book and the ideas it spawned. Instead, they focused attention on the more immediate effect on the electric industry of the highly publicized campaign launched in 1964 by President Johnson's wife, Lady Bird, to beautify the nation.

President Johnson was quick to expand on his wife's initiative. In a message to Congress in February 1965, he asked for action to preserve and enhance the natural beauty of the American countryside and to make U.S. cities more attractive places to live. He also announced plans for a White House Conference on Natural Beauty, to be chaired by Laurance Rockefeller.

Underground installation of utility transmission lines was one of five problems the president wanted the conference to consider in depth. The conference would also address the need to abate pollution of the nation's rivers, but the president expected to "continue to conserve the water and power for tomorrow's needs with well-planned reservoirs and power dams."

I sent a letter to President Johnson telling him APPA members were "eager to participate" in his campaign and urging him to include public power representatives in the White House conference.

APPA endorsed the president's desire to "identify and preserve free-flowing stretches of our great scenic rivers before growth and development make the beauty of the unspoiled waterway a memory." However, an April 1965 editorial in *Public Power* magazine said the president's proposal raised questions about the care required to identify the streams that would be protected from further development.

We feared a ban on future hydroelectric power development. The editorial questioned "the wisdom of burning up non-renewable fossil fuel resources instead of more completely harnessing the flow of our rivers." Recent floods in the Pacific Northwest and Northern California emphasized the need for construction of flood control projects that might be prohibited on rivers included in the wild rivers system.

True conservation is something more than fencing off areas of the natural environment," the editorial said.

"Today's Americans can be thankful that President Theodore Roosevelt and Gifford Pinchot[1] viewed planned, orderly development as a part of their fight for conservation.

---

[1] Former governor of Pennsylvania and an adviser to TR on conservation.

There is room in America for a National Wild Rivers System. But there is also room—and need—for the continued beneficial development of our rivers, including some not presently harnessed. The two concepts do not need to be mutually exclusive.

Despite our differences with the Johnson administration on the question of wild rivers, we supported the White House Conference on Natural Beauty, held in Washington May 14 and 15, 1965. R.J. McMullin, a former APPA president and general manager of the Salt River Project in Phoenix, and Samuel B. Nelson, general manager of the Los Angeles Department of Water and Power, were named to a conference panel on underground installation of utility facilities.

After two days of meetings, the utility panel recommended widespread extension of underground installations to new residential areas, along with improved appearance of overhead facilities and public education about the high cost of putting transmission lines underground.

McMullin said underground transmission was impractical except in metropolitan high-rise areas, where it could be justified by extremely high load density. Undergrounding cost as much as 50 times more than overhead transmission, he said.

Rep. Richard Ottinger, D-N.Y., in August 1965 introduced three bills to "attack the mounting problem of overhead transmission lines." The bills would offer tax incentives to utilities for undergrounding power lines and provide federal funding for research. Congress did not act on the Ottinger bills. Instead it focused on funding research to reduce the cost of new underground transmission lines.

In May 1966 the Senate Commerce Committee held hearings on a bill to broaden the Department of Interior's authority to develop a research program. The bill was not enacted into law, but agitation for underground power lines continued for the remainder of the 1960s. In June 1968, Laurence Rockefeller's Citizens' Advisory Committee on Recreation and Natural Beauty issued a report to the president recommending electric utilities adopt a goal of undergrounding distribution lines in new residential subdivisions by 1975.

By the mid-1960s serious differences began to arise between public power and environmental advocates over hydroelectric power projects. To bring lower cost power to New England, public power groups espoused construction of a dam in Maine at the Rankin Rapids site on the St. John River, below the mouth of the Allagash River. Environmental groups opposed the Rankin Rapids site because they wanted the Allagash River to remain wild. In response, the federal government moved the site of the proposed dam to the Dickey-Lincoln School site, which would not affect the Allagash River. Conflicts also arose over proposals to build the Bridge and Marble Canyon dams on the Lower Colorado River.

In an effort to improve our relations with environmentalists, I spoke at a meeting of the National Wildlife Federation in December 1965. Relocation of the storage dam to the Dickey-Lincoln School site represented a cooperative effort of public power and conservation groups to save the Allagash River in its wild state and could "make it possible to have our cake and eat it too," I said.

I told federation members their aims and those of APPA members "are in many instances in harmony." It is the relatively few conflicts between the groups that "tend to attract the most attention and I believe that is unfortunate," I said. But I did not gloss over emerging differences over legislation to designate certain rivers as wild. APPA did not quarrel with the purposes of such proposals and in fact supported a wild rivers bill. However, pending legislation raised questions about the care required to identify streams that would be protected from development.

•

In his first major speech since becoming chairman of the FPC, Lee White spelled out a broad environmental role for the electric industry when he addressed the APPA annual conference in May 1966:

> While the availability of a low-cost reliable source of power is a most legitimate goal of the industry, we would do a disservice to the public, and the industry as well, if we were to take the myopic view that this is all the American public desires or expects from us.
>
> The public and its elected representatives have already begun to insist that the industry take steps to improve the aesthetic aspects of electric power facilities and to minimize the air pollution and stream polluting effects of electric power production and to develop fully the scenic and recreational potential of hydroelectric projects on the nation's navigable streams.
>
> These are not inconsequential matters to be taken lightly. They represent proper aims and purposes of a society seeking to create the best possible environment for itself and for future generations. Taking a cue from recent developments in the automobile and drug industries, the power industry would be wisely counseled to exert every effort to make prompt improvements in each of these areas.

The National Conference on Air Pollution called further attention to environmental issues. Much of the emphasis at the conference was on automobiles, which were estimated to emit 85 million of the 135 million tons of pollutants poured into the atmosphere annually. However, 12.5 percent of the nation's air pollution stemmed from generation of electric energy, White said at the conference. Extensive research in post-combustion pollution control, nuclear power, relocation of generating plants and additional consumption of natural gas would be required to improve pollution control, he said.

•

Dam-building sustained two blows in mid-1967. Interior Secretary Udall opposed construction of Rampart Canyon Dam in Alaska and the Senate Interior Committee reported a bill authorizing development of the Lower Colorado River, including the Central Arizona Project, but without the Hualapai (formerly Bridge Canyon) Dam. Environmentalists opposed Rampart Canyon Dam because of its potential damage to wildlife and fisheries. The Department of Interior's formula for mitigating these effects inflated the cost of the project, adversely affecting its economic feasibility.

Environmental groups claimed Hualapai Dam would flood the Grand Canyon. In fact the dam would back water for only 13 miles along the border of the Grand Canyon National Park, in an area not visible from any public vantage point within the Grand Canyon.[2]

In the July 1967 issue of *Public Power*, I devoted my column to comments on dams and conservation. I wrote:

> I ask those who regard themselves as conservationists: Are you focusing on the really important issues in opposing dams that are located away from population centers and that actually enhance the opportunity for mankind to enjoy nature? Wouldn't your efforts be spent to better advantage if you directed your ire at the developers who destroy the trees in areas where people live...the auto manufacturers who have done little to curb air pollution...the industries that have polluted our rivers...and the entrepreneurs who have decimated our beaches?...
>
> Yes, we need to preserve the beauty of nature in remote areas that

---

[2] Ironically, as a substitute for the energy that would not be produced at Hualapai Dam, environmentalists, led by David Brower of the Sierra Club, agreed to the construction of a large coal-burning steam plant at Four Corners, at the intersection of New Mexico, Arizona, Colorado and Utah. Later, astronauts traveling in space observed that the plume of smoke from this plant was one of the most distinct landmarks they could observe in space.

people must journey to to enjoy. But in my opinion the vastly more important need is to preserve the beauty of nature in the environment where people live and work. People should be able to live in surroundings of natural beauty; they should not have to travel hundreds of miles to enjoy nature.

Those who are interested in conservation might also take note of the fact that the production of electric power by falling water is our only renewable energy source. The failure to build Hualapai Dam or the Rampart Canyon project does not diminish the need for electric power by one kilowatt-hour; the need will remain, and it will be filled by the burning of coal or uranium—both of which are not renewable energy sources, and both of which, unfortunately, add somewhat, at this time, to environmental pollution problems.

...It is true, of course, that hydroelectric power does not have the capacity to provide all or even a major portion of our energy requirements. But where hydro power can be developed in a feasible manner, it would seem to me to be contrary to the principle of conservation to burn other fuels as a substitute for our only non-polluting, renewable energy resource.

•

Siting large new power plants was another new issue in the 1960s. In January 1969 the Energy Policy Staff of the White House Office of Science and Technology warned that coordinated planning of power plant siting was essential to avoid serious contamination of the nation's air and water. The White House predicted utilities would triple their power generating capacity within 20 years, mainly by constructing power plants of 2,000 to 3,000 mw each. Hundreds of acres of land would be required for each facility and without careful advance planning on sites and adequate emissions control equipment, the power plants would exacerbate environmental problems and jeopardize health and safety.

In May 1969, President Nixon urged APPA members to become more active in environmental matters. In a message read at the APPA annual conference's opening session, the president said:

> Your industry's concern can no longer be limited to simply meeting the nation's power needs at the lowest possible cost. Your expanding responsibility demands that you be alert to the impact of your activities on our surroundings, our health and the public welfare—especially the municipally owned segment of your industry.

FPC Vice Chairman Carl Bagge, who spoke at the conference, delivered a stronger message. Public concern for protection of aesthetic values is not a fad that "a fickle public might forget when it finds another cause," he said. Bagge urged APPA to establish a Committee on the

Environment, a suggestion the board of directors promptly adopted. In little more than a month, the committee, chaired by former APPA president R.J. McMullin of the Salt River Project, had met and adopted a proposed 15-point program. Recommendations included:

- Establishment of January 1, 1971 as a target date for underground placement of distribution lines in new residential areas and encouragement of federal grants to help local utilities convert existing facilities from overhead to underground;
- Consolidation of transmission facilities by using "utility corridors" to reduce the number of lines and rights-of-way;
- Joint action by utilities in generating and transmission to obtain the benefits of large-scale facilities and to minimize the total environmental effect of separate power plants and power lines;
- Increased research on the disposal of pollutants and wastes from generating facilities;
- Utilization of potential hydroelectric sites, regarded as pollution-free sources of energy with multiple-purpose benefits, including recreation, and
- Research and development on non-polluting electric vehicles.

·

In July 1969, S. David Freeman, director of the Energy Policy Staff of the White House Office of Science and Technology, urged more electric industry research to combat air pollution. Freeman spoke at the Seven States Air Pollution Conference in his hometown of Chattanooga. He pointed out that air pollution in the United States was caused almost entirely by energy use. Less than 5 percent of the nation's energy came from hydro power or atomic energy, neither of which polluted the atmosphere. The remainder contributed to air pollution, which was causing economic damage of $10–$20 billion a year, he said. Automobiles and other forms of transportation contributed 60 percent of total emissions then considered harmful (primarily in the form of carbon monoxide). Power plants and industry accounted for 30 percent of air pollution, primarily in the form of sulfur oxides. Space heating and refuse disposal accounted for the remaining 10 percent.

Freeman called on the electric utility industry to attack the problem with an accelerated research program.

"Low-cost electricity is not really low-cost if it does not include a reasonable component to assure that its production does not harm the environment and to assure that it will continue to be low-cost in the future," he said. "Surely the electric consumer should be expected to devote at least 1 percent of his electric power bill to research and development to combat air pollution and for other research activities."

•

As its reach continued to broaden, the environmental movement advocated policies that conflicted with a basic tenet of public power: "more power at lower cost." That philosophy was founded on the assumption that availability of an abundance of low-cost energy led to a more productive economy and a higher standard of living.

To implement this philosophy, public power utilities were in the forefront of efforts to promote the sale of electricity. As long as there were economies of scale in building power plants and high-voltage transmission lines, load promotion went hand-in-hand with rate reduction. Greater consumption made it possible to build larger, more efficient power plants, which in turn resulted in lower costs and rates. When this philosophy was first espoused, the electric industry and the public did not recognize the long-term environmental consequences of building more fossil-fired generating plants

Environmental groups contended that if utilities stopped promoting the use of electricity, fewer new generating plants would be needed, utilities could more easily fulfill their customers' demands, and the threat to the environment would be lessened.

I devoted my column in the January 1970 issue of *Public Power* to environmental issues. I acknowledged that power production presented threats to the environment and that more attention should be paid to efficiency, both in conversion of basic energy sources to electricity and in end use. However, because of the importance of electricity to society, the public policy emphasis should be on accelerating research to reduce environmental problems. Environmental problems could not be solved by restricting electricity consumption if no limitations were placed on the use of other energy sources, I said.

I addressed the issue of "want" versus "need"—whether demand was being stimulated for "non-essential" products that used energy.

> Who is to decide what is an important or an unimportant use of electric energy?
> What may appear to some to be a frivolous waste of a resource would be regarded by others as a necessity. Many things that we use are not essential, but they contribute to the comfort and enjoyment of living, and have freed us from drudgery so that we can have more time to spend on more satisfying and productive endeavors.

Furthermore, is it rational to limit the generation of electric power while at the same time permitting the building of other industries, or automobiles, or other . . . sources of pollution?

Placing a subjective value on the uses of electricity could not be done without applying the same standards to virtually all other uses of our productive capacity, I wrote.

To implement a national policy of establishing priorities on the end uses of our resources would probably require the involvement of government in our economy to an extent rarely if ever before undertaken. However laudatory the objectives of such a policy, those espousing it should give careful consideration to the question of whether or not they would be creating a far worse situation in the long run than the condition they are seeking to correct.

I questioned whether market forces should be used to limit use of electricity through a radical change in the industry's traditional rate structure. For many years, the electric industry had used declining block rates. The cost of the first, relatively small, block of electricity was relatively high so the utility could recover its investment in facilities as well as the cost of production. Rates for additional blocks were progressively lower, to reflect the fact that economies of scale made it possible to generate, transmit and distribute larger quantities of energy at lower cost.

Public power utilities had been leaders in promoting the use of declining rate blocks. We felt this approach to rate design was economically justifiable and socially desirable. Now, with increased emphasis on conservation, some suggested an inverse rate structure. Lowest rates would apply to a relatively small block of power needed for essential uses, while higher rates would be charged for consumption of larger blocks of energy. The theory was that progressively higher rates would discourage frivolous uses.[3]

"But considering the growing affluence of our society, would this really be the case?" I asked. "And would such a policy be justifiable in any event? Would not such a rate structure permit the affluent to enjoy

---

[3] Re-reading my comments some three decades later, I found that I had ignored what became more obvious in the decade after they were written; namely, that the less expensive sources of energy had already been tapped, and economies of scale in generation had reached an end. Meeting future demands resulted in higher marginal costs and therefore warranted a reversal in the declining block rate policy.

luxuries (albeit 'frivolous' ones) while at the same time penalizing the less affluent?"[4] I wrote:

> the solution to the problem, it seems to me, lies in a general upgrading of the education of the people of the country and a reordering of our national priorities—processes that go far beyond the question of whether or not a particular use of electric energy constitutes a "want" rather than a "need."

•

By the beginning of a new decade in 1970, a confluence of factors had focused increased attention on the environment. Environmental organizations had become more active and vocal. Young people involved in the movement against the Vietnam War also took up the cause. They rebelled against the acquisition of more and more consumer goods that required the exploitation of natural resources. Power shortages were anticipated in some regions, causing concern about utilities' ability to meet growing demands and leading to resentment of utility advertising and load promotion. Some groups and members of Congress expressed anger that utilities, according to some estimates, were spending seven times more for sales expenses and advertising than on research to reduce pollution.

The new decade began on an auspicious note when President Nixon chose New Year's Day 1970 to sign the National Environmental Policy Act, which Sen. Gaylord Nelson, D-Wis., described as "the most important piece of environmental legislation in our history." NEPA called for formation of a Council on Environmental Quality to advise the president on environmental matters. CEQ was charged with reviewing environmental impact statements, which NEPA required of all federal agencies planning projects with major environmental ramifications.

In his State of the Union Address on January 22, 1970, President Nixon proposed to make "the 1970s a historic period when, by conscious choice, [we] transform our land into what we want it to become."

On February 10, President Nixon continued his activist role, sending Congress a 14-page environmental message that spelled out his recommendations for "total mobilization" against pollution. The program included 23 major legislative proposals and 14 new measures that would be implemented by executive orders by the president. Nixon

---

[4] It was not until 1973 that Congress enacted legislation providing for a subsidy to low-income energy consumers.

recommended establishment of nationwide air quality standards and proposed the Clean Air Act.

Two months later, the first Earth Day celebration was held on April 22. The event surpassed the wildest expectations of its sponsors, Senator Nelson and Rep. Paul McCloskey, R-Calif. Peaceful demonstrations with a theatrical flair, teach-ins, displays and other events were held on the mall in Washington and elsewhere and gave impetus to environmental actions by the federal government.

In May 1970 the National Academy of Engineering and the National Research Council released a joint report recommending an immediate federal and industrial research effort to control sulfur oxides, which it described as the nation's second worst pollutants. Electric power plants were the main source of sulfur dioxide emissions.

APPA took heed of the increasing concern about the environment. The May 1970 issue of *Public Power* was devoted largely to articles about the impact of environmental concerns on public power. An article by R.J. McMullin, chairman of the APPA Committee on the Environment, pointed out that public power utility managers were finding that environmental factors involved future tangible and intangible costs and benefits and therefore should be included in any benefit-cost ratio. Public power utilities, he added, also were anticipating that environmental concerns and reliability could be interrelated. He recommended public power leaders "think environment" and seek to lead the industry in environmental protection.

Dave Freeman of the White House energy policy staff warned that "if public power does not hear the voice of the people on this issue, then in a real sense it will no longer be public power." The greatest mistake the electric industry could make would be to assume that electricity is so much of a necessity that concerns over the environment could be ignored, he said. Freeman proposed "a new form of competition in the industry— a race to see which utilities can make the greatest contribution to protecting the environment, rather than destroying it."

●

On July 9, 1970, President Nixon sent Congress a reorganization plan calling for establishment of the Environmental Protection Agency. The new organization was to consolidate responsibility for environmental matters within one agency. On November 9 the president appointed 38-year old Assistant Attorney General William D. Ruckelshaus as the first EPA administrator and EPA opened its offices on December 2, 1970. "It was not long before the media were portraying William Ruckelshaus as a knight in shining armor, charging out to do battle with the wicked polluters of America," wrote Jack Lewis in the November 1985 issue of the *EPA Journal*.

Thus began a new era for the power industry. In the preceding decade APPA tried to prepare its membership for the vast changes brought about by increasingly demanding laws and regulations enacted to clean up the environment. As public, nonprofit institutions, APPA member utilities generally were more receptive to environmental concerns than other sectors of the industry. However, it was not easy to change doctrines that had developed over many decades. Legislation and regulations to protect the environment met resistance from some managers and policy-makers imbued with the tradition of providing an abundance of power at the lowest possible cost. In the face of the popularity of low electric rates, utility officials found it painful to accept the large expenses associated with reducing pollution. Imbued with the American ethic of advertising and promotion of consumer goods—and having seen a phenomenal rise in the American standard of living—public power managers and policy-makers found it hard to reverse course and curtail load promotion.

Perhaps the hardest reality for public power utilities to confront was the realization that, largely because of opposition of environmental groups, the nation had reached the end of the era of building multipurpose water resource projects. To give up the opportunity to further develop these sources of non-polluting, renewable energy was a pill many public power advocates had difficulty swallowing.

Nevertheless, by concentrating on energy efficiency, public power systems found that conservation made sense economically, and did not have to lower the standard of living. Additional generating capacity continued to be needed, but more emphasis was placed on renewable resources. In some cases conservation was a less expensive alternative than building a new power plant, and at the same time furthered the nation's environmenatal objectives.

Radin when he was briefly assigned as a photographer in the Signal Corps during World War II.

Radin at age six, while growing up in Chattanooga.

Radin (right) and his older brother, Jacob, in front of their home in Chattanooga.

Radin's wife, Sara as a reporter for The Chattanooga Times in 1944.

Radin and younger son, Bill, who accompanied Alex to World Energy Conference in Istanbul.

Radin with older son, Jay, when Jay received his doctorate in clinical psychology at the University of Michigan.

Grandsons Andrew and Sam, when Sam graduated from Emory University.

Son Bill; Bill's wife, Ruth; Alex's wife, Carol; Alex; Jay's wife Mary; and Jay.

At World Power Conference in Tokyo in 1966. Left to right: G.O. Wessenauer, manager of power, TVA; Radin, and Lee White, chair of the Federal Power Commission.

At a dam site in Siberia during study by Senate committees of water resources development in Soviet Union in 1959. Radin is sixth from left. To his left are Sens. Frank E. (Ted) Moss, D-Utah; Ernest Gruening, D-Alaska, and Ed Muskie, D-Maine.

Meeting of officers of Electric Consumers Information Committee with former president Harry Truman. Left to right: Clyde Ellis, general manager, National Rural Electric Cooperative Association; John Edelman, head of Washington office of Textile Workers Union of America; Truman and Radin.

Meeting of officers of APPA and NRECA with President Kennedy in 1961. Front row, left to right: Agriculture Secretary Orville Freeman, J. Dillon Kennedy, manager of Jacksonville, Fla., Electric System and president of APPA; Interior Secretary Stewart Udall, President Kennedy; Clyde Ellis, general manager, NRECA, and Radin.

At APPA congressional reception in Washington. Left to right: Radin; S.R. Finley, superintendent of Chattanooga Electric Power Board; Sen. Lee Metcalf, D-Mont.; Kirby Billingsley, commissioner and subsequently manager, Chelan County Public Utility District, Wenatchee, Wash.; and Frank King, manager, Gas & Electric Department, Holyoke, Mass. Finley, Billingsley and King served as presidents of APPA.

At ceremony on the steps of the Capitol commemorating the first day of issue of a postage stop honoring Sen. George Norris, R-Neb. Postmaster General Day presents first day of issue to Radin. Seated at right is Speaker of the House Sam Rayburn.

At meeting in Pacific Northwest. Left to right: Owen Hurd, manager of the Benton County PUD, Kennewick, Wash., who was subsequently manager of the Washington Public Power Supply System, and a president of APPA; Sen. Wayne Morse, D-Ore., and Radin.

Dedication of Oahe Dam on Missouri River in South Dakota. To left of podium (from left to right) are Secretary of the Interior Stewart Udall; Radin, and President Kennedy.

Thirteen past presidents attended reception for Radin at his retirement. Left to right: R.J. McMullin, Salt River Project, Phoenix, Ariz.; John Kelly, Gainesville, Fla.; Frank King, Holyoke, Mass.; Calvin Henze, Florida Municipal Power Agency; Robert McKinney, Cowlitz County PUD, Longview, Wash.; William Corkran, Easton, Md.; Jack Pfister, Salt River Project; Earl Brush, (partially hidden) Lansing, Mich.; Radin; Jack Spruce, San Antonio, Texas; Charles Duckworth, Garland, Texas; Jim Baker, Shrewsbury, Mass.; Durwood Hill, Nebraska Public Power District, and Stan Case, Fort Collins, Colo.

Members and staff of the Monitored Retrievable Storage Review Commission inspect spent fuel storage facilities in Sweden. From left to right: Jane Axelrad, executive director and general counsel; Dr. Frank Parker, Radin, and Dr. Dale Klein.

Radin with Sen. Henry M. (Scoop) Jackson, D-Wash.

Radin at retirement party with Joe Swidler, former chairman of the Federal Power Commission, and Mrs. Swidler. In background is Carol Radin.

Two of the U.S. Senators who attended the reception for Radin in Washington at his retirement. Left, Sen. Ted Stevens, R-Alaska; right, Sen. Slade Gorton, R-Wash.

Sen. George McGovern, D-S.D., and Radin.

Radin greets President Jimmy Carter at meeting of Consumer Federation of America.

Radin and Larry Hobart, Deputy Executive Director, APPA.

Radin is greeted at White House by President Reagan at an industry meeting in support of the Clinch River Breeder Reactor.

Judy Sheldrew (left) representative of governor of Nevada; DOE official, and Radin at Yucca Mountain spent fuel repository in Nevada.

Radin and Alan Richardson (left), then legislative director of APPA, meet with then-Rep. Al Gore Jr., D-Tenn.

Chapter 34

Touting The Promise of Electric Vehicles

As environmental problems attracted growing attention, APPA took the lead in promoting development of electric vehicles. Studies showed about 50 percent of air pollution could be attributed to transportation. APPA saw electric cars as both environmentally friendly and a way to promote sale of electricity. Generating electricity to charge batteries for electric vehicles produced air pollution, but such pollution could be controlled more easily from a single electric generating station than from millions of automobiles. Furthermore, pollutants from power plants could be dispersed in remote locations rather than in congested urban areas.

Advocacy of electric vehicles served our interests in another way. The vehicles could be charged largely at night during off peak hours, when generating plants were not fully used. Consequently, electric vehicles could provide a desirable new load for electric utilities and little new generating capacity would be required.

Our efforts began late in 1965, when the APPA board of directors appointed an Electric Vehicle Committee to study the possibilities of battery-powered vehicles. The committee was chaired by Claud Erickson, general manager of the Lansing, Michigan, municipal electric utility. Erickson had a long-standing interest in electric vehicles and had written a book about their history, portions of which were published in *Public Power* magazine.

At its annual conference in May 1966, APPA adopted a resolution calling for a "large-scale research and development effort to bring the electric vehicle to market." The following month, I testified before the Senate Subcommittee on Air and Water Pollution of the Senate Commerce Committee, advocating large-scale research and development on electric vehicles.

Sen. Warren Magnuson, D-Wash., chairman of the Senate Public

Works Committee, wrote an article for *Public Power* magazine favoring electric vehicle research. In late August 1966 he, Sen. Edmund Muskie, D-Maine, and Sen. Jennings Randolph, D-W.Va., introduced legislation to provide federal funds to step up research, development and demonstration of electric-powered vehicles. Similar bills were introduced in the House, and newspapers and consumer magazines began to publish articles on the subject.

By the fall of 1966 there was a flurry of activity on electric vehicles. Ford Motor Company said it had an advanced concept of a battery-powered car in early stages of development, and *The New York Times* reported General Motors Corporation was developing a similar type of vehicle.

Interior Secretary Stewart Udall predicted that half the motor vehicles in the nation might be electrically operated within 20 years. In November, Secretary of Health, Education and Welfare John W. Gardner said internal combustion engines were on a "collision course" with the American people unless their exhaust fumes could be eliminated.

On October 4, 1966, APPA attracted national attention when Dr. J.E. Goldman, director of Ford Motor Company's scientific laboratory, met in Washington with the association's Electric Vehicles Committee to discuss details of the company's newly developed sodium-sulfur battery system. This innovation was heralded as the breakthrough in development of a practical electric auto. The meeting also featured reports from the General Electric Company, the U.S. Public Health Service and a British authority on battery-operated motor transportation. A number of federal government officials and representatives of major press associations, newspapers and newsmagazines were on hand as APPA provided the forum for the first public briefing on the new battery following Ford's initial press announcement.

In late October, General Motors Corporation unveiled two experimental electric vehicles in Detroit, but did not share Ford's optimism about electric vehicles.

"I don't think the air pollution problem is going to end piston engines," said GM Executive Vice President Edward N. Cole.

GM's demonstration featured operation of a battery-powered 1966 Corvair and a GMC van powered by a fuel cell. The Corvair was propelled by 13 trays of silver-zinc batteries that cost $15,000, and other parts of the system cost $7,500.

•

In June 1967 two bills on electric vehicles were the subject of joint hearings before the Senate Commerce and Public Works committees. S. 451 by Senator Muskie would authorize the Department of Health, Education and Welfare to study means of transportation, including electric vehicles, that would not contribute to air pollution. S. 453, sponsored by Senator Magnuson, would direct the recently formed Department of Transportation to undertake research, development and demonstration of electrically powered vehicles.

A day before the hearing, a large crowd, including many senators and representatives, attended a demonstration of electric vehicles in the garage of a Senate office building. The event attracted television coverage. APPA distributed buttons with the inscription, "Drive Better Electrically."[1]

At the hearing, I testified that development of electric vehicles provided an opportunity to help solve air pollution, traffic congestion, noise and other environmental problems. Several senators and representatives also testified in favor of the bills. Officials of the Department of Transportation, the Department of Health, Education and Welfare, and the Department of Commerce generally agreed with the bill's objectives, but opposed the use of federal funds to speed development of alternative non-polluting vehicles. Two of the three major automobile manufacturers did not oppose the bills, but expressed reservations about the need for such legislation.

In October 1967, the Department of Commerce released an advisory panel report that claimed a practical electric car was 10 years away. The panel's chairman, Richard S. Morse of the Massachusetts Institute of Technology, said General Electric Company's experimental electric vehicle "is essentially a golf cart" with limited range.

Consumer advocate Ralph Nader—who had first come to public attention because of his criticism of the safety of GM's Corvair—contended electric vehicles were feasible. However, he claimed that the "elephantine" automobile industry "has such a vested interest in existing technology of the internal combustion engine that nothing beyond glacial-like movements can be expected of its management." Prof. Lloyd Orr of Indiana University told the Senate Antitrust and Monopoly Subcommittee that the Big 3 auto producers (General Motors, Ford and Chrysler) viewed with apprehension any innovation that threatened to weaken or destroy

---

[1] This was a take-off on a then-prominent electric industry slogan, "Live Better Electrically."

the foundations of their concentrated power.

At the end of 1967, a report was issued indicating "significant progress" on an alternative vehicle that would prove to be the direction in which the automobile industry was heading. The Department of Housing and Urban Development displayed a model of a vehicle that would be powered by a hybrid gas-electric engine that was projected to reduce emissions to one-tenth those produced by conventional internal combustion engines. The hybrid would be capable of a top speed of 60 miles per hour and have an operating range of up to 100 miles. The vehicle's motor was described as a two-cylinder gasoline engine coupled with an electric motor operated by a battery. The car could be operated in one of three modes: by gas engine alone, battery alone, or a combination of the two.

Despite technical and economic problems encountered in producing a relatively inexpensive battery that did not have the weight of lead acid batteries, APPA continued to promote electric vehicles. We planned to showcase them at the annual conference in Washington in May 1969.

To attract press attention, we arranged to have one of our principal speakers—Senator Muskie—ride in an electric car from the Capitol to the Washington Hilton Hotel, where press photographers were to greet him upon his arrival. An electric car was delivered to the Capitol, whereupon the senator, the driver, and Larry Hobart of the APPA staff were to proceed to the hotel. Unfortunately, midway to the hotel, near the corner of Connecticut Avenue and K Street in a busy section of downtown Washington, the car broke down and, said Hobart, "just wouldn't go." Senator Muskie and Hobart had to hail a cab to proceed to the conference. This ignominious experience considerably dampened APPA's enthusiasm for electric vehicles.

Chapter 35

Giant Power and Joint Action

Municipally owned electric utilities perennially faced the challenge of maintaining their independence and viability in the face of competition from much larger private power companies.

Although municipally owned utilities are far more numerous than the power companies (there are about 2,000 public power utilities and 240 power companies), the average municipal utility is considerably smaller than the average power company. Large cities such as Los Angeles, Memphis, Jacksonville and Seattle own and operate their electric utilities, but the median number of customers for municipal utilities is 1,870, compared to 190,000 for private power companies.

After World War II smaller municipal utilities, because of their size, were unable to take advantage of economies of scale in electric generating facilities. The municipal utilities could not afford to build large generators on their own and power companies did not pass along their lower costs to municipal wholesale customers, frequently charging them rates higher than those offered to their retail customers. Wholesale power costs account for more than 75 percent of operating and maintenance expenses, so the disadvantage in bulk power costs made municipal utilities vulnerable to power company attempts to buy them out.

In July 1952 Donald C. Cook, chairman of the Securities and Exchange Commission, announced that the commission would study and make recommendations on the integration of electric systems. The study would be conducted under the authority of the Public Utility Holding Company Act of 1935 and would cover all utilities—publicly, cooperatively and privately owned. Cook said he did not favor the complete elimination of all small utilities, but he added this ominous note:

Nevertheless, there is such a thing as too small a company. The utility business is big business. It does not exist in this country as a competitive industry in which, as a matter of national policy, the entities are kept comparatively small in order to stimulate competition. As regulated monopolies, utilities are to be encouraged to operate as efficiently and economically as possible and today this means companies of fairly large scope.

Cook said he did not want to get involved in the public-versus- private power controversy, but we were not reassured. He had emphasized acquisition as a means of achieving integration of small utilities with larger ones. However, most of the smaller utilities were publicly or cooperatively owned and would be the most likely targets for acquisition by large private power companies.

APPA publicized his remarks, pointing out the potential threat his study posed to the continued operation of smaller utilities. I wrote an editorial for *Public Power* magazine describing the pitfalls of Cook's plan and met personally with him. After our meeting, I received a letter from him in which he expressed appreciation for the "fine coverage" in *Public Power* of his speech announcing the SEC study. However, he said he was "exceedingly disturbed" at our implication that the studies would damage publicly owned utilities.

> I think you have given undue weight to my treatment of acquisitions as one means of accomplishing the efficiencies of integration, particularly when viewed in the context of publicly owned utilities. There are, as you know, a very large number of small, uneconomic privately owned companies and the examples used in my speech dealt with situations of this type.

I was not comforted by his letter, because I had no doubt that the municipally and cooperatively owned utilities would bear the brunt of pressure to be acquired by large private power companies. Consequently, APPA continued to foster opposition in Congress and elsewhere against the Cook proposal. In October 1952, APPA General Counsel Northcutt Ely wrote Cook saying the SEC had no authority under the holding company act to include municipal and other local publicly owned electric utilities in the study. PUHCA was enacted "to protect the public, investors and consumers from enumerated evils from the economic effect of complex, unwieldy and undesirable activities of privately owned public utilities," Ely said.

Cook responded that Ely's views would be "very carefully studied and analyzed before any final decision on your request is reached." Shortly thereafter, the study was dropped, and Cook left the SEC with the change in administration in 1953.

•

Removal of the threat from the SEC study did not end our concerns about the basic problem: achieving the economies of scale while retaining the benefits of local control of electric service.

In the ensuing years, APPA devoted substantial efforts to two major campaigns to obtain lower bulk power costs. One was focused on the creation of joint action agencies formed by municipal utilities to give them a mechanism for constructing larger, more economical power generating stations than the individual utilities could build separately. The joint action agencies also could participate more readily in power pooling arrangements or negotiate on a joint basis for the purchase of wholesale power from power companies.

A second avenue—called giant power—was to advocate federal policies that would foster the development of large-scale regional and inter-regional power pools and transmission lines that would make low-cost power available to consumer-owned electric utilities.

Although there had been previous discussion of both approaches, the seminal event for these activities was a speech by Leland Olds at APPA's annual conference in New York City in June 1957. Olds had been chairman of the Federal Power Commission from 1939-1949 and subsequently became director of Energy Research Associates, a consulting firm.

Olds believed social good could be achieved through increased use of electrical energy and freedom of consumers to choose their source of electricity, be it from privately or publicly owned utilities. He foresaw the continued growth in demand for electricity and the efficiencies and lower costs that could be obtained by building large power plants interconnected by high-voltage transmission lines.

Olds was alarmed by the prospects for the future of municipally owned electric utilities and rural electric cooperatives. Hundreds of consumer-owned electric utilities obtained bulk power from small diesel or coal-fired generating stations or they purchased it from power companies. Neither alternative offered bulk power at costs that compared favorably with those of the larger, interconnected power companies, which were forming pools that excluded municipal utilities and rural electric cooperatives.

Olds also was disturbed by the power companies' efforts to seek exemptions from PUHCA for companies combining to own giant generating stations and transmission grids. In 1956 advocates of the PUCHA exemption testified that technical advances made it desirable to build large generating units and transmission lines that necessitated utility mergers.

Commenting on the power companies' proposed mergers, Olds said "the greatest challenge to local publicly owned electric systems and rural electric cooperatives, as well as to the people of the country as a whole, is to take whatever steps are necessary to bring giant power under effective democratic control so as to make it the servant of all." He offered this vision of the future:

> Giant power must mean great regional power reservoirs, created and constantly expanded through cooperation of federal, state, municipal, private and cooperative electric power agencies. Such regional wholesale power supply pools must be fed by a combination of hydroelectric plants, built as parts of federal comprehensive river-basin programs, huge steam plants located in the country's well-distributed coal fields and corresponding atomic giants located away from urban areas, all integrated with the power supply of local systems.
>
> These giant power reservoirs, under federal and state law, must be required to assume full responsibility for meeting the growing wholesale power requirements of all retail power systems, whether private, public or cooperative, at the lowest possible cost in accordance with the postage stamp rate principle.[1]

Olds said preference to public and cooperative utilities in marketing federal power "must be preserved in full force and effect as a safeguard against any future attempt of private monopoly to gain control." As an additional safeguard, public and cooperative electric utilities should work toward joint ownership of their own generating and transmission systems to take advantage of economies offered by larger and more efficient generating stations, pooling reserves and saving capacity through diverse loads, Olds said.

Leland Olds died of a heart attack on August 3, 1960 at the age of 69. His death was a great loss to me personally as well as a loss to public power. A gentle, caring man with an unyielding dedication to principle, he was a beloved friend as well as a mentor.

---

[1] Under postage stamp rates, power is delivered at a consistent price regardless of the distance it travels.

One of Olds' most important legacies was his vision for creation of a giant power cooperative, which he unveiled at a Mid-West Electric Consumers Association meeting in Rapid City, South Dakota, in 1959. Olds proposed that the consumer-owned utilities of the Missouri River Basin create a regionwide wholesale giant power source to meet their rapidly expanding needs. His proposal was referred to the Power Supply Committee of the Mid-West Electric Consumers Association and in August 1960 the committee submitted a detailed report to more than 600 officials of publicly and cooperatively owned utilities at a Giant Power Conference at Sioux Falls, South Dakota. The conference was held shortly after Olds' death and was dedicated to his memory.

The committee proposed forming a giant power cooperative to build 1,250 mw of new generation and 1,200 miles of transmission lines in the eight-state eastern Missouri Basin. The new cooperative would supply the major power needs of the region's municipal systems and rural electric cooperatives by building base-load thermal plants and high-voltage transmission lines. The new facilities would be integrated with federal power installations in the area.

The giant power cooperative envisioned by the plan became the Basin Electric Power Cooperative, headquartered in Bismark, N.D. Organization of the cooperative was a boon for the rural electric cooperatives and public power utilities in the region. However, it was a loss for APPA, because the co-op selected Jim Grahl, APPA's deputy executive director, as its first manager. Jim and I had been personal friends and neighbors as well as colleagues and I valued his contribution to APPA. However, I appreciated the challenge the new position offered him and fully supported his decision.

Jim remained faithful to the ideals of Leland Olds and public power, and built an outstanding organization. He was before his time on environmental matters. When Basin was organized, the environmental movement was not in full flower and federal and state legislation had not been adopted to require reclamation of strip-mined land. Nevertheless, Jim insisted on sound reclamation practices in the strip-mining of lignite, the fuel to be used in Basin's first generating plant. He also advocated using the most advanced methods of emission control available at that time. He employed union labor, and bent over backwards to provide power for municipal utilities and rural electric cooperatives.

In May 1962 the cooperative received a $36.6 million loan from the Rural Electrification Administration for the construction of its first unit, a

200-mw plant on the banks of the Missouri River near Stanton, North Dakota. The plant was to be the largest lignite-fueled plant in the Western Hemisphere. Although the generating station was built by the cooperative, it was important to the municipal utilities and public power districts of the region, 37 of which were members of Basin Electric. The public power utilities obtained three-year firm power contracts for power surplus to the initial needs of the cooperatives and these were to be extended as additional units were built. Appropriately, the station was named the Leland Olds Power Plant and I had the privilege of being one of the speakers at its dedication in November 1965.

•

Olds' vision of giant power encompassed a leadership role of the federal government in providing power supply as well as initiatives by local public power systems and rural electric cooperatives in forming joint action organizations.

At a meeting of the American Economic Association in December 1957, Leland Olds unveiled a national power supply plan calling for the establishment of four or five regional wholesale power supply systems that would provide low-cost electricity for all of the nation's electric distribution systems. He described his proposal as an answer to the challenge of the new age of giant power.

Pointing to growing power requirements, Olds said meeting the supply challenge with the greatest economy would require the separation of the wholesale power supply and distribution functions of the electric business. He proposed economic power planning in two fields. Wholesale power supply planning would "emphasize the mass-production portion of the business and, because of the far-flung nature of the regional combinations involved, will be chiefly the responsibility of the federal government." Distribution planning would "emphasize the mass-consumption portion of the business and, because of its local character, will be chiefly the responsibility of state regulatory agencies."

The proposed power supply systems would serve all publicly, privately and cooperatively owned utilities in a region, and could be set up as nonprofit corporations, jointly owned by the local electric utilities they served. Financing would be mainly with bonds.

The wholesale power supply systems "must have utility responsibility for keeping capacity constantly ahead of the requirements of the distribution systems and for supplying all such systems, without regard to ownership, at standard 'postage stamp' rates," he continued. "Provision should be made, under contract or otherwise, for integrating usable existing generating plants of participating systems into the grid operation."

Olds proposed that the regional wholesale supply corporations be regulated by a federal commission. If the utilities in a region were unable to agree on setting up a regional grid system, the commission would submit plans to Congress to establish a federal wholesale power supply system for the region.

Olds discussed his proposal with the Electric Consumers Information Committee, which I chaired, and the committee decided to name a Giant Regional Power Legislation Committee to work with him to prepare legislation to carry out his concept. Olds chaired the legislative committee. I was a member, along with representatives of National Rural Electric Cooperative Association, the National Farmers Union, and the AFL-CIO. The committee was augmented by several federal government and congressional staffers who met with us unofficially. By December 16, 1958, Olds had prepared two alternate bills. In Olds' words, both "would establish clearly the congressional intent to assure ample supplies of low-cost power in such a way as to meet the expanding requirements of the nation without fostering giant monopoly in the electric power field."

The first bill would establish three federally owned regional wholesale power corporations, for the Northeast, the South and the West. The corporations would own and operate the giant regional power pools. They would be given authority to plan, finance, construct, purchase, contract for the use of, condemn, and otherwise use facilities for the generation, transmission, and wholesale marketing of power to meet all requirements of the region served. The federal wholesale power corporations would provide power for private, public and cooperative electric utilities as well as, in certain instances, large power-using industries. The corporations would be financed by the issuance of bonds.

The second bill, an alternative to the first, would provide for joint private ownership of regional wholesale power corporations. It would establish the regulatory framework for creation by local utility companies of jointly owned regional wholesale power corporations. It would direct the Federal Power Commission to make continuing surveys of the power supply situation in the United States and long-range plans for meeting the country's growing power requirements. FPC would divide the country into not more than eight power supply regions for the purpose of preparing specific plans as a basis for certificating jointly owned regional wholesale power systems for regions other than those served by the Tennessee Valley Authority and the Bonneville Power Administration.

FPC would be empowered to issue certificates of convenience and necessity for the jointly owned regional wholesale power systems, based on the intent of Congress that the corporations were to assume utility obligation to provide all electric distribution systems, however owned, with ample power at the lowest possible cost.

In the event that the local electric companies failed to establish a jointly owned regional wholesale power corporation in any region, FPC could order the formation of such a corporation. Alternatively, the commission could propose to Congress a plan for establishing a federal regional wholesale power corporation for that region.

Olds said the second bill would preserve the TVA and BPA market areas against "encroachment" by jointly owned regional wholesale power corporations and "would recognize these two federal agencies as the wholesale power systems for their regions, to provide federal public yardsticks of costs and technological progress." The bill would require privately owned electric utilities to divest themselves of ownership of generating facilities, ultimately transferring the facilities that could be economically used to the regional corporations.

Although the second bill was not as far-reaching as the first, both would have made extraordinary changes in the organization of the nation's electric industry. The Electric Consumers Information Committee panel that reviewed Olds' proposals was sympathetic to his objectives, but had a great deal of concern about the reach of some of the proposals, such as the disposition of generation and transmission facilities owned by the local publicly and cooperatively owned utilities.

Our committee held a number of meetings to discuss the Olds proposals, but could not reach agreement. Meanwhile, Olds became ill, and the election of John F. Kennedy as president and the appointment of one of our colleagues, Ken Holum, as assistant secretary of the Department of the Interior, opened up new opportunities for the federal government to carry out some aspects of giant power, at least for the West.

•

We did not have to wait long for the new administration's initiative. In a message to Congress on February 23, 1961, the president directed the secretary of the interior "to develop plans for the early interconnection of areas served by that department's marketing agencies with adequate common carrier transmission lines..."

Subsequently, the Department of the Interior established a Coordinating Interconnection Committee to implement the program. An interconnection between the systems of the Missouri River Basin and the Southwestern Power Administration was one of the first considered by the committee.

On December 15, 1961, the completion of a task force report led to the authorization and construction of the Pacific Northwest-Pacific Southwest intertie as a cooperative effort among federal, public and private utilities. Concurrently, other studies were made to investigate the feasibility of an extra-high-voltage intertie between the Pacific Northwest and the Missouri River Basin systems.

Early in 1967 the federal power marketing agencies recognized the need for a comprehensive, consolidated long-range planning study of the Western and Middle Western power systems to demonstrate the benefits that could result from interconnections. In April 1967 Ken Holum appointed a steering committee to conduct the long-range study and prepare a report, which became known as "Transmission Study 190." The completed report was transmitted to Holum in March 1968.

Twelve plans were investigated, four alternating current and eight direct current. All 12, the committee declared, would operate satisfactorily during normal as well as emergency conditions for exchanges of 3,000 mw. An analysis showed that all were economically feasible. Depending upon the type of lines built (alternating or direct current), costs were estimated to range from about $717 million to $1.5 billion.

The study showed that seasonal variations in loads and related resource requirements by 1980 would permit diversity exchanges between the Pacific Northwest and the central part of the United States. The magnitude of the interchange was shown to be 3,000 mw of seasonal diversity exchange between the western and central areas of the United States, eastward in the summer and westward in the winter. The study also estimated 600 mw of time-zone diversity exchange for transfer in each direction during the winter between the Pacific Northwest and the Eastern Missouri River Basin. Equal or greater diversities could be expected to exist between other western and central areas or systems.

The steering committee concluded that technology existing at that time made it feasible to consider the fully integrated operation of the Pacific Coast interconnected systems with the Interconnected Systems Group located east of the Rocky Mountains.

After the report was issued, the Interior Department proceeded with discussions with the electric industry about going forward with the plan. However, by the fall of 1968 the election campaign was well under way, and the election of Richard Nixon as president in November and the appointment of a new secretary of the interior ended further serious discussions by the administration.

Nevertheless, Congress continued to express interest in a nationwide grid system. In June 1970, Sen. Lee Metcalf, D-Mont., testifying before the Senate Judiciary Subcommittee on Antitrust and Monopoly, advocated a common carrier transmission grid for wheeling electric power from central pools to distribution systems in various regions of the country. In July 1971, bills were introduced in the Senate and House authorizing creation of a new federal corporation, the National Power Grid Corporation, to build and operate a national electric transmission grid and to authorize regional generation and transmission agencies. Senator Metcalf introduced the bill in the Senate, and an identical bill was introduced in the House by Rep. Robert O. Tiernan, D-R.I., and cosponsored by Representatives Herman Badillo, D-N.Y., and James Abourezk, D-S.D.

The National Power Grid Corporation would be responsible for construction and operation of large-scale generating plants and a nationwide system of extra-high-voltage transmission lines. The corporation would be directed by a three-member board of directors, consisting of one representative each of private power companies, publicly owned utilities and consumers. Power from the national grid would be sold at wholesale and transmitted at postage stamp rates by regional bulk power supply corporations.

The bill directed the corporation to select sites for plants and transmission lines with "all possible weight to the protection of the environment" and to invest a minimum of $250 million annually in research, principally to minimize environmental effects of electric power production. The corporation would supply power by contracting with existing utilities or by building its own plants. Transmission facilities would be acquired either by negotiation with existing owners or construction of new lines.

At a press conference held when the bill was introduced, Representative Tiernan said he expected "violent opposition" from the investor-owned utilities. However, Senator Metcalf said the bill would provide "a concession to the power companies" by giving them one seat on a three-member board "to let them in on the action."[2]

---

[2] Senator Metcalf was considered the nemesis of the private power companies. In 1967 he and his executive secretary, Vic Reinemer (who later became editor of *Public Power*) published the book *Overcharge*, which infuriated the power companies. Metcalf and Reinemer also were credited with coining the term "IOUs" to describe the investor-owned utilities. The companies at first shunned the use of the term, but in time it became generally accepted.

Representative Abourezk was elected to the Senate in 1972. About two weeks later, he was the principal speaker at the annual meeting of Basin Electric Power Cooperative. Noting Leland Olds' advocacy of giant power and leadership in forming the cooperative, Abourezk announced he would once again cosponsor the national power grid legislation.

Bills to establish a national power grid were introduced in both houses of Congress in late February 1973. Senator Metcalf again was the chief sponsor, but this time he was joined by a larger group of supporters, including Senators Mike Mansfield, D-Mont.; George McGovern and Abourezk (both South Dakota Democrats); Hubert Humphrey, D-Minn.; Frank Moss, D-Utah; and William Hathaway, D-Maine. Representative Tiernan introduced companion legislation in the House.

Again, little action was taken on the proposal. However, Senator Metcalf and his supporters did not give up. They introduced similar bills in 1975 and asked the Congressional Research Service to study the technology for coast-to-coast transmission of electricity and the economic and environmental impact of such a system. Published in 1976, the CRS study generally was unfavorable to the concept of a national power grid. It concluded there was not enough load diversity among the time zones to justify a national grid, that most of the seasonal load diversity was already used and the remainder was too scattered to justify a grid. The study also concluded regional reserve pools would evolve into a national grid within 10 years and that reserves might be reduced, without jeopardizing reliability, by 1 to 3 percentage points as a result of a strong national power grid.

However, the study acknowledged that utilities that did not have access to power pools would benefit from a national grid open to all, and that FPC needed authority to order wheeling of power. The study also noted that reducing reserves to a level of 15 percent of projected annual peak demand would yield present value savings over 10 years of about $20 billion. (Reserves were averaging about 20 percent at that time.)

Undaunted by the lack of progress in advancing his legislation, Senator Metcalf and several cosponsors again introduced the national power grid bill in August 1977. This time, the trigger for their action was a systemwide blackout of the New York City metropolitan area on July 13 and, 14. Senator Metcalf said the legislation would insure "more efficient use of electrical energy and insure against the kind of blackouts which again paralyzed the nation's largest city last month."

Again, little progress was made in advancing the national power grid legislation and, with Senator Metcalf's death in 1978, there was no longer a driving force for the legislation. But the agitation for the national power grid concept served a useful purpose. Pressure for enactment of such legislation was an important factor in forcing voluntary regional power pools, such as the Mid-Continent Area Power Pool and the New England Power Pool, to open up their membership to local public power utilities and rural electric cooperatives.

•

Olds' vision for nationwide giant power was never realized. But APPA's efforts to promote formation of municipal joint action agencies within states were more fruitful. During the 1960s and 1970s, we directed our most immediate attention to formation of these agencies. One of the first efforts to create these organizations began in the 1950s, when Ken Billington, executive director of the Washington Public Utility Districts' Association, spearheaded a movement to create a joint action agency in the state of Washington.

Billington and other public power leaders knew the federal government could not be relied upon to provide all of the future needs of the public utility districts and other consumer-owned electric utilities in the Northwest. They concluded it would be prudent for the public agencies to establish their own organization to supply a portion of the region's growing requirements. State law authorized the formation of a joint action agency by the PUDs, and on August 8, 1956, 17 of the state's 19 PUDs filed an application to create the agency. Washington Public Power Supply System was established on January 31, 1957.

Other early efforts at joint action were centered in Pennsylvania and Ohio, where municipal and cooperative utilities created the Penn-Ohio Power Development Association in 1958. The purpose of this group was to purchase the share of power allocated from the Niagara Falls power project to Pennsylvania and Ohio, and to transmit this power to members of the organization over its own transmission lines.

APPA's annual conference in Washington in 1959 added impetus to the drive for joint action. Joseph Swidler, former general counsel of the Tennessee Valley Authority, who later became chairman of Federal Power Commission, was one of the featured speakers and urged joint action of publicly owned electric utilities. He cautioned, however, that public power utilities in a number of states were handicapped by state laws that failed to provide authority for pooling power supply resources by consumer-owned utilities. He called on consumer-owned utilities in each state to study legislation with a view to making improvements.

In my report at the annual conference, I announced that APPA planned to offer more assistance to members in securing ample low-cost power through "modern, efficient and, where possible, integrated power supply sources."

At APPA's 1960 annual conference, a panel discussion was devoted entirely to the issue of joint action. One panelist, Mayor Maurice A. TePaske, of Sioux Center, Iowa, coined a phrase—"Tie or Die." It became the motto for joint action.

Establishment of Basin Electric Power Cooperative was one of the earliest fruits of Leland Olds' advocacy of comprehensive regional power supply for consumer-owned electric utilities. Concurrently, APPA accelerated its efforts to promote the formation of joint action agencies by local public power utilities.

APPA took a major step forward in promoting joint action by adding Herbert Blinder, a power supply planning engineer, to the APPA staff in 1961. Herb had worked for the Sacramento Municipal Utility District. I met him when he came to Washington to testify before congressional committees on behalf of the Trinity River power project in California. I was impressed with his broad view of power supply and his ability to articulate technical issues in a manner understandable to laymen as well as engineers.

Herb and Larry Hobart of the APPA staff visited state and regional affiliates of APPA to preach the gospel of joint action. It was not an easy sell. Some smaller utilities that operated their own generating stations were skeptical of the joint action concept because they felt it would lead to a loss of their autonomy. Just how cool some APPA members felt toward joint action was demonstrated during one of the early road show performances in Missouri. After flying to a nearby airport, Larry and Herb rented a car and drove to the locale of the meeting, a building that appeared to be a combination ballroom and bar. They arrived at noon, the appointed hour, and found the room empty. After waiting at least half an hour, one person showed up. Without identifying himself, he sat down with Larry and Herb, pulled a bottle of liquor out of a paper bag and shared it with them. Still, he did not identify himself. Finally, Larry said they were there to meet with a group of municipal utility leaders about joint action and asked if that was the reason for his presence. He said it was, but said little else.

Gradually, about a dozen men arrived. Larry and Herb set up a screen and made a presentation on the virtues of joint action. The audience listened, but asked no questions. Once Larry and Herb finished, the group departed without further word.

Despite this cold reception, Larry and Herb persisted and gradually the joint action concept won acceptance among APPA members. In *Public Power* magazine in July 1968, Herb reported there was a definite trend toward joint action among the nation's local publicly owned electric utilities. Five years later a *Public Power* magazine survey identified 45 joint action projects. By September 1978, joint action in some stage of development had increased to include more than half of all local publicly owned electric utilities. At the beginning of the 21st century, 69 joint action agencies, covering most of the United States, existed.

Chapter 36

Emergence of an Energy Crisis

The Nixon administration is best remembered for the Watergate break-in, the Vietnam War, and turbulent social upheavals. But in the annals of the energy industry, the Nixon years bring to mind fuel shortages, steeply rising prices and the Arab oil embargo.

The earliest manifestations of an emerging problem involved the availability of coal, the fuel used to produce about 50 percent of the nation's electricity. During the first nine months of 1969, U.S. coal consumption increased by 20 million tons and production declined by 25 million tons, compared with the comparable period of 1968. Coal companies were reluctant to develop new mines because they expected nuclear power to absorb a major part of future markets. They also claimed utilities had underestimated their coal requirements.

In March 1970, I wrote to President Nixon asking for government interventions. The inability of electric utilities to obtain adequate coal supplies posed a threat of a severe power crisis, I said. Widespread brownouts and blackouts were likely. I urged the president to ask the Federal Power Commission to survey utility coal stocks; to ask the Interstate Commerce Commission to study ways to speed up coal shipments, and to direct the White House Office of Emergency Preparedness to prepare for possible action to assure continued operation of coal-fired generating units. I also asked the president to advise the attorney general to investigate possible antitrust violations resulting from oil company control of major coal companies.

Shortly thereafter, presidential assistant Peter Flanigan responded, saying the administration was reviewing my recommendations.

In May, the Office of Emergency Preparedness confirmed APPA's reports of possible energy shortages. OEP Director Gen. George A. Lincoln released survey results indicating deteriorating energy supply circumstances in the East. Coal production "may be inadequate to rebuild stocks to normal levels" and some utilities "may face real shortages this summer," Lincoln said.

In addition, natural gas supplies were tight. Lincoln said the government would take several actions, including streamlining Interstate Commerce Commission procedures to give priority use of hopper cars to coal shipments and curtailing production at the Atomic Energy Commission's gaseous diffusion plants, which consumed large quantities of electricity.

•

At APPA's annual conference in Memphis in May 1970, member utilities reported on their difficulties obtaining coal. One speaker, Dr. Bruce Netschert, director of the Washington office of National Economic Research Associates, warned of the "recent wave of horizontal integration in the fuels industries. Oil companies bought coal companies, entered the uranium business and purchased large interests in coal and oil shale lands, he said. These were "ominous" developments for electric utilities, because they "cannot help but decrease competition among the fuels," he said.

At that conference, the APPA board of directors created an Emergency Committee on Coal, which met in Washington with Nixon administration officials.

Only two of the 10 largest coal companies in the United States were independently owned. The remaining eight—which accounted for almost 43 percent of industry production—were owned by oil companies, other mineral firms, or large industrial concerns with stakes in the energy field.

I called for a Department of Justice investigation of antitrust implications of the concentrated ownership in the fuels industry and suggested Congress authorize the federal government to develop oil and natural gas resources. "Such a federal 'yardstick' type of operation should have as beneficial an effect on the oil and gas industry as public power has had on the electric industry," I said.

At a Senate hearing in July, James Watson, manager of power for the Tennessee Valley Authority, said TVA would have four or five plants out of coal in the upcoming winter if the coal shortage situation did not improve. TVA had only a 12-day stockpile, he said.

Federal Power Commission Chairman John Nassikas said fuel problems confronting the electric industry "have increased rapidly within the last 12 months," and the energy crisis "could be resolved only by a comprehensive national energy policy."

Some Congressmen began to express concerns about the fuels situation. In August 1970, Rep. William R. Anderson, D-Tenn., a former Navy submarine commander, introduced a resolution calling on the House Interstate and Foreign Commerce Committee to conduct "a full and complete investigation and study of the high price of coal." TVA had recently announced an "earth-shaking 25 to 30 percent rate increase" for its wholesale power because coal prices had doubled in a year's time, Representative Anderson said.

In September, Sen. Albert Gore Sr., D-Tenn, introduced a bill to discourage further consolidation of coal companies and limit coal exports. His bill also would amend federal antitrust laws "to insure the coverage of conglomerates involving the fuel industry."[1] Later that month, Senator Gore testified in the Senate in support of a bill he and 59 other senators had introduced to establish a National Commission on Fuels and Energy. President Nixon could help end the "artificially induced" shortage of coal and other fuels "with two strokes of a pen"— by temporarily limiting coal exports and by changing oil import quotas to permit increased supplies to enter the country, he said. In addition, the president could institute antitrust action "to restore some semblance of competition" and "use the moral force and power of his office to bring some of the big oil companies into line."

James A. Garvey, vice president of the National Coal Association, said only 20 percent of the coal industry's productive capacity was owned by the oil industry. He blamed the shortage of coal on the Atomic Energy Commission's "oversell" of nuclear power, and criticized TVA and Duke Power Company for deciding to "go nuclear."

In late September, unseasonably high temperatures sent electric loads soaring, causing blackouts and brownouts in wide areas throughout the East. Emergency Preparedness Director Lincoln urged consumers to limit power uses to essential needs.

As the winter of 1970 approached, Dr. Paul McCracken, chairman of President Nixon's Council of Economic Advisers, warned consumers might have to reduce energy use by 10 percent to conserve coal, oil and gas in the face of a threatened fuel shortage. No section of the country was "immune from concern," he said.

A joint statement issued by Dr. McCracken and OEP Director Lincoln

---

[1] Ironically, after his defeat for re-election in 1970, Sen. Gore became an officer of a major coal company, Occidental Petroleum Company.

listed a series of steps to give "reasonable assurance" of adequate fuel supplies for the winter. The main thrust of their statement was an appeal to fuel suppliers to boost production and delivery schedules and to increase prices to stimulate production.

In early October 1970, in testimony before the House Select Committee on Small Business, I said the McCracken-Lincoln proposals were "timid" and promised "small results at best."

Citing reports from municipal electric utilities of fuel price increases of as much as 136 percent, I expressed doubts about "whether a general price increase will result in an equitable distribution of supply to all potential consumers." I urged the administration to allocate fuels to meet high priority needs, such as schools, hospitals, public facilities and electric power generating facilities. Fuel producers were entitled to a fair profit, but there was "no inherent right on the part of private holders of vital natural resources to obtain a price that bore little or no relationship to the cost of production or to withhold these resources until guaranteed excessive prices," I said.

In October, Federal Trade Commission Chairman Miles W. Kirkpatrick said the commission staff would determine whether there had been "collusion or other unlawful conduct" in the oil industry to withhold natural gas from the market. He said the commission also would give "priority treatment to current merger activity in the energy field," and investigate anticompetitive behavior of oil, gas, electricity and coal companies.

•

Because of the worsening coal supply situation and rapidly increasing coal prices, a 25-member delegation from the Tennessee Valley Public Power Association and the Emergency Committee for the Tennessee Valley met in mid-December with U.S. Attorney General John Mitchell and other officials to seek remedial action. On the night before their first meeting, I attended a briefing session and press conference at a Washington hotel. National Coal Association Vice President Brice O'Brien asked for time to address the group. The gracious southerners agreed and, to their chagrin, O'Brien launched into a spirited attack. I could feel the tension and amazement in the audience as O'Brien said, "We raised the hell out of the price of coal..and you've got to pay it...The days of cheap energy are gone." The cost of producing coal had risen $2 a ton "so if you want coal, you are going to pay $3 a ton more. To hell with the TVA...Don't sue us, you are wasting your time and money," he said.

Despite O'Brien's threat, the delegation proceeded with its appointments. After the meetings, Attorney General John Mitchell asked them to name a committee to work with the Justice Department. The TVPPA delegation was also pleased with its meetings with the Federal Trade Commissioners, who reported on their investigation of the energy industry.

Several days after the Tennessee Valley group was in Washington, Stephen Dunn, outgoing president of the National Coal Association, announced NCA Vice President O'Brien was not representing the association when he spoke to the group. NCA did not control coal prices and O'Brien "is now on extended leave of absence for reasons of ill health," Dunn said.

•

The predicted energy shortages occurred. In late January 1971, five of seven utilities in the New York Power Pool reduced voltages by 5 percent and power companies in New England asked consumers to reduce non-essential uses of electricity. Washington, New York and other major areas in the Northeast had power shortages. Millions of New York residents endured seven voltage cutbacks in three weeks; New England residents had eight cutbacks in the same period.

In March 1971, representatives of the Emergency Committee for the Tennessee Valley and the Tennessee Valley Public Power Association came to Washington again and formally asked the Justice Department to investigate possible price fixing in the coal industry. The group also wanted the Federal Trade Commission to investigate the merger between Consolidation Coal Company and Continental Oil Company. At a meeting with Assistant Attorney General Richard W. McLaren, who headed the Justice Department's Antitrust Division, the group presented preliminary findings of a study of coal prices conducted by S. Robert Mitchell, an economist who had recently retired from the Antitrust Division staff after 22 years of service. Mitchell's study indicated it was unlikely that recent coal price increases (an average of 60 percent during the previous 18 months) could be justified on economic grounds. A grand jury investigation was warranted on the question of whether the spiraling price increases resulted from conspiratorial action, he said.

In May, APPA and National Rural Electric Cooperative Association recommended municipal and cooperative utilities consider filing class action suits against coal companies for damages from price-fixing. During the preceding 10 years, seven of the 10 largest independent coal companies were acquired by non-coal energy corporations. Four of the acquisitions were by petroleum companies that also produced natural gas.

Later that month, the FTC announced an in-depth investigation of antitrust factors involving concentration of ownership and interfuel competition among the nation's major oil, natural gas, coal and electricity producers. The commission would study: (1) the nature and extent of interfuel competition; (2) concentration in the energy sector; (3) the relationship between concentration levels and profitability, as a possible indicator of market power; and (4) effects of structural change on new investment and research and development within the energy sector.

Meanwhile, the FTC ruled Kennecott Copper Corporation's acquisition of Peabody Coal Company violated the Clayton Antitrust Act. The commission ordered Kennecott to sell Peabody within six months and directed it not to acquire any coal assets for 10 years without prior FTC approval. Kennecott was the nation's largest copper producer and Peabody was the nation's biggest coal producer, the FTC noted. The coal industry "is experiencing a steady trend toward rising concentration...This trend, unless halted, foreshadows ominous developments in the coal industry, with production and sale of coal concentrating in fewer and fewer hands," the commission said.

This good news was countered by a letter I received from Assistant Attorney General McLaren, advising me that the Justice Department would not investigate coal pricing.

•

In summer 1971, higher fuel prices and warnings about energy shortages precipitated several congressional hearings. At year's end, the House Small Business Committee castigated the Justice Department for failing to block anticompetitive takeovers of large coal companies by oil companies. "Increased concentration in the energy market could reduce competitive raw fuel alternatives available to electric utilities, with the resulting higher fuel prices forcing them to raise power rates to record high amounts," the committee said in a report prepared by its Special Subcommittee on Small Business Problems.

In a speech to the American Mining Congress in early 1972, C. Howard Hardesty, vice president of Continental Coal Company, blasted APPA, consumer protection groups, "self-dealing politicos," the House Special Subcommittee on Small Business Problems, Ralph Nader, and the FTC for criticizing the fuels industry. Hardesty accused the House Subcommittee on Small Business Problems of "mounting a highly biased attack upon the association of oil companies with coal companies." The subcommittee's report abounded "with wholly unsubstantiated innuendoes of monopoly and collusion," he said.

Hardesty called APPA "an association dedicated to fragmenting the coal industry" and criticized us for giving the FTC information related to the Continental Oil-Consolidation Coal merger. "It is clear from the record that a special interest group has exerted a powerful and effective influence on the supposedly impartial activities of the Federal Trade Commission," he said.

"Only the [fuels] industry can be relied upon as a source of "unbiased and informed" information, Hardesty said. "Self-styled" consumer protection groups, "self-dealing politicos," Congress and regulatory agencies were unreliable and the news media were a "yeasty breeding ground for compounding error among some of the media representatives who cite unsupported allegations as truths," he said.

•

In the fall of 1972, new predictions of an energy crisis surfaced. Industry and government experts warned that declining U.S. supplies of petroleum and continued shortages of natural gas could bring another energy crisis and more price increases.

Many blamed the oil shortages on the government's restrictive oil import quotas. This became an issue in the 1972 presidential campaign. The Democratic candidate, Sen. George McGovern of South Dakota, called for an end to quotas. Reacting to increasing demands from Congress and McGovern, President Nixon authorized a 35 percent increase in imports, but only for the remainder of the year. Sen. Edward M. Kennedy, D-Mass., described the president's action as "a piecemeal and shortsighted solution to the oil crisis in New England." The real solution was to scrap the oil import quota system permanently, he said.

•

When President Nixon began his second term in 1973, I predicted in a column in the January-February issue of *Public Power* that Congress and the administration would consider certain changes in policies and a reorganization of government agencies dealing with energy. I did not foresee the event that created the greatest disruption in energy supply in that decade and marked the beginning of a major shift in world geopolitical policy, the Arab oil embargo of October 1973.

In mid-April 1973, President Nixon sent his energy message to Congress. It stressed energy production, but also called for voluntary energy-use labeling of major home appliances and automobiles. He also called for establishment of an Office of Energy Conservation in the Department of the Interior. The president ended the 14-year oil import quota program by substituting phased imposition of "license fees" on crude oil imports and petroleum products above 1973 levels. He called for legislation to deregulate new natural gas prices and directed the interior secretary to triple the annual acreage leased on the outer continental shelf by 1979 for oil and gas drilling.

President Nixon asked Congress "to act swiftly" on his proposed legislation to remove restrictions on construction of the controversial Alaska oil pipeline. The adminstration expected to proceed with a pilot project on oil shale leasing programs "if the environmental risks are acceptable." He said he expected leasing of geothermal fields on public lands could begin after a final environmental analysis and urged that "the highest national priority be given to expanded development and utilization of our coal resources." The nation needed to reduce reliance on fossil fuels and move swiftly to develop nuclear power, he said.

Elimination of oil import quotas was "one of the most welcome—and overdue—recommendations," I said. But deregulation of "new" gas prices was unnecessary. "There is no evidence that natural gas producers have been forced by regulation to sell their product at a loss, or even at an inadequate profit margin," I said. "Natural gas producers have been guaranteed a rate of return of about 15 percent."

•

During the remainder of President Nixon's term,[2] the combination of insufficient domestic supplies and the embargo resulted in intense debate on oil allocations, emergency restrictions, decontrol of natural gas prices, and formation of a federal fuels corporation.

Because of tightening oil supplies, the administration and Congress gave immediate attention to the need for an oil allocation program. President Nixon advocated a voluntary scheme, while Senator Jackson wanted a mandatory program. Jackson introduced a bill to create a Federal Office of Emergency Fuel Allocation to assure adequate fuel supply to municipal, county and state governments. It would establish priorities, protect independent suppliers, and prevent non-competitive practices in the petroleum industry.

Early in June 1973, the Senate passed a bill to require the president to establish a mandatory fuel allocation program. However, the president's

---

[2] President Nixon's term came to an abrupt end when he resigned on August 9, 1974, after the House Judiciary Committee had passed three articles of impeachment largely as a result of the president's involvement in the cover-up of the break-in of the Democratic National Committee at the Watergate. Gerald R. Ford was sworn in as president the same day.

energy assistant, former Colorado Gov. John A. Love, said the administration continued to oppose mandatory government allocation of oil and would stick by its voluntary program. The bipartisan, six-state New England Congressional Caucus promptly denounced the administration's decision, calling it "myopic and unresponsive to the threat of an oil shortage this winter."

I criticized the administration's policy as designed "to protect the interests of the big oil companies rather than small consumers by placing primary reliance on a voluntary program, which has proven to be a failure insofar as local public power systems are concerned." I told the Federal Oil Policy Committee that the absence of price controls made price gouging inevitable.

Support grew for a mandatory program and in September attorneys general from 35 states called on Congress to break up the nation's major oil companies and to compel them to submit to a mandatory oil allocation program.

In late September, amid growing concern about prospects for the winter, APPA representatives met with Governor Love in his large, ornate office in the Executive Office Building, next door to the White House. The tall, handsome, affable former governor gave us a friendly hearing, but was non-committal about a change in the administration's position.

Early the following month, the White House announced it would impose a mandatory, but limited, fuel allocation program, which Senator Jackson described as "a piecemeal approach to a larger problem."

In mid-October 1973 the House passed an emergency petroleum allocation program that was tougher than the one approved by the Senate. The House-passed bill applied to heavy residual oil burned by electric utilities, crude oil, gasoline and other fuels. The bill also ordered the president to give top priority to essential services, including those provided by electric utilities.

While the nation fretted about adequate supplies of oil, major petroleum companies reported record profits during the third quarter of 1973. Exxon, the world's largest petroleum company, showed an 80 percent increase in net income from the same period a year earlier, and Gulf Oil Company registered a 91 percent gain.

•

On October 6, 1973, Egypt and Syria launched a surprise attack on Israel. The invasion began on Yom Kippur, the holiest day of the year for Jews and came to be known as the Yom Kippur War. Caught unaware, the Israelis initially suffered serious setbacks and were using up war materiel at an alarming rate. Fearful that the supply of arms by the Soviet Union to the Arab countries would tilt the military balance against Israel, the United States agreed to provide large-scale military aid to Israel.

When the Arab countries learned of the U.S. aid program, they quickly retaliated by cutting off oil supplies to the United States. The Arab nations had long considered using this tactic, but the war with Israel provided a propitious opportunity to deploy the weapon, because the United States had become increasingly dependent upon Middle Eastern oil, and did not have ready access to reserves to offset the loss of imported oil.[3]

Ironically, the first announcement of what later was regarded as a momentous event was reported on page 18 of the October 21 *New York Times*. Perhaps the story did not receive more prominent attention because the embargo began the same day as the infamous "Saturday Night Massacre," when Attorney General Elliott Richardson resigned because he refused to carry out President Nixon's order to fire the Watergate special prosecutor, Archibald Cox. President Nixon then dismissed Cox, abolished the office of special Watergate prosecutor, and discharged William D. Ruckelshaus, the deputy attorney general.

The story was also downplayed because the full impact of the embargo was not apparent at its inception. The *Times* said precise calculations were not available, but cutbacks of Arab oil might total a million barrels a day of crude oil. Total U.S. consumption of crude oil and refinery products was estimated at 17 million barrels a day.

Daniel Yergen, in his book, *The Prize*, said the United States understood the dimensions of the loss only after the fact. "In the midst of the cutbacks, there was great uncertainty about how much oil was available, combined with an inevitable tendency to exaggerate the loss," he said. "The confusion resulted from the contradictory and fragmentary nature of information and from the massive disruption of established supply channels, all overlaid by rabid and violent emotions."

In the turmoil resulting from the embargo, gas was in short supply, prices of oil and gasoline shot up, and angry motorists had to line up at service stations to obtain gasoline. President Nixon made a nationally televised address in early November to outline a broad new energy program. He said he would prevent utilities from converting from coal to oil for power production, and asked for prompt enactment of legislation to relax environmental regulations to permit burning of high-sulfur coal

---

[3] In 1973 the United States depended upon imported oil for 36 percent of its requirements. By 2001, U.S. dependence on foreign oil had increased to 56 percent.

and oil. He also proposed "energy conservation fees or taxes" on natural gas and electricity consumption.

The president proposed "Project Independence," comparing it to the Manhattan Project, which produced the atomic bomb, and Project Apollo, which enabled the United States to put a man on the moon six months ahead of the goal enunciated by President Kennedy. He called for long-term research and development programs to make the United States energy-self-sufficient by 1980.[4]

A week after President Nixon's nationwide television address, Congress approved the Emergency Petroleum Allocation Act, which the president signed on November 27. The bill covered the full range of petroleum products, including heavy residual oil burned by electric utilities, and went beyond the administration's program, which gave priority fuel allocations only to the Defense Department. The bill extended priorities to essential services, including municipal, county and state governments and electric utilities.

Two days before signing the allocation act, the president again appeared on television to outline a series of sweeping energy conservation measures. Pending passage of legislation giving him authority to impose a mandatory ban, he asked for a voluntary halt on Sunday sales of gasoline and a reduction in highway speed limits to 50 miles per hour. The president also wanted to ban many types of commercial and decorative lighting.

While Congress was considering the oil allocation legislation, it debated a broader National Energy Emergency Act. The emergency legislation, sponsored by Senator Jackson, was passed by the Senate shortly before the president signed the allocation legislation. It gave the chief executive sweeping powers to deal with a critical nationwide energy shortage, including the discretionary authority to ration and allocate scarce fuels and to require energy conservation compliance by business, government and the public. The Senate bill would prohibit any power generating facility from converting from coal to oil or gas and would require that power plants with "ready capability and necessary plant equipment" burn coal.

The bill permitted restrictions on non-essential energy uses. It required the president to issue a plan within 90 days to develop the nation's hydro

---

4 According to Daniel Yergen's *The Prize*, Nixon's staff told him achieving energy independence by 1980 was impossible, but Nixon was so embroiled in the Watergate controversy that he seized upon this prediction to divert attention from Watergate.

power resources by providing for "expeditious" completion of projects already authorized and for planning other projects.

By mid-December the House had passed a modified version of the National Energy Emergency Act, which established a coal allocation program. After a failed attempt to pass a windfall profits tax on oil and gas companies, a Senate-House conference committee approved a "prohibition on inequitable prices" for domestic crude oil, residual fuel oil and refined petroleum products.

APPA supported the price rollback. Officers and staff of the association met with Deputy Federal Energy Administrator John Sawhill and gave Congress the results of a survey of APPA members. The survey showed prices for residual fuel oil had risen as much as 400 percent in a 12-month period. Distillate fuel prices rose as high as 260 percent. We also told Sawhill about the substantial price increases and difficulties APPA members were experiencing in obtaining coal.

A revised emergency bill won quick congressional approval. However, administration officials, including Secretary of the Treasury George Schulz, said the price rollback would dampen new investment required to produce more oil. As expected, President Nixon vetoed the bill, primarily because of his objections to the rollback of crude oil prices. The Senate sustained the veto by a vote of 58 to 40.

The president said the rollback would discourage production of petroleum products and "result in reduced energy supplies, longer lines at the gas pump...and serious damage to jobs in America." At a news conference, he said "the back of the energy crisis has been broken," and he called on Congress to enact other energy legislation, including a proposal to deregulate natural gas prices.

About two weeks after the president's veto was sustained, the Arab oil-producing nations announced their intention to end the embargo.

•

Under prodding by APPA, members of Congress and consumer groups, the Federal Trade Commission investigated anticompetitive practices of oil companies. In July 1973 the FTC filed a formal complaint against the nation's eight largest oil companies. They were charged with participating in anti-competitive activities involving a conspiracy to monopolize crude oil refining, creating a shortage, requiring consumers to pay higher prices, and forcing hundreds of independent dealers out of business, thereby providing excess profits to the firms.

The FTC issued the complaint against companies known as the "Big Eight": Exxon, Texaco, Gulf Oil, Mobil Oil, Standard Oil of California,

Standard Oil of Indiana, Shell Oil, and Atlantic Richfield. It charged that since at least 1950, the eight companies had monopoly control of oil refining in the Eastern and Gulf Coast states and parts of the Midwest. The commission said the "Big Eight" had accumulated "profits and returns on investments substantially in excess of those they would have obtained in a competitively structured market." FTC figures showed the 1973 first-quarter profits of the companies were more than 29 percent higher than for the previous year.

Deputy Treasury Secretary William E. Simon, who also headed the president's Oil Policy Committee, tried to persuade the FTC to withdraw its antitrust action against the companies. He told FTC Chairman Lewis Engman the antitrust case could worsen the energy crisis and reiterated oil industry arguments placing primary blame for the fuel shortage-cost spiral problems on federal laws and policies.

The FTC staff was not intimidated by Simon. In February 1974, the staff recommended the eight companies be compelled to divest themselves of at least 40 percent of their refinery capacity and all of their pipelines as a means of increasing competition in the industry.

•

Still another major effort to correct the problem of energy shortages centered on the concept of creating a federal fuels corporation. One of the principal proponents of this idea was Consumer Federation of America's Energy Policy Task Force, chaired by Lee C. White. White originally made the proposal in 1969 when he was chairman of the Federal Power Commission, but the effects of the 1973 Arab oil embargo provided a more receptive climate for this idea. Modeled after the Tennessee Valley Authority, the corporation would drill for oil and gas on public lands to provide a "yardstick" for acquiring reliable data on petroleum production and as "a competitive spur to the privately owned petroleum industry."

In mid-November 1973, two weeks after White had testified before the Senate Commerce Committee urging the creation of a Federal Oil and Gas Corporation, Sen. Adlai E. Stevenson III, D-Ill.,[5] and nine Senate colleagues introduced a bill to create such an entity. The corporation would develop publicly owned oil and gas resources on federal lands; stimulate competition in the petroleum business; provide data on actual costs of producing oil and gas; and contribute additional fuel supplies that the federal government could allocate to essential public needs, including

---

5 Senator Stevenson's father was a former governor of Illinois and an unsuccessful Democratic candidate for the presidency in 1952 and 1956.

national defense.

With the worsening oil situation, support for creation of a federal oil and gas corporation continued to grow. By March 1974 almost 100 congressmen had sponsored a companion House bill. APPA endorsed the legislation. The pluralistic ownership in the electric industry worked well and could bring similar benefits to the oil and gas industry, we said. However, once the oil embargo ended, support for creation of a federal oil and gas corporation dwindled.

•

By the time Gerald Ford became president in August 1974, prices of all fuels continued to escalate and were regarded as a primary cause of inflation that was sweeping the country. President Ford held a summit conference in Washington in September 1974. Prior to the conference, the administration organized separate meetings of various sectors of the economy to make recommendations. I was one of four electric utility representatives invited to speak at the "pre-summit" meeting of administration officials in Dallas. Secretary of the Interior Rogers C.B. Morton chaired this session, which was devoted largely to natural resources and energy.

Fuel was the largest single expense for utilities and sharp increases in fuel prices during the past few years were kicking up electric rates and the cost of other products, I said. I called for federal action to halt runaway fuel prices. Between April 1973 and April 1974, the price of coal rose 62.4 percent. During the same period, oil prices increased 169.4 percent and natural gas prices went up 30.9 percent. These price escalations were not justified by increases in costs of labor, safety or other production expenses, I said.

During the same period, coal company profits had risen sharply. From the first quarter of 1972 to the comparable period in 1973, Consolidation Coal Company profits increased 118 percent; Peabody Coal Company, 83 percent; Amax Coal, 53 percent; and Utah International, 24 percent. Despite these large profits, coal production had not increased; in 1971, 1972 and 1974, it was lower than in 1970. I recommended government price controls if the coal companies did not halt such large price hikes voluntarily.

I also suggested more vigorous enforcement of antitrust laws, more intensive conservation efforts, leadership by the Department of the Interior in planning inter-regional high-voltage electrical interconnections and development of hydroelectric power resources.

Shortly after the summit, President Ford addressed a joint session of

Congress to describe his "new mobilization" against inflation. He called for eliminating oil- and natural gas-fired generating plants from baseload capacity and converting them to coal or nuclear fuel by 1980. The Federal Energy Administration was directed to call a meeting of utilities, the coal and nuclear industries, and state and federal regulatory agencies to establish within 90 days a schedule for phasing out sufficient oil-fired plants to conserve one million barrels of oil daily. Although 500 coal-fired power plants would not be in compliance with existing anti-pollution regulations by June 1975, President Ford said he would allow them to continue to burn coal, but they might require waivers from the Environmental Protection Agency. He also recommended:

- reducing energy use;
- increasing the investment tax credit for investor-owned utilities from 4 percent to 10 percent to assist them in "overcoming their financial problems";
- deregulation of natural gas rates "to stimulate production";
- legislation to facilitate increased use of coal;
- maximum production of the Naval Petroleum Reserves in California and full-scale exploration and development of naval oil reserves in Alaska;
- enactment of a nuclear plant licensing bill "to expedite licensing and construction power costs and accelerate U.S. energy self-sufficiency";
- passage of a windfall profits tax on oil; and
- creation of the federal Energy Research and Development Administration.

About two weeks after the president's address to Congress, the Ford Foundation released the report of its Energy Policy Project. The 511-page report, *A Time to Choose—America's Energy Future*, was conducted by an independent staff of economists, engineers, scientists, writers and attorneys, under the direction of S. David Freeman, formerly of the White House energy policy staff. I served on a 20-person advisory board for the study.

Freeman relished exploration of new ideas and his staff presented papers that challenged some of the most hallowed principles of the establishment. Advisory board meetings were marked by lively debate. Freeman made it clear that he would listen carefully, but the board was to be strictly advisory, not a board of directors.

Much of the debate centered on the future growth rate of energy use. Many board members representing the energy industry were imbued with the traditional concept of the inevitability—if not desirability—of continued growth in energy consumption. Some of the most vigorous arguments were between Freeman and William P. Tavoulareas, president of Mobil Oil Company At an advisory board retreat near Denver, Tavoulareas objected to staff projections of energy growth and the need for greater emphasis on conservation. As the meeting was breaking up, an exasperated Tavoulareas thundered, "I'm going to get in my jet and tell the pilot to fly back to New York as fast as he can and to hell with the amount of fuel he burns up."

The Ford Foundtion recommended the United States reduce its annual growth in energy consumption from 4.5 percent during the preceding eight years to about 2 percent. Energy conservation could be achieved without adversely affecting the economy or lifestyle, the report said. Projected energy growth could level off to zero in 10 years, it said. It recommended establishment of regional grids to meet power needs efficiently and reforms in industry structure to separate electric generation and transmission from local distribution operations.

In later years, a number of the concepts advocated by the Ford Foundation gained wide acceptance, but they were regarded as heresy by many in the energy industry in 1974.

I supported most of the report's recommendations, but took exception to the general tenor of the document. In separate views published in the report, I said it "overcompensates in the direction of decrying the detriments of energy production, without giving sufficient recognition to the benefits that have been derived from the use of energy, and the importance of adequate sources of energy to the future of our society."

•

In mid-November 1974, the Federal Energy Administration released a 776-page *Project Independence* energy report. It also advocated conservation programs and called for measures to reduce energy growth to 2 percent annually by 1985. The FEA report did not make specific recommendations, but offered policy options. It was expected to provide the basis for a major presidential message early in 1975 and future policy-making decisions on energy. Significantly, the report did not affirm former President Nixon's objective of energy self-sufficiency by 1980. Complete independence from foreign oil "is simply not warranted economically or politically," even by 1985, the report said.

The reduction to 2 percent energy growth could be attained by imposing mandatory fuel-saving standards for automobiles, appliances and buildings and by redesigning electric rates, FEA said. Banning use of natural gas and oil for heating new buildings would transfer demand to electricity and reduce dependence on oil imports, the report said.

President Ford made an unexpected nationally televised speech on energy issues prior to his State of the Union address in January 1975. He proposed an increase in import fees on each barrel of foreign crude oil, a more comprehensive program of energy conservation taxes on oil and natural gas, deregulating natural gas prices and removing price controls on domestic oil.

"We need, within 90 days, the strongest and most far-reaching energy conservation program we have ever had," the president said.

He acknowledged energy prices would rise under his program, but said it would achieve two important goals: discouraging unnecessary use of petroleum products and encouraging development and substitution of other fuels and newer energy sources. The president predicted that by 1985, the United States would be "invulnerable" to foreign energy disruptions or oil embargoes.

A few days later President Ford delivered his State of the Union address and described a long and varied list of proposals for a national energy program. He said he would ask Congress "to authorize and require tariffs, import quotas or price floors to protect our energy prices at levels which will achieve energy independence." In effect, the president was suggesting the price of domestic fuels be raised to match oil prices set by the Organization of Petroleum Exporting Countries.

•

President Ford faced formidable obstacles to enactment of his program. Congressional elections in November 1972 gave Democrats resounding majorities in both the House and Senate. Almost immediately after the president proposed to impose higher taxes on oil imports, a joint resolution introduced in both chambers sought to prevent him from raising the oil import tariff without congressional approval.

Consumer Federation of America claimed the president's program would force consumers to pay $30 billion in additional fuel costs while receiving tax reductions and direct payments amounting to $19 billion. In late January 1975 the Library of Congress released a study contending that President Ford's energy program could cost consumers about $50 billion in 1975 in higher fuel prices, averaging about $723 annually per household.

The APPA Legislative and Resolutions Committee adopted a resolution supporting congressional action to suspend the president's authority to raise the tariff on oil imports. An import fee would "boost the costs of all fuels, require significant increases in the cost of electricity, and add to general inflation," the resolution said.

The confrontation between the administration and Congress on oil pricing lasted through most of 1975. On December 18, 1975, three days after price controls expired on oil, the president signed S. 622, the Energy Policy and Conservation Act of 1975. The measure brought together five bills that Congress had been considering most of the year. The struggle behind the passage of the bill emphasized the dichotomy between the administration's determination to raise prices to reduce oil consumption and congressional preference for conservation, energy efficiency and alternative energy.

Chapter 37

Crisis Begets a National Energy Policy

Events preceding the 1976 presidential election campaign made it obvious energy policy would be a major issue for the next administration. To help shape policy during the campaign and in a new administration, the APPA board of directors on September 28, 1976 adopted an energy policy statement and sent it to both presidential candidates. APPA recommended creation of a Department of Energy and establishment of a federal fuels corporation, and proposed the federal government provide uranium enrichment services, nuclear fuel reprocessing and radioactive waste storage. Conservation could save energy and dollars and the federal government should promote conservation by implementing new concepts and advancing development of renewable energy, APPA said. Price rationing should not be used to encourage conservation. Instead, the federal government should fund programs to help consumers conserve energy. The APPA board also recommended the federal government expand generating capacity at its existing hydroelectric dams, where feasible, and build new projects.

Subsequent events proved APPA prophetic in identifying issues that commanded the attention of the newly elected President Carter.

•

On February 2, 1977, less than two weeks after he took office, President Carter made his first nationwide television address. Energy was the centerpiece of his "chat" with the American people. Seated casually before a low fire in the presidential library, the president wore a sweater, slacks and tie. The sweater symbolized his effort to ask the American people to make sacrifices by turning down their thermostats to 65 degrees during the day and 55 degrees at night, to conserve energy.

"The United States is the only major industrial country without a comprehensive, long-range energy policy," the president said.

President Carter directed his energy assistant, Dr. James Schlesinger,[1] to develop a national energy policy by April 20. Then, he would ask Congress to enact comprehensive legislation emphasizing conservation. The energy wasted in the United States "is greater than the total energy that we are importing from foreign countries," the president said. He called for policies to develop coal in an environmentally sound way and to emphasize research on solar energy and other renewable energy sources. The president said he would ask Congress to create a new Energy Department to centralize responsibility for energy policy, adding:

> We must face the fact that the energy shortage is permanent. There is no way we can solve it quickly. But if we all cooperate and make modest sacrifices, if we learn to live thriftily and remember the importance of helping our neighbors, then we can find ways to adjust and to make our society more efficient and our own lives more enjoyable and productive. Utility companies must promote conservation and not consumption. Oil and natural gas companies must be honest with all of us about their reserves and profits. We will find out the difference between real shortages and artificial ones. We will ask private companies to sacrifice, just as private citizens must do.

Two days later, Schlesinger spoke to an APPA audience at a luncheon meeting in Washington. He said "massive" conservation by the American people would be needed to resolve the nation's energy problems and conservation must be the "keystone" of U.S. energy policy for the next 10 to 15 years. Electric utilities, he said, must play a major role in the turnaround from a production-oriented system that had led to "highly wasteful" energy use. Although he stressed the need to improve efficiency by 30 to 50 percent, Schlesinger said the United States also should make a major effort "to move power plants away from the use of oil and natural gas to coal."

While finalizing specific recommendations for new energy policies, President Carter recommended a reorganization of agencies dealing with energy. In late February 1977, the administration released plans to create a new Department of Energy that would consolidate the functions of all or part of nine existing federal agencies into a single cabinet-level department. The reorganization bill submitted to Congress would abolish

---

[1] Schlesinger, a Republican, had held a number of important positions in the federal government: assistant director of the Office of Management and Budget, chairman of the Atomic Energy Commission, and director of the Central Intelligence Agency.

the Federal Power Commission, the Federal Energy Administration and the Energy Research and Development Adminstration and transfer those agencies' programs and personnel to the new department.

APPA was disturbed about a proposal to transfer to DOE the Interior Department's Bureau of Reclamation and the federal power marketing administrations—Bonneville, Southwestern, Southeastern and Alaska power administrations. We wanted these organizations to retain their identities if they were incorporated in the new department.

We were also troubled about the plan to transfer the Federal Power Commission, an independent agency, to the Department of Energy. Under the reorganization plan, FPC would be absorbed by a new Economic Regulatory Administration, which would be part of DOE and headed by a single administrator appointed by the secretary of energy. The agency would be authorized to issue rules to simplify procedures. A Hearings and Appeals Board, consisting of three presidential appointees serving four-year terms, would review all cases involving wholesale power rates, natural gas prices and hydroelectric licensing.

In testimony to the Senate Governmental Affairs Committee in March 1977, I supported creation of a Department of Energy, but opposed the transfer of Federal Power Commission functions to DOE. About 900 local publicly owned electric utilities purchased wholesale power from power companies regulated by the FPC. Transferring FPC's functions could harm consumers by eliminating quasi-judicial hearings on rates. I also urged the committee to preserve the organizational identities of the federal power marketing agencies and recommended the Bureau of Reclamation stay within the Interior Department because of the multipurpose nature of western water projects.

Several days after I testified, I met with Schlesinger at his office in the Executive Office Building to discuss the role of the FPC. An intelligent, highly articulate and determined individual, Schlesinger argued strongly that the government could greatly influence energy policy by setting rates. Depending upon the policies followed, rates could either encourage or discourage the production and use of fuels. Consequently, DOE needed to have a strong role in determining wholesale rates for natural gas and electricity, he argued.

I countered that the FPC should be a non-partisan, independent body and its quasi-judicial proceedings were essential to its role in protecting the public. After we had debated the subject for almost an hour without reaching agreement, I thought our discussion of the issue had come to an end.

However, at 8 o'clock the following morning, a Saturday, Schlesinger telephoned me at home. He wanted to continue to discuss the FPC's future. We largely restated the views we had expressed the previous day and again were unable to reach agreement. Although we disagreed, our exchange gave me a better understanding of Schlesinger's point of view and heightened my opinion of his thoughtful, hands-on approach to resolving problems.

Meanwhile, opposition to moving FPC to DOE was growing. Virtually all segments of the electric industry as well as the National Association of Regulatory Utility Commissioners and a number of senators and representatives opposed the proposal.

Congress took heed of the opposition. Ultimately, FPC was transformed into the Federal Energy Regulatory Commission, but its independent role was virtually unchanged. Congress did grant DOE some budgetary review responsibility over FERC, and gave DOE authority over exports and imports of gas and electricity.

The act creating DOE also retained the identities of the power marketing agencies. However, APPA's recommendation that the Bureau of Reclamation remain intact within the Department of the Interior was not followed. Instead, Congress separated the bureau's power marketing function from its other responsibilities and created the Western Area Power Administration within DOE to market power produced by the Bureau of Reclamation, except for power generated at bureau dams in the Pacific Northwest. Power from these facilities was marketed by Bonneville Power Administration. All of the power marketing agencies were then transferred from Interior to DOE.

•

Seated behind a massive desk in the Oval Office, President Carter presented his nationally televised energy message on Monday, April 18, 1977. Unlike his sweater-clad February chat, the president this time wore a dark suit and spoke in a soft, serious manner. The speech later became best known for the president's description of efforts to resolve the energy problem as "the moral equivalent of war," except, he said, "we will be uniting our efforts to build and not to destroy."

> Tonight I want to have an unpleasant talk with you about a problem that is unprecedented in our history. With the exception of preventing war, this is the greatest challenge that our country will face during our lifetime.
> The energy crisis has not yet overwhelmed us, but it will if we do not act quickly. It's a problem that we will not be able to solve in the next few years, and it's likely to get progressively worse through the rest of this century.

The president set the stage for a special message on energy he sent to Congress two days later. Recognizing the political difficulties of gaining acceptance of a program that emphasized reductions in energy use, Carter acknowledged that some of his listeners might doubt that the nation faced energy shortages. The 1973 gas lines were gone and homes were warm again.

"But our energy problem is worse because more waste has occurred and more time has passed by without our planning for the future," he said. "And it will get worse every day until we act."

The oil and gas the nation relied upon for 75 percent of its energy were "simply running out," the president said. Domestic production had been dropping steadily at about 6 percent a year, while imports had doubled in the previous five years. The nation's economic and political independence was becoming increasingly vulnerable and unless we reduced oil consumption, the world would be demanding more oil than it could produce in the 1980s, he said.

The United States was "the most wasteful nation on Earth," President Carter said. "We waste more energy than we import. With about the same standard of living, we use twice as much energy per person as do other countries like Germany, Japan, and Sweden." He set several goals for the nation to meet by 1985:

- Reduce the annual growth rate in energy demand to less than 2 percent;
- Reduce gasoline consumption by 10 percent below its current level;
- Cut oil imports in half;
- Establish a strategic petroleum reserve of one billion barrels, more than a six-month supply;
- Increase coal production by more than two-thirds to more than one billion tons a year;
- Insulate 90 percent of American homes and all new buildings; and
- Use solar energy in more than 2.5 million homes.

The president followed up his address with release of a detailed energy program. He intended to rely on taxes to achieve conservation—a prescription that was sure to engender tremendous opposition in Congress.

Another foundation of the program was a prohibition on use of natural gas or oil in new power plants. Instead, the president recommended increased dependence on coal as a power plant fuel. He advocated a greatly expanded role for electric utilities and state regulatory commissions in promoting conservation.

President Carter sent Congress a 283-page draft bill, "The National Energy Act of 1977," with the hope that Congress would pass it before adjourning in October. However, the bill dealt with many complex, controversial issues, requiring referral of various sections to a number of House committees. To coordinate congressional consideration, the House created a special 37-member Ad Hoc Committee on Energy, chaired by Rep. Thomas L. Ashley, D-Ohio. In the Senate, the bill was referred to the Energy and Natural Resources Committee, chaired by Sen. Henry M. (Scoop) Jackson, D-Wash.

•

APPA generally supported the bill, but it covered a wide scope and we needed to concentrate our efforts on provisions that would directly affect our members. Behind the scenes, we worked closely with congressional sources and with the White House staff, especially S. David Freeman,[2] on provisions of special interest to APPA. In July, the APPA Executive Committee met with Schlesinger for 90 minutes to discuss the legislation.

Responding to the administration's pressure for quick action, the House approved the National Energy Act by a vote of 244 to 177 in August, only three months after the president had proposed the legislation. Quick action by the House limited the time opponents had to mobilize their forces. Consequently, some of the controversial sections favorable to public power slipped through the House without significant change.

A provision of special importance to APPA would authorize the newly created Federal Energy Regulatory Commission to order utilities to interconnect with other utilities and to transmit power from one utility to another. This would facilitate more efficient use of generating and transmission facilities. APPA earlier had pressed for granting such authority to the Federal Power Commission to give wholesale customers more choices in buying power. Without recourse to the commission's power to order wheeling and interconnections, municipal utilities were captive customers of their neighboring private utilities.

Another provision of the House-passed bill would prohibit private

---

[2] Freeman had served as an energy adviser to Carter during the campaign. After Carter's election, Freeman was a member of a small staff, headed by Schlesinger, that developed Carter's energy program.

power companies from "pancaking" wholesale rate increases. This referred to the power companies' practice of imposing a second or third rate increase before the first rate hike had been approved by FPC. Under the bill passed by the House, no filed rate could take effect until FERC issued a final order, thus ending FPC's practice of suspending rate increases but letting them be imposed, subject to a possible refund, pending the commission's final decision.

The House bill also outlawed "price squeezes," which occured when a wholesale supplier charged a municipal utility a wholesale rate higher than the supplier's retail rate. However, the House deleted a provision that would have extended to non-nuclear power facilities a preconstruction antitrust review similar to that conducted for nuclear power plants.

The House bill retained the major elements of the administration's bill. It also would establish minimum standards for utility rates and tax U.S. oil to increase its controlled price to the uncontrolled world price while providing rebates to the public. After voting down an amendment to deregulate natural gas prices, the House approved the administration's formula for federal controls, but at a higher $1.75 price ceiling (from $1.45) per thousand cubic feet of gas.

The House eliminated provisions to increase gasoline taxes and to provide rebates for small, energy-efficient automobiles.

•

The Senate split the massive energy bill into five parts, covering energy conservation, power plant and industrial fuel use, public utility regulatory policies, natural gas policy and energy taxes.

Private power companies were stunned by the House-passed bill, and quickly mustered their forces to launch an all-out campaign in the Senate to undo the work of the House. As Senate committees prepared to hold hearings on the legislation, Edison Electric Institute President W. Donham Crawford in August 1977 called a press conference to distribute a highly critical, 70-page analysis, which described the House bill as a "disaster." Provisions allowing the Federal Power Commisison to require wheeling of power by private utilities were "a clear sop to public power," he said. He denounced sections giving FPC authority to order interconnections and pooling and banning "pancaking" wholesale rate increases and "price squeeze" actions.

The APPA staff knew we would have great difficulty holding gains made in the House. We therefore mobilized APPA members and allied organizations to retain provisions important to APPA and electric consumers.

In September, I testified before the Senate Subcommittee on Energy Conservation and Regulation in support of antitrust review of all new power plants. Responding to an argument made by opponents, I pointed out that only two nuclear plants had been delayed for about two months each because of such review. Language calling for anticipatory antitrust review could be "carefully drafted to guard against construction delays." I also asked the Senate to support provisions barring "pancaking" of rates, "price squeeze," prohibiting discrimination between wholesale and retail customers in the event of curtailments, and encouraging cogeneration.

Larry Hobart of the APPA staff testified before the subcommittee in support of provisions to give the Federal Power Commission authority to order wheeling and interconnections. Unfortunately, when the Senate split the energy legislation into five bills, provisions regarding wheeling, interconnections and pooling were referred to a subcommittee of the Senate Energy and Natural Resources Committee headed by Sen. J. Bennett Johnston, D-La., who supported private power company positions.

The subcommittee dropped the House provisions on wheeling and interconnections. However, Senator Johnston recognized that these were contentious issues. In the Senate floor debate, he called wheeling "complicated," and added:

> the committee did not want to use the power of the federal government...to permit what some utilities regard as piracy—that is, to require a utility to wheel the power from some other utility's generating plant to one of its own wholesale customers; in effect, to require a utility to furnish the rope to hang itself or risk losing some of its retail or wholesale customers.

Reiterating that the goals of the bill were to conserve energy, to use facilities efficiently, and to provide equitable rates for consumers, Senator Johnston said: "Wheeling has nothing to do with that."

The Senate committee also rejected the House provisions on "pancaking" and "price squeeze."

Natural gas pricing posed the biggest stumbling block to Senate passage of the entire package of energy legislation. The gas industry pressed hard for decontrol of the price of producing natural gas. Consumer groups, including APPA, opposed decontrol on the grounds that it would result in rapid price escalation and would not necessarily increase production. Opponents also feared decontrol would inflate other fuel prices. As a compromise, President Carter proposed an increase in the price of "new" natural gas, while retaining federal regulation of "old" gas.

Despite the agreement worked out by the White House and the Senate leadership, the bill triggered a bitter and prolonged filibuster aimed at delaying or blocking price decontrol. Senators Howard Metzenbaum, D-Ohio, and James Abourezk, D-S.D., led the filibuster, but the Senate ultimately passed the bill by a vote of 50 to 46.

•

By mid-October 1977 both houses of Congress had completed work on the energy bills, but the 38-member conference committee faced the daunting task of reconciling sharp differences between the Senate and House versions. Natural gas deregulation and energy taxes were the most divisive issues. The House had voted to increase the price cap on natural gas, but to continue federal regulation. The Senate had voted to raise prices and to deregulate onshore gas after two years and remove controls on offshore gas after five years. The House bill would lead to $50 billion in new federal energy taxes for conservation and other purposes, with a complicated rebate mechanism. The Senate bill would provide $40 billion in federal tax incentives to encourage conservation and increase energy production, research and development.

The conference committee continued to wrestle with the controversial provisions throughout much of 1978. Conferees did not reach an agreement until October, in the closing hours of the 95th Congress.

The bill enacted by Congress authorized the Federal Energy Regulatory Commission to order transmission services subject to a number of restrictive conditions. FERC would have to find that its order would be in the public interest, would conserve a significant amount of energy, promote the efficient use of facilities and resources, or improve reliability. The commission could not require wheeling if it would place an undue burden on an affected utility, impair reliability, or impair the ability of a utility to adequately serve its customers.

Not satisfied with these conditions, the power companies proposed—and Congress adopted—additional restrictions. First, FERC could not issue a wheeling order unless it first determined that it would "reasonably preserve existing competitive relationships." Second, no utility could be ordered to wheel electricity that would replace electricity provided under an existing contract, or that would replace electricity already provided to the applicant by the utility. And finally, FERC could take no action that would "likely result in a reasonably ascertainable, uncompensated economic loss" for the affected parties.

APPA was sorely disappointed by the final action on wheeling and interconnection provisions. Power granted FERC was rendered relatively inconsequential because the commission's authority was hemmed in by so many limitations.[3]

To reduce demand, the National Energy Act of 1978 required larger electric utilities—those with annual retail sales exceeding 750 million kwh—to make certain conservation services available to their customers. For example, utilities had to offer to inspect residential buildings and identify energy conservation measures. They had to offer to help customers install conservation measures by arranging financing and suppling lists of vendors who could provide these services. Conservation measures listed in the bill included weatherstripping, storm doors and windows, insulation, furnace efficiency devices, thermostats, load management devices, and wind and solar devices.

The law pushed utilities to stop using oil and natural gas for generating electricity. Existing power plants could not use gas after 1990 and, if coal-capable, could be ordered to stop using gas before then. Plants could not increase the proportion of gas to oil that they used from 1974 to 1976, or switch to gas if none were used in 1977.

To stimulate natural gas production, Congress allowed the price of "new" gas to rise immediately from $1.50 per mcf to $2.09 per mcf. Thereafter the price would increase by the rate of inflation plus 3.7 percent in the early years and 4.2 percent in the later years. New gas prices were decontrolled in 1985.

An Energy Department program created by the law encouraged development of small hydro power projects at existing dams not then used for power generation.[4] The law authorized federal loans for up to 90 percent of the costs of feasibility studies and 75 percent of project costs.

•

Passage of the law demonstrated how changing circumstances could quickly make a law irrelevant or inappropriate. While Congress debated the bill, natural gas supplies were short. However, by the time the bill was

---

[3] In the long run, our efforts were not in vain. A decade and a half later, Congress reconsidered the issue in conjunction with adoption of the Energy Policy Act of 1992. Bolstered by support of large industrial customers and growing interest in competition, APPA and its allies succeeded in securing broader wheeling and interconnection authority, similar to that proposed by President Carter.

[4] For the purposes of this legislation, a small hydro power project was defined as one that could be developed at an existing dam site and would have not more than 15 mw of capacity.

enacted, there were reports of a gas "glut." [5] Only a month after the National Energy Act of 1978 became law, Schlesinger, whom President Carter appointed to be the first secretary of energy, said the Department of Energy would urge oil-burning electric utilities and industry to switch to natural gas for the short run because of the nation's huge surplus of gas.

In late February 1979 I appeared on a panel on the PBS television program, the MacNeil/Lehrer report, to discuss the natural gas "glut." I said that if this surplus were to last only for three to four years, as predicted, surplus gas should be sold to utilities rather than to residential customers, because utilities had alternative sources of fuel, whereas residential consumers generally did not have alternate fuel capability.

Troubled by the continued high level of oil imports, President Carter announced early in 1979 that he planned to phase out oil price controls on June 1, as authorized under existing law. To counter this effort, bills were introduced in both houses of Congress to extend mandatory controls for at least two years. Sponsors of the legislation, including Senator Jackson, chairman of the energy committee, said deregulation would have a devastating inflationary effect on the economy by adding multi-billion dollar increases to energy costs.

APPA was one of 117 consumer, labor, public interest and other organizations that formed a coalition opposed to oil price decontrol. Decontrolled oil prices would force public power utilities using oil to increase electric rates. Deregulation also would kick up prices of other fuels, notably coal, resulting in further hikes in power costs, we argued.

Congressional opponents of oil decontrol could not block the president's actions and President Carter deregulated "old" oil on June 1, angering some members of Congress and organizations that had supported him.

In the context of this series of events, the president met with leaders of consumer, environmental and other organizations at the White House early in June. I was one of a dozen people who participated. Reflecting on the event more than two decades later, I found the meeting memorable not for what was accomplished, but for the first-hand impression I gained of President Carter as a person and as a leader.

The president knew our group opposed oil price deregulation. He

---

[5] Embarrassed by the sudden shift in gas supplies from shortages to a "glut," industry sources coined the terms "overdeliverability" or "bubble" to describe the new market situation.

urged us to support other efforts, such as increased conservation and a windfall profits tax on oil companies. Nevertheless, the issue of oil price decontrol arose and several participants voiced their strong opposition in a tone I did not regard as appropriate for the occasion. President Carter listened carefully, was polite, soft-spoken and retained his composure, but did not respond in kind. He merely said he considered his action necessary to induce increased oil production and additional conservation.

As our group left the West Wing, news reporters surrounded us on the White House lawn. I remained in the background during the press conference and struck up a conversation with Betty Furness,[6] former consumer adviser to President Johnson, who had also attended the meeting. Betty and I were both astonished by the contrasts in style between Presidents Johnson and Carter. We agreed that no exchange such as we had just witnessed would have occurred in President Johnson's presence. No one would have had the temerity to speak to President Johnson in the manner in which some of our group had addressed President Carter. If we had raised strong objections to a position he was considering, President Johnson would have expressed his views in no uncertain terms. Betty and I also agreed that President Johnson would have taken advantage of the occasion by giving the group specific marching orders on what to do to advance his position.

Although I admired President Carter for his integrity and dedication to public service and have respected the role he has played since leaving the White House, this experience gave me an insight into an aspect of his leadership style that subsequently contributed to defeat in his reelection campaign.

•

Changing conditions and shortcomings in the National Energy Act of 1978 induced the Carter administration to propose new measures to meet the energy crisis. The administration was alarmed by the continued high level of oil imports and rapidly rising fuels prices, which were contributing to rampant inflation. Borrowing costs rose sharply.

On July 15, 1979, less than a year after adoption of the comprehensive energy legislation of 1978 and after a week of

---

6 A former actress, Furness had gained nationwide recognition for her commercials for Westinghouse consumer products during breaks at nominating conventions of the Democratic and Republican parties in the 1950s. She had an engaging manner of talking about refrigerators and electric ranges while making an appealing "pitch" for the company's products, and became a celebrity in her own right.

contentious debate among his advisers at Camp David, President Carter came off the mountain and again went on national television to propose new energy programs. The president said the energy problem had snowballed because of a "crisis of confidence" that permeated the country.

He proposed an immediate ceiling on oil imports so the United States would never use more foreign oil than it did in 1977. That required utilities to cut oil consumption in half by 1990. Additionally, the president asked for:

- Creation of an Energy Security Corporation to oversee development of synthetic fuels and other sources of energy to replace reduced oil imports;
- Establishment of the nation's first solar bank to help achieve the goal of 20 percent of the nation's energy from solar energy by the end of the century;
- Creation of an Energy Mobilization Board, which would have authority to cut through regulatory delays to expedite completion of energy projects; and
- An accelerated conservation program to involve "every state, county, city and citizen" and requiring stronger conservation efforts and larger public transportation systems.

Congress debated elements of the president's newest energy program for more than a year. At the adjournment of the 96th Congress late in 1980, some portions of the program had been adopted, with changes, while others died. Congress passed the Energy Security Act, which had two major objectives: (1) reducing dependence on foreign oil by stimulating production of synthetic fuels, and (2) promoting renewable energy and conservation. The first goal was to be achieved principally by production of synthetic fuels from coal, shale and tar sands as well as hydrogen from water. Congress authorized a $3 billion "fast start" program of loans and guarantees to initiate development. This would become a standby program once the U.S. Synthetic Fuels Corporation was established. The federally owned corporation would have a 17-year life, during which time it could obligate up to $88 billion in financial assistance. Production goals of 500,000 barrels of crude oil equivalent per day by 1987, increasing to two million barrels per day by 1992, were established. Although Congress approved the legislation, the corporation was never activated. President Carter lost his bid for re-election in 1980 to Ronald Reagan, who opposed government involvement in energy markets.

Congress passed the Crude Oil Windfall Profits Tax Act of 1980, designed to collect $230 billion. Some of that amount would be dispersed in the form of increased tax credits for installing solar, wind or geothermal energy equipment. It provided new credits for cogeneration and ocean thermal equipment and for hydroelectric generating facilities at existing dams with generating capacity of 25 mw or less.

•

The energy legislation adopted during the Carter administration constituted the most comprehensive energy policy in U.S. history. However, the policy failed to achieve its long-term goals of reduced dependence on imported oil, greatly increased conservation and widespread use of alternative or renewable fuels.

Within a decade, natural gas—once considered too short in supply and too valuable for other purposes to be used as a fuel for power plants—became the fuel of choice for electric utilities. Increased quantities of gas were brought to market to meet greater demand of utilities and other users. Utilities valued gas as a power plant fuel because of its clean-burning qualities, efficiency and the lower capital costs and relatively short time frame for installing gas turbines.

The law, together with increased availability of natural gas, did spur reduced utility use of oil. In 1977, 17 percent of all electricity produced in the United States was oil-fired. By 1987, that proportion dropped to 5 percent and to 2 percent by 1997. However, the 1978 law did not reduce overall U.S. reliance on imported oil. OPEC failed to convince its members to limit oil production and the price of foreign oil remained relatively low. By 2001, the United States relied on foreign oil for 60 percent of its domestic requirements, up from 44 percent in 1978.

Chapter 38

The Ups and Downs of Nuclear Power

Undaunted by setbacks in the legislative battle over the 1954 amendments to the Atomic Energy Act and encouraged by optimistic predictions about the future of nuclear energy, APPA continued to press for an opportunity to participate in nuclear power development.

In July 1955, the APPA board of directors voted to establish an Atomic Energy Service. The inauguration of this service, headed by James L. Grahl, ushered in a period of intensive activity by APPA to promote civilian development of nuclear power. First, we attempted to convince AEC of the need to fashion demonstration programs to promote the development of smaller reactors—those having a capacity of about 50 mw or less—which would be most adaptable for use by the majority of APPA member utilities. Second, we intensified efforts to get the federal government to build a few large reactors and thereby bear the substantial risks of demonstrating the economic and technical feasibility of building nuclear power plants.

To accomplish our first objective, we advocated that the commission undertake the responsibility of financing and building reactors on the sites of municipal electric systems or rural electric cooperatives. These utilities would purchase the steam produced by the reactors and use it at the site for driving conventional generating units that the utilities would install. Through this joint effort, small utilities could become knowledgeable about nuclear technology and the integration of such technology in their systems.

As a result of continued prodding from APPA and the National Rural Electric Cooperative Association, AEC offered limited opportunities for smaller utilities to participate in demonstration programs. In response to proposals, AEC selected the municipal utility of Piqua, Ohio, and rural electric cooperatives in Elk River, Minnesota.; Chugach, Alaska, and Big

Rapids, Michigan, for demonstration projects. AEC also approved a proposal by Consumers Public Power District of Nebraska (now known as Nebraska Public Power District) to construct a 75-mw sodium-cooled graphite moderated reactor. Another participant was the Puerto Rico Water Resources Authority (now known as the Puerto Rico Electric Power Authority), which partnered with the AEC to building a nuclear superheated power reactor.

•

Although the demonstration program was useful, APPA and allied organizations felt progress on development of nuclear energy was insufficient. We also believed the government's heavy reliance on the power companies—which received government subsidies for development of nuclear energy—would result in the companies becoming the principal beneficiaries of technological progress supported largely by public funds. We thought the nonprofit segments of the electric industry, as well as the private power companies, should reap the benefits of nuclear energy and that the AEC itself should take the initiative to advance this technology and make it available to all segments of the industry for the benefit of all electric consumers.

Reflecting these and other concerns, Sen. Albert Gore, D-Tenn., and Rep. Chet Holifield, D-Calif., introduced identical bills in 1956 calling for a federal program for the construction of six prototype atomic power reactors in various sections of the country. APPA and other organizations participating in the Electric Consumers Information Committee enthusiastically supported the Gore-Holifield bill. In testimony before the Joint Committee on Atomic Energy (JCAE), Samuel B. Morris, general manager of the Los Angeles Department of Water and Power and chairman of the APPA Atomic Energy Committee, said the issue in atomic energy was not public vs. private power, but rather "whether we as a nation are seriously interested in the vigorous development of economic atomic power." He added that "private and consumer-owned utilities and the federal government all should go ahead with projects."

AEC Chairman Lewis L. Strauss opposed the bill because, he said, it "would divert scarce technical skills from activities [that] promise greater results in subsequent years." Private power companies also opposed the bill, arguing it was unnecessary and would intrude on the role of private enterprise.

Despite strong opposition, the Gore-Holifield bill was favorably reported by the JCAE by a 14-0 vote, and in mid-July 1956 the Senate approved the measure by 49-40. However, the bill was amended considerably before its passage to remove many of the objections of private power companies and other opponents.

Instead of building six large reactors in different geographic regions, the bill approved by the Senate did not specify the number of reactors that would be built. Sen. Clinton P. Anderson, D-N.M., chairman of the JCAE, said the bill envisioned three large prototype reactors to develop 100 mw of electricity or more, plus two smaller reactors.

The bill also was amended to avoid controversy over marketing power that would be produced by the federally owned reactors. Under the Atomic Energy Act, AEC was required to give preference to local public agencies and rural electric cooperatives in the sale of power generated by the commission. To avoid this issue, the Senate provided that the large reactors would be built at AEC's major production facilities, with power to be used by AEC itself.

Although we were disappointed that the bill had been watered down, APPA and our allies were heartened that the measure was still alive. However, Representative Holifield warned that we could expect a tough battle in the House. In addition to the opposition of the Eisenhower administration and power companies, the bill faced a fight from coal companies, who stepped up their campaign after the Senate's action.

The final vote on July 24, 1956 climaxed a hectic seven-hour debate during which the House adopted a series of crippling amendments. Nevertheless, 27 Democrats, mostly from districts with strong coal interests, joined 176 Republicans to defeat the bill by a margin of 203-191. Seventeen Republicans joined 174 Democrats in voting for the measure.

•

The Gore-Holifield bill was the high water mark for efforts to initiate a federal program to build demonstration nuclear power plants. After its defeat, continued efforts were made in behalf of greater federal activity, but they were unsuccessful.

To forestall federal activities, private power companies intensified their efforts to build large nuclear power plants. Recognizing they did not have the resources individually to build large plants, the smaller municipal utilities conceived a plan whereby, as a group, they could buy an ownership share in large plants built by private power companies.

Two test cases initiated in 1967 by groups of municipal utilities in New England and North Carolina were the prelude to the introduction of a bill by Senators George Aiken, R-Vt., and Robert Kennedy, D-N.Y., that would amend the Atomic Energy Act to "insure a reasonable opportunity for all electrical utilities to participate in the benefits of nuclear power and prevent monopoly in the field of electric generation and distribution."

The Aiken-Kennedy bill provided that no electric utility would be granted a nuclear plant license by AEC unless all other interested parties, including public, private and cooperative entities, were offered an opportunity to participate in ownership of the facility. The bill also would require a nuclear license applicant to agree to make the lifetime output of energy from the facility available on "fair and non-discriminatory terms" to all persons. An applicant would be required to build a plant of sufficient capacity to meet reasonable demands of all other electric utilities in the region and to make adequate transmission capacity available to all owner-participants and purchasers of energy.

In May and June 1968, momentum for the bill picked up as hearings were held in the Senate. In my testimony, I pointed out that because of the economics involved, only a few major utilities could afford to construct nuclear plants. Failure to foster joint action, I said, would lead to increased concentration and control of generation.

Robert Gerdes, chairman of Pacific Gas and Electric Company and president of the Edison Electric Institute, testified against the bill. He said it would "open the door to a vast expansion of federal power throughout the United States." He acknowledged that nuclear technology had been developed by federal tax funds, but said this "does not justify preferential treatment of government agencies and cooperatives."

A report by the Justice Department on the Aiken-Kennedy bill charted a new course. The Justice Department said a nuclear power plant designed to produce electricity for wholesale or retail distribution was a commercial operation and the Atomic Energy Act should be amended to recognize this fact. As recipients of commercial licenses for nuclear power plants, power companies would be subject to antitrust scrutiny. The Justice Department also said it should give antitrust advice on any proposed nuclear power plant before a license was issued.

Taking into account the Justice Department's comments, Senator Aiken and others introduced a new bill to require the Atomic Energy Commission, with the advice of the attorney general, to conduct a pre-licensing review of nuclear power plants to determine whether proposed facilities would create or maintain antitrust violations.

In mid-April 1970 the JCAE held hearings on S. 212 and similar bills. APPA Assistant Executive Director Larry Hobart and I testified in favor of the proposed legislation, along with representatives of the National

Rural Electric Cooperative Association, Massachusetts municipal utilities, ElectriCities of North Carolina, Mid-West Electric Consumers Association, AFL-CIO and Consumer Federation of America.

Spokesmen for Southern California Edison Company, Carolina Power & Light Company, Consumers Power Company and other privately owned utilities vehemently opposed the bill. They asked that it be altered so all pending license applications would escape antitrust scrutiny. They also challenged assertions that they should make available to small electric utilities a portion of the ownership or output of nuclear power plants and asked Congress to eliminate from the Atomic Energy Act all preference provisions that gave priority for power output to consumer-owned utilities.

Despite vigorous opposition of the private power companies, the Aiken bill was enacted into law in 1970.

The prelicensing antitrust review worked as intended. As a result of the Justice Department's review, a number of municipal utilities and rural electric cooperatives obtained part ownership of nuclear power plants. This, however, turned out to be a mixed blessing because of the increasing difficulties and rising costs of nuclear power. The consumer-owned utilities became obligated to amortize a portion of the costs of plants that later became uneconomic.

However, the antitrust review had other long-range beneficial effects. The Justice Department uncovered anticompetitive power company activities that were outside of the realm of nuclear power and many of these were corrected.

•

By 1970, serious challenges to nuclear power had emerged. Eugene Water & Electric Board in Oregon was the first public power utility to feel the brunt of opposition. In November 1968, Eugene voters approved issuance of $225 million in bonds to develop nuclear or other thermal facilities, individually or by participating with other utilities. Eugene moved ahead on plans for a 1,000-mw nuclear power plant in which the municipal utility would have 50 percent ownership. Portland General Electric Company would own 30 percent and Pacific Power & Light Company, 20 percent.

Opposition to the nuclear facility mounted, mainly because of a campaign launched by an anti-nuclear group known as the Eugene Future Power Committee, led by faculty and students at the University of Oregon in Eugene. Actions of the Eugene Future Power Committee and its supporters resulted in a vote on May 26, 1970 of 11,750 to 10,892 in favor of a city charter amendment that would prevent the Eugene Water and

Electric Board from spending any funds until January 4, 1974, at the earliest, on the design or construction of the proposed nuclear power plant. In the interim, EWEB could do only ecological, meteorological and siting studies. This was the first step in the ultimate demise of the project.

Meanwhile, national environmental groups intensified their campaign to stop the development of nuclear power. Consumer advocate Ralph Nader and Friends of the Earth filed suit in June 1973 against the Atomic Energy Commission, seeking shutdown of 20 of the nation's large (greater than 400 mw) nuclear power plants in 12 states because of alleged violations of the Atomic Energy Act and safety regulations.

To build public support for his anti-nuclear campaign, Nader in November 1974 sponsored a national "Critical Mass '74" conference in Washington. One speaker at the event, Dr. John Goffman, a medical physics professor at the University of California and outspoken nuclear power critic, called for a moratorium on construction of nuclear power plants. Their continued construction would result in production of "unmanageable" amounts of radioactive fissionable materials, he said. He also warned that terrorists might have access to radioactive wastes from power plants, which he said were already sufficient to permit production of 30 atomic bombs annually.

Subsequent congressional hearings, issuance of reports by scientific groups and other activities drew increasing public attention to issues dealing with the safety of nuclear power.

•

Criticism of nuclear power intensified after March 28, 1979. At about 3 a.m., alarms sounded in the control room of the 880-mw Three Mile Island nuclear power plant near Harrisburg, Pennsylvania, operated by Metropolitan Edison Company. Although there were no injuries or fatalities, for several days residents of the surrounding area were in a high state of anxiety because of the possible danger of a hydrogen gas explosion. No evacuation was ordered, but Pennsylvania Governor Richard Thornburgh advised pregnant women and preschool children within a five-mile radius of the plant to leave the area.

The accident dominated the headlines and news broadcasts for several days and aroused new concerns about the safety of nuclear power. Some anti-nuclear activists advocated the immediate shutdown of all nuclear power plants. For the most part, the reaction of public officials was cautious. President Carter said a shutdown was unthinkable and a number of congressional leaders supported this view. The accident, in fact, pointed up the important role nuclear power played in the U.S. electric industry and in the economy. At that time, nuclear power provided 12.5 percent of the nation's generating capacity, but some regions were far more heavily dependent on nuclear energy. (Wisconsin received 40 percent of its electricity from nuclear energy, the Chicago area 42 percent, and New England 38 percent.)

Although the government did not shut down nuclear power plants, studies of the accident and the lessons learned from it were initiated by a presidential commission, the Nuclear Regulatory Commission, congressional committees, the Electric Power Research Institute and an ad hoc committee of the electric industry.

In early May 1979 the APPA Executive Committee established a new APPA Task Force on Nuclear Policy, adopted a resolution expressing the association's position on Three Mile Island, and supported a proposed technical study of the accident by a newly created Nuclear Safety Analysis Center, under the direction of the Electric Power Research Institute.

The Executive Committee advocated a complete fact-finding investigation of the TMI accident by Congress and the executive branch. It also supported continued operation of existing nuclear power plants and construction of units planned at that time, "with whatever modifications in operation or design are needed in light of Three Mile Island to properly protect workers and the public..."

The most definitive assessment of the accident came from the President's Commission on the Accident at Three Mile Island. Chaired by John G. Kemeny, president of Dartmouth College, the group became known as the Kemeny Commission.

The commission issued its report on November 2, 1979. The fundamental causes of the accident were people-related, not equipment-related, Kemeny said at a press conference. The accident was triggered by an equipment failure, deficient training, inadequate and confusing operating procedures and a control room inadequate for managing an accident. The Kemeny Commission called for a major reorganization of the Nuclear Regulatory Commission from a five-member group to an agency with a single administrator and said the attitude of the nuclear industry toward safety and regulation must change dramatically. It called for establishment of accredited training institutions for operators and their immediate supervisors and said reactor operators should be required to graduate from such institutions. In response to the TMI accident, the nuclear power industry established the Institute for Nuclear Power Operations, a self-policing organization that sets standards and monitors the performance of nuclear power plants.

•

The Tennessee Valley Authority had embarked upon a massive program of planning and constructing 17 nuclear power units. Washington Public Power Supply System planned to build five nuclear power plants in Washington state. Both utilities were harmed by changing conditions that called into question the viability of their large-scale projects.

TVA's nuclear program received its first jolt on March 22, 1975, when a fire in the cable room of the Browns Ferry Nuclear Plant shut down units 1 and 2 for more than a year.[1] Subsequently, falling demand for electricity, sharply escalating construction costs, rising interest rates and construction delays prompted TVA to reconsider its nuclear power efforts. In 1979 TVA deferred construction of four of its 17 units and in March 1982 the TVA board voted to defer construction of three more nuclear units.

By August 1982 TVA had cancelled four units that had been deferred—Hartsville A1 and A2 and Yellow Creek 1 and 2. Studies showed that under the utility's highest load growth assumptions, power from the plants would not be needed until near the end of the century.

"At over $10 billion without interest, the cost of Yellow Creek would be more than we have spent to build the entire TVA power system in operation today, including interest," said TVA Manager of Power Hugh Parris. TVA was looking at alternatives and concluded that by the end of the century, the difference between nuclear and coal-fired generation would be "just too close to call," Parris said.

Cancellation of the four units left TVA with five operating units and four under construction. Subsequently, work was suspended or terminated on the four plants under construction. As of 2002, five TVA nuclear plants, with a capacity of 7,205 mw, were operating.

•

A similar reevaluation occurred in the Pacific Northwest. The Washington Public Power Supply System, a joint action agency, was the center of attention. In April 1969, as electric loads in the Northwest were growing rapidly and the federal government could no longer

---

[1] Because of safety concerns, Browns Ferry 1 was shut down again in March 1985, and it was not until 2002 that the TVA board of directors decided to complete work on that unit. It was expected to go into service again in 2006, when it will add 1,240-mw to TVA's nuclear plant capacity.

supply the increasing demands of the region's utilities, the Joint Power Planning Council[2] agreed on a plan to build seven large thermal generating plants, each having a capacity of at least 1,000 mw. One of the plants was to be a nuclear facility built by the Supply System.

By 1977, WPPSS had embarked on the construction of two additional nuclear plants with financing guaranteed by the Bonneville Power Administration. These plants were referred to as WNP (Washington Nuclear Plants) 1, 2 and 3. Construction of the three plants initially was expected to cost about $6 billion, making their financing program one of the largest of any local public power agency in the United States. In July 1977, WPPSS issued $230 million in bonds, reported at that time to be the largest single competitive municipal bond sale in history. The agency attracted a low 5.713 percent interest rate, thanks to its strong reputation in the bond market and the BPA backing for the bonds. Financing of two additional plants—WNP 4 and 5—was to be backed by commitments from participants in the venture, primarily publicly and cooperatively owned utilities. Although BPA did not back the financing of WNP 4 and 5, the agency strongly supported the need for the plants. In June 1976, BPA Administrator Don Hodel (who later became, successively, secretary of the Departments of Energy and Interior in the Reagan administration) issued a "notice of insufficiency" that said BPA would not guarantee to supply all of the power needs of the region's public and cooperative electric utilities after June 1983. In a letter to the consumer-owned utilities, BPA declared, "Only by utilities signing these agreements [to build WNP 4 and 5] can these generating projects be constructed on the schedule required to meet loads of Northwest utilities after July 1, 1983."

By July 1976, 88 of these utilities responded to a solicitation for WNP 4 and 5 power contracts and committed themselves to purchase the output of the plants.

Within the next few years, a number of events placed the Supply System's nuclear power program in a different light. Anti-nuclear sentiment in the region rose. Costs of construction and financing escalated, resulting in sharp rate increases. Load forecasts declined as economic conditions deteriorated and consumers turned to conservation. While emphasizing that the output of WNP 4 and 5 ultimately would be needed, Robert Ferguson, managing director of the Supply System, in June 1981 recommended a one-year moratorium on construction of the

---

[2] The Joint Power Planning Council consisted of 105 publicly and cooperatively owned utilities, four private power companies, and Bonneville Power Administration.

plants. He noted that a newly completed budget put the cost of completing all five plants at $23.8 billion, compared with an estimate of $6.67 billion when financing for the projects began in the 1970s. With interest rates on tax-exempt municipal bonds rising to 15 percent, Ferguson observed that funding all five projects at nearly $24 billion "presents a very, very difficult problem in today's financial market." Subsequently, the 88 participants in the WPPSS financing agreed to "mothball" plants 4 and 5 for two years.

As electric rates continued to rise under the burden of higher construction and interest costs, a ratepayers' revolt erupted in the service areas of the utilities supporting the nuclear power construction program. Facing increasing financial difficulties and a hostile public environment, the Supply System in 1983 suspended work on two additional nuclear plants. Work continued only on WNP 2, which was 98 percent complete, but the utilities were committed to paying off the debt it had incurred, whether or not the plants were completed.

On June 15, 1983, the Washington State Supreme Court issued a momentous decision affecting WPPSS. The court ruled that the public utility districts and municipalities that had signed contracts to participate in the financing of WNP 4 and 5 had no authority to enter into such contracts. The ruling meant the utilities were not required to make payments to WPPSS for the $2.25 billion in bonds sold to finance construction of WNP 4 and 5.

When the Washington State Supreme Court on July 22 refused to reconsider its June 15 decision, the other shoe dropped. On July 25, 1983, WPPSS defaulted on $2.25 billion in bonds for WNP 4 and 5, creating the largest municipal bond default in U.S. history.

I knew many of the public utility district commissioners who had approved the WPPSS construction program and I felt for them as they agonized over the unfortunate turn of events. Some of the commissioners and managers undoubtedly relished the role of being in the "big time" power arena, and enjoyed being wined and dined by Wall Street bond houses. However, the overwhelming majority of commissioners felt nuclear power was necessary to carry out their responsibilities to provide an ample supply of reasonably priced electricity to the people of their communities. The part-time commissioners were honest, conscientious farmers, ranchers and small businessmen who were dedicated to fulfilling their financial and civic obligations. In their personal lives, they would sacrifice to repay their debts. They did not want to default, but felt they had no alternative in view of the court's decision.

With the benefit of hindsight, it is clear that WPPSS—which had a staff of about 100 people when construction of the first three units began—was not prepared to oversee a massive construction program for a technology that had not yet matured. Like many others, the Supply System had been oversold on the status and promise of nuclear technology. I do not ascribe ulterior motives to Bonneville Power Administration, but I believe the agency was culpable, too, for using a hard sell to persuade the utilities to embark upon the ambitious nuclear power effort.

•

The final national nuclear power issue in which APPA was actively involved before I retired occurred in the 1970s when the Atomic Energy Commission proposed to construct a 300- to 500-mw demonstration breeder reactor.

Milton Shaw, AEC director of reactor development and technology, appeared before the APPA board of directors in late July 1971 to ask for the association's participation in building the breeder, which he said could be completed for $400 million to $500 million. The federal government would contribute $130 million and the utilities $300 million. The utilities' share would include $40 million from the public power sector. AEC would fund basic research, which was estimated to cost about $2.4 billion.

Shaw, who appeared with his trademark briefcase chock full of transparencies to be used in an overhead projector, was a persuasive advocate. He said the breeder, which would produce about 30 percent more nuclear fuel than it consumed, was environmentally the least objectionable method of meeting the nation's future energy supply.

Early development of the breeder, Shaw said, would reduce demand for uranium fuel for conventional light water reactors and, as a result, might curtail the upward price trend for uranium. The breeder also would diminish the need for additional fossil fuel generation.

The APPA board of directors was impressed and voted to participate in the program. To reach the goal of $40 million of voluntary contributions from the public power sector, the board asked the association's members to contribute voluntarily 0.0025 cents per kwh of 1970 retail sales.

All segments of the utility industry heartily endorsed work on the breeder reactor, but the project met early opposition from the environmental community. In October 1971 the Scientists' Institute of Public Information described AEC's environmental defense of the breeder reactor as "superficial, misleading and inadequate." Nevertheless, AEC and the utility industry proceeded with the project. In January 1972 AEC selected a joint proposal by Chicago's Commonwealth Edison Company and the Tennessee Valley Authority to build and operate the breeder. Commonwealth Edison would supply the project manager and manager of engineering and TVA would operate the plant, which would be located in the TVA area. Clinch River, Tennessee, was later selected as the site for the facility and the plant became known as the Clinch River Breeder Reactor.

AEC Chairman Dr. James R. Schlesinger said the plant could be operating by 1980. He called it "our best hope today for meeting the nation's growing demand for economical, clean energy. Because of its highly efficient use of nuclear fuel, the breeder reactor could extend the life of our natural resources from decades to centuries with far less impact on the environment than power plants which are operating today."

AEC officials said the breeder could reduce by 1.2 million tons the amount of uranium required to supply U.S. energy requirements in the next 50 years. Conventional nuclear power plants of that era required 150 tons of uranium annually, but it was estimated that a breeder of the same capacity would use only 1.5 tons.

With the strong support of the Nixon and Ford administrations, work continued on the breeder reactor and ground was broken at the Clinch River site in Tennessee. However, with the election of Jimmy Carter as president, the fortunes of the breeder turned. The breeder required the recycling and reprocessing of plutonium produced in nuclear power plants. President Carter was concerned that reprocessing could result in proliferation of the production of weapons-grade plutonium. Consequently, in April 1977 he announced his decision to "defer indefinitely" commercial reprocessing and said a major project at Barnwell, South Carolina, would "receive neither federal encouragement nor funding for its completion" as a commercial plutonium reprocessing and recycling facility. Construction of the Clinch River project was suspended.

APPA and other segments of the electric utility industry supported retention of the breeder reactor demonstration program. In June 1977 we told the Senate Energy Research and Development Subcommittee that the project would increase the energy derived from potentially recoverable domestic uranium from an estimated 1,800 quads with light water reactors to 130,000 quads with the breeder.

Studies indicated a 1,000-mw coal plant would disturb 28,000 acres of land over its lifetime while a breeder of the same capacity would disturb 640 acres in the same period, we said. A 1,000-mw coal plant would require 25,000 railroad cars per year to supply fuel while the 1,000-mw breeder would require 50 railroad cars per year.

Regarding the nuclear weapons proliferation argument, we said:

> While there is no question that this problem is real, APPA believes that the argument is specious. The nuclear genie is already out of the bottle. Perhaps a dozen countries in the world have the capability of producing nuclear weapons today. This is not 1947, and the U.S. does not possess a nuclear monopoly. What is needed is international control over these materials, not a unilateral moratorium on the Clinch River Breeder.

The battle for appropriations for the Clinch River project continued for several years, but support for the breeder declined as additional problems arose. In July 1981 a report by staff of the House Energy and Commerce Committee pointed out that the cost of the project had risen from $669 million in 1973 to more than $3.2 billion in 1981. The report also complained that the rules for the government's obligation had changed significantly, to the disadvantage of the government. The original government-industry agreement provided for the government to pay $100 million plus no more than 50 percent of the remainder of the project's costs. Subsequently, the agreement was renegotiated, limiting the industry's liability to about $250 million and saddling the government with "an open-ended commitment to pay for the remainder of the project, including cost overruns," the subcommittee staff said.

As new questions were raised about the economics and viability of the project, my attitude toward the project cooled. I was also disillusioned by my experience as a member of the board of directors of the Breeder Reactor Corporation, which was established to oversee the industry's participation in the project. This was my first experience as a member of the board of directors of a private corporation and I was astonished at the manner in which the board operated. Meetings usually were held at a hotel at the Chicago airport, and convened at a noon luncheon. After hearing brief progress reports, members of the board were confronted with a two- or three-inch thick notebook containing various documents, filed under tabs, which required approval. There was obviously no time for board members to read the documents. Instead, a member of the board would call out, "Tab 1," whereupon there was an immediate motion for approval, and the motion was approved by voice vote. This process continued until all of the tabbed items were approved. There was rarely discussion of any of the items, and the entire meeting was usually completed by 2 or 2:30 p.m.

I complained regularly to the chair about not receiving the materials in advance, but to no avail. Apparently, this was the customary means of conducting a corporate board meeting. I fault myself for not being more aggressive in opposing this procedure.

Although Clinch River Breeder Reactor was cancelled in 1979, hopes for Clinch River revived somewhat with the election of Ronald Reagan, who was a strong supporter of nuclear power. A last-minute effort to resuscitate the project came on July 21, 1983, when a group of industry and labor officials met at the White House with the president. I was one of the participants. President Reagan strode into the meeting wearing a light-colored suit and was his customary ebullient self. Even though I was not in his ranks of admirers, it was difficult not to be taken in by his charm. The president read a formal statement expressing support for the project, then shook hands with each person for the customary "photo op." After the meeting, we were treated to an elegant luncheon in the state dining room. Despite President Reagan's support, Congress refused to approve appropriations to continue work on the project.

•

When I retired from APPA on June 30, 1986, the nuclear power program, initially heralded as offering so much promise for mankind, was in disarray. No one talked, except in jest, about nuclear power being too cheap to meter. Not a single order for a new nuclear power plant had been placed since 1978, and no new orders were in prospect.

A combination of factors accounted for nuclear power's disfavor. Economics were probably the single most important element. Construction costs had risen sharply and the long period required for completion magnified the expense of interest during construction.

The lack of standardized designs was a big problem. Other factors contributing to the decline were safety concerns, as demonstrated by the Three Mile Island accident and the subsequent, far more serious, accident at the Chernobyl plant in the Soviet Union in 1986; the greater availability and declining costs of natural gas; and the problem of permanent storage of nuclear waste.

Competition between public and private power played an important role in encouraging utilities to rush prematurely to develop nuclear power. Because the technology was developed by the federal government, power companies feared nuclear power would become a province of public power, with the output of the federal nuclear plants sold on a preferential basis to local public power and rural electric cooperative utilities. Thus, in the minds of private power executives, nuclear power posed an even greater potential threat than the federal hydro power program because the development of nuclear resources was not limited to areas of the country that were susceptible to development of hydroelectric power. I think this fear was misplaced, but it was real in the minds of many leaders of private power companies. They rushed prematurely into nuclear power to prove they were capable of developing the technology and to discredit the need for a federal initiative. The strategy proved self-defeating because it led some power companies to amass huge debts that became stranded investments.

Chapter 39

Assaults on Preference and Other Federal Power Policies

During the last few years before I retired, APPA confronted challenges to fundamental policies the association had espoused for decades. Many of these issues, in which I had personally been involved, centered on the federal power program, which had been the source of reasonably priced wholesale power for more than 600 local publicly owned electric utilities and a like number of rural electric cooperatives.

The Reagan administration wanted to abolish the traditional policy of pricing federal power at cost in favor of selling electricity at market prices, which would have greatly increased federal power rates. The administration also proposed selling the agencies to private companies.

Preference rights of municipal utilities and rural electric cooperatives to purchase federal power were challenged. At the same time, private power companies initiated an aggressive campaign in Congress to take away the preference rights of municipal utilities in obtaining licenses for hydroelectric power projects when existing licenses expired.

Since its inception, the federal power program consistently encountered strong opposition from private power companies. Under federal law, municipal utilities and rural electric cooperatives have preference in purchasing the electricity output of federal dams. When they were unable to change the law, the private power companies sought other means to negate the preference clause. They pushed to have federal power priced at the going rate in the market. Federal law required government-produced power to be sold at cost, on the grounds that the government was generating electricity to provide a public service, not to produce a profit. Supporters of the federal power program also argued that the sale of power at cost-based rates would establish a competitive "yardstick" for the electric industry.

Private utilities contended market rates would provide greater revenues to the federal government. However, their real objective was to deprive preference customers of the benefits of federal power and to eliminate the competitive pressures preference customers exerted by selling electricity at lower rates.

The power companies found a sympathetic ear in William Niskanen, a member of the President's Council of Economic Advisers, who headed an administration group studying the possibility of raising federal power rates. At a meeting with APPA representatives in September 1982, Niskanen acknowledged the administration was considering abandoning cost-based pricing of federal power. He said he was not interested in the historic and statutorily directed method of pricing federal power, but wanted "economic efficiency in allocation of resources."

Congressional delegations from areas served by federal power marketing administrations were irate when they heard of Niskanen's plans. A caucus of about 15 representatives from the Tennessee Valley and the Pacific Northwest, led by Rep. Al Gore Jr., D-Tenn., summoned Niskanen to a hearing before the caucus. In a testy exchange with the caucus, Niskanen accused members of Congress of lying about the administration's study. He said his task force would not recommend "specific changes in rates," but would suggest policy changes. He repeatedly maintained that any changes in policies would require congressional action Niskanen refused to make available copies of the task force's working documents.

To bolster our opposition to a change in pricing policy, I released a study by the APPA staff showing that local public power utilities that purchased federal power from the Tennessee Valley Authority and the power agencies would have increased their rates by $860 million if market prices had been in effect in 1981. The higher rates would have resulted in a 300 to 400 percent increase in wholesale power costs.

As members of APPA and the National Rural Electric Cooperative Association continued to bombard Congress with opposition to a proposed change in federal power marketing policies, high-ranking members of the Reagan administration began to distance themselves from the proposal. In November 1982 Secretary of the Interior James Watt told APPA and NRECA he did not favor raising the rates of federal power marketing agencies. However, he acknowledged there was political pressure within the Reagan administration and in the Congress to drop cost-based rates in favor of "market value" pricing. Budget Director David Stockman also indicated the administration was pulling back on the study. In a letter to 40 members of Congress, Stockman said the administration had suspended work on the pricing studies.

In December 1982, Congress passed an amendment to halt the Reagan administration's attempts to study market pricing or other methods that would deviate from the long-standing cost-based policy. The amendment, attached to an appropriation bill, prohibited the federal government from studying any non-cost-based approach to pricing federal power unless Congress expressly authorized it. Although the spending bill expired at the end of the 1983 fiscal year, the prohibition on pricing studies remained in effect.

•

While we fought market-based rates, we also faced a proposal to sell the five federal power agencies: Bonneville, Western Area, Southeastern, Southwestern and Alaska power administrations. The impetus for this came from a report submitted in July 1983 by the Task Force on Privatization of the President's Private Sector Survey on Cost Control (PPSSCC).

The task force was one of several appointed by the PPSSCC, headed by J. Peter Grace, chairman of W.R. Grace Company The task force estimated sale of the PMAs would yield the federal government $25 billion over five years. Although state and local governments would have the right of first refusal in the sale of federal assets, the task force said the greatest benefits to the federal government would result from sale of the agencies to private power companies or private industry.

"Not only would the federal government be relieved of the operating losses associated with PMA facilities and receive a lump sum purchase price, but any private firms' earnings on such assets would be taxable," the task force said.

In its final report to President Reagan in December 1983, the PPSSCC (known as the Grace Commission) also advocated selling federal power at market rates.

Shortly thereafter, I wrote to President Reagan objecting to the Grace Commission's recommendations. The hydroelectric projects operated by the power agencies "are multipurpose projects, constructed not only to generate electricity but to provide flood control, irrigation, navigation, municipal water supply and recreation," I said. "The federal government can manage these facilities to ensure that there is a reasonable balance among the public purposes to be served. In contrast, if the projects were sold, the purchasing entities would want to maximize power production at the expense of other uses."

Any short-term gain to the government that might result from sale of the projects would be more than offset by the future loss of a revenue-producing asset, I added.

Power generated at federal projects was inexpensive because it had no fuel costs and the projects were built years ago, when construction and financing costs were lower, I said. Power sold at market rates would be based on electricity produced at coal, oil, nuclear and natural gas plants, all more expensive than falling water. Consequently, the market price of federal hydro power would be artificially inflated.

I also pointed out that using the market rate as the standard would increase power rates nationwide, because the low-cost public power yardstick would disappear.

The Reagan administration in February 1986, in the budget proposal for fiscal 1987, released details of its plan to sell the power agencies. The administration said it would send Congress legislation to sell the agencies later that year. The plan envisioned selling the Bonneville and Southwestern power administrations by 1988. The Alaska, Southeastern and Western Area power administrations would be sold by 1991.

The National Governors Association immediately opposed the proposal. In February, the governors adopted a resolution that said sale of the agencies would "seriously jeopardize the economic vitality of individual states, entire regions of the country and the nation as a whole by forcing up electric costs for consumers."

At a press conference in March, I pointed out that federal power customers would pay as much as $12.6 billion more a year for electricity if the agencies were sold to private companies. This increased cost—390 percent—would result if the five agencies were sold for $65.9 billion, as a conservative research group, the Heritage Foundation, had suggested. At the press conference I released findings of an economic study commissioned by APPA, which showed that selling the power agencies would affect more than 265,000 manufacturing, commercial and service businesses in 34 states where federal power was sold. The affected businesses employed 3.2 million people and had annual sales of more than $325 billion.

In May, the House of Representatives adopted an amendment to an appropriations bill that would force DOE to curtail many of its activities aimed at selling the PMAs. The amendment had the bipartisan sponsorship of Representatives Vic Fazio and George Miller (both Democrats from California), Virginia Smith, R-Neb., and Dick Cheney, R-Wyo. The amendment would permit DOE to spend up to $400,000 to prepare proposed legislation enabling investigation of a sale, but it could not expend resources on an implementation plan. The amendment also would prohibit DOE from studying the sale of the Tennessee Valley Authority.

In June, the Senate adopted a more restrictive bill that completely barred the expenditure of funds for such studies. Subsequently, Senate-House conferees agreed on the Senate language and in June 1986, my final month with APPA, the Congress passed the bill, ending efforts to sell the power agencies.

•

Another attack on the preference policy occurred in 1981 in New York state, when John Dyson, chairman of the Power Authority of the State of New York, announced he would ask the state Legislature to create a Residential and Rural Electric Authority (RREA), an agency that would act as a preference claimant for hydroelectric power produced at the St. Lawrence and Niagara power projects. However, the new agency would resell the power to the private power companies, which would distribute it to all of the state's rural and domestic customers.

The New York Municipal Electric Utilities Association (MEUA) immediately attacked PASNY's proposal. James Pullen, general manager of the Jamestown, New York, Board of Public Utilities, called the proposal an attempt to circumvent the federal Niagara Redevelopment Act, which required that 50 percent of the output of the project was to be sold to preference customers.

In a speech at the annual meeting of the New York MEUA in September 1981, I described the Dyson plan as "a conduit to turn over valuable hydroelectric resources to investor-owned utilities." The proposal threatened national power policies, consumer rate stability and continuing competition in the electric utility industry, I said.

In January 1982, 120 representatives of public power utilities in the state went to Albany to tell members of the New York Senate and Assembly that the Dyson plan would harm New York's economy. MEUA President John Gilbert told legislators the proposed RREA could not achieve its stated aims of significant rate relief to private power company customers, aid to industry, protection of municipal electric systems, and reducing dependence on oil. Instead, the proposal would devastate the economies of the municipalities currently served by preference power and would undermine the industrial base and adversely affect the state's economy.

Finding little support in the state Legislature to establish the RREA, Dyson urged individual cities to set up municipal distribution agencies (MDAs) that would apply to PASNY for an allocation of hydro power, which they would distribute through power companies. A number of cities and counties served by private power companies authorized creation of these paper agencies, which would own no distribution facilities.

In January 1985, PASNY announced it would accept applications for power from MDAs in the service territories of three of the state's major power companies. MEUA charged that the PASNY proposal clearly violated an August 1984 ruling by the U.S. Court of Appeals for the Second Circuit, which held that federal preference law applied to municipal and cooperative electric utilities. The association subsequently asked a federal court to enjoin PASNY from allocating hydro power to the municipal distribution agencies.

In March 1985, in a decision hailed by MEUA as a "total victory" for public power, FERC ruled, 4-1, that agencies allocated electricity from PASNY's Niagara Project must distribute electricity to retail customers to qualify as "public bodies" under the Niagara Redevelopment Act. The 2nd Circuit U.S. Court of Appeals upheld FERC's ruling in June 1986.

•

While PASNY was attempting to change power marketing policies by advocating the establishment of paper agencies to act as preference claimants for hydro power, a similar effort was going forward in Utah. In April 1983 Utah Power & Light Company asked the Western Area Power Administration to consider its application for an allocation of power from the Colorado River Storage Project and Hoover Dam, along with requests from preference customers. The company said it would ask the cities it served at retail to apply for hydro power that would be sold to UP&L. In turn, the company would resell the electricity to residential consumers within the boundaries of those cities.

"One group of consumers living, by geographic happenstance, in an area served by a preference entity receives power at very reasonable, if not low, rates, and similar consumers living elsewhere suffer very high and increasing rates," UP&L said.

Robert Partridge, executive vice president of the National Rural Electric Cooperative Association, and I wrote to WAPA Administrator Robert McPhail calling the UP&L proposal a "direct frontal attack on preference" that "seeks to wholly negate a well established and litigated doctrine of federal law and public policy." The preference policy had been enunciated in some 30 separate statutes enacted during the past 77 years, we said.

Removal of the institutional competition in Utah fostered by application of the preference principle would leave UP&L in a position to "institute rate increases and service policies in a freer manner, to the detriment of its own consumers, " APPA said.

The depth of feeling about this issue was demonstrated in October 1983 when WAPA held a public hearing on the UP&L proposal. More than 175 persons—predominantly supporters of consumer-owned electric utilities—testified. APPA Deputy Executive Director Larry Hobart testified that the preference policy rested on five basic concepts:

> (1) Power generated...by the federal government is public property since natural resources...are employed; (2) useful social purposes are served by ensuring that the advantages of public projects flow to electric ratepayers through governmental or other nonprofit institutions rather than through the toll gate of private firms organized to benefit stockholders; (3) the electric industry...best serves the nation if diversity of ownership exists so as to encourage yardstick competition...(4) local governmental and cooperative utilities are in general smaller than privately owned companies, and their reliance on power purchased from private companies should be reduced by making available to them excess power from federal projects; and (5) local control and independence over power distribution is a worthwhile goal which is advanced by access to the electricity sold by federal power marketing agencies...

NRECA Deputy General Manager Charles Robinson cited statistics to demonstrate why availability of low-cost federal power was critically important for rural electric cooperatives. He pointed out that cooperatives in Utah served 3.7 customers per mile of distribution line compared with 32.6 customers per mile for UP&L. Co-op revenues per mile were $5,294 compared with $46,017 for UP&L, and the average investment required to serve each customer in Utah was $3,045 for the co-ops and $1,977 for UP&L.

UP&L attorney Donald Holbrook charged that WAPA's marketing policies to preference customers—which served 23 percent of Utah's population—failed to meet "the most widespread use" requirements of federal law. He said circumstances in the electric industry had changed since preference laws were enacted. Strict regulation and the high cost of power had pushed some private power companies to "hover close to the edge of insolvency."

In September 1984 WAPA turned down UP&L's bid for preference power, saying it was not persuaded by arguments that existing application of the preference laws violated the "widespread use" policy of federal reclamation law or the Constitution. WAPA said it met the widespread use mandates by marketing CRSP power in six states. The marketing policy had been consistently set forth by Congress in an effort to promote "yardstick" competition through sales of federal power, the agency said.

•

Another attack on preference policies during the early 1980s targeted hydroelectric licenses – an issue that probably commanded more of my attention than any other during the last few years of my work at APPA. Under the Federal Water Power Act of 1920, Congress gave preference to municipalities in obtaining an original license for a project. Power companies did not challenge these preference rights. However, as time approached for the expiration of original licenses, heated controversy arose over whether municipalities had preference rights in the issuance of new licenses for those that had expired.

To clarify the preference rights of municipalities in relicensing, the city of Bountiful, Utah, in 1978 filed a petition with FERC asking the commission to issue a declaratory order interpreting the preference clause of the Federal Water Power Act. UP&L's 50-year license for a 2,500-kw hydroelectric project on the Weber River had expired, and both Bountiful and UP&L had filed competing applications for a new license. Subsequently, a similar contest arose between the city of Santa Clara, California, and Pacific Gas & Electric Company, when both filed for new licenses for a project built by PG&E on the Mokelumne River in California. FERC consolidated both cases into a single action. APPA filed a brief supporting the position of Bountiful and Santa Clara.

In August 1979, FERC staff counsel James V. McGettrick filed an initial brief with the commission stating that municipalities had preference in relicensing against original license holders. Pointing to the legislative history of the Federal Water Power Act, he wrote:

> The most important point to be understood from study of the act's historical background is that the act was the culmination of a long struggle by supporters of the conservation movement to protect the interests of the public against what was seen as unbridled exploitation of the nation's water resources for private profit.

In February 1980 FERC held oral argument on the issue of preference in relicensing. APPA General Counsel Northcutt Ely was the lead witness in the day-long hearing. He told the commission a municipality needed only to show that its plan was at least as well adapted to the conservation and utilization in the public interest of the water resources of the region to qualify for preference in licensing.

"Preference is simply a tie breaker. If both plans are equally well adapted, the tie is broken in favor of the preference holder," Ely said. "There is not a word in the statute to support the hypothesis that the original licensee has any priority over an equally qualified plan."

Private power companies argued that an original licensee of a hydro project had priority to renew its license for 50 years. The companies said use of the words "new licensee" in Section 7(a) of the Federal Power Act supported their contention that there was a difference between original and new licensees.

In June 1980 FERC ruled that preference should be accorded to municipalities in relicensing just as in the issuance of an original license. The commission said a public interest test should be considered by FERC, but—all other factors being equal—preference to municipalities should be a "tie-breaker" in granting new licenses for an existing project when there were competing applications by public and private entities.

The FERC decision subsequently was upheld by the 11th Circuit Court of Appeals. In February 1983 several private power companies asked the U.S. Supreme Court to review the appeals court's opinion. Normally, FERC would be expected to oppose such a request, since its original decision had been upheld by the court of appeals. But four new commissioners were appointed to FERC between 1980 and 1983. Their views differed from their predecessors' and the new commissioners asked the U.S. solicitor general to urge the Supreme Court to remand the case for further commission action. The solicitor general, however, advised the Supreme Court that the commission was ready to reverse its earlier decision—without even the benefit of the extensive hearing procedure followed by the previous commission. The solicitor general therefore suggested the case be sent back to the 11th Circuit for further consideration.

On July 6, 1983, the U.S. Supreme Court let stand the September 1982 decision of the U.S. Court of Appeals for the 11th Circuit, which upheld FERC's decision declaring that municipalities had preference in relicensing.

•

While the generic Bountiful case was grinding through the legal mill, FERC was considering the specific application by the public utility districts of Cowlitz and Clark counties, Washington, to take over the expired license for the 136-mw Merwin Dam on the Lewis River. The dam, originally licensed to Pacific Power & Light Company, was in the service area of the two PUDs, which filed an application for the license by creating the Clark-Cowlitz Joint Operating Agency (CCJOA).

The Merwin Dam relicensing application was the first actual relicensing case to come before the commission. FERC hearings on Merwin Dam opened in September 1982 and Clark-Cowlitz supporters were encouraged when the commission's staff filed a brief supporting the PUDs. The staff brief said the commission should issue a license to the PUDs. It also agreed with the PUDs' contention that they should pay PP&L a takeover price based on the power company's original investment of $16.5 million, rather than the $800 million cost of building a new coal-fired plant to replace its lost capacity, as PP&L had requested. The latter point was extremely important to the PUDs. If they had to pay $800 million for the plant, the takeover would not be cost-effective.

Robert McKinney, manager of the Cowlitz County PUD, said PP&L had had the right to operate the project and had earned a profit on it. "Now, it must once again become a public asset," he said.

In September 1983, despite the Supreme Court action to let stand a lower court decision upholding the commission's earlier policy supporting preference on relicensing, a majority of the commission, by a 3-2 vote, reversed FERC's 1980 declaratory order on preference in relicensing. All of those voting for the change were Reagan appointees and were not members of the commission when it issued the original declaratory order. The commission then voted unanimously to award the license for Merwin Dam to PP&L rather than to the PUDs.

In discussion during the meeting, commissioners favoring a change in policy argued that the Federal Power Act was silent on the issue of preference in relicensing, although it clearly provided for preference in original licensing. They also contended that the electric utility industry of the 1910s and 1920s was dominated by holding companies and shareholders and was very different from the industry of the 1980s, which they claimed was tightly regulated.

CCJOA and its supporters then went on a roller coaster ride of appeals. After FERC turned down a request for a rehearing, the CCJOA, joined by APPA and a number of municipal electric utilities, asked the U.S. Court of Appeals for the District of Columbia Circuit to review FERC's decision to reverse its relicensing policy and to award the Merwin Dam license to PP&L. At the same time, Bountiful and Santa Clara asked the U.S. Court of Appeals for the 11th Circuit in Atlanta to enforce its December 6, 1982 judgment upholding FERC's June 1980 declaratory order on preference in relicensing.

The cities charged that the commission—after unsuccessfully seeking

U.S. Supreme Court remand of the 1980 ruling—proceeded to do "precisely what it was denied the authority to do" in a way that demonstrated "either a reckless disregard bordering on contempt" for the court's decision "or an abysmal ignorance of the most basic elements" of the judicial process.

The commission told the 11th Circuit Appeals Court it was not bound by the court's previous ruling because the 1980 FERC ruling was a declaratory order.

Supporters of the CCJOA were jubilant when a three-judge panel of the U.S. Court of Appeals for the District of Columbia Circuit in late October 1985 ruled in favor of CCJOA. The court said the Federal Power Act clearly called for municipal preference in relicensing as well as original licensing, and FERC violated legal principles barring relitigation of issues when, in September 1983 it reversed its policy on preference in relicensing.

Noting that it is "amply evident" that established legal principles barred FERC from relitigating the Bountiful decision, the court said the commission's most recent interpretation of the Federal Power Act "is unsupported by either the statute's language or its legislative history. Even giving FERC the deference normally accorded an agency's interpretation of its governing statute, the commission's proffered reading would have to be rejected."

But CCJOA's elation was short-lived. In January 1986, the full U.S. Court of Appeals for the District of Columbia Circuit voted to reconsider the ruling of its three-member panel. The court acted at the behest of FERC and the Department of Justice, which joined FERC in seeking the rehearing because it was concerned about the language in the panel's decision related to a federal agency's right to reverse itself.

•

While these legal maneuverings were going on, the battle over relicensing policy went before Congress. At the behest of the private power companies, Rep. Richard Shelby, D-Ala.,[1] in November 1983 introduced a bill (H.R. 4402) to amend the Federal Power Act to eliminate preference in relicensing and to direct FERC to issue new licenses to utilities holding existing licenses.

APPA had expected that the power companies would seek legislation as well as FERC action to support their position. We were, however,

---

[1] Rep. Shelby was elected to the U.S. Senate in 1986. He changed his party registration to Republican in 1994.

surprised and dismayed by the extent of the bill's initial support. Forty-four representatives signed on as cosponsors. Having considered ourselves and our allies as representatives of consumers, we found it galling that the power companies, which had drafted the bill, wrapped themselves in the cloak of consumers and titled the bill, "Electric Consumers Protection Act of 1983."

I issued a statement declaring that, if adopted, the bill "would result in a perpetual grant of public resources to private companies" and would constitute "a serious threat to a fundamental public policy regarding use of the nation's resources." I vowed that the association would "oppose the bill with every means at our command."

Thus began one of the most intensive lobbying campaigns in which APPA and its members had ever been involved. Coincidentally, the association's current officers had a special interest in the case. APPA's president was Robert McKinney, general manager of the Cowlitz County PUD, an applicant for the Merwin license. The association's vice president was Gordon Hoyt, general manager of the Anaheim Department of Public Utilities, which, along with other California cities, applied for two of the expiring licenses in California.

A week after the Shelby bill was introduced, three members of the House—Representatives Al Swift and Don Bonker (both D-Wash.), and Albert Gore Jr., D-Tenn.—sent a letter to all members of the House warning that the bill "threatens to rekindle the long dormant public-private power battles." They said the bill was "not a simple proposition, or a minor amendment to existing law," and added:

> Congress struggled with water power legislation for nearly 15 years, spending six years on various bills, which eventually culminated with the passage of the Federal Water Power Act of 1920. An overriding concern throughout this period was that private parties not be granted a right in perpetuity to control, use and profit from this public water resource. In stark contrast, H.R. 4402 would result in a perpetual grant to private parties.

Representative Gore also introduced a separate bill, titled "Electric Utility Competition Act of 1984," which would extend preference in relicensing to rural electric cooperatives. It would also require the Justice Department to conduct an antitrust review of a utility at the time of a

---

[2] Sen. Howard Metzenbaum, D-Ohio, later said on the floor of the Senate that the bill should have been called the "Private Utility Protection Act."

project relicensing. APPA and NRECA supported the Gore bill.

In intense lobbying campaigns, one of the first objectives of each side is to line up allies. The power companies scored early on this front when the influential National Association of Regulatory Utility Commissioners adopted a resolution generally supporting their position, both in relicensing and in the method of calculating compensation for a project that was to be relicensed to another party. NARUC expressed concern that the "millions of customers" of private utilities "would incur higher electric rates for the sake of far fewer state or municipal electric customers if the utilities were forced to transfer their hydroelectric projects to these preference entities under a possible interpretation of the Federal Power Act."

APPA needed not only to build alliances with other organizations, but also to shore up support within the association's membership. Far more members were affected by preference in marketing federally produced power than preference in relicensing. They felt the association should not expend its resources on the relicensing issue, but instead should save its ammunition for a battle on preference in power marketing.

To counter this concern, I said, at a meeting of the Mid-West Electric Consumers Association in December 1983, that attacks on preference in relicensing were part of a "larger-scale battle against the entire preference concept, including preference in federal power marketing."

> These issues go to the heart of fundamental principles in the access and distribution of benefits from development of public resources. If we fail to make a strong defense of preference in relicensing I believe we invite further incursions on the principle of preference in power marketing.

The pace of the legislative battle accelerated in 1984 with the announcement that hearings would be held on the Shelby bill in mid-May before the House Commerce Committee's Conservation and Power Subcommittee. In anticipation of the hearings, 14 public power, rural electric cooperative, consumer, environmental and labor organizations held a press conference on May 9, 1984 to announce their opposition to the Shelby bill.

At a news conference, the organizations said they would mount a nationwide campaign to show that the proposed legislation was "not in the public interest, not in the consumer interest, against competition in the electric power marketplace, and not in the interest of environmental protection or the proper management and use of public resources."

The hearing on May 17 was a tense occasion, given the sharply opposing views of the contesting parties. The hearing room was crowded to overflowing with witnesses, a myriad of lobbyists, and observers. Present were officers of some of the nation's largest power companies, as well as officials of APPA and representatives of other public power, consumer, labor and environmental groups.

Because APPA and its members took a leading position on the issue, I was one of the principal witnesses. The Shelby bill would give investor-owned power companies a perpetual right to use and profit from public waterways, I said. "The well-documented benefits of competition in relicensing—yielding plans to increase project capacity and improve environmental and recreational attributes associated with the project—will be foregone."

Robert McKinney testified that CCJOA's efforts in the Merwin application demonstrated that existing law provided sufficient incentive to promote licensing competition and that further legislation was not needed.

> Surely without the [Federal Power] Act's preference, it is unrealistic to expect that CCJOA or any other municipality could responsibly spend public money on relicensings. Yet the act is not overly one-sided in favor of public licensings. Preference alone does not bring forward a competing municipality but rather a municipality's belief that it can satisfy the act's requirement to develop and utilize the water resources in the best interest of the region.

Gordon Hoyt told the subcommittee the Anaheim Department of Public Utilities had joined in filing competing applications for the Rock Creek Cresta and Haas-Kings River projects, both of which had been previously licensed to PG&E. Even though FERC had not yet set either of these proceedings for hearings, relicensing competition, or the threat of it, had already prompted PG&E to propose improvements that would benefit all consumers, regardless of the final outcome of the case. Power potential would be upgraded by 51 percent, and improvements would be made in water quality and environmental and recreational facilities.

PG&E Chairman Fred Mielke said Santa Clara bought almost half of its wholesale power from PG&E and therefore, along with PG&E's retail customers, benefited from fuel savings made possible by the company's Mokelumne project. The city also purchased more than half of its wholesale power from federal hydro projects. Consequently, he said, the city's 40,000 customers enjoyed much lower rates than PG&E's customers, along with higher levels of lower cost hydro power factored into their electric bills.

"Nonetheless, the city of Santa Clara claims it should have 'preference' for the project over PG&E and its customers. We believe there is absolutely no justification for such a position," Mielke said.

At a subsequent House hearing, Santa Clara City Manager Donald R. Von Raesfeld said PG&E initially proposed no new or additional development in its application for a second license for the Mokelumne project. However, as a result of Santa Clara's competing application, the company belatedly proposed project improvements. This change was a direct result of competition, Von Raesfeld observed.

•

After the House hearings, two anti-preference bills were introduced in the Senate. Sen. Malcolm Wallop, R-Wyo., and 10 cosponsors offered a bill similar to Shelby's that would eliminate municipal preference and require that any licensee that lost a license be "justly compensated by the new licensee." Sen. Bennett Johnston, D-La., introduced a bill to eliminate preference but leave intact compensation provisions of existing law, which provided that a licensee be paid a sum equal to its net investment in the project if the license were transferred to another party. Congress took no action on relicensing in 1984 and the bills were introduced again in 1985.

Environmental consequences of hydroelectric licensing and production entered the legislative debate in 1985 and dominated discussion at a June hearing of the House Subcommittee on Energy and Power. William Knapp of the U.S. Fish and Wildlife Service told the panel competition for licenses would enhance the quality of environmental improvements. Russell Shay of the Sierra Club agreed.

Asked by Rep. Michael Bilirakis, R-Fla., why he favored municipal preference when the concept of preference appeared to be inconsistent with competition, Shay said experience had shown that competition existed only when there was municipal preference.

The hearing was the prelude to increasingly aggressive demands by environmental groups to incorporate provisions in the pending legislation to give more recognition to environmental factors in the issuance of licenses for hydroelectric power projects.

•

The first congressional committee vote on relicensing occurred on October 2, 1985, when the Senate Energy and Natural Resources

Committee adopted a bill eliminating public preference in relicensing and establishing a preference for original licensees. The bill approved by the Senate committee made it clear FERC must consider fish and wildlife mitigation and enhancement as well as irrigation, flood control and water supply matters in evaluating the public interest standard in both licensing and relicensing proceedings. The bill also established economic criteria that would skew decisions for a new license in favor of large power companies. Sen. Howard Metzenbaum, D-Ohio, who had asserted that preference was essential for preserving competition, cast the lone dissenting vote on the committee.

I issued a statement expressing disappointment that the committee had not supported preference or other public interest provisions, such as access to wheeling and antitrust review.

Our disappointment turned to jubilation on October 22, 1985, when the three-judge panel of the D.C. Circuit Court of Appeals ruled that the Federal Power Act clearly called for municipal preference in relicensing. After the decision was announced, I said the court's action in the Merwin Dam case placed congressional consideration of this issue in an entirely different perspective. To counter the power companies' contention that existing law was ambiguous, I said, "That argument — which was used to cloak their goal of obtaining perpetual licenses to public resources — no longer has validity."

Anticipating a markup soon on the Shelby bill by the House Energy Conservation and Power Subcommittee, I sent a letter to all members of the subcommittee pointing out that the Appeals Court's opinion undermined the power companies' arguments that they were "vested with a right to enjoy and profit from this public resource in perpetuity."

I also observed that the power companies had grossly exaggerated the extent and the cost to consumers of a change in licenses. The cost would not amount to the billions of dollars claimed by the investor-owned utilities. Furthermore, any costs would be more than offset by the public benefits that would be achieved by encouraging greater competition in the electric utility industry.

Although the House Energy and Power Subcommittee was due to mark up the Shelby bill in late November, action was stalled because of negotiations between the CCJOA and Pacific Power & Light Company over the Merwin Dam license. The Court of Appeals' decision opened an opportunity for a compromise over the competing license applications for the dam, and the subcommittee was prepared to endorse in legislation whatever agreement the utilities reached. However, as Congress neared adjournment, no settlement had been worked out and the subcommittee postponed action until 1986.

•

In January 1986, the situation took an unexpected turn when the full D.C. Circuit reversed the three-judge panel, vacating the October ruling. We were stunned by the court's action. PP&L suspended negotiations with the CCJOA. On January 29, 1986, the House Energy Conservation and Power Subcommittee approved the Shelby bill. It left to the courts the disposition of the license to the Merwin Dam project, which was to be treated according to existing law. Nine other pending competitive license applications involving contests between publicly and privately owned utilities would be subject to the bill's provisions eliminating preference.

By April, it had become obvious that the power companies had a steamroller moving the bill. The measure went to the Senate floor on April 11. Although proponents had the necessary votes to pass the bill, opponents put up a valiant fight and the debate at times became acrimonious.

•

Senator Johnston, a major advocate of the bill, was especially upset by the efforts of Sen. John Melcher. D-Mont., to amend the bill in order to improve small utility access to wheeling of electric power. Over a three-day period, Senator Melcher offered a series of amendments dealing with wheeling rights, thereby delaying a vote on passage of the bill.

However, with the exception of a relatively minor amendment having to do with a utility's application for a wheeling order, all of Senator Melcher's proposals were defeated. Nevertheless, in the face of the obvious hostility of the bill's proponents, Senator Melcher plodded ahead in what was described as a "mini-filibuster" that infuriated Senator Johnston.

On April 17, the Senate approved the bill by a vote of 83-14, and four days later the companion House bill was approved by voice vote. Unlike the experience in the Senate, where debate continued during four days, the House debated and voted on the bill during a single afternoon.

Both the House and the Senate removed the preference for public agencies in relicensing. However, the Senate substituted a preference for the incumbent licensee, while the House rejected an explicit preference for existing licensees, and instead provided that licenses should be awarded after a competitive process based on a public interest standard. The House also did not incorporate economic impact criteria biased toward large private utilities, such as those included in the Senate bill. The House bill had no comparable provisions.

•

The actions in April virtually ended my involvement in relicensing legislation. I retired on June 30, 1986, and conferees who would work out differences between the Senate and House bills were not named until late June.

I was saddened that APPA and its members had lost the last major congressional battle fought during my watch. However, it was apparent from the beginning that we were waging an uphill battle. Nevertheless, we thought the fight had to be made on the grounds of the broad public interest and, more specifically, in the interests of APPA members.

Our campaign was handicapped by the fact that relicensing applied directly to a relatively small segment of the APPA membership. We emphasized that the contest over relicensing preference threatened to be a prelude to an effort to do away with preference in marketing federal power. Although many APPA members understood and appreciated this threat, it did not activate a sufficient number to become involved in the legislative effort.

The congressional battle also demonstrated that in a major contest, the power companies could amass lobbying, public relations and other resources that overwhelmed what we had to offer.

Nevertheless, the intensive fight that APPA made in behalf of relicensing preference played an important role in bringing about a more public interest orientation in the bill that was enacted. Without APPA's efforts, the legislation would likely have contained a preference for incumbent licensees. Although the measure signed into law was skewed in favor of existing licensees, it did not provide for an outright preference to the incumbents and it required FERC to take public interest considerations into account in awarding a license.

The controversy over APPA's fight to preserve preference also gave environmental groups more political leverage than they otherwise would have had to obtain support for their amendments.

Finally, APPA's efforts were worthwhile because they sent a strong signal to Congress and the power companies of the magnitude of the battle they would face if an effort were made to eliminate preference in federal power marketing. Even Senator Johnston declared on the floor of the Senate that no one should make the mistake of thinking that the relicensing bill was "the first step toward privatizing the federal power marketing administrations, for example, or doing away with the power marketing preference enjoyed by public power. I certainly would oppose any such effort."

Other senators and representatives offered similar assurances.

•

Congress finally passed the relicensing legislation and it was signed into law on October 16, 1986. As finally agreed upon by Senate-House conferees, the bill removed the preference to public agencies in relicensing, but did not disturb preference in original licensing, which was never at issue.

There has not been a single contested application for relicensing since the bill was passed. When the bill was being considered by Congress, competitive proposals had been filed for 10 relicensing applications.

The Merwin Dam case, one of the principal factors that instigated the congressional fight on relicensing, was not resolved until almost two years later. On August 11, 1987, by a 4-3 vote, the full U.S. Court of Appeals for the District of Columbia Circuit ruled that FERC acted lawfully when, in September 1983, it reversed a 1980 interpretation of the preference rights of municipalities in relicensing hydroelectric projects and awarded a license for the dam to PP&L.

The majority opinion was written by Judge Kenneth Starr (who later served as special prosecutor in high profile cases involving President Clinton). Starr said the CCJOA's challenge to FERC's earlier interpretation of the Federal Power Act "involves fundamental issues of the power of an administrative agency to change its interpretation of law and to take regulatory action based upon that new interpretation." The agency has that right and the commission's latest interpretation was reasonable, the court majority held.

In November 1987 the CCJOA asked the U.S. Supreme Court to review and reverse the Circuit Court of Appeals' ruling that the license for the Merwin Dam project should be awarded to PP&L, but on February 29, 1988 the high court declined to review the appeal.

"The process has run its course. It's over," said Cowlitz County Public Utility District General Manager Robert McKinney when informed of the Supreme Court's action. "I think we served the public interest in pursuing this. That project is better today due to competition. We solved fish, flood and wildlife problems at Merwin Dam. We did what we could within the limits of a public agency."

Chapter 40

Working As A Consultant

After retiring from APPA, I opened an office as a consultant. My major clients were two regional associations—the Tennessee Valley Public Power Association and the Northwest Public Power Association—and a state association, the Washington Public Utility Districts Association. I also chaired advisory committees of the Consumer Energy Council of America, headed a federal commission on nuclear waste and handled special projects for individual publicly and cooperatively owned utilities.

My first assignment for TVPPA was to evaluate and make recommendations on the governing structure of the Tennessee Valley Authority. In the late 1980s, TVA's nuclear power program was in disarray and was subject to a great deal of criticism.

Caught up in the post-World War II enthusiasm for the promise of nuclear power and desirous of freeing itself from increasing dependence on coal-fired energy, TVA in the 1960s and early 1970s had embarked on an overly ambitious scheme to build 17 nuclear power plants. By 1986, eight of these units had been cancelled, four were still under construction, and five operating reactors had been shut down for major repairs and modifications.

The nuclear plant debacle raised questions about the management and governance of the agency. In response, Rep. Ronnie Flippo, D-Ala., proposed legislation to restructure the TVA board of directors, which consists of three full-time directors responsible for policy and management. No regional representation is required in the appointment of directors. Each director is named by the president, subject to Senate confirmation, and serves a nine-year term.

The federal pay cap was another major problem for the agency. The cap greatly limited TVA's ability to pay the salaries required to attract highly specialized nuclear engineers.

Representative Flippo proposed the establishment of a nine-member board of directors, which would be responsible for policy-making, not day-to-day management. Eight directors would be appointed by the president, subject to Senate confirmation. They would serve three-year terms, part-time, and would be selected from the seven states that comprise the Tennessee Valley. The eight presidential appointees would select a CEO who would serve ex officio as a member of the board and whose compensation would be determined by the board of directors.

TVPPA asked me to review this legislation and recommend a position on it. I raised questions about some features of Representative Flippo's bill, but I agreed with his conclusion that the existing three-person, full-time board of directors was not in the best interests of TVA or its power distributors.

Like Representative Flippo, I recommended splitting the agency's policy- making and management responsibilities. Policies would be determined by a part-time board consisting of 11 members, of whom eight would be selected from the states in the Tennessee Valley. However, I proposed that three board members come from outside the Tennessee Valley, to reflect the national interest in TVA, since it is a federal agency. Management would be turned over to a full-time chief executive officer appointed by and responsible to the board of directors. However, unlike the Flippo proposal, the CEO would not serve as a member of the board.

Although I felt restructuring the board of directors would be desirable, I did not recommend that this step be taken immediately because it could distract TVA's attention from pressing problems involving its nuclear power program. Furthermore, I did not believe Congress could pass a bill that could be implemented in time to be helpful in the immediate future.

In developing my report, I worked closely with a special TVPPA committee and the association's executive director and I felt they supported my recommendations. However, I did not take into account the influence of the TVA board of directors on the distributors who comprised TVPPA's membership. Even though I did not recommend immediate action on Flippo's proposal, the TVA board was concerned about congressional consideration of any important changes to the TVA Act at a time when the utility was subject to so much criticism because of its nuclear power program. Also, the board did not want to be relegated to a part-time status without any executive responsibilities.

Members of the TVA board used their influence with TVPPA members, and especially the then-president of the association. When my report was submitted to the TVPPA board of directors, it was merely accepted without any recommendation for action and I was discharged for a time from any further responsibilities with TVPPA.

Nevertheless, congressional sentiment grew for restructuring the TVA board. After I completed the report, a congressional subcommittee held hearings on restructuring TVA and the municipal utilities of Memphis and Nashville engaged me to testify on their behalf in favor of the proposal. Again, the TVA board exerted its influence. Immediately before I was to testify, a member of the board persuaded Rep. Jamie Whitten, D-Miss., powerful chairman of the House Appropriations Committee, to appear ahead of me. His objections to the proposal killed any further action by the subcommittee.

Criticism of TVA continued. Because of the disarray of the nuclear program and concern about TVA's large debt, the Southern States Energy Board, chaired by Virginia Gov. Gerald Baliles, created an Advisory Committee on TVA to look into the agency's problems and recommend remedial actions. TVA supporters viewed the advisory committee with skepticism. The CEO of Virginia Power Company had been sharply critical of the federal utility. Friends of TVA thought Governor Baliles might use the committee to initiate a vendetta against TVA and urge privatization of the agency. However, Governor Baliles appointed a broad spectrum of prominent people involved in the electric utility industry, as well as academicians, businessmen, former government officials and an official of the Consumer Federation of America. I was appointed to the committee, as was Michael Browder, general manager of the Bristol Tennessee Electric System.

The 16-member committee held its first meeting in Knoxville, Tennessee, where TVA is headquartered, on January 5 and 6, 1987. Sen. Albert Gore Jr., D-Tenn., spoke at the opening session and sent a shot across the bow. While acknowledging that TVA faced serious problems, he recounted the agency's contributions to the region and the nation and warned the committee: "TVA is not for sale and never will be…Privatization is a political idea, not an economic one."

The committee was divided into three subcommittees. I was assigned to the Organization and Management Subcommittee, chaired by Fred Smith, chairman and CEO of Federal Express, which is headquartered in Memphis. A copy of my 1986 report to TVPPA on the reorganization of TVA's policy-making and management structure was distributed to each member of the subcommittee. The subcommittee—and ultimately the full committee—adopted recommendations that largely paralleled those that

Representative Flippo and I had proposed. The committee advocated the establishment of a larger board, consisting of nine part-time directors who would be appointed by the president and confirmed by the Senate. They would be responsible for policy-making and oversight of TVA's management, but day-to-day management would be vested in the CEO, who would be appointed by the board.

The report also advocated elimination of TVA's statutory pay cap, which, it said, "has made it virtually impossible for TVA to compete for and retain needed managers and specialized technical personnel, especially for the nuclear power program."

The report received wide publicity, but Congress did not act upon it. However, in 1997, Sen. Bill Frist, R-Tenn., introduced a bill patterned largely after the recommendations of the decade-old Southern States Energy Board report. Senator Frist's bill attracted considerable support, including endorsement by *The Chattanooga Times*, but the TVA board of directors continued to oppose the concept and Congress took no action on the bill.

Although I do not believe organizational structure is the answer to all problems, I continue to feel a change such as that proposed by Representative Flippo, Southern States Energy Board and Senator Frist would be desirable. As *The Chattanooga Times* pointed out in an editorial on October 13, 1997, the "TVA chairman, with varying participation by his two colleagues, makes policy decisions, runs the agency as a super-CEO and functions as the agency's own regulatory overseer." The editorial continued:

> The lack of insulation between policy and management has gotten TVA into much trouble. Many missteps could have been avoided if decision-making had involved a wider, collaborative effort and real separation of power.

•

Another of my most challenging assignments as a consultant was my appointment as a member of the Monitored Retrievable Storage (MRS) Review Commission.

In response to increasing public concern about the disposition of the growing volume of nuclear waste from the nation's nuclear power plants, Congress passed the Nuclear Waste Policy Act of 1982. The legislation favored geologic disposal for the permanent storage of nuclear waste and established a procedure for siting, constructing and operating two permanent geologic repositories. The act also directed DOE to study the need for and feasibility of a monitored retrievable storage facility, as well as a proposal for constructing one or more MRS facilities for temporary storage of nuclear waste.

Both aspects of the program—the geologic repositories and the MRS facility—were highly controversial. A site near Oak Ridge, Tennessee, was selected for an MRS, but met strenuous opposition from the state of Tennessee and local residents. Aside from objections to the location, opponents argued that an MRS, once built, would become a *de facto* permanent repository and would take the pressure off the government to build a geologic repository for permanent storage of spent nuclear fuel.

It became apparent that the 1982 plan would not work, so Congress revisited the issue and adopted the Nuclear Waste Policy Amendments Act (NWPAA) of 1987. At that time, about 20,000 metric tons of commercial spent nuclear fuel were stored at more than 70 nuclear plant sites. It was expected that existing nuclear plants would produce approximately 87,000 metric tons of spent fuel during their lifetimes.

NWPAA designated Yucca Mountain, Nevada, as the sole candidate site for a permanent repository for nuclear waste and it was expected that the necessary approvals could be obtained so the repository would be ready to accept waste by 1998. That date was later pushed back to 2003, then to 2010. By 2002, some observers predicted that even the 2010 date was too optimistic. The Yucca Mountain facility faces the daunting task of isolating radioactive waste from the environment for 10,000 years—longer than recorded history.

To defuse the controversy over the MRS, the NWPAA "annulled and revoked" the plan to build the facility at Oak Ridge, Tenn., and created the Monitored Retrievable Storage Review Commission to study and report on whether an MRS should be a part of the nation's nuclear waste disposal system. The NWPAA authorized construction of an MRS, but directed DOE to delay site surveys until after the MRS Review Commission had submitted its report.

In further efforts to respond to critics, the NWPAA contained several other limitations on the MRS. It stipulated that construction of an MRS could not begin until the Nuclear Regulatory Commission issued a license for a repository. The practical effect of this condition was to make it impossible for an MRS to be operational for more than three years before the opening of the repository. Another limitation restricted the amount of nuclear waste that could be contained in the MRS to a quantity that was far short of what was needed for a permanent repository.

Congress gave the speaker of the House of Representatives and the president pro tempore of the Senate power to appoint the three members of the commission. To my surprise, Rep. Morris Udall, D-Ariz., whom I had known and worked with since he came to the Congress in 1961, nominated me to serve as one of the three commissioners. I had no expertise in the field of nuclear waste and therefore felt reluctant about accepting the assignment. However, recognizing that it would be an interesting learning experience, I accepted. Dr. Victor Galinsky, a former member of the Nuclear Regulatory Commission and former head of the Physical Sciences Department of the Rand Corporation, and Dr. Frank Parker, professor of environmental and water resource engineering at Vanderbilt University, were also named to the commission.

After the appointments were announced, the commissioners met to discuss how we would proceed. We quickly selected Galinsky as chairman. However, a few weeks later, Galinsky, without conferring with Parker or me, withdrew from the commission, for reasons that were not made entirely clear. He had considerable experience in nuclear energy and I was greatly disappointed at his decision.

After a delay of a month or more, Dr. Dale Klein, an associate professor of nuclear engineering at the University of Texas, was appointed to fill the vacancy. Klein was well qualified to be a member of the commission, not only because of his background in nuclear engineering, but also because of his research in thermal analysis of nuclear shipping containers.

Galinsky's withdrawal and bureaucratic problems caused a six-month delay in getting the work of the commission under way. Galinsky's departure required election of a new chairman. After several weeks' delay, the commissioners agreed upon me as the chairman. I was reticent about accepting this responsibility, mainly because of my lack of technical expertise. On the other hand, the decisions we were to make had a significant political component and I recognized the value of my experience in dealing with the Washington bureaucracy and in managing an organization. The commissioners were sworn in on June 14, 1988 in the offices of House Speaker Jim Wright, D-Texas. We assembled a small, capable staff and contracted out various studies, but adopted a hands-on approach. We acted as a collegial body, met approximately every two weeks and gathered information in the interim. We held public hearings in four cities and met with officials in Sweden, Switzerland, France and the Federal Republic of Germany about the methods they were employing for both interim and permanent storage of nuclear waste.[1]

For almost a year the commission conducted public hearings and compiled information. We discussed the findings of our staff and consultants, but kept an open mind. Once we completed this intensive study phase, the commission and key staff members held a retreat near Charlottesville, Virginia, to make decisions. It soon became apparent that there were differences of views of members of the commission. Klein felt strongly about the advantages of an MRS. Parker, too, believed there was merit in an MRS, but that interim storage facilities of a more limited size and purpose would be more appropriate (and doable) at that time. For safety and economic reasons, I felt an MRS could not be justified. I also was sympathetic to the argument that building a full-scale MRS removed pressure to build a permanent repository.

We all agreed on one conclusion: that linking construction of a monitored retrievable storage facility to construction of a repository—as proposed by DOE and required by the NWPAA—could not be justified. Under such limitations, an MRS could not be operational for more than three years prior to the opening of the repository. Hence, its value would be greatly diminished.

As chairman, I felt strongly that the commission should make every effort to reach a consensus. The other commissioners agreed.

At our retreat, we agreed on five conclusions. First, from a technical perspective, both the MRS and the no-MRS options were safe, although neither was completely without risk. In the absence of an MRS, utilities could store nuclear waste on-site in above-ground casks when they had used all available space in the "swimming pools" in which they had stored waste. Such casks were already commercially available and we visited sites where they were used. The dry casks were considered to be safe for 100 years.

Second, we concluded an MRS would be more costly than a system without an MRS, although the economics would become more favorable if the repository were delayed and the MRS could accept spent fuel as soon as possible.

Third, no single discriminating factor would favor the MRS over the no-MRS option, but, cumulatively, there were a number of advantages to a central storage facility. These advantages, however, were predicated on

---

[1] An independent study of eight other countries conducted for the commission showed that all ultimately planned permanent storage in a geologic repository, but at a later date than that anticipated by the United States for its repository.

an MRS that was not limited in size nor linked to the repository schedule.

Fourth, we agreed that an MRS with the limitations imposed by current law could not be justified. If the opening of the repository were delayed beyond 2003, the date then projected by DOE, most nuclear utilities would have to make other arrangements for temporary storage, obviating the need for an MRS.

Fifth, we decided some interim storage facilities, substantially more limited in capacity and built under different conditions than the MRS, would provide for emergencies and other contingencies.

These conclusions led us to make three recommendations. First, we said Congress should authorize construction of a federal emergency storage facility with a capacity limit of 2,000 metric tons of uranium. Such a plant would serve as "a safety net of storage capacity for emergency purposes," we said in our report. The emergency storage facility could be used for decontamination of affected parts of reactors and for storage of debris.

Second, we recommended that Congress authorize construction of a user-funded interim storage facility with a capacity of 5,000 metric tons of uranium. This could be used by utilities that lacked space for life-of-plant storage as well as utilities unable to obtain a license for additional storage. The facility also could provide storage for spent fuel retained at sites where utilities no longer operated nuclear power plants.

Finally, we recommended Congress reconsider the subject of interim storage by the year 2000, to address uncertainties that existed when our report was prepared and to evaluate the performance of the two facilities we recommended.

Our recommendations were a compromise. We did not support an MRS of the scale proposed by DOE, nor did we advocate a strictly no-MRS option. Instead, we supported two limited-capacity facilities that would provide for emergencies or other immediate needs for interim storage. This was as far as we could go in light of the statutory linkages between the MRS and the permanent nuclear waste repository and the fact that we could not demonstrate an urgent need for a full-scale MRS at that time, based on safety or economic considerations. Like most compromises, our proposals satisfied neither proponents nor opponents.

On November 1, 1989, the day our report was released and a day before a scheduled hearing on the report by the Senate Committee on Energy and Natural Resources, members of the commission briefed some of the principals involved in this issue. Because the Tennessee congressional delegation had so vehemently opposed the location of an

MRS at Oak Ridge, we first met with Sen. Al Gore Jr., D-Tenn., and Craven Crowell,[2] chief of staff for Sen. Jim Sasser, D-Tenn. Because Parker was from Vanderbilt University, in Senator Gore's home state, we asked him to take the lead in the presentation.

Despite the fact that we did not recommend a full-fledged MRS and supported facilities for severely limited purposes, Senator Gore was hostile to our recommendations and minced no words in expressing his displeasure at our responses to his sharp interrogation. He made it abundantly clear he opposed *any* interim storage facilities. Later that day, Senators Gore and Sasser issued a joint press release highly critical of our report.

We were scheduled to meet that day with Sen. J. Bennett Johnston, D-La., chairman of the Senate Energy and Natural Resources Committee. However, at the last minute, Senator Johnston was detained because of a highly controversial issue pending on the Senate floor. We met instead with members of the committee's staff.

Our inability to meet with Senator Johnston proved crucial to the proceedings the following morning before the Senate committee. Senator Johnston was a strong advocate of an MRS and he dismissed our recommendations for the limited storage facilities and the problems we had in justifying an MRS in view of the statutory linkage with the permanent waste repository. He gave us a hard time. Had we been able to meet privately with him in advance, as we had planned, we might have allayed some of his concerns. As it was, the negative reaction we received at the hearing, plus the opposition of Senators Sasser and Gore, sealed the doom of our report. We received some support from electric utilities, but their enthusiasm was dampened by our recommendation against building an MRS. Environmental groups, too, were unhappy, because they felt our advocacy of the limited storage facilities would open the door later to a full-scale MRS.

Although my fellow commissioners and I were disappointed at the response to our work, I did not regret spending time on this project. I learned a great deal and enjoyed working with my colleagues. We produced a comprehensive report that contained a great deal of valuable information that deserved serious consideration.

However, I was not naïve. I had observed on many occasions that commissions of this nature frequently issue reports that are promptly

---

[2] During the Clinton administration, Crowell was named chairman of TVA.

ignored. In Washington, special study commissions often are appointed to delay action on a controversial issue or to assuage special interests. Nevertheless, it was disillusioning to see 18 months' effort dismissed so handily by members of Congress who had ordered the study.

•

I thought completion of the MRS commission report marked the end of my involvement in the nuclear waste issue. However, in 1994, Secretary of Energy Hazel O'Leary asked me to represent her on a special study of the administrative and financial operations of the Yucca Mountain project.

The governor of Nevada opposed the project and complained about the Department of Energy's administration of it. To allay his concerns, Secretary O'Leary proposed an independent study of the administrative and financial aspects of the project. The study would be overseen by one representative of the governor and one representative of the secretary of energy.

Again, I was reluctant to accept the assignment. However, I had known Mrs. O'Leary for many years and had been friendly with her and her late husband, Jack O'Leary, an able public servant who had been deputy secretary of energy in the Carter administration. I therefore accepted and worked with the governor's representative, Judy Sheldrew, a member of the Nevada Public Service Commission. Our responsibilities consisted primarily of setting forth the scope of work of the study, engaging consultants to conduct it and overseeing the work of the consultants.

Although the state of Nevada opposed the Yucca Mountain nuclear waste project and DOE supported it, I believe Ms. Sheldrew and I succeeded in making the report objective. The consultants' report found some areas where changes were desirable and our lead consultant and I personally went over the recommendations with Secretary O'Leary. She asked questions, took copious notes and seemed determined to see that the report's recommendations were taken seriously. In a subsequent meeting with the staff of the Office of Civilian Radioactive Waste Management, I was pleased to see that the staff was systematically reviewing our report and following up on our recommendations.

My experience with the MRS commission and the administrative and financial review of the Yucca Mountain project brought into sharp focus the relative lack of attention paid to the important problem of nuclear waste disposal during the period after World War II, when so much emphasis was placed on development of nuclear power. I recall very little discussion about nuclear waste disposal during those glory days. It was generally assumed that nuclear waste would be reprocessed, even though reprocessing would reduce, but not eliminate, the volume of radioactive waste. Reprocessing later was dropped as a national policy because of concerns that it would facilitate proliferation of weapons-grade plutonium.

Disposition of nuclear waste did not receive the serious attention of Congress until on-site storage was rapidly filling up at the nation's nuclear power plants and nuclear power opponents seized on the lack of a permanent means of safely storing nuclear waste as a potent argument to halt the growth of nuclear power.

The lesson to be learned from these experiences is that society must make every effort to explore the long-range consequences of new technology before vast sums of money and energy are spent to develop the technology—especially if there is potential for harm as well as good.

Chapter 41

Summing Up—Public Power

Today's public power industry is far different from the one in which I became actively involved in 1948, and public power of tomorrow will not bear a close resemblance to what exists today in terms of such characteristics as assets owned, sources of generation and focus on new issues. Events of yesterday and today may indicate what the future portends, but public power must hold fast to its mission and the underlying philosophy that has guided it for more than a century.

When I joined the APPA staff, the major issue was federal water power development. That program was high on the national political agenda, because it was a key element in efforts to stimulate the economy. It was significant to APPA because it offered the prospect of providing a dependable, low-cost source of wholesale power to many local publicly owned electric utilities.

Clearly, the era of federal power development has ended. The most economical sites for multipurpose water resource projects have been developed, and government spending priorities have turned in other directions. Furthermore, opposition of environmental groups would make it difficult, if not impossible, to obtain congressional approval for developing new sites, even if they were economically feasible.

Yet, a vast infrastructure of dams, transmission lines and appurtenant facilities is in place. Although federal power represents only about 10 percent of the nation's total generating capacity, its importance in certain regions far exceeds that figure. In the West, many municipal utilities and rural electric cooperatives depend largely or entirely on federal power for their wholesale supplies and federal transmission lines provide an essential link between regional electric generating facilities. In the Tennessee Valley, TVA is the sole supplier of electricity to 159 municipal electric utilities and rural electric cooperatives, and to important large industries and government installations.

Although controversies about the federal power program are not likely to be of the magnitude of those that occurred in the past, there will continue to be agitation regarding the role of the federal power systems. Public power and rural electric cooperative utilities must defend this program, because it provides an essential source of power and acts as a competitive force in the electric industry. At the same time, public power groups must resist power company efforts to weaken or eliminate the preference provision in federal law that gives consumer-owned utilities first rights to purchase federal power.

At some time in the future, Congress undoubtedly will be confronted with plans to sell the federal power systems, or at the very least reorganize them. Supporters of the federal power program therefore should be prepared to support the continued existence of this program while examining possible structural changes in the power marketing administrations (PMAs). It would also be well to take a constructive new look at the PMAs' future role, such as serving in a more expansive manner as leaders in energy conservation and development of renewable resources.

•

Another issue that consumed much of my attention over the years was federal regulation of wholesale rates charged by private power companies. This issue was vital to APPA because a vast majority of the local public power systems and rural electric cooperatives depended upon private power companies for their wholesale supply of energy. Without federal regulation, these small utilities were at the mercy of their power company suppliers as to the rates and conditions under which they purchased wholesale power.

The vitality of regulation has ebbed and flowed, depending upon prevailing political and economic pressures and the orientation of the president making appointments to regulatory agencies. Recently, in response to accusations that the Federal Energy Regulatory Commission was not enforcing the law in the debacle in California resulting from deregulation, the commission took a more hard-line stance. In the same vein, scandals involving Enron, WorldCom, Tyco and other companies stimulated the Securities and Exchange Commission to become more aggressive regulators. However, I have little doubt that as the spotlight of publicity shifts to other subjects, there will again be a relaxation of regulation.

Organizations such as APPA have played a valuable role in focusing public attention on the need for enforcement of such laws as the Federal Power Act and the Public Utility Holding Company Act, and must continue to be actively involved in such efforts in the future.

Some will question whether deregulation will eliminate federal regulation of wholesale sales. I think the answer to this question is "no." In enacting the Energy Policy Act in 1992, Congress permitted FERC to decontrol wholesale rates, provided it found that there was workable competition in the wholesale market. In the absence of such competition, FERC continued to have responsibility to impose just and reasonable rates.

Unfortunately, FERC ignored the prerequisite of workable competition in the wholesale market and refused to intervene when wholesale prices shot up in California in 2001. It was only under pressure from Congress, the state of California and customers that FERC imposed conditions that brought some degree of stability to the California market.

The electric industry is in interstate commerce and it is vital to the nation. I believe it will always be subject to federal control. But the degree and effectiveness of that control will depend on the amount of pressure exercised by those affected by regulation, such as local public power utilities and consumer organizations.

•

In the early years of my career, economies of scale in generation and transmission were highly touted. To make the most economical use of the large generating stations, it was desirable to build high- or extra-high voltage transmission lines that would electrically link regions and ultimately the nation. Leading planners in public power promoted the concept of Giant Power to make the most efficient and equitable use of these large facilities.

Because small municipal electric utilities could not individually finance and build such large units, APPA encouraged them to form joint action agencies to take advantage of economies of scale. Over a period of years, publicly owned utilities organized some 65 joint action agencies. These agencies successively participated, frequently in concert with large private power companies, in the financing and construction of generating plants having individual units as large as 1,000 mw of capacity.

Although many of these ventures proved successful, the industry found in the 1970s that the economic limits of very large generating stations had been reached, if not exceeded. The high capital costs incurred during long construction periods, the extensive loss of revenue and threat to reliability that occurred when a very large unit was taken out of service and other problems placed a cloud over the feasibility of such ventures. At the same time, the availability of low-cost natural gas and improvements to gas turbines demonstrated the desirability of building smaller gas turbine units, which could be brought on line faster and with greater flexibility than the very large units.

Meanwhile, society's rapidly increasing dependence on an uninterrupted supply of electricity, coupled with the threat of terrorist activities, has placed added emphasis on the desirability of building smaller, distributed generation. The interruption of service of these generating plants would not have such widespread effects as the outage of very large units.

Recognizing environmental as well as economic factors, some joint action agencies have significantly shifted their emphasis on the sources of power they are providing their members. A notable example is Energy Northwest, which in its previous incarnation as the Washington Public Power Supply System attracted national publicity in 1983 when it defaulted on $2.25 billion in municipal bonds because of its unsuccessful attempt to build five nuclear power plants. In a turnaround from the past, the agency in 2002 completed a 48-mw wind project, which is believed to be the largest such development by a public power utility in the United States. The agency also has installed a solar power station. Vic Parrish, CEO of Energy Northwest, told me his objective is for Energy Northwest to be a "carbon-less" energy company, with one-third of its operating capacity to come from wind energy.

Having established the benefits of working together for power supply, joint action agencies have expanded their services to include training, purchase of equipment, public communications, engineering and project management, lobbying, fuel purchasing, legal assistance, demand-side management, rate design, equipment testing and other services. Undoubtedly, joint action agencies will continue to expand the scope of their activities to meet emerging needs. They will also have the flexibility to fulfill their traditional role of power supply, whether economics and societal considerations call for large or small generating units.

•

Throughout the history of the electric industry, there has been conflict between public and private power. The controversy probably reached its zenith during the New Deal, when the federal government promoted multipurpose water resource projects. To facilitate marketing of power, Congress required the federal government to give priority in access to federally produced power to public power systems and rural electric cooperative utilities. This policy was based on the principle that nonprofit agencies should have preference in obtaining federal power in order to prevent monopolization of public resources and to facilitate the most widespread use of those resources.

The activities of the federal government in building low-cost generating facilities while at the same time giving preference to municipalities and rural electric cooperatives sent shock waves through the private power industry, which already was reeling from financial scandals perpetrated by Samuel Insull and his holding company empire.

This was the exciting, heady atmosphere I encountered when I reported for work at APPA in 1948. Although some conflict continues to exist between public and private power interests where their competitive positions intersect, tensions eased as the federal power program stopped expanding. However, controversy continues to erupt from time to time in specific localities where efforts are made to convert a private power company to public ownership, or vice versa.

There is no merit in promoting controversy for the sake of controversy, but there is value to society in having active competition between publicly and privately owned utilities. The people in any given area should have the right to choose what type of institution provides the essential service of electricity. They should have the option of making that choice between a private power company and a consumer-owned institution such as a publicly or cooperatively owned electric utility. When the people of Long Island, New York. found they could obtain lower cost electricity and better service through a publicly owned utility, they were able in 1998 to exercise that choice through the creation of the Long Island Power Authority. This public power agency purchased the facilities of the former private power company, Long Island Lighting Company, and reduced rates for its almost one million residential customers by 16 percent and cut rates to its approximately 100,000 commercial customers by 8 percent.

•

Having spent 38 years with the American Public Power Association, I cannot refrain from a few words about this organization. I am proud of the role of APPA as an institution. It has achieved influence considerably beyond the size of its membership or resources. I attribute its success in large part to the integrity of its membership and staff and its ability and courage to take positions that are beneficial to society but not necessarily in the mainstream of public opinion. Because it has had the fortitude to espouse views that differed from those of the large privately owned giants of the industry, APPA has often been at the center of controversy. In this connection, I am reminded of two statements by one of my mentors, Gordon Clapp, an early chair of the Tennessee Valley Authority. He wrote:

> The TVA is controversial because it is consequential—let it become insignificant to the public interest, an agency of no particular account, and people will stop arguing about it.

> Let no one forget that electric service is a public service, no matter who owns and operates the properties that supply and distribute power…

Acting on the basis of what it deemed to be in the public interest, APPA has espoused many controversial positions. It has won battles and lost some. However, even when the association didn't prevail, the influence we exerted often resulted in the adoption of alternatives that moved in the direction of our goals. For example, in the 1960s, APPA felt the electric industry was not adequately supporting energy research. Consequently, the association advocated the initiation of a federal tax through which all electric utilities (including public power utilities) would contribute to a fund for research. Private power companies were hostile to the concept, but the pressure exerted by APPA and others stimulated the creation of a voluntary industry-funded Electric Power Research Institute.

Similarly, when the 1965 Northeast blackout and subsequent events prompted APPA to call for the establishment of federal reliability standards, the investor-owned utilities responded by creating another voluntary organization—the North American Electric Reliability Council—to fulfill this need, at least in part.

I am confident APPA will continue to be a leader in advocating innovative concepts to benefit its members and society.

•

The biggest challenge facing local public power utilities will be to remain true to their historic commitment to the communities they serve while adapting to changing demands and the advent of new or improved technologies in the generation and delivery of electric power.

They will also be challenged to provide such power in as efficient and environmentally benign a manner as possible.

Fortunately, local public power utilities are favorably positioned to promote innovations. Because they are generally smaller, they are not burdened with a bureaucratic decision-making process. New ideas flow more easily to the top channels of command. And informed citizen-owners can demand changes that are in the public interest. In recent years, public power utilities have demonstrated their responsiveness to new citizen demands by inaugurating telecommunications services that were not provided adequately by private companies.

Local public power utilities have another essential attribute that enhances their contribution to society. As public agencies, they must provide essential information about their operations to the public. In short, public power offers the transparency that was denied stockholders, the government, employees and the general public in the events that led to the downfall of Enron, WorldCom and other corporations that abused their public trust.

Public power utilities can take advantage of their flexibility of operation and at the same time live up to their heritage by giving increased attention to protecting the environment. Public power attained national recognition by its association with the conservation movement espoused by President Theodore Roosevelt early in the 20th century. Conservation of that era did not have the breadth or scope of the environmental movement of today, but today's emphasis on protecting the environment is a natural progression from the conservation movement of the Roosevelt era.

Although a number of actions have been taken in recent years to protect the environment, pressure exists for additional measures. The major unresolved environmental issue is that of global warming. Opinions continue to differ about the extent of the danger of global warming and the measures that should be taken to combat it, but the issue cannot be ignored. Additional steps—many of which will affect electric utilities—are being demanded. It would be prudent for public power to anticipate the changes that are needed rather than react to pressure after the fact.

In view of constantly increasing requirements for energy, conservation of the nation's energy resources is of greater importance than ever before. By taking the lead in demonstrating efficiency and greater reliance on renewable resources, public power can continue to be on the cutting edge of energy policy and serve as a national if not international model, while it retains its traditional philosophy and mission. Thus, it will continue to be locally owned and controlled. It will seek to provide a public service—electricity—at the lowest possible cost to the consumer while giving cognizance to societal needs. It will continue to operate in the sunshine. It will continue to be oriented toward meeting the needs of the communities it serves. And it will continue to provide that essential yardstick by which the public, regulators and policy-makers can measure the performance of private power.

Chapter 42

Summing Up – Private Life

This book begins with an account of my life before I joined the APPA staff. It seems fitting to close with reminiscences of important personal events that occurred during my career.

Aside from marriage, there is probably no more meaningful experience than becoming a parent—an event that Sara and I first experienced in 1947, a year before I became involved with public power. Our first son, Jay, was born that year. Our second son, Bill, was born in 1952.

Although Jay and Bill came into the world under different circumstances, the joys (and occasional pains) of caring for them were similar. No human experience compares to holding and feeding a baby and feeling its warm, precious body against yours. Reading to a child is a special pleasure, as you sense his concentration on the words and substance of a story. His first words, first haircut and first days at school are memorable. Up to the age of about 4 or 5, one of the most endearing experiences for me was to hold Jay's or Bill's hand as we strolled through the zoo or crossed a street. Holding their little hands made me feel protective and created an emotional as well as physical bond between my sons and me.

Introducing the children to experiences important to me was meaningful. When Jay was about three years old, I took him to a children's concert at a nearby high school. It was a special thrill to have him sit on my lap and listen as the strains of live symphonic music filled the hall. However, this introduction to classical music was premature; Jay quickly grew bored and fidgeted during much of the performance.

He enjoyed some recorded music. His favorite was Prokofiev's *Lieutenant Kiji Suite*. I would hold him on my shoulders and he called out, "kiki, kiki" as the music played. Another of his favorite activities while I carried him on my shoulders was to pat my bald head and exclaim, "popo, popo."

I eagerly anticipated the time when I could introduce Jay to my favorite food, ice cream. After we finally acquired a second-hand car, Sara and I one weekend drove to an ice cream parlor in the recently opened Shirlington shopping center in Virginia. However, Jay was too young to sit down and relish the taste of ice cream; he was impatient with the slow service and had difficulty handling his spoon. The outing did not live up to my expectations.

I had many similar experiences with Bill, but in a different environment. When we moved to Hollin Hills, I became an ardent gardener and Bill followed me as I worked. One of his favorite pastimes was to crawl into a large bucket that I carried with me as I weeded.

Regrettably, I did not engage in sports with Jay and Bill. I tossed balls with both boys, but I had not been active in athletic events and felt I was unable to participate with them in playing baseball, football, or swimming. Nevertheless, both boys took part in sports. I related to my sons in other ways. I helped Jay with his newspaper deliveries. Although he conscientiously delivered the afternoon paper each day, the Sunday edition was heavy, so I arose early Sunday mornings and drove him on his neighborhood route. Somewhat to Jay's displeasure, Bill insisted on accompanying us on these rounds. After we finished, we treated ourselves to breakfast at a local restaurant, then walked on a trail along the Potomac River. It was idyllic.

One of the favorite times Bill and I had together was on Saturday mornings, when I frequently took him to the APPA office while I edited *Public Power* magazine. Bill was intrigued as he watched me paste up a "dummy" for the magazine—a process made obsolete by the computer. While I worked, he went to another desk and designed his own versions of *Public Power* covers and illustrations for articles. I have kept his drawings and continue to derive pleasure from them. I am proudest of one headed, "Hall of Heroes." It shows, standing on pedestals, George Washington, Abraham Lincoln, Thomas Jefferson, Theodore Roosevelt and Alex Radin.

Bill was also a big booster of APPA and prepared ads promoting APPA membership. One ad pictured George Washington declaring, "I think I'll join APPA." The ad explained that Washington would have given such advice if he had not died.

Both Jay and Bill were excellent, conscientious students, but their extracurricular interests diverged. Jay was a star basketball player and made the varsity team when he was a sophomore. Because of his height, sturdy physique and ability, fans in the stand would exhort the team to pass the ball to "Big Jay." I was an excited spectator and very proud of his accomplishments.

Jay's basketball activities resulted in an incident that reflected some of the stresses and strains of that period. Although public schools had been desegregated, public facilities still had not been opened to all—as Jay and some of his teammates painfully learned when they went to a neighborhood restaurant, the Dixie Pig, after a Friday night game. One member of the team was black and the restaurant refused to seat the black student. Jay and his friends—stunned, angered and disbelieving— promptly left. When he returned home and related the incident to Sara and me, Sara was so upset she wrote a strong letter to the restaurant. She did not receive a response.

At about age 13, Bill started playing the guitar seriously, and soon became known for his proficiency. While he was in high school, he played with groups at restaurants. Thus began his lifelong interest in music, which ultimately led to a 13-year professional career and a graduate degree in music at the University of Southern California.

•

One day as I was driving out of Hollin Hills to work, I saw a group of children walking to a nearby school and it struck me that the time would come when Jay and Bill would complete public school, go off to college, and leave home. I felt a sudden, deep sense of loss.

That painful time came in 1965, when Jay left home to begin his college career at the University of Michigan, less than a year after Sara had died. Bill and I drove him to Ann Arbor. I don't know how we managed to get all of his things, plus suitcases for Bill and me in our small Corvair (the General Motors car that Ralph Nader described as "unsafe at any speed"). However, at that time freshmen did not bring computers, stereos, small refrigerators and other such paraphernalia to college.

Jay's return home for Christmas holidays and summer vacations was joyful. His friends came over and it was a pleasure to see them and talk with them about their experiences at college. However, Sara's absence left a noticeable void for me, Jay and his friends, some of whom had felt close to Sara and had confided in her.

At the height of the Vietnam War, Jay came home from college to participate in antiwar marches in Washington. He often invited classmates to stay with us. Their spirit of activism was stimulating. I frequently marched with them and was proud that they were sufficiently concerned about national events to make their voices heard.

By the time Bill entered the University of Wisconsin, the Vietnam War was at its height. Student reaction generally was hostile and the University of Wisconsin was one of the schools where opposition was most virulent. I accompanied Bill when he enrolled at the university, saw him settled in his dormitory, then flew back to Washington. A terrible pall of sadness overcame me as my plane lifted off the ground in Madison. The realization hit me that for the first time in more than two decades, I would return to a house without either of my children being present.

Except for summer vacations, my sons did not live with me after they went to college. However, I kept in close touch with them and followed their personal lives as well as their professional careers.

Both Jay and Bill have been successful in their chosen professions. After completing his undergraduate work at the University of Michigan and taking off two years to teach at a high school in a Washington suburb, Jay returned to the University of Michigan to earn a doctorate in clinical psychology. He has remained in Ann Arbor and is highly regarded in his private practice. His sons, Sam and Andrew, also have been a source of pleasure as I have watched them mature and gained insights from them into the views of a new generation.

After receiving his master's degree in music, Bill decided to choose another career and became a successful executive recruiter, or "head hunter." He has written five books about executive recruiting and career development that have sold well and he conducts training seminars for those in the profession. Although he does not play guitar professionally, except for limited engagements, he enjoys playing regularly with friends and is an accomplished musician.

•

Having experienced the close companionship of 22 years of married life, I was receptive to finding a way to recreate such a relationship after Sara's death. During the 1965 Christmas holidays—slightly more than a year after Sara died—I was invited to a neighborhood party that changed the course of my private life. I was introduced to Fran Overstreet, whose husband had died recently of cancer of the pancreas, the same disease that had killed Sara. Fran was an attractive, lively woman and we shared a number of interests. Her late husband, a college professor, was a Russian scholar and had written a book about the Communist Party in India. She and her husband had lived in India and the Soviet Union. While her husband was studying at Moscow University under a Fulbright scholarship, Fran studied Russian. When she returned to the United States, she worked for a while as a Russian translator, then got a job with the Neighborhood Youth Corps, one of Lyndon Johnson's Great Society programs.

The Great Society era was an exciting time in Washington. It reminded me of FDR's New Deal era. Fran and I had similar political leanings and found that our friends and social interests were compatible.

In the spring of 1966 we began discussing marriage. She had two children—a girl and a boy—who were roughly the same ages as my children. Fran and I had some trepidation about blending our respective families. However, my older son, Jay, was already in college, and her daughter would soon go away to college. My principal concern was with Bill, whose interests and personality were not compatible with those of Fran's son. However, I was optimistic that we could work out differences between the two. Even so, I felt somewhat guilty about the arrangement, but rationalized it on the grounds that a family environment for Bill would be better than the two of us living alone. I talked about my feelings with Bill. He seemed accepting, but understandably apprehensive.

When I discussed my marriage plans with Jay, I sensed discomfort on his part, but I did not believe it would be a major problem, because he would be away at college much of the year.

There was another difficulty. Fran was not Jewish and I knew this would upset my mother. However, Fran consented to have a rabbi marry us.

We were married in July 1966 at the Sheraton Carlton Hotel in Washington. Although we had a large reception afterwards, only relatives and close friends were invited to the wedding ceremony. I felt good about the symbolism of our four children holding up each of the four poles of the *chupeh*, the traditional canopy under which the bride and groom are married in a Jewish ceremony. To my delight, the rabbi gave an eloquent sermon that made an analogy between a successful marriage and the themes and harmonies that could be achieved by different musical instrumentalists playing together.

About a week after the wedding, we moved into a new house in Hollin Hills. Although either of our respective homes would have been adequate to accommodate our merged family, we felt each house tied us to memories of the past and that we should begin life anew in a different environment.

During the first few years of marriage, despite difficult moments, we had a rich life and I was grateful for Fran's companionship. We entertained a great deal, both for friends and for occasions connected with my work. I felt that, to a considerable extent, I had reconstituted my life with Sara.

At Christmas 1975, what appeared to be a relatively insignificant event again changed the course of my life. As a present, Fran gave me a subscription to a series of National Symphony Orchestra concerts at the Kennedy Center. Fran did not share my love of classical music, but knew of my interest and thought I might carpool to the concerts with Carol Tefft, a neighbor who also had symphony tickets. Fran had been a friend of Carol's and had introduced me to her. Carol's husband, Clark, occasionally played poker with Fran.

I found Carol to be a warm person, easy to talk with and I was comfortable being with her, but there was no romance between us, nor was there between Fran and Clark. The series of concerts gave Carol and me an opportunity to know each other better.

Coincidentally, during that winter and spring, the relationship between Fran and me deteriorated seriously. There had been increasing strains between us for several years and in early summer 1976, after a great deal of agonizing, I decided to divorce Fran. She did not contest the action and immediately left our home when I told her I would proceed with the divorce.

Before we broke up, I had purchased tickets to an opera to be performed at the Kennedy Center. Since Fran and I had separated, I invited Carol and asked her to have dinner with me before the performance. I was anxious to talk about the traumatic experience I had in breaking up with Fran and Carol lent a sympathetic ear.

I continued to go with Carol to the remaining NSO concerts that season and we talked more intensely and personally on the drives back to Hollin Hills. An exceptionally open person, Carol also began to tell me about some of the difficulties that she was having at home. I felt closer to her, but there was no immediate romance. Occasionally, on a weekend I would call and ask whether she and Clark would like to join me at a movie. She usually accompanied me, but Clark did not; he was not a movie fan.

I enjoyed the occasions I was with Carol. Many of our interests were the same, especially art and music. Carol was an artist, had a studio in her home, and taught art at a private school near Alexandria, Va. We had friends in common and shared values about politics, society and people. I found her easy to be with. She had no pretenses, and I felt she had many of the characteristics that I had prized in Sara, especially her warm, compassionate nature and her interest in people. (It is perhaps prophetic that her birthday–November 20—falls on the same day that Sara died.)

By the end of the summer, Carol had decided to leave her home and rent an apartment in Alexandria. I began to see her more often, but insisted that our budding relationship should not be a deciding factor in whether or not she would separate permanently from Clark. However, she decided to end her marriage, regardless of what happened between us. So Carol and I spent more and more time together. What began as a friendship blossomed into a full-blown, ardent romance.

A warm-hearted, supportive companion, she immeasurably eased my transition to bachelorhood. Soon, I was inviting her to spend weekends with me and we went on trips together. Later, she moved into my apartment and we were married there, in the presence of members of the family, in September 1979. It has been a comfortable, sustaining relationship. We are each other's best friends, sharing our feelings and our love for each other. She has endeared herself to my sons and to my family and has brought together our respective families. She is a true companion who has enriched my life in many ways.

•

Looking back, I feel I have much to be thankful for. Although I have experienced major tragedies—the death of my father at a young age and the death of Sara when she was only 41 years old—I also have had good fortune. Perhaps the greatest gifts I have had were the unqualified love and acceptance of me by my mother and father and the example of integrity that they demonstrated. My brother has been a model of compassion and honesty and, along with my father, introduced me to the joys of music. From Sara I gained an appreciation of art and sensitivity to people. I cherish Carol for her warmth and companionship, her integrity and her sense of values.

I am indebted to my sons for their love and caring concern and closeness between us and for the joys they and my grandchildren have brought me. We have a great deal of contact and a mutually supporting relationship. Carol's children and grandchildren likewise have added an important dimension to my life.

I have been fortunate, too, in having a circle of friends who have been supportive and intellectually stimulating.

The chance events that brought me to APPA have been fortuitous. APPA gave me an opportunity to grow personally and professionally, and at the same time enabled me to promote and protect policies and programs that were beneficial to the American people. Most important, I did not have to sacrifice principles. Reflecting on recent revelations about the greed and unethical behavior of many corporate executives, I am especially grateful that never once in my career with APPA was I asked to do anything that could be considered unethical. Nor was I ever personally pressured to take positions with which I strongly disagreed. And finally, I am indebted to colleagues for their friendship and professional guidance and assistance.

It's been a good ride. APPA gave me the opportunity to visit countries I had never dreamed of seeing and to travel to the smallest hamlets as well as the largest cities of the United States. It permitted me to know and work with people in the highest stations of life as well as with those unsung heroes who conscientiously carry out their public service responsibilities.

I have been blessed.

The most important sources of information were newsletters and magazines published by the American Public Power Association. The author reviewed every issue of these publications from their inception in 1942 through June 1986. APPA files, including minutes of meetings of the board of directors, also were important, as were numerous newspaper articles, primarily from *The Washington Post* and *The New York Times*. Other sources included the following:

Ashworth, William. *Hells Canyon – The Deepest Gorge on Earth*. New York: Hawthorn Books 1977.

Billington, Ken. *People, Politics and Public Power*. Washington: Washington Public Utility Districts' Association, 1988.

Cook, Blanche Wiesen. *Eleanor Roosevelt, Vol. 1*. New York: Penguin, 1992.

Douglas, William O. *Go East, Young Man: the Early Years; The Autobiography of William O. Douglas*. New York: Random House, 1974.

Dyke, Richard W., and Francis X. Gannon. *Chet Holifield – Master Legislator and Nuclear Statesman*. Maryland: University Press of America, 1996.

Electric Consumers Information Committee. *The People's Fight for Low Cost Power: Report of the Electric Consumers Conference, Washington, D.C., May 26-27, 1952*.

Ellis, Clyde T. *Notes and Diary from U.S.S.R. Trip 1959 from Clyde Taylor Ellis Papers, 1933-1976*. University of Arkansas Libraries, Fayetteville, Ark.

Gruening, Ernest. *Many Battles – The Autobiography of Ernest Gruening*. New York, Liveright, 1973.

———. *The Public Pays; A Study of Power Propaganda*. New York: Vanguard Press, Inc., 1964.

Holum, Ken. *A Farmer Takes a Stand*. South Dakota: Center for Western Studies, 1987.

King, Judson. *The Conservation Fight, From Theodore Roosevelt to the Tennessee Valley Authority*. Washington: Public Affairs Press, 1959.

Library of Congress. Congressional Research Service. *National Power Grid System Study: An Overview of Economics, Regulatory, and Engineering Aspects*. Washington, D.C.: U.S. Government Printing Office, 1976.

Lyons, Barrow. *Tomorrow's Birthright; A Political and Economic Interpretation of Our Natural Resources*. New York, Funk & Wagnalls Co., 1955.

Miller, Gary K. *Energy Northwest: A History of the Washington Public Power Supply System*. N.p.: Xlibris, 2001.

Monitored Retrievable Storage Review Commission. *Nuclear Waste: Is There a Need for Federal Interim Storage?* Washington, D.C.: U.S. Government Printing Office, 1989.

Neville, Peter. *A Traveller's History of Russia and the U.S.S.R.* New York: Interlink Books, 1997.

Owen, Marguerite, *The Tennessee Valley Authority*. New York: Praeger, 1973.

Power Authority of the State of New York. *St. Lawrence Power Project Data – Statistics*. New York: Power Authority of the State of New York, n.d.

Radin, Alex. *Report and Recommendations on a Legislative Proposal to Restructure the Tennessee Valley Authority*. Washington, D.C.: Radin & Associates, 1987.

Rowley & Scott and Tally, Tally & Bouknight. *Artificial Restraints on Basic Energy Sources – An Abridged Version of Report to APPA and NRECA*. N.p., 1971.

Schwarz, Jordan A. *The New Dealers – Power Politics in the Age of Roosevelt*. New York: Knopf, Inc., 1993

Scott, Pamela and Antoinette J. Lee. *Buildings of the District of Columbia*. New York: Oxford University Press, 1993.

Southern States Energy Board. Advisory Committee on the Tennessee Valley Authority. *TVA: A Path to Recovery*. Georgia: Southern States Energy Board, 1987.

Tollefson, Gene. *BPA and the Struggle for Power at Cost*. Oregon: Bonneville Power Administration, 1987.

U.S. Department of the Interior. *Transmission Study 190*. Washington, D.C.: U.S. Government Printing Office, 1968.

U.S. House. Committee on Interior and Insular Affairs. Subcommittee on Irrigation and Reclamation. *Hells Canyon: Hearings on H.R. 5743*. 82nd Cong., 2nd sess., 1952.

————— . Committee on Public Works. *Steam-Electric Generating Plants in Pacific Northwest: Hearings on H.R. 4963*. 82nd Cong., 1st sess., 1951.

————— . *TVA Self-Financing*. 86th Cong., 1st sess., 1959. H. Rept. 271.

————— . Subcommittee on Flood Control. *Tennessee Valley Authority Financing: Hearings on H.R. 3236 and H.R. 4266*. 85th Cong., 1st sess., 1957.

U.S. Joint Committee on Atomic Energy. *Hearings on H.R. 13731 and H.R. 13732, to Amend the Atomic Energy Act of 1954 Regarding the Licensing of Nuclear Facilities*. 92nd Cong., 2nd sess., 1972.

————— . *Hearing on Proposed Arrangements for Electric Generating Facilities at Hanford New Production Reactor*. 87th Cong., 2nd sess., 27 September 1962.

————— . *Hearings on Prelicensing Antitrust Review of Nuclear Powerplants*. 91st Cong., 1st sess., 1969 and 91st Cong., 2nd sess., 1970.

U.S. Senate. Committee on Commerce. *Exemption of Certain Public Utilities from Federal Power Commission Jurisdiction: Hearings on S. 218.* 89th Cong., 1st sess., 1965.

————. Subcommittee on Communications. *The Speeches of Senator John F. Kennedy – Presidential Campaign of 1960.* Washington, D.C.: U.S. Government Printing Office, 1961.

————. Committee on Interior and Insular Affairs and Committee on Public Works. *Relative Water and Power Resource Development in the U.S.S.R. and the U.S.A. Report and Staff Studies.*
86th Cong., 2nd sess., 1960.

————. Committee on Interstate and Foreign Commerce. Subcommittee on the Nomination of Leland Olds. *Hearings on Reappointment of Leland Olds to Federal Power Commission.* 81st Cong., 1st sess., 1949.

————. Committee on Public Works. *Amending the TVA Act.* 1957. S. Rept. 575.

————. *Revenue Bond Financing by TVA.* 86th Cong., 1st sess., 1959. S. Rept. 426.

————. *Revenue Bond Financing by TVA,* 86th Cong., 1st sess., 1959. S. Rept. 470.

————. Subcommittee on Flood Control. *Amending the TVA Act Hearings on S. 1855, S. 1869, S. 1986 and S. 2145.* 85th Cong., 1st sess., 1957.

Yergin, Daniel. *The Prize: the Epic Quest for Oil, Money, and Power.* New York: Simon & Schuster, 1991.